FOUNDATIONS OF CHARITY

Foundations of Charity

Edited by

CHARLES MITCHELL

School of Law, King's College London

and

SUSAN R MOODY

Charity Law Research Unit, University of Dundee

•HART•
PUBLISHING

OXFORD – PORTLAND OREGON

2000

Hart Publishing
Oxford and Portland, Oregon

Published in North America (US and Canada) by
Hart Publishing c/o
International Specialized Book Services
5804 NE Hassalo Street
Portland, Oregon
97213-3644
USA

Distributed in the Netherlands, Belgium and Luxembourg by
Intersentia, Churchillaan 108
B2900 Schoten
Antwerpen
Belgium

Hart Publishing Ltd is a specialist legal publisher based in Oxford, England. To order further copies of this book or to request a list of other publications please write to:

Hart Publishing Ltd, Salter's Boatyard,
Folly Bridge, Abingdon Road, Oxford OX1 4LB
Telephone: +44 (0)1865 245533 or Fax: +44 (0)1865 794882
e-mail: mail@hartpub.co.uk
WEBSITE: http//www.hartpub.co.uk

British Library Cataloguing in Publication Data
Data Available
ISBN 1 84113–130–X (hardback)

Typeset by Hope Services (Abingdon) Ltd.
Printed and bound in Great Britain on acid-free paper by
Biddles Ltd, www.biddles.co.uk

Foreword

LORD GOODHART, QC

Our definition of "charity" for legal purposes remains rooted in the wording of the preamble to an Elizabethan statute. Four hundred years on, the nature and function of charities have changed immensely. Within the last few decades, for example, charities have passed from being seen as bodies doomed to extinction by an ever-expanding welfare state to being major providers of welfare services funded by the state. But no consensus has yet been reached in the debate about the adoption of a modern definition of charity.

Charles Mitchell and Sue Moody are to be congratulated on putting together a valuable collection of essays on different aspects of the charity debate by a diverse group of (mostly young) academic lawyers and philosophers. Dealing with specific issues which feature in the debate, Michael Chesterman questions the justification for tax relief on some kinds of charity, and calls for greater freedom for charities to act politically; Alison Dunn also sees politics and charity as being more closely linked than is currently recognized by the law; Charles Mitchell discusses the implications of the Charity Commissioners' ongoing Review of the Register for the development of the English law of charitable status; and Patrick Ford considers the Scots law of public trusts as a model for the reform of the English law. At a level more removed from current controversies, Sue Moody argues that the work of volunteers is a central and essential element of charity; Mark Freedland calls for a revision of the dividing line between public and private law as they relate to charities; and Rob Atkinson notes the dangers of state interventionism in the internal affairs of charities, particularly in relation to religious sectarianism. Finally, in chapters which are more philosophical than legal, John Gardner discusses the relationship between charity and justice, public spiritedness, and loyalty, while David Stevens defends the Christian view of charity from secular criticism from both left and right.

This scholarly and wide-ranging book is an important contribution to the debate on charity. It will stimulate thought and promote well-informed action. It deserves to be widely read by people with a practical as well as an academic interest in charities.

Preface

CHARLES MITCHELL AND SUSAN R MOODY

It is almost four hundred years since the idea of charity was first given statutory legal form in England, in the Preamble to the Statute of Charitable Uses 1601. The definition of charity contained in the statute, and developed in subsequent case law, continues to have a profound impact not only on the law regulating charitable trusts, but also on the management and organisation of a major part of the voluntary sector in the United Kingdom. There are currently around 180,000 charities registered with the Charity Commission in England and Wales, and around 27,000 recognised by the Inland Revenue in Scotland, and although the problems of defining the voluntary sector are notorious, these figures suggest that charities probably represent well over half the voluntary sector organizations in the United Kingdom. All these bodies derive their privileged status from the Preamble and judicial interpretation of its four heads of charity, namely the relief of poverty, the advancement of education, the promotion of religion, and purposes beneficial to the community which do not fall under the first three heads. Their status gives them particular fiscal advantages and, in theory at least, wins them a special place in public sentiment, encouraging charitable donations and voluntary activity by citizens. It also places significant limitations on the type of work they are permitted to undertake, on their involvement in political campaigning, and on their internal organisation. In addition, they are required to meet certain standards of accountability and financial management. Their compliance is monitored through a regulatory framework designed specifically for charities. Given the advantages of charitable status (in particular the tax exemptions to which registered charities are entitled) it is understandable that organisations should have to meet certain criteria in order to qualify, and that their continued adherence to "charity" should be monitored. However, it may be questioned whether the law should continue to support "charity" at all. The word increasingly carries with it somewhat antiquated and even unpalatable connotations of "do-gooding", moral superiority, a patronising relationship between donor and recipient and the maintenance of inequality and power imbalances within society. It seems to offer little scope for reciprocity and inclusiveness. Derived from a Western Christian tradition it may seem ill-suited to the pluralist, multi-cultural, secular society which characterises Britain in the twenty-first century.

However, while the term charity may be out of step with contemporary thinking, the idea of giving a privileged place to voluntary organisations is, if anything, becoming more widespread. With the rediscovery of "civil society", the demise of Communism in Eastern Europe, and the impact of globalisation, many countries are looking to find ways of developing and enhancing a robust, independent voluntary sector. The creation and maintenance of a "buffer zone" between states and markets is currently a major pre-occupation across the world. In addition, the voluntary sector is seen as providing ways of increasing citizen involvement in social activity, encouraging social inclusion, and harnessing skills for public benefit. Charities in the United Kingdom have been at the forefront of social change, pioneering many of the services which were subsequently taken up by the Welfare State in the 1940s. They continued to develop initiatives under the new regime (in advice-giving, environmental protection, and housing, for instance), when many thought that they would cease to have any substantial role. They adapted well to the major changes which followed the Griffiths Report and are now the major provider of social services in Britain. Some charities also perform a key role in identifying and representing new areas of concern and, within legal limits, actively encouraging developments which challenge current orthodoxies. Nevertheless, they are under considerable pressure, on the one hand from government to meet its policy agenda, and on the other from businesses which compete with them in the market for the delivery of services. As the least powerful player the voluntary sector needs some protection from such pressures.

Legal regulation offers one way of securing the position of the sector and giving it space within which to flourish. The demands of the "contract culture", the danger which undue government influence can pose for the independence of the voluntary sector, and the potential for erosion of altruistic values represented by encroachment of the market are all very real threats. A regulatory system which acknowledges such difficulties and affords some protection for "charity" is not only desirable but essential. However, even if one accepts that voluntary organisations should be given special status and therefore specific regulation, the current English legal position, particularly in relation to the definition of charity, may not offer the best framework for the encouragement of charitable endeavour. It has long been criticised as being out of step with modern thinking, containing anomalies which erode public support for charities (such as charitable status for public schools and private hospitals), and failing to accept the legitimate role which the voluntary sector should be playing in political debate. The English courts and the Charity Commissioners have been able to widen, or at least to offer a more contemporary interpretation of, "charity" in recent times (for example, by extending charitable status to organisations designed to further race relations, and by withdrawing it from gun clubs). Yet there are still voluntary bodies which continue to be excluded, such as campaigning organisations, and self-help organisations such as credit unions and some housing associations. Two recent major reports on the voluntary sector, the Kemp and the Deakin Reports, were severely critical of the current legal definition of "charity", and proposed changes which would, in effect, substitute a test of public benefit for the artificial and convoluted position which has been the legacy of the common law. The Charity Commissioners have been active in this area, and have been consulting interested parties about extending "charity" to include certain types of activity which are currently excluded, such as urban and rural regeneration and the relief of unemployment. Central government has also pledged its support for the voluntary sector, through Compacts for each part of the United Kingdom.

The time is right, therefore, for a fundamental reappraisal of the assumptions which inform English legal notions of "charity". The major umbrella organisation for charities in England and Wales, the National Council for Voluntary Organisations (NCVO), has been co-ordinating an extensive programme of work reviewing the structure and operation of the law relating to charitable status. As part of this critical examination, and with generous financial support from the Economic and Social Research Council and the Modern Law Review, NCVO and the School of Law at King's College London organised a colloquium in September 1998 designed to reconsider the "foundations of charity". By focusing on underlying theoretical issues rather than concentrating on practical proposals and detailed law reform it was hoped that the contributors would introduce new and challenging ways of defining charity. The contributors were deliberately drawn from a diverse group of academic scholars to avoid the rather narrow and perhaps insular approach to "charity" sometimes taken by specialists in the law of trusts. They ranged from established experts in charity law and policy, such as Professor Michael Chesterman, to a social policy analyst, Professor Jane Lewis. They included contributions from five different jurisdictions—Australia, Canada, England and Wales, Scotland, and the United States—and the contributors drew on a wide variety of subject areas aside from the law for their inspiration—Jurisprudence, Public Law, Political Philosophy, Social Policy, and Theology. Their individual contributions were informed and enriched by two pre-colloquium meetings and by questions and issues raised at the colloquium itself.

This collection of essays contains most of the papers given at the colloquium. There is an additional contribution from Patrick Ford on the Scottish law of public trusts as a model for reform of the English law of charity, which the editors feel casts an interesting new light on the subject. We are grateful to the editors of those journals—the *Modern Law Review*, the *Northern Ireland Legal Quarterly* and *Trust Law International*—who allowed us to reproduce work already published elsewhere. It was disappointing not to be able to include Jane Lewis's contribution (because permission to do so was refused by the journal editors), but it is referred to in several of the chapters in this book and can be found at (1999) 10(3) *Voluntas* 255. On behalf of all the contributors to this collection, we would also like to thank Margaret Bolton, of NCVO, and Professor John Gardner, formerly of King's College London, for their work in organising the Foundations of Charity Colloquium, and we would also like to thank all those who attended the colloquium for their stimulating input.

While each of the contributions to this collection deals with specific issues there are certain over-arching themes which can be discerned in many of the chapters. First, and most fundamental, there is the issue of values. Does "charity" have anything unique to offer which citizens should value and the law seek to uphold? Professor John Gardner's contribution dissects this important philosophical issue and distinguishes charity from other "virtues" such as justice, public-spiritedness, and loyalty. He takes issue with the economists' view that human behaviour is self-regarding, and also with the legal reformers' wish to align charity with public benefit, a proposal which is also examined from a comparative perspective by Patrick Ford. In Professor Gardner's view, charity should rather be understood as a spontaneous response to the needs of others, arising not from obligation but from an unquestioning spirit of altruism. Professor David Stevens, in contrast, urges us not to neglect the essential links between religion and charity, and puts forward the idea of a common or universal good as the core of charitable activity, drawing on Thomism and its modern gloss from Finnis. His conclusion is that liberal secular ideas cannot encompass the notion of charity, because altruism and love are foreign and distasteful to liberal theory. Abandonment of the religious dimension of charity impoverishes the concept and makes it redundant.

Another theme is the role of charity in empowering and activating. For almost a century charities have been prevented from political campaigning except within narrow limits. Dr Alison Dunn questions this approach from the standpoint of liberation theology, pinpointing the strong links between the impetus to do good and actions to increase social justice. She sees the distinction between political and non-political action as a false one and suggests ways in which political involvement could be beneficial to charity and the wider society. Sue Moody also looks at activism within charities, in the form of voluntarism or self-giving. She claims that "charity" should encourage voluntary action and looks at a variety of philosophical perspectives which, she believes, support this view, including the work of John Locke, Kantian philosophy, notions of civil society and communitarianism. She applies their understanding of self-giving in charity to English charity law and suggests ways in which the law could support and encourage voluntarism.

A question for lawyers and political scientists is the location of charity in the body politic. Are charities creatures of private law or do they have a public dimension? Professor Mark Freedland argues that it is unsatisfactory to locate charity solely within the private sphere, as common law legal systems have tended to do. He demonstrates that the law of charity could be used to rethink the public/private distinction (defining it in a more multi-dimensional way), and provides a useful example of ways in which public and private modes of regulation can be applied to the same area. Professor Rob Atkinson's discussion has a similar theme, as he examines the implications of state intervention in voluntary bodies' internal disputes, and considers the extent to which such intervention may be justified according to the nature of the voluntary body and the nature of the state in question. Dr Charles Mitchell's contribution, too, requires us to think about the relationship between the state and the voluntary sector, by asking whether unelected judges and Charity Commissioners are the worst—or the best—people to decide whether particular sorts of voluntary activity deserve state subsidy.

The final theme underlying the papers is the role of charity in the Welfare State. In particular, Professor Michael Chesterman develops his seminal work on the origins of trust law and the role of charities in social welfare, *Charities, Trusts and Social Welfare* (London, Weidenfeld and Nicolson, 1979). He takes two key aims for charity identified in his book, that is "promoting wealth distribution through tax reliefs" and "ensuring relative autonomy", and tests out whether changes in charity law and administration over the last twenty years have furthered these aims. He suggests that English charity law since 1979 has hindered the achievement of these objectives. In Australia, on the other hand, legal developments have contributed to these aims, particularly by restricting favoured tax status to public benevolent institutions only and in legal decisions on political campaigning.

This collection offers the reader the opportunity to explore the meaning of charity in law from a wide variety of perspectives, and to consider how it is intimately bound up with the nature of our moral and political communities. The contributors challenge some long established notions of what should be regarded as "charitable" and present innovative ideas for a more just and effective definition of charity. We believe that everyone with an interest in the voluntary sector will be stimulated by their arguments, as we have been ourselves.

Contents

Notes on Contributors

Rob Atkinson received his undergraduate degree in history and philosophy from Washington and Lee in 1979 and his law degree from Yale in 1982. After clerking a year for Judge Donald S Russell on the United States Fourth Circuit Court of Appeals, he practised law in Washington, DC, with the firm of Sutherland, Asbill, and Brennan. In 1987 he joined the Faculty of Law at Florida State University, where he has been a Professor since 1996; his specialities are professional responsibility, property, and nonprofit organizations.

Michael Chesterman has been a Professor of Law at the University of New South Wales since 1979. Previously, he was a member of the Faculty of Laws at King's College London, and a Professor of Law at the University of Warwick. He is the author of *Charities, Trusts and Social Welfare* (London, Weidenfeld & Nicholson, 1979) and co-author of Moffat and Chesterman, *Trusts Law: Text and Materials* 1st edition (London, Butterworths, 1988).

Alison Dunn is a Lecturer in Law at the University of Newcastle-upon-Tyne. She has written widely in the area of charity law, and is the editor of *The Voluntary Sector, the State and the Law* (Oxford, Hart Publishing, 2000).

Patrick J Ford is a Scottish solicitor and Lecturer in Law at the University of Dundee. After reading Classics and English Law at Cambridge, and Scots Law at Edinburgh, he practised as a private client solicitor for fifteen years, developing a special interest in charities. In 1994 he left private practice in Edinburgh to join the Charity Law Research Unit at Dundee and is working on a doctoral thesis comparing the Scots, English and French approaches to voluntary sector regulation.

Mark Freedland is Professor of Employment Law in the University of Oxford and Law Tutor at St John's College Oxford. His writing and research are in the fields of Employment Law and Public Law; the Law of Trusts is one of his teaching subjects. It is from that combination of subjects that he approaches the Law of Charity; in particular, he takes the view that Public Law affords significant novel insights into Charity Law.

John Gardner is Professor of Jurisprudence in the University of Oxford. He has previously held appointments at King's College London and at Columbia University in New York City. He has published widely on problems of moral philosophy that are relevant to legal doctrine.

Charles Mitchell is a Lecturer in Law at King's College London. His research and teaching interests include charity law, trusts law, and the law of restitution. He has written various articles on these subjects, and a book, *The Law of Subrogation* (Oxford, Clarendon Press, 1994).

Susan R Moody is a Senior Lecturer in Law at the University of Dundee and a founder member of the Charity Law Research Unit there. For five years she ran a major Scottish charity and has continued to be actively involved in the Scottish voluntary sector. She has particular research interests in volunteering and the law, and she is a trustee of the Lloyds TSB Foundation for Scotland.

David Stevens is an Associate Professor of Law at McGill in Montreal. He is the author of publications on charity law, corporate law, and private law. He was the director of the Ontario Law Reform Commission Report on the Law of Charity (1996). He is also a tax associate at the law firm Goodman and Carr in Toronto.

1

The Virtue of Charity and its Foils

JOHN GARDNER

1. THE VARIETY OF MORAL VIRTUES

> [T]hat moral virtue, that we can truly measure by civil laws, which is different in different states, is justice and equity; that moral virtue which we measure purely by natural laws is alone charity. Furthermore, all moral virtue is contained in these two.[1]

HOBBES' RESTRICTION OF the range of moral virtues to two may be thought excessively parsimonious. What about honesty, loyalty, courage, considerateness, tolerance, public-spiritedness, conscientiousness, trustworthiness, and all the rest? Hobbes evidently thinks that these are not distinct moral virtues. But is that because they are not *virtues*? Or because they are not *moral*? Or because they are not *distinct*? "A bit of each", seems to be Hobbes' answer. But Hobbes doesn't stop to offer any very illuminating explanations. One has the impression that, like many other philosophers of the modern age, he finds the diversity of moral virtues a philosophical embarrassment. He hopes to tidy things up without making the kind of fuss that would only serve to draw attention to their untidiness.

Why would this be? Here is one obvious explanation. As well as varying in the spirit in which they act (warmer or colder, more spontaneous or more deliberate, with more levity or more gravitas, etc.), people with different moral virtues vary in how astute they are, and how much importance they attach, to different sub-groups of moral reasons. They have, to put it another way, different moral *priorities*. In particular, what one person is disposed to regard as sufficient moral reason in itself to ϕ, another may well regard as insufficient. Hence people with different moral virtues often react differently to the same situation—one is inclined to ϕ and the other to μ—sometimes to the point of mutual antagonism or mutual frustration. When the only alternative to a betrayal is a deceit, for example, some (more loyal) will baulk more at the betrayal ("what is a little white lie when my friend's reputation is at stake?"), whereas others (more honest) will baulk more at the deceit ("what friend worth his salt would have me tell lies merely for the sake of his reputation?"). Since each applies these distinctive priorities not only to herself but also to others—they are, after all, *moral*

[1] Thomas Hobbes, *De Homine*, in W Molesworth (ed), *The Latin Works of Thomas Hobbes* (London, Bohn, 1839–1845), vol 2, 116–17.

priorities—the two will sometimes look askance on each other's actions. But in that case (the thinking goes) surely they can't *both* be right? Surely at least one of them must be morally misguided, treating some reason as a sufficient reason for action when it is actually insufficient? Surely, in other words, it must be the case that either the more honest person is being *too* honest or the more loyal person is being *too* loyal? Otherwise we are landed with the embarrassing conclusion that the more loyal person is justified in doing as he does while the more honest person is no less justified in objecting, and *vice versa*.

Something like this line of thought led many philosophers of the modern age to attempt to isolate one single trait of character which is the *master* moral virtue, the one which consistently alights on the correct overall priorities for any moral agent and in the process (so to speak) *arbitrates* between the more selective moral priorities of virtues like loyalty and honesty. To fill this space some utilitarians alighted on a rather austere kind of public-spiritedness which has come to be known as "impartial benevolence" or "responsible benevolence";[2] Kant and some of his followers, meanwhile, opted for variations on the rather different, but no less austere, theme of diligence or conscientiousness.[3] Insofar as other traits like honesty and loyalty are moral virtues at all, according to these tidy modern views, they are not *distinct* moral virtues but merely subsidiary aspects of the relevant master-virtue. On the Kantian view, for instance, a loyal person is strictly speaking morally virtuous only insofar as he is *diligently* (i.e. duty-observingly) loyal. If he is so loyal that his astuteness to the interests of his friend or his party or his country displaces, rather than subserves, his astuteness to considerations of duty pure and simple, his loyalty necessarily becomes, in Kantian eyes, a moral limitation rather than a moral virtue. Now he is loyal *to a fault*. Thus when his loyalty has him act differently from the way that the perfectly diligent person would act (i.e. has him breach his duty for any reason other than that he has another more pressing duty[4]) his action may very well be morally excused but it cannot possibly be morally justified. And there are well-known parallel utilitarian suggestions: justice, insofar as it is a moral virtue at all, is merely an aspect of the virtue of impartial benevolence, for one should always keep the interests of all in view even when judging among the few, etc.

These well-known Kantian and utilitarian abridgements of moral character are bound together by two shared assumptions, both of which are false. First, both assume that direct moral success is automatically superior to indirect moral success. Whether it be thanks to lack of information, weakness of will, or other obstacles within or beyond themselves, there exists a wide range of cases over which people are more likely to hit the moral target—to act exactly as

[2] This custom-designed utilitarian virtue is nicely discussed in W Frankena, "Beneficence/Benevolence", (1987) 4 *Social Philosophy and Policy* 1.

[3] For a subtle rendition of the Kantian virtue, see B Herman, *The Practice of Moral Judgment* (Cambridge, Mass, Harvard University Press, 1993), chap 1.

[4] Kant thought that moral duties cannot conflict and so would omit the qualification. I include it because this aspect of Kant's thought has no direct bearing on the issue at stake here.

morality would have them act—if they aim instead at something else. And *habitually* aiming at something else may sometimes maximise one's hit rate over time, thus fully justifying one's occasional misses (even when those could have been avoided by taking a direct aim). In a way these "misses" are none other than bigger hits. This was the insight of rule-utilitarians like Mill and Sidgwick, who accordingly kept open their lists of distinct moral virtues.[5] The honest or loyal person who overshoots the moral target in a given case is not being too honest or too loyal if the consequence of her being that honest or that loyal is that she hits the moral target more often than she would if she were to have compromised her honesty or her loyalty sufficiently to hit the target in this particular case. This immediately opens up logical space for a more honest person and a more loyal person to look askance at each other's actions without forcing us to the conclusion that either the former is too honest or the latter too loyal. All else being equal both may be justified (and not merely excused) in their actions and reactions, for in being pre-disposed to act and react as she does, prioritising some sub-group of moral reasons for action out of proportion to their real moral priority, each improves her overall hit rate judged not only according to her priority but according to the *real* moral priority.

But even in saying this we are granting the second false assumption underlying the "master virtue" view. We are talking as if there *is* always a "real moral priority", some singular moral target that should ideally be hit (whether directly or indirectly) in each case. In reality there is often no such thing. There are many distinct non-derivative moral values, and these are not comprehensively ranked in respect of their relative importance. So there is no unified master-prioritisation by which to judge, and hence to rank, the diverse moral priorities of the honest person, the loyal person, the diligent person, the public-spirited person, and so forth. While some prioritisation of moral reasons is certainly the work of the reasons themselves—without this there could be no such thing as an error of judgment, no such thing as a vice or fault, etc.—nevertheless there comes a point at which the reasons abdicate responsibility for their own prioritisation and leave the reasoner to his or her own devices. Different moral virtues, on this more Aristotelian view, are among the reasoner's own devices: they are dispositions to prioritise different sub-groups of moral reasons within the bounds fixed by the independent prioritisations imposed by the reasons themselves (after these have been adjusted for the possibility of indirect success).[6] This does not mean that one can never be too honest or too loyal, etc.

[5] J S Mill, *Utilitarianism* (ed R Crisp, Oxford, Oxford University Press, 1998), chap 5; H Sidgwick, *The Methods of Ethics* 7th edn (London, Macmillan, 1907), chap 11.

[6] There is a controversy over whether this really *is* Aristotle's view, or rather a reconstruction of what he ought to have thought given his other views. After all he does seem to pledge allegiance at NE 1144^b32 to 1145^a2 to the Platonic thesis of the unity of the virtues, according to which to possess one moral virtue is to possess them all. The tension is helpfully discussed, but not solved, by T Irwin in "Disunity in the Aristotelian Virtues", in J Annas (ed), *Oxford Studies in Ancient Philosophy: Supplementary Volume 1988* (Oxford, Clarendon Press, 1988) 61. My own interpretation of the "unity" passage is that it commits Aristotle only to the following theses: (a) that there is a

One is indeed too honest if one tends to spill one's thoughts on any subject, however sensitive, as soon as one is asked to. One is likewise too loyal if one tends to stand by people however nasty they turn. These are dispositions which violate the independent constraints of moral reasons, systematically overshooting even their own moral targets and thereby undershooting all others. But one is not, on the other hand, too honest merely because one's honesty compromises one's loyalty, or too loyal merely because one's loyalty compromises one's honesty. One is not too loyal or too honest merely because in hitting one target one misses another. Nor is this merely thanks to the logical space opened up by the insight of the rule-utilitarians. It is for the deeper reason that one cannot but continue to prioritise among moral reasons even after those moral reasons have ceased prioritising themselves, and so one cannot hope, even in principle, to hit every moral target only according to the order in which the target ought, morally, to be hit. Beyond a certain point, there *is* no such order independently of the customised way in which one's moral character represents it.

These remarks are directed against those modern philosophers who famously mined for the fool's gold of a single master moral virtue. But so far they do not seem to speak to Hobbes' more quirky proposal. For Hobbes, after all, there are two distinct moral virtues. If he has got this far, you may ask, then why not further? Why not three or seven or fifty? After all, even to recognise the existence of two distinct moral virtues he must surely have managed to overcome the embarrassment of which I spoke, the embarrassment at the thought that two people, one charitable and the other just, might both be entirely justified in objecting to, maybe even frustrating, each other's actions. Surely he must already have conceded either the Millian point or the Aristotelian point? And surely, with either of those points conceded, the further diversification of moral character beyond justice and charity poses no further philosophical threat? Philosophically, isn't it just more of the same? True enough. Which makes one wonder whether Hobbes really *has* conceded either the Millian or the Aristotelian point, i.e. whether, in treating justice and charity as distinct, he really *has* reconciled himself to the possibility that a just person and a charitable person could be at odds with each other, without it following that either the first is too just or the second too charitable. One wonders whether there isn't perhaps some significance in Hobbes' choice of *these* two moral virtues to appear on his official list.

Perhaps the relationship of the just and the charitable is a special one, not analogous to that between the loyal and the honest, and so not opening the same philosophical can of worms. Could it be that, although they clearly act in different spirits, the impeccably just person and her charitable counterpart some-

"threshold" moral virtue (the virtue of responsibility) such that if one does not exhibit it at all then one also exhibits no others; and (b) that to exhibit the threshold virtue impeccably is to exhibit all others *in some measure* though not necessarily impeccably, so long as any shortfall in one is owed to impeccability in another. Obviously this is not the place to defend this interpretation or to defend the view (as I think, correct) that it yields.

how end up not being at odds when it comes to the prioritisation of moral reasons? In which case Hobbes's view aligns with the "master virtue" view, to which it merely adds an interesting twist. There is one ultimate set of moral priorities (*contra* Aristotle) and they are indeed to be served directly (*contra* Mill and Sidgwick), but there is nevertheless a moral division of labour, such that different people, acting in different spirits, deal with different parts of the moral operation, and (unless in error) never step on each other's toes. So neither justifiably shuns the other's justifiable actions, and the philosophical embarrassment of the opposite situation is avoided. In one sense, to be sure, the two virtues are distinct, for they involve acting in different *spirits*, and that means that, true enough, they cannot be impeccably manifested at the same time by one and the same person. But in another sense they are not distinct. Their rational priorities are mutually consistent and join up to form a single master set. It is, if you like, one master virtue with two subsidiary branches. Elsewhere Hobbes hints that this is the view he really has in mind. He talks as if there is only *one* real moral virtue—namely charity—of which justice is but a (more reliable, more organised) official or public branch.[7]

Even if one rejects all such "master virtue" views (having recovered from the modern philosopher's embarrassment at the thought of mutual antagonism even among the morally unimpeachable), one may well still be tempted by the idea that the virtues of justice and charity, impeccably manifested, might indeed have some kind of special integrated or arbitrated relationship with each other. Isn't there, after all, a sense in which these two virtues are aspiring to occupy the very same moral space, identically defined? Aren't the just and the charitable both aspiring to provide answers to the moral question of *who gets what from whom*? Even if we grant that different and sometimes mutually antagonistic or frustrating priorities must emerge from people being concerned with different moral questions, it might still seem reasonable to expect compatible priorities among those who are especially concerned with the very *same* moral question. So if we temporarily narrow our moral attention down to the question of who gets what from whom, mightn't we expect morality *then* to give us a set of master priorities by which to judge people's own personal priorities—or in other words a kind of *localised* master-virtue (even if it is one requiring a division of labour between two temperamentally distinct types of agents)? I think this is a common view, especially among today's political philosophers who (under the influence of a myopic conception of the role of social organisation in human life) often do narrow their moral attention down to this one moral question.[8] Arguably this is all that Hobbes himself is doing, for arguably he too regards the question of who gets what from whom as the key moral question facing what he

[7] Thomas Hobbes, *The Elements of Law* (ed Gaskin, Oxford, Oxford University Press, 1994), 90–91, and (for the avoidance of doubt) 101.

[8] Most famously it is the question that dominates John Rawls' *A Theory of Justice* (Cambridge, Mass, Harvard University Press, 1971) and the vast literature that it has spawned.

calls "civil society" (in fact, arguably today's myopic conception of the role of social organisation in human life is mainly his fault).

But even with our attention artificially narrowed down to this one moral question, the "master virtue" view is still, in my view, a profoundly mistaken one. There is no comprehensive prioritisation of priorities to be found that would arbitrate between the different moral priorities of the just and the charitable. Their quarrels—and quarrels they certainly have—are not signs that one or other of them is necessarily going too far, acting beyond her justified remit, usurping the other's role, etc. Like the honest and the loyal, the just and the charitable may well resent or frustrate each other's actions without any necessary implication that one of them is being too just or the other too charitable. Nor is this only for Millian reasons, i.e. because there are different indirect methods for hitting the same moral target. It is also for the deeper Aristotelian reason that, even in respect of the narrow question of who gets how much of what, there are various moral targets to aim at, multiple ultimate moral values at stake that are not transitively ranked by importance.

2. CHARITY AND JUSTICE

> [W]e feel ourselves to be under a stricter obligation to act according to justice, than agreeably to friendship, charity, or generosity; . . . the practice of these last mentioned virtues seems to be left in some measure to our own choice, but . . . somehow or other, we feel ourselves to be in a peculiar manner tied, bound, and obliged to the observation of justice.[9]

Smith is not alone in observing and trusting these feelings. One familiar account of the marriage of justice and charity portrays charity as justice's Stepford Wife. If one wants to turn one's case for getting more of something into a priority case, the story goes, one had best appeal direct to justice; charity is good-natured but not very assertive. Many thoughts conspire to lend appeal to this view. One is Hobbes' thought, encountered above, that the priorities of the just, unlike those of the charitable, are suitable to be "measured by civil laws". If true (and we return to the question in part 5 below) doesn't this suggest that the priorities of the just are somehow more important, more insistent, or more fundamental than those of the charitable, and so fall to be satisfied first? And here is another apparently corroborating thought: Although people may well be regarded as too charitable, it sounds odd to say of someone—in the way that I did towards the end of the last part—that she is "too just".[10] Perhaps one can never be too just. If that is right, then someone could in principle be insufficiently just thanks to being too charitable, but not the other way round. Could this apparent asymmetry be significant? It may be thought that it points to a dramatically one-sided

[9] Adam Smith, *The Theory of Moral Sentiments* (eds Raphael and Macfie, Oxford, Clarendon Press, 1976), 80.

[10] Thanks to Janis Rosenthal for alerting me to this line of thought.

relationship between the just and the charitable. A more just person may justifiably baulk at what a more charitable person does, but not the other way round, for the more just person cannot be too just. And this in turn may seem to lend plausibility to the idea of an overarching moral prioritisation of the respective priorities of the just and the charitable. The moral priorities of the charitable play second fiddle. They can be overridden by but they cannot override those of the just.

How could this be so? Here are some well-known ways of distinguishing charity from justice which are supposed to explain and secure the kind of prioritisation between them that Smith claims to find reflected in ordinary moral experience. All are mistaken.[11]

Duty versus supererogation

Some think: If one does whatever impeccably just people do, then one does no more than one's moral duty, whereas what the charitable do is necessarily beyond the call of duty.[12] This would establish the lexical priority of justice on the assumption that one cannot justifiably fail to do one's duty in order to do something beyond the call of duty instead. In fact this assumption is false. If I break my promise to meet you for lunch because I stop off to save a drowning child from the canal at great personal risk, I act supererogatorily and yet my consequent breach of duty is amply justified.[13] But be that as it may, the proposed mapping of the justice/charity distinction onto the duty/supererogation distinction distorts both virtues. What is certainly true—and important—is that the just are concerned, in a way in which the charitable are not, with people getting what is due to them from those from whom it is due. Possibly (let us concede for the time being) this does entail that the moral priorities of the just person are dominated, as those of the charitable are not, by duties. But even so, her actions *qua* just may go well beyond performing her *own* duties. They may include supererogatory actions of enabling, encouraging, persuading, cajoling, or even compelling others to render (and receive) their due. One may exhibit how just one is in campaigning tirelessly at great personal cost to organise

[11] Some of the views to be encountered here were also attacked by Allen Buchanan in "Justice and Charity", (1987) 97 *Ethics* 558. However, his criticisms often do not square with mine. More sympathetic to my approach, although less detailed, are the remarks of Robert Goodin in *Protecting the Vulnerable* (Chicago, Chicago University Press, 1985), 16–17.

[12] e.g. A Gewirth, "Private Philanthropy and Positive Rights", (1987) 4 *Social Philosophy and Policy* 54, 55. Gewirth speaks of "philanthropy" but his definition of this includes all charitable giving as well as philanthropy in the strict sense discussed in part 3 below.

[13] See F Kamm, "Supererogation and Obligation", (1985) 82 *Journal of Philosophy* 118. To avoid begging any questions, my example in the text is one in which the conflict is not between justice and charity. Meeting you for lunch would not be a just thing to do (although it would be a considerate thing to do) and saving the child need not be unusually charitable (although it might be exceptionally courageous).

appeals for people on death row, to secure compensation for impoverished victims of wrongdoing, etc.

Conversely, people are sometimes only doing their duty in acting charitably. Or so, at any rate, they are apt to claim. Some, like Mother Teresa, even regard it as their duty to *devote their lives* to charitable endeavour *qua* charitable. It is one thing to say that these people are overzealous in holding themselves to have such an extensive duty of charity, but quite another to accuse them of defying logic in supposing that they could have any duties of charity at all. Could it really be true that the long history of such commitment to charitable endeavour, believed by the committed to be no more than their duty, is not only morally misguided but also conceptually confused? That defies belief. What might seem more credible, perhaps, is the thought that people only have duties of charity if they are sufficiently charitable types. That is to say, the value of the charitable spirit in which Mother Teresa acted made duties of actions that would not otherwise have been duties. By contrast, it may be said, we all have our duties of justice (e.g. to compensate those whom we have wronged) whether or not we are remotely just people. But that still cannot be right. It is a condition of the existence of any duty that it is possible in principle to perform it for no other reason than that it is one's duty. But performing a duty of charity for the sole reason that it is one's duty is inconsistent with performing it charitably. If one does this, one is not being charitable, but rather diligent or conscientious. One lacks the spirit of spontaneous fellow-feeling that animates one's charitable friends. It follows that being charitable cannot be a necessary condition of being under a duty of charity. You may object that the diligent or conscientious person's "cold charity" has a rather poor reputation. True enough. But the explanation cannot be that such people are not doing their duty. A much more likely explanation is that they are doing it in a morally second-rate way, i.e. for second-best reasons and in a second-best spirit. *Pace* Kant and his followers, diligence is more like a fall-back virtue than a master-virtue. (All this is consistent, by the way, with the possibility that some duties of charity bind only those who occupy certain roles, e.g. social workers, teachers, followers of certain religions, clerics, etc. The same is true of duties of justice, some of which only bind judges, others of which only bind parents, etc. That a duty is a moral one does not entail that it is *everyone's* duty.)

Rules versus decisions on the case

According to a different view, there may be duties of charity as well as duties of justice, but whereas duties of justice are embodied in rules, duties of charity arise one at a time, according to the merits of particular cases. The just person uses rules to settle who gets how much of what, but the charitable person is disposed to react *ad hoc* to localised variations in people's predicaments. This puts justice in the moral driving seat, it is thought, granted only the everyday assumption that even when we reason on the merits we must at least play by the rules.[14] In fact, this latter assumption is groundless. Adherence to sound rules, even those establishing moral duties, is often just one of several justified ways to proceed. This is an elementary implication of what we learn from Mill and Sidgwick. But in any case, justice and charity cannot be differentiated according to the ruliness or unruliness of their respective priorities. That I make it my rule always to give everyone the benefit of the doubt in thinking about what is to be done for them or done to them makes me a decidedly charitable person. A just person might well be prepared to allow that rule, or even insist on it, in the particular context of criminal trials where someone is up against the might of the state, but would resist applying the rule more generally. Isn't this charitable rule (the just person might say) a kind of abdication of judgmental responsibility when those before us are all ordinary folk with their competing requests and requirements, and giving one the benefit of the doubt means (in effect) denying it to another? Isn't this rule a recipe for failing to give everyone their due? The debate here is not about *whether* rules are to be used but about *which* rules are to be used. Indeed in such a debate it might well be the just person rather than the charitable person who would be the first to abandon her resort to rules in favour of deliberation on the merits of the particular case. Solomon's most famous judicial intervention, after all, was tailor-made for a particular case and involved no rule-following on his part. Here we see the face of *equity*, which Hobbes classified, you will recall, as one of the faces of justice, not one of the faces of charity. And rightly so.

Perfect versus imperfect duties

Unlike duties of justice, it is sometimes said, duties of charity leave it to the duty-bearer to determine the particular occasions for compliance, so long as an adequate measure of compliance is chalked up over time.[15] The latter are imperfect duties, whereas the former are perfect duties. Perfect duties surely take priority when they arise, the thinking goes, for (in view of their built-in flexibility) one generally has *other* opportunities to perform the imperfect ones without doing so at the expense of fulfilling perfect ones. One may doubt whether this distinction between types of duties is a distinction of substance, and (even if it is) whether it has the advertised implication for prioritisation.[16] But even if the distinction works as its proponents say it does, it clearly fails to mark the

[14] A story along these lines emerges from L Lomasky, "Justice to Charity", (1995) 12 *Social Philosophy and Policy* 32.

[15] The view is most closely associated with Kant: see his *Groundwork of the Metaphysic of Morals* (ed Paton, New York, Harper and Row, 1964), 89–91. There is more than one way to use the expression "imperfect duty": see O O'Neill, "The Great Maxims of Justice and Charity", in N MacCormick and Z Bankowski (eds), *Enlightenment, Rights, and Revolutions* (Aberdeen, Aberdeen University Press, 1989) 297, 301–2. However I have interpreted it as Kant appears to interpret it in explaining why duties of charity are imperfect. For another interpretation, cf n 21 below.

[16] See J Waldron, *Liberal Rights* (Cambridge, Cambridge University Press, 1993), 14–16.

difference between duties of justice and duties of charity. Recall the parable of the Good Samaritan. Even if the priest and the Levite have no duty of justice to help (even if the traveller in trouble has only himself to blame, even if helping would mean letting the original malefactors off the hook, even if the priest and the Levites have already done more than their bit for the sick and needy today, etc.) it remains their duty of charity to help. If they do indeed have this duty, it is a duty of charity that is as perfect as could be. It is a duty to go to the aid of this particular traveller right here, right now. In fact, in this case the duties of justice seem to be the less perfect ones if any are, for they are the ones that seem to be chalking up credits and debits over time. Only a just person—dare I say someone who is *too* just, to the point of being a bit of a stickler?—would think, in a situation like this, about whether someone going to the injured traveller's aid would be doing more that his due, or whether the traveller is asking for more than his due. "Who cares?", a more charitable person would respond, "Can't you see he's in serious trouble? We can quibble later about what's due to whom and from whom. Now is the time to lend a hand, no further questions asked." This imaginary exchange brings out that the "imperfect" view of duties of charity is actually *the just person's myopic view of what duties of charity are like*. It is a view which (predictably enough) turns duties of charity into (relatively unspecific) duties of justice instead, structured by the idea of *giving one's due over time*. This idea of giving one's due is the very idea that impeccably charitable people tend to regard as a distraction.

From these refutations there starts to emerge a positive picture of how the moral priorities of the just and the charitable really do contrast, a picture in which the sub-groups of moral reasons to which these character types are respectively astute differ not in their *force* but in their *content*. Of this emerging picture, however, various elements call for further explanation. The most important is the mysterious concept of the *due*, which the just person regards as central but the charitable person regards as distracting. My explanation of the Samaritan case suggests that A can have a duty towards B even though, in the fulfilment of it, A will give more than her due and B will get more than his due. How can we make sense of this paradoxical-sounding suggestion? Here are a couple of explanations which get us closer to the truth about justice and charity, even though neither is spot on.

Deserts versus needs

One explanation has the just person caring primarily about what people *deserve*, whereas the charitable person cares first and foremost about what people *need*.[17] If "due" means something like "deserved", then the idea of a duty

[17] See T Campbell, "Humanity Before Justice", (1974) 4 *British Journal of Political Science* 1. In allying Campbell with the view in the text I do not distinguish, as in a fuller analysis one should, between the humane and the charitable. My excuse is that Campbell also fails to keep them distinct.

without dueness no longer sounds so paradoxical. One could have a duty of charity based on need which competes for attention with a duty of justice based on desert. This would also harmonise nicely with another point already mentioned. As we saw, the just often disagree with the charitable about whether and how to *judge* people. As compared with the just, the charitable tend to help others more often and more freely but they also judge others less often and less harshly. What exactly is the connection between these two tendencies? The proposal now under scrutiny explains. Since they give priority to the deserved, the just begin by judging *people* in order to judge how much those people ought to contribute or receive. Whereas the charitable think that such a judgmental outlook misses the more pressing problem of meeting people's needs, which are typically quite unrelated to their deserts.

This explanation is half right. It is right regarding the charitable and their attitude to desert. But the explanation is wrong regarding the just and their attitude to need. "To each according to his needs" is a principle of justice, not a principle of charity. That is because of the special work done by the words "according to". The just person cares about needs as well as deserts, but she cares about needs *on the model of deserts*. She treats needs as reasons for deciding *among* people (or groups of people) as possible recipients or contributors. To put it another way, she sees every action of contributing to others as a kind of adjudication in their favour. Others (including her) are (in effect) the losers, she says, so the question always arises whether the right people were favoured. If she ends up favouring the wrong people (the less needy, the less deserving, or whatever) it is always a failure for her *qua* just. But for the more charitable type it is still a success so long as help was indeed rendered to people who did indeed need it. This is not to say that faced with the choice between meeting a more urgent and a less urgent need, where all else is equal, we might as well opt to deal with the less urgent need, for that is no less charitable. On the contrary: that would be irrationality and cannot be justified as the action of a charitable person any more than it could be justified as the action of a just person. But the question is not whether such an irrational adjudication is justified. The question is whether all actions of helping the needy are to be conceived by those facing them as primarily raising questions of this adjudicative type, i.e. whether their success is to be judged by applying the just person's test of success rather than the charitable person's.

Plainly the answer is no. Even if we assume (wrongly) that there is an overall transitive ranking of different kinds of needs, and even if we assume (wrongly) that "to each according to his needs" is the only sound principle of justice, it does not follow that *using* this sound principle of justice as one's own principle is the only way justifiably to set about meeting people's needs. We know from the rule-utilitarians that direct success is not the only kind of success, nor always the most reliable. The charitable may say that (even applying the test of whether each does receive *according to* her needs) we do better on the whole by worrying about people's needs as we notice them (i.e. simply by being astute to them *as needs*) than we would by always worrying about whether we have indeed noticed them in the right order (i.e. by being astute to them as possible grounds for adjudicating among different competing claims on our time and energy and money). "Even if we do get some of them in the wrong order," the more charitable may say to their more just friends, "at least we were out there meeting them, whereas you guys were still sitting around quibbling about *who* should meet *whose* needs, and which *first*, and so forth. Didn't you notice that meanwhile some people were *dying*? What kind of sense of priority is that?" Of course, as one would expect in a quarrel among those with different moral virtues, this scathing remark puts an excessively negative spin on what the just were doing. Unlike the depressing sticklers who take their concern with what is due too far (and sometimes do indeed quibble people to death), impeccably just people know where to draw the line. But still they draw the line differently from their more charitable friends. For they *do* think that adjudicative concerns—identifying who has the strongest claim and meeting it first—have a higher priority in sound reasoning than the charitable person is prepared to allow. Over a range of cases more charitable people will justifiably be shocked that their more just friends were willing to see A's needs go unmet merely because A had already had a lot of needs met as compared with B, or B had already made his contribution to A's needs and it was now C's turn to do something for a change, etc. Meanwhile the more just types will justifiably get sniffy at the tendency of the charitable to go off and meet people's needs willy nilly, without giving much weight to such important objections.

A fortiori once other adjudicative criteria, such as desert, are put back into play so that the just person has an even larger stock of adjudicative objections to draw on, and can accuse the charitable not only of overlooking the more needy, but also of letting the guilty off the hook or rewarding the malefactors, etc. At this point we leave behind the mainly Millian disagreement between the two characters and embark on what can only be a deeper Aristotelian one. For now there are clearly multiple moral targets to hit and they cannot be comprehensively ranked independently of the moral characters of those who do the ranking. In particular there are undeserving people in dire need (e.g. child-murderers held for years in intolerable psychological conditions on death row) and deserving people with less pressing needs (e.g. innocent people who have been ripped off and lost part of their life-savings). It is logically impossible to reduce these two cross-cutting dimensions of morality—the evaluation of people and the evaluation of their predicaments—to a single-value moral project. As the failures of Kant and the classical utilitarians showed, doing so cannot but be reductive in respect of one or other of the two dimensions. Either one follows the utilitarian path and ends up missing out (or rather instrumentalising to the point of unrecognisability) the moral evaluation of people, or else one follows the Kantian path and ends up missing out (or rather relegating to the supposedly subordinate domain of prudence) the moral evaluation of their predicaments. Either way one has lost sight of an essential aspect of morality. I am not saying, I should stress, that this is the only irreducible schism to be found among ultimate moral concerns. Nor am I saying that the just are more Kantian in their priorities and the charitable more utilitarian. I am only saying that sometimes their differences of priority may bring that old philosophical division to mind, reminding us that *some* moral schisms are beyond being explained away as merely Millian or Sidgwickian differences.

Rights versus goals

But maybe (some will say) there is a more direct connection with the old philosophical dispute. Couldn't the difference between the two characters under discussion perhaps be summed up by saying that, to the extent that both care about helping others, the just care about honouring people's *rights* to be helped whereas the charitable downplay those rights in favour of the *goal* of helping? The contrast between rights and goals is a well-known false contrast.[18] It also has nothing much to do with the struggle between Kant and the utilitarians. All the same, it might have something to do with the struggle between the just and the charitable. A right to charity is admittedly an odder thing to claim than a right to justice. Could this point to an easy way of restating the relevant notion of "dueness"? Maybe what is due to me from you is no more and no less than what I have a right to as against you. In which case there can be a duty to provide more than is due to another, as in the Good Samaritan story, if and only if there can be duties not based on that other's rights. And indeed there can be such duties. Many moral duties, such as my duty to pay my taxes and my duty to vote and my duty not to pollute the river, are not rights-based. Maybe duties of charity belong in the same class?[19]

Well actually, they cannot *quite* belong in the same class. The duties just mentioned are not rights-based duties because they are not duties to serve any distinct person's (or any distinct group of people's) interests.[20] But the moral duty of the priest, the Levite, and the Samaritan is clearly a duty to serve the interests of the forlorn traveller. Isn't that enough to make it a rights-based duty of charity? I think it is: the duty is owed to the traveller, it is based on his right. So there is indeed a right to charity here. The oddness of talking about such rights is not semantic but pragmatic. We live in such legalistic times that when we think about rights to charity, we tend to think first about the traveller *claiming* such a right against someone. Thinking in those terms, we cannot but transpose the

[18] Rights are possible goals. Cf A Sen, "Rights and Agency", (1982) 11 *Philosophy and Public Affairs* 3.

[19] Mill, *Utilitarianism*, above n 5, 305. Mill regards this as a restatement of the view that duties of charity are imperfect duties. This shows another possible interpretation of the expression "imperfect duty". However my argument shows that duties of charity are still not imperfect ones even on this interpretation.

[20] I borrow my explanation of the nature of rights from J Raz, *The Morality of Freedom* (Oxford, Clarendon Press, 1986), chaps 7 and 8.

whole issue into an adjudicative idiom. Now there is an imaginary *dispute* about what should be done, a *competition* for the energy or time or money of others, and someone has to be the winner and someone else the loser. At this point the duty can no longer be conceived or discussed as a duty of charity, for it has been transformed by the adjudicative context. If it is to be recognised as a duty in this context, it can only be recognised as a duty of justice. For those who think that rights *are* claims, this sets up a logical obstacle to the idea of a right to charity.[21] But rights are not claims. They are reasons why others have duties to serve the interests of the right-holder. They can be mentioned, discussed, infringed, honoured, and acted on, as well as being, and without being, claimed. So while the thought of *claiming* a right to charity may be close to oxymoronic (thanks to the overtone of dispute or contest) the idea of *having* such a right, or *honouring* one, or *violating* one, is not. Accordingly, the relevant notion of "getting (or giving) one's due", the one that preoccupies the just and differentiates their priorities from those of the charitable, is not that of having one's rights honoured. It is close to the notion of having one's rights honoured *in the resolution of a dispute or competition*. To the extent that talk of rights is regarded as the natural language of disputes and competitions, it may seem natural to think that justice is the virtue of those who care most about rights. And to the extent that morality is seen as a kind of adjudicative framework for disputes and competitions, the just may be seen as bearers of the most important moral virtue, even (perhaps) the *master* moral virtue. But in fact the second view is as distorted a view of morality as the first is a distorted view of rights. While life is competitive and yields many disputes, resolving these is not the whole art of life. In fact much of the art of life (taking in not only charity but also, as we will see, loyalty and public-spiritedness) is the art of remaining charmingly oblivious to them.

The remarks of this part go well beyond an attack on the dismissive "Stepford wife" view of the virtue of charity. They tell against all views which portray the virtues of justice and charity as standing in a special harmonious relationship with each other, whether thanks to lexical ranking or otherwise. That the two virtues stand in a special relationship cannot be denied. But it is the stormy relationship of *foils*. Of course, only two characters closely bound together can be foils. And so it is with the just and the charitable. Of any just action or reaction there is an intelligible charitable variation, and *vice versa*. And whoever can be treated justly can also be treated charitably, and *vice versa*. This was the idea conveyed in the thought, with which we embarked upon our comparison of the two character-types, that both aspire to provide answers to the moral question of *who gets what from whom*? We can now see that this way of bringing out their common starting-point was misleading. With its undertone of a pending

[21] Cf O'Neill, "The Great Maxims", above n 15, who notices that performance of a duty of charity cannot be *claimed* and regards that as supporting the view that such a duty is not rights-based. But then she makes a subtle modification which gives her error away. She articulates her view as the view that duties of charity, unlike those of justice, are not based on "claimable rights". Quite so: but this does not show that they are not based on rights.

adjudication this is already a just person's way of putting the question. So it predisposes us to a just person's answer.[22] But it nevertheless helps to remind us that the just and the charitable are not just occasionally and accidentally at odds over tricky cases, in the way that the honest and the loyal find themselves at odds over some tricky cases where one must deceive to avoid betrayal and *vice versa*. On the contrary, the just and the charitable are *set up* to collide; to be more charitable *is*, you might say, partly a matter of being at odds with one's more just friends. One can see why this fact might strike some as frustrating. In an age when so few react to the serious problems of strangers for anything other than morally unimpressive reasons, such as making a profit out of their misery, why can't all the "caring and sharing" types join forces, stop quarrelling, get on with the business?[23] The answer—if I may end this part by simplifying and thereby slightly parodying the distinction between the two virtues—is that the just person's sharing is a fair-weather friend to the charitable person's caring. Unlike the care of the charitable, the care of the just, *qua* just, tends to run out once people have given or taken their share.

3. CHARITY AND PUBLIC-SPIRITEDNESS

> [G]ood dispositions are those which are suitable for entering into civil society; and good habits (that is, moral virtues) are those whereby what was entered into can best be preserved. For all the virtues are contained in justice and charity.[24]

We already noted the myopic Hobbesian tendency to think that *who gets what from whom* is the main or even the only issue facing "civil society". We might reply that there are, on the contrary, many civic virtues, such as neighbourliness and public-spiritedness, the priorities of which have nothing much to do with who gets what. But this reply grants Hobbes' further assumption, spelt out in the passage just quoted, that charity and justice are indeed to be listed among the *civic* virtues. In reality they are not. They are virtues of what might be called the *humanitarian* class. Their default constituency is that of all human beings.[25]

[22] Cf Charity Commission, *The Hallmarks of a Well-Run Charity*, leaflet CC 60 (London, Charity Commission, 1999), para (g): "a charity should be ready [publicly] to explain and justify the policies and practices it has chosen to adopt." Does this also predispose to a just person's explanation or justification?

[23] Cf F Gladstone, *Charity, Law, and Social Justice* (London, Bedford Square Press, 1982), 32. In an attempt to marshal the troops Gladstone claims that charity, like justice, is a virtue of "equal and unconditional concern". The obvious objection is that equal concern—if the word "equal" is to mean anything—cannot be unconditional. It has to be conditional on the recipient's not already having had her (equal) share.

[24] Hobbes, *De Homine*, above n 1, 117.

[25] All living creatures? I think not. I think it is impossible to be either just or charitable towards donkeys or squirrels. At any rate one cannot be charitable towards them unless one can also be just towards them, which requires in turn that they be moral agents (and thus can be judged morally on what they do). The question of whether the constituency of moral agents goes beyond humanity cannot be discussed here, and anyway does not affect the main point.

The just *qua* just may care as readily about prisoners of conscience on the other side of the globe, the charitable as much about starvation on another continent. The slogan "charity begins at home" is not, you will notice, something that the charitable tend to say. It is normally a complaint of the rather uncharitable who wish that the charitable would be more loyal and less charitable. If I am charitable or just, however, people are *people*, never mind whether they are *my* people. This is not to deny, of course, that some just people and some charitable people, occupying certain specialist roles, have their energies diverted into the problems of smaller constituencies than the whole of humankind. Of course there are divisions of moral labour with specialised duties attached. Judges have special duties of justice as between litigants, teachers have special duties of charity towards their pupils, etc. That is not the point. The point is that to be impeccably just or impeccably charitable, across even these small constituencies, one must exhibit the capacity to look upon those involved as human beings with none of whom one has any special personal bonds—no special loyalties, if you like—beyond those of shared humanity. As we saw in the previous part, there are two contrasting ways of doing this, which are foils to each other. The charitable person emphasises human *commonality*, the fact that all human beings are by their nature needy, vulnerable creatures, in the same boat, all at risk of drowning, be it through natural disaster, disaster brought about by others, even disaster of their own making. The just, by contrast, emphasise human *separateness*, the fact that all human beings have their own distinctive interests which may conflict, and which need to be adjudicated, so that lines constantly need to be drawn between disasters made by another and disasters of one's own making, or between greater and lesser disasters, etc. Although sometimes the disasters in question may be local to particular societies, they need not be. Unlike a specifically civic virtue, justice and charity can be exhibited no less perfectly in one's global relations, and without any buttressing belief in the existence of a global civil society. In fact, the suggestion of a global civil society is usually a piece of propaganda designed to capture the work of some people with civic virtues for the wider humanitarian cause. It is an attempt to globalise the more parochial virtues by conjuring up the image of a global parish. Often this is the reaction of the just or the charitable who are justifiably frustrated with those whose virtues lie in their relations with a narrower, often more parochial, constituency. These in turn divide into two main groups. First there are those, like the loyal and the patriotic, whose virtues lie in their relationship with a *particular* person or group of people, or a *particular* society. These people are foils to the just and the charitable alike, and I return to them in the next part. But secondly there are those, notably the public-spirited and the neighbourly, whose virtue lies in their relationship with and participation in aspects of civil society *as such*, never mind which *particular* society. These people are not exactly foils to the just and the charitable, but nor are they simply more of the same. The label "civic virtue" is, in my view, most helpfully reserved for this group. A common tendency to assimilate the humanitarian virtue of charity to the civic virtues, and in particular to confuse it with public-spiritedness, has some unhappy contemporary consequences.

Duties of charity may, as we saw, be rights-based. Not so duties of public-spiritedness. This is because the distinctive priority of the public-spirited is the provision and maintenance of public goods, such as sensitive policing, public education, a vibrant artistic culture, fine cityscapes, good government, etc. They care, in Hobbesian terms, about how civil society can best be preserved or improved. Although public-spiritedness takes many forms—including participation in local politics, giving up a lucrative city job to work in the civil service, working in the community garden, etc.—those who are public-spirited in how they use their own resources have the special title of *philanthropist*. The philanthropic and the charitable are particularly easily confused.[26] The main reason is that tackling some human deprivations can also be a public good. It is not only the formerly poor who are better off for the eradication of poverty, nor only those educated by it who are better off for a strong culture of public education. We are all better off for inhabiting a less fractured, or as the case may be more cultivated, society. I do not mean that we will each see further benefits, e.g. higher wages or reduced crime, thanks to more cordial social relations or a more skilled workforce or something like that. I mean that living in a less fractured or more cultivated society (or a more politically active or more tolerant society, etc., as the case may be) *is* the benefit. It is the very fact that this is a benefit to all if it is a benefit to any that makes it a public good, and thus a matter of interest to the public-spirited. By contrast it is the different fact that it helps the poor or illiterate (or the disenfranchised or the victimised etc.) that makes it of interest to the more charitable person.

One can quickly see the scope here for another fair-weather friendship. The public-spirited person, especially the philanthropist, may well be a reliable dispenser of what I referred to earlier as "cold charity"—cold, because it is not a human deprivation *as such* that animates her to get involved, so much as the broader social advance that comes of dealing with that deprivation. Her spirit is that of earnest concern rather than that of spontaneous fellow-feeling: she cares about *the problem of poverty*, say, more than about *the plight of the poor*. To the more charitable person she is missing the point. And yet, precisely as the just and the charitable may productively collaborate up to a point, so may the charitable and the public-spirited. In English law, notice, the concept of charity has been adapted to blur the boundaries between the virtue of charity on the one hand and that of public-spiritedness on the other. The requirement that, to be legally charitable, activities must be "for the public benefit" is one that equivocates between a charitable person's interpretation (that a wide enough constituency of people must stand to have their deprivations ameliorated) and a public-spirited person's interpretation (that a public good must be served,

[26] e.g. J Waldron, *Liberal Rights*, above n 16, 15; M Chesterman, *Charities, Trusts and Social Welfare* (London, Weidenfeld and Nicolson, 1979), 2.

whether or not by ameliorating anyone's deprivations).[27] Many tensions in the law of charity reflect this ambivalence. Most notoriously: Is educational provision "for the public benefit" (e.g. in fee-paying schools and the elite universities) even when it doesn't tackle anybody's educational deprivations?[28] The problem arises because here the two virtues part company; more charitable types (often here with the support of their more just friends) reckon that their more public-spirited friends have lost the plot (and likewise when the latter open another art gallery or opera house, beautify another landscape or stately home, etc.). While some people are in such great need, aren't there more pressing things to be done than supporting esoteric research or operatic excellence, especially if the main enthusiasts for these goods are the already advantaged? Possibly. Maybe some people are being *too* public-spirited, at the price of not being charitable enough. Or possibly their public-spiritedness is a failure even in its own terms (what they thought to be a valuable public good really isn't one). On the other hand maybe these are cases in which the impeccably charitable and the impeccably public-spirited simply part company, in which there are two incompatible and mutually incomprehensible ways to be morally unimpeachable. Be that as it may, the law talks as if this is not an issue by fudging the difference between the two virtues and calling them both "charity".

This is one of several legal fudges which lead to schisms among organisations involved in (legally) charitable pursuits. Some quite justifiably have no wish to be associated with others. A common proposal is that purely public-spirited activities (such as setting up orchestras or running art galleries) ought also to have to meet an *additional* test of genuine charitability (say, of working mainly to bring musical or artistic training or experience to those hitherto deprived of it) before they can join the world of "charity".[29] The fact that, in using the label "charity", the law is probably misleading some people into thinking that this is *already* the test, gives power to the moral elbow of this proposal.[30] On the other

[27] To judge by the remarks of Lord Wilberforce in *Re Resch's Will Trusts* [1969] 1 AC 514, the two types of public benefit (which he calls "direct" and "indirect") both count independently towards charitable status, so that enough of one, or enough of the other, or enough of a mixture of the two, will do. I should add that the law judges the public benefit of the objectives that the contributor *expressed* herself to have, and does not look behind these to see if she also had some ulterior reason. Obviously this additional move allows some whose actions are *neither* charitable *nor* public-spirited (but rather e.g. prudent uses of tax allowances) to be classed as legally charitable as well.

[28] Compare *Re Macduff* [1896] 2 Ch 451, 471 (Lindley LJ), with *Governors of Campbell College Belfast* v. *Commissioner of Valuation for Northern Ireland* [1964] 2 All ER 705.

[29] See e.g. Chesterman, above n 26, 338–9, where he relies, interestingly, on the key distinction between charity and philanthropy that he denies on page 2. He pursues a variation on this theme in his contribution to this volume at 253–61.

[30] An interesting example concerns animal welfare. Many people support animal welfare causes under the heading of charity (meaning their actions to alleviate the suffering of animals). The law, however, accords these causes charitable status only *qua* public-spirited, i.e. only for their contribution to civilised human life by their war against human cruelty: *Re Wedgwood* [1915] 1 Ch 113. That the donors may be in error to regard their actions as genuinely charitable in the moral sense (see text to n 26 above) does not eliminate the worry that the error is being exploited by the law's use of the label "charity" to describe a cause recognised in law only for its public-spiritedness.

hand, the fact that people systematically undervalue public goods (because their benefits are diffuse) provides a strong counterargument (viz. that unless they are sneaked in under some other heading, public goods will be inadequately supported). On top of this there is the complicating factor that a strong institutional arrangement to support (genuinely) charitable action is *itself* a public good, to which the public-spirited often do contribute thanks to the fact that they are legally bundled in with the charitable and to some extent collaborate in their activities. And then there is the question of whether truly charitable activities must also reciprocate by meting the "public good" standard (which may pose new problems for, e.g., emergency overseas famine-relief projects). Obviously this is not the place for a full critique of the law of charity. Like most law it represents a great deal of political compromise and has to be approached in that light. Its interest to us here is mainly that the ambiguity of the "public benefit" test captures nicely, and yields nice illustrations of, the inevitable instability of the alliance between the charitable and the public-spirited.

Would another way to put the contrast be to say that the charitable have a more *individualistic* outlook than the public-spirited? After all it is sometimes thought to be the hallmark of moral individualists that they do not see value in public goods as such, but only in the further benefits they bring to particular people. On this basis it is often said that justice is a virtue with individualistic priorities.[31] Maybe charity too? I find the label "individualist" misleading in this context, and misleading as applied to justice as well as to charity. Among the things that can be treated justly or charitably are not only people but also *groups* of people. It is possible to be charitable towards whole nations, or to be just in one's dealings with aboriginal peoples, etc. Possibly, when one is just or charitable towards a group, what one provides them with is sometimes a public good. But notice how one must *regard* it in order to be just or charitable. One must regard it as giving the group its due (to be just) or as going to the group's aid (to be charitable). The mere fact that it is a public good does not suffice as a reason for providing it, as it does for the public-spirited. You may say that in this last sentence I am back-tracking from my suggestion that public-spiritedness is a civic virtue. Couldn't one be public-spirited in building a school or a church for another society but one's own? Of course. My suggestion that the public-spirited have a civic virtue, recall, was not the suggestion that they contribute specifically to the shape of their *own* society. It was that their interest lies in contributing to the shape of *some* society, and (unlike the charitable and the just) not merely to some of the groups or individuals that inhabit it. Even though they are not humanitarian—they do not see people merely as human beings, but rather as inhabitants of a society—there is no built-in element of partisanship towards any *particular* people or any *particular* society in the civic virtues.

[31] See e.g. M Sandel, *Liberalism and the Limits of Justice* (Cambridge, Cambridge University Press, 1982), 168–73.

4. CHARITY AND LOYALTY

> Charity is that virtue by which part of the sincere Love we have for our selves is transferr'd pure and unmix'd to others, not tied to us by the Bonds of Friendship or Consanguinity, and even mere Strangers, whom we have no obligation to, nor hope or expect any thing from.[32]

Mandeville's remark brings us to another group of virtues which *do* involve the extra element of partisanship—for a particular person or group or nation or culture—and it is this element of partisanship that makes these virtues true foils to both justice and charity. Moreover these partisan virtues—notably loyalty, solidarity, and patriotism—are virtues of notoriously problematic standing in eyes of moral philosophers. The austerity of the Kantian and utilitarian "master-virtue" proposals came partly of the thought that loyalty, solidarity, patriotism, etc. are the chief moral *enemy*, moral vices masquerading as virtues, fit only to be slain by an authentic moral virtue that knows no deep attachment to any person or group of people over any other. Part of their bad reputation comes, of course, of the fact that loyalty, solidarity, and patriotism have been systematically tarnished with the brush of their own immoral excesses. Patriotism is not a virtue, it is said, because some nations are vile and their so-called patriots are actually sad chauvinists, solidarity is not a virtue because it creates the hostile climate of class or family antagonisms, loyalty is not a virtue because it leads to some people covering up each other's war crimes, etc. All that such examples really show, of course, is that it is possible to be too loyal or too patriotic or too solidary to the point of vice, exactly as it is possible to be too just or too charitable to the point of vice.[33] They do not show that patriotism and solidarity and loyalty are not moral virtues any more than the fact that some people are appalling sticklers for what is due shows that justice is not a moral virtue, or the fact that some are soppy sentimentalists who lavish support on cuddly causes shows that there is no moral virtue in charity.

Nevertheless it is important to grasp just how sharply these virtues do contrast with justice and charity. One can be loyal etc. only to someone or something *in particular*. It has to be the very thing that it is. No substitute will do, even one that has all the same rationally significant properties. It is no good reminding me, as a patriotic Scot, that in every significant way Sweden is no less fine a country than Scotland. The point is that it is not Scotland, and Scotland is my country. And even if this fellow you have introduced me to is just as splendid as my friend, and in just the same situation, and making just the same

[32] Bernard Mandeville, "An Essay on Charity and Charity-Schools", in *The Fable of the Bees* (ed Kaye, Oxford, Clarendon Press, 1924), vol 1, 253, 253.

[33] Cf A MacIntyre, "Is Patriotism a Virtue?", in M Rosen and J Wolff (eds), *Political Thought* (Oxford, Oxford University Press, 1999) 269, whose analysis makes the concept of an "immoral excess" of patriotism hard to accommodate, thus giving succour to those who regard patriotism as a vice.

request for assistance, and even if he would be a great friend, he is *not* my friend, and that means that I don't have the same duties towards him as I do towards my friend. My friend is invested with special value, and his good is made a special priority, simply because *he is the one* that is my friend. One may, of course, be just or charitable in respect of one's friends (or one's family or country or social class etc.). But to do so in the right spirit one must have the capacity to overcome one's attachment to them, temporarily to abstract oneself and think of them as just like other people. Often, happily, this can be done without disloyalty. But there is a constant risk of conflict thanks to the opposition between seeing human beings *simply as* human beings and seeing them as the particular human beings they are (or as defined in terms of the particular affiliations they have). So often—and again it is no mere accidental conflict—one cannot be impeccably loyal except at the price of compromising one's justice or one's charity, and *vice versa*.

In the case of charity, the directness of this collision is sometimes overlooked thanks to the theological association of charity with *love*, of which Mandeville reminds us. If the spirit of charity is a kind of love then surely all the virtues of successful love—including loyalty—are naturally at ease with it? At any rate, it belongs to the same family of virtues, what we may call the *warm* virtues (contrasted with the colder virtues of justice, diligence, etc.).[34] The problem with this line of thought is brought out by Aquinas.[35] Just as we may show austere Kantian "philosophical respect" for those whom we rightly despise, so we may have a kind of "philosophical love" for those who are nothing to us personally, even for those we rightly hate. It is the love of common humanity. It is not the love of particular people, which by its very nature depends on the contrastive purchase of there being others out there who are *un*loved. And the virtue of loyalty is the virtue which supplies this contrastive purchase, which prioritises the good of the object of one's affections and in the process deprioritises the good of others. If one wants to think of charity as a kind of loyalty to (or solidarity with) one's fellow human beings, so be it. But in the process one misses the key point about loyalty. One misses the fact that loyalty is a virtue of selective attachment. If there are none to whom one has no loyalty at all then there are none to whom one is loyal either. Whereas charity prizes its own indiscriminateness as between particular (i.e. nominate) people. One can, of course, be a charitable enthusiast for certain *causes*, and to that extent loyalty and charity may go hand-in-hand. But notice that those causes cannot entail loyalty to any particular (nominate) beneficiaries without losing their charitable character. And notice too that one is not very charitable if one's loyalty to a cause means that one denigrates or bemoans other charitable causes (for then one is not being very charitable in judging those who support them).

[34] Cf Rob Atkinson's discussion in this book at 135–8 of "fellowship" and "intimacy" as distinguishing features of the non-profit sector.

[35] *Summa Theologica* II-II, Q25.

Again the conflict between charity and loyalty is familiar from contemporary debates about the law of charity. At the slightly permeable margins of charitable status, in English law, lie self-help groups and other mutual benefit organisations.[36] It is often said that they must be brought into the centre of things from the wasteland of uncertain legal status. They are more democratic or grass-roots, they epitomise the way forward for the charitable sector, they replace the old idea of charity as something graciously passed down from on high with the more modern and less demeaning idea of people being helped to help themselves, etc. Now, no doubt the proliferation of more complex types of deprivation does mean that beneficiary involvement in organised charitable pursuits is a guard against various kinds of ignorance and blunder. But notice that the idea of mutuality as a paradigm goes much further than this. It moves away from the idea of a common humanity in the direction of an idea of special loyalties to those with whom one shares a predicament, including special duties of reciprocity of the kind that characterise personal friendship, marriage, and neighbourly and collegial relations. Genuine charitable people—as opposed to pseudo-charitable self-aggrandisers—expect none of this reciprocity. It is nothing to them if their help goes unthanked and even unrecognised. To have helped one's fellow human beings is enough. The Good Samaritan, for instance, asks nothing in return. His intervention is unconditional. Some loyalty, of course, is equally unconditional, like that of parents for their children. It too asks for nothing in return. But still it is the foil of charity: you are *you*, brother, you are *one of us*, you are *part of the family*, you are *not* just another human being, a stranger, nobody in particular. In this contrast between the charitable and the loyal, unlike the contrast between the charitable and the public-spirited, the English law of charity has remained largely true to its name and has resisted moves to embrace the dramatically contrasting "one of us" paradigm. It has hesitated over beneficiary-trustees, beneficiary-members, beneficiary-contributors, and all the other trappings of mutualism.[37] If mutualism is the one true way forward, then the law of *charity*—properly so called—is clearly on its way out. For this is not charity but a form of loyalty or solidarity.

Three cheers for that, some will say: it is indeed time we said goodbye to the law of charity properly so called. It is demeaning for people to rely on charitable help and patronising for others to dispense it. Even charity's classification as a moral virtue, which has been taken for granted throughout this essay, is really a sad vestige of long-defunct status relationships. It is time we saw it for the moral weakness it really is. Insofar as people in need want anything from strangers, it is sometimes said, they want no more than their due. Beyond that they would rather rely on their "own people" to help them (e.g. in mutual aid or familial relationships). People just don't want charity.[38] Personally, I am never

[36] *Re Hobourn Aero Components Ltd's Air Raid Distress Fund* [1946] Ch 194.

[37] Cf Charity Commission, *Users on Board: Beneficiaries Who Become Trustees*, leaflet CC 24 (London, Charity Commission, 2000).

[38] It is not clear whether the same people also don't want to be treated mercifully or humanely. These virtues have something in common with charity and something in common with justice.

sure what to make of such objections. Are they really moral objections, which carry with them the implication that others are demeaning themselves (and hence acting unjustifiably, albeit perhaps excusably) if they collaborate with the charitable by accepting help from them? Not only don't people want charity, in other words, but anyone who does shouldn't? If so, does this extend to all, or only to some (e.g. only to those who have a claim of justice against those very people now offering them charity, or only to those who accept charity from people who are ignorant of the real character of their predicaments, or only to those who are too craven or gracious in their reactions to the charitable)? Sometimes the objections seem not to be directed at the charitable at all, but rather at the cold charity of the public-spirited ("they treat us like some kind of social disgrace") or of the diligent ("we are just another pang of conscience to them"). Perhaps general alienated cynicism (possibly coupled with facile psychoanalytical beliefs about subconscious ulterior motives and/or facile economistic views about the nature and role of self-interest in human life[39] and/or facile ideological attachments to ideas of false consciousness) leads some people to interpret the acts of the genuinely charitable as acts of cold charity or (worse still) as people's self-serving attempts to ingratiate themselves or to feel good about themselves?[40] In which case the objections are not objections to *charity* but rather to the *lack* of it. On other occasions the objections seem rather to be only to *misguided* charity, i.e. to charitable intervention which fails in its own terms by not meeting people's real needs or by upsetting the people it aims to help by making clumsy assumptions about their needs and the best way to meet them. In which case the protest, again, is not against charity itself but against its aberrations. And yet there remains a strand of thought which does appear to rail against charity itself, demanding that it be recognised for the vice it really is. At any rate, if philosophers find charity less morally problematic than partisan virtues like loyalty, solidarity and patriotism, the reverse is clearly true for non-philosophers. This explains why many will defend charity only at the price of making it seem closer to other moral virtues—such as justice and solidarity—than it really is, i.e. by dressing it up as one of its foils.[41]

If there is a problem with charity it is clearly located in the *expressive* rather than the instrumental side of the virtue's value. I doubt whether (in the grand

[39] Cf David Stevens' critique of economics as a guide to public policy on the voluntary sector in his chapter in this book at 49–51; this subject is also addressed by Sue Moody in her chapter at 84–6.

[40] e.g. M Mauss, *The Gift* (trans Cunnison, London, Cohen and West, 1954), 63: "Charity wounds him who receives and our whole moral effort is directed towards suppressing the unconscious harmful patronage of the rich almoner." So presumably the ordinary charity of ordinary (non-rich) people who forgo a pint at the pub to help someone who fell ill on the bus, or who put the last pound of their weekly pension towards a disaster appeal, is not wounding. In which case one may wonder why there could not be better-off people who are similarly motivated, i.e. who do not exhibit the "unconscious" attitude expressed here. One thing that is notable is how little charity Mauss himself is exhibiting in his interpretations of others, and he is not alone.

[41] In my view the contributions of Alison Dunn and Sue Moody to this volume are examples. Dunn (chap 3) draws charity towards justice and Moody (chap 4) draws it towards solidarity.

scheme of things) the moral virtues vary much in respect of their purely instrumental contributions to the state of the world, as conceived independently of the presence of the virtues themselves. Where they vary importantly lies in what the exhibition of those virtues expresses. Acting for certain reasons and in a certain spirit not only improves one's chances (rule-utilitarian style) of bringing certain value to the world, but also plays a constitutive role in *shaping* the value that one thereby brings. For the fact that they were virtuously performed lends meaning, and hence expressive value, to one's actions, at least when they were successful in their own terms.[42] This in turn contributes to the Aristotelian diversification of value, for it is part of the nature of these expressive values that they cannot be created other than by different people with different virtues (so that they cannot be reduced to any common overarching value that all the virtues conspire to yield). Sometimes some actions associated with some virtues, if they are distinctive enough, actually take on some of the associated meaning even when not performed for the relevant reasons or in the relevant spirit. But be that as it may, the expressive value of the actions that manifest it is crucial to each moral virtue's status as a virtue. It is a moral virtue only if it expresses a morally acceptable attitude to those whose good it prioritises. Those who challenge the status of charity as a moral virtue may be denying that this is true of charity in one of two ways. They may be denying that the "philosophical love" of the charitable is a morally acceptable attitude to others. Or they may be doubting whether charitable actions truly succeed in expressing that attitude. The second possibility strikes me as an incoherent objection. It would have the implication that what some people mean by their actions is not among the things that those actions could conceivably mean. It seems to me that this makes it logically impossible to mean them, which turns this into another cynical objection portraying the charitable as insincere. As for the first possibility it requires more investigation. But it seems highly unlikely to me that an attitude according to which we are all in this boat together, according to which we are all human beings in common, could end up being a morally unacceptable one. The very idea bites at the heels of the concept of morality.

5. THE JUSTICIABILITY OF CHARITY

> [T]hat moral virtue, that we can truly measure by civil laws, which is different in different states, is justice and equity; that moral virtue which we measure purely by natural laws is alone charity. Furthermore, all moral virtue is contained in these two.[43]

I repeat this passage because we never got round to discussing Hobbes' thought that charity is a virtue which cannot be "measured by civil laws". It is important

[42] A common mistake is to reduce all such expressive value to symbolic value by thinking that it is only the attempt and not the success that counts.

[43] Thomas Hobbes, *De Homine*, above n 1.

to grasp what the point is that Hobbes is making here. It is not that charity is a private person's virtue, beyond the concern of state officials and institutions. On the contrary, Hobbes believes, and rightly so, that public officials and institutions (including legal officials and institutions) should be charitable as well as just.[44] Nor is Hobbes making the obvious point that law cannot make anyone act charitably, where this implies acting for charitable reasons and in a charitable spirit.[45] Of course it can't. But in *this* sense the law can't make anyone act justly either, or honestly, or loyally, or even diligently. It can't make anyone exhibit *any* moral virtue. All it can do is get people to *emulate* morally virtuous behaviour, by getting them to perform their duties of justice (e.g. their duty to pay damages to those whom they wronged), or their duties of honesty (e.g. their duty not to defraud), or their duties of considerateness (e.g. their duty to drive carefully), etc. What Hobbes is suggesting is that, in the case of charity, it is beyond the capacity of the law *even to do this much*, i.e. even to get people (albeit uncharitably) to perform their duties of charity. Why on earth would this be?

This chapter points to an answer. It is not (as some have imagined) that there are no duties of charity, nor that duties of charity are unruly, or imperfect, or not rights-based. It is that law cannot give effect to duties of charity—such as the Good Samaritan's duty—without subjecting them to adjudicative testing in the courts. Such testing is the law's only mechanism for settling (i.e. settling in any given case) the proper extent of the duties that it recognises. And viewing a duty of charity through this adjudicative lens means changing its moral classification. It means giving effect to it, if one gives effect to it, as a duty of justice rather than a duty of charity. A duty of charity cannot be made an object of adjudication without losing its identity as a duty of charity. As lawyers are wont to put it, a duty of charity is not *justiciable*. And that means precisely that it defies "measurement by civil laws".

Notice that this is not, as it stands, an attack on the *legitimacy* of laws such as Good Samaritan laws imposing duties of easy rescue. A common mistake is to think that since duties of charity are not justiciable, any law which requires that we do what charitable people would do is an illegitimate excursion by the law beyond its proper jurisdiction. This mistake helps to ground many pompous right-wing objections to the welfare state. The source of the error is the confusion of a logical point with a moral one. To say that charity is not justiciable is *not* to say that duties of charity cannot legitimately be transformed into legal duties. It is merely to say that they cannot be transformed into legal duties *without also being transformed into duties of justice*. The latter transformation may well be morally unobjectionable. There is no reason to think that once a duty of charity, always a duty of charity. Perhaps it is high time some were turned into duties of justice, for there is a shortage of charitable people, or

[44] Thomas Hobbes, *Leviathan* (ed Oakeshott, Oxford, Basil Blackwell, 1960), 227.
[45] Cf the remarks of M Rothbard cited by Waldron in *Liberal Rights*, above n 16, 227–8.

the most charitable people around here are unfortunately overlooking these particular duties, etc. Moreover, there is no reason to think that once duty of charity, *only* a duty of charity. Perhaps contributing to the elderly poor having a decent holiday once a year is both my duty of charity (boy, do they need it) and my duty of justice (it's the least we can do in return for all they did for my generation). Perhaps, indeed, it is also a duty of public-spiritedness (it cheers the country up), of trustworthiness (they were promised a happy old age by governments we supported), of loyalty (they are after all *our* elders), and so on. In which case there are plenty of grounds for legislating their holiday entitlement; the case for doing so is overdetermined without even relying on the charitable case. (It is also subject, of course, to many possible countervailing considerations; I do not deny that there might be some. I deny only that Hobbes' point is one of them.)

Although the non-justiciability of charitable priorities does not pose any obstacles to the meeting of people's needs by law (e.g. through ordinary social security or health care laws) it clearly does put a logical question mark over another body of legal doctrine, namely the law of charity itself. If the priorities of the charitable person are not justiciable then how is such a thing as the law of charity possible? One answer familiar to lawyers: charity in the legal sense is quite distinct from charity in the moral sense, so these questions about the justiciability of charity don't arise when "charity" is understood as a legal term of art. But this is simply not true. The connections between the legal concept of charity and the moral concept are close. It is true, as we saw, that many public-spirited activities are also regarded in law as charitable, but not to the systematic exclusion of charitable ones.[46] On the contrary, the law's trick, for better or for worse, is to lend support to public-spirited activities on the back of genuinely charitable ones.

The simpler answer, and the right one, is that the law of charity creates only legal *powers* to do the charitable thing, not legal duties to do so. The legal duties imposed on others when those powers are exercised (i.e. the duties imposed on charitable trustees, and the directors of charitable corporations, and their auditors and regulators, etc.) are not themselves, and do not purport to be, duties of charity. On the contrary, as the word "trustee" suggests, they are mainly legal duties of trustworthiness (to keep faith with the objects of the charitable contribution), with which are associated some duties of prudence (directed towards maximising the net value of the contribution). While duties of trustworthiness and duties of prudence are not themselves duties of justice, and may conflict with duties of justice, it does not follow that they are not justiciable. Charity has to be understood in opposition to justice—as justice's foil—but trustworthiness and prudence (and most other moral virtues) can be understood independently of both and can be made subject to the constraints of justice without entirely selling out their distinctiveness. Thus it is possible to provide legal support for

[46] Text to nn 27 and 28, above.

people to perform their moral duties of charity, by giving them legal powers that can be used to impose legal duties on others to perform moral duties that are *not* duties of charity, and yet to do so for charitable ends. This allows the courts to pass the buck of deciding how far these duties extend—pass it back to the charitable person—and hence to avoid destroying them as duties of charity by attempting to render them justiciable. Of course the question will still arise, and must still be rendered justiciable, when the legal power of the charitable person has been exceeded, i.e. when a given object lies outside the bounds of the charitable. This is not a surprise. For one can of course be *too* charitable, and at that point it is the job of other virtues (including justice) to rein one back in. The courts must merely avoid the temptation to rein the charitable in too soon, as if there were no possibility of an impeccably charitable person doing something, with perfect justification, at which a perfectly just person (such as the best judge in the world) would baulk.

2

Rescuing Charity

DAVID STEVENS

This he said, not because he cared for the poor; but because he was a thief.[1]

1. INTRODUCTION

IN HIS 1995 book on Mother Teresa, *The Missionary Position: Mother Teresa in Theory and Practice*,[2] Christopher Hitchens decided to "pick on a wizened, shriveled old lady, well stricken in years, who has consecrated her entire life to the needy and the destitute".[3] It seemed astonishing, Hitchens wrote, that no one had decided "to look at the saint of Calcutta as if, possibly, the supernatural had nothing to do with it"[4] Mother Teresa had described her own activity as follows:[5]

> There is always the danger that we may become *only social workers* or *just do the work for the sake of the work*. . . . It is a danger if we forget to whom we are doing it. Our works are only an expression of our love for Christ. Our hearts need to be full of love for him, and since we have to express that love in action, naturally then the poorest of the poor are the means of expressing our love for God.

A self-professed ethical humanist, Hitchens distorts and denies this claim in his book, largely on the basis that it is simply fraudulent, the fraud consisting equally in the fact that Mother Teresa's true objective was to proselytize but also, and more importantly for present purposes, in the fact that in so characterizing her life's work, Mother Teresa had not really identified anything of value. When measured against the standards of modern medical science and modern techniques of poor relief—"social work"—her efforts and the efforts of her order, the Missionaries of Charity, fell, in Hitchens's estimation, well below the level of acceptability.

A reputed author of science fiction in Canada, "Spider" Robinson, wrote an article in Canada's national newspaper in which he labelled as "arrogant" the

[1] John 12:6.
[2] London, Verso, New Left Books, 1995.
[3] *Ibid*, xi.
[4] *Ibid.*
[5] *Ibid*, 31 (emphasis added).

recent statement by the Vatican that Catholics are not permitted to doubt the official teachings of the church.[6] His position was supported by the claim that it is arrogant in matters of religion to take the position that one's own is truthful, and by implication, that others are less than one's own in some respects.

In a 1996 pamphlet of the Fraser Institute, Canada's neo-conservative policy institute, the author asked rhetorically: "If you were going to give $1,000 to the charity of your choice, would you send a cheque to the government?" Then he answered:[7]

> No one actually believes that governments are more effective at distributing charity than charities themselves, even though government programs have more fanfare. . . . There is nothing charitable in forcing citizens to participate in a government spending adventure. The idea that it is good to share with others is very different from the idea that government should confiscate your wealth and redistribute it according to a political formula.

A recent article by a colleague at the University of Toronto used social choice analysis to demonstrate (skillfully) that trust is needed to make markets efficient.[8] What was striking about the argument was the need to make it. Had economists previously thought it possible to analyze the market or any other behaviour without it?

At a recent tax conference in Toronto there were gathered many of Canada's leading tax academics and lawyers. I sat beside a tax practitioner at lunch who has spent a career in tax law. He related how difficult a job Revenue Canada auditors have keeping up with the complex tax provisions designed by the Department of Finance. He said that he was able to negotiate a settlement of taxes in his own case recently due to the willingness of a quota driven Revenue Canada official to collect as much as possible, as efficiently as possible. He also observed that the settlement, from his point of view, was advantageous because it prevented further investigation into his affairs, which might have revealed such facts as the use of his expense account to purchase gas for the boat at the cottage and to pay for the green fees of his weekend golf. In his view—probably the view of most Canadian taxpayers—his obligation to pay taxes was based not so much on the legal provisions supporting their imposition, but on the likelihood that he would be caught and not be able to negotiate his way out.

In the first story, what many would portray as true charity is ridiculed as pointless. In the second, religion is abolished because it is denied the possibility of making truth claims. In the third, an attack on the welfare state is justified in the name of charity. In the fourth, social science discovers moral virtue, after a long period of believing, apparently, that it is perfectly feasible to ignore it in

[6] The article appeared in July 1998 in the *Toronto Globe and Mail*.

[7] E Levant, *Youthquake* (Vancouver, Fraser Institute, 1996); available on the web at: www.fraserinstitute.ca/publications/books/youthquake/index.html.

[8] B Chapman, "Trust, Economic Rationality and the Corporate Fiduciary Obligation", (1993) 43 *University of Toronto LJ* 547.

any theoretical account of society. The last story illustrates the decline in at least one aspect of civic virtue, the obligation to pay taxes.

The argument in this chapter is prompted by the configuration of views exhibited in these five stories. Reading them without nuance and accepting them as illustrative of modern opinion on charity and the welfare state one might draw the following conclusion. There are three views on charity. One, following Hitchens, claims that charity is mainly about the material result of works—poor relief or social work—and political consciousness-raising in regard to the plight of the poor. This view emphasizes the receiver's side of the charity equation. On this view, religion is an illusion (according to Robinson). The issue is how to deliver poor relief, etc., as effectively as possible, and the clear preference is in favour of state level mechanisms. The second view, taken from the Fraser Institute, claims that the welfare state is an abysmal social and economic failure. It clamours not so much for a return to charity but to the material preconditions of charity, individual liberty and the sanctity of property. In advancing this argument it deploys a conception of charity that emphasizes the giver's side of the equation—the sentiment in favour of giving—without, however, defending it or suggesting that a charitable disposition is a good thing to have. On this view religion is merely a well-spring of moral sentiment. The issue is wasted tax dollars. These wasted dollars could be used more effectively by taxpayers pursuing their own charitable endeavors. The third view, according to the social sciences, claims that conventional morality, including the moral virtues and in particular the virtue of charity, are unintelligible, at least to the extent that they cannot be reconstructed on the objective principles of social science. The fundamental explanatory concept of much of social science is rational self-interest. On this view, religion is merely an object of sociological interest, not the experience of something real. The issue is the intellectual puzzle of altruism, which, with religion, is abolished at the outset, by hypothesis for some, as an article of faith by many.

One notable outcome of this configuration of views is the modern citizen's lax attitude toward the obligation to pay taxes: there is no reason to support the welfare state offered in the first view except the now-defeated ideology of socialism; what remains of moral sentiment clearly suggests that it is morally justifiable not to pay taxes; and, in any event, moral virtue exists only in the very limited version of it understood by economic man, namely, that portion of it derivable from the concept of self-interest or justifiable as an instrument of welfare maximization. Therefore, the only personal reason to pay taxes is the prudential one of not getting caught.

Opposed to these three views are the beliefs of a person such as Mother Teresa. Her statement of her position points to two elements of the charitable act which are generally well-recognized as essential to its meaning. First, on the giver's side, there is the element of love of persons for their own sake, in her terms, the love of God. Second, on the receiver's side, there is the fact that charitable acts promote the good of persons; in her case, mainly by simply recognizing their dignity as persons.[9] Her view is essentially religious. According to Mother Teresa, the love of God is the foundation of charity.

The relationship between her perception and the modern ones is interesting. Social science regards her life's project as strange or delusional; the views of the left and the right agree, but would use the religious understanding that underlies her project by, basically, consuming its social product. In the case of the left, it is the material product, poor relief, etc.; and in the case of the right, it is the spiritual product, moral sentiment. The left thus appropriates and distorts the receiver's side of her equation, and the right appropriates and distorts the giver's side. Hitchens puts the position of the traditional left well:[10]

> It was once well said, of the criticism of religion, that the critic should pluck the flowers from the chain, not in order that people should wear the chain without consolation but so that they might break the chain and cull the living flowers. . . . If we ever get off of our knees and cull those blooms, there will be no need for smoking altars and forbidding temples with which to honour the free-thinking humanists, who scorned to use the fear of death to coerce and flatter the poor.

Edward Gibbon stated the view of the *traditional* right. Commenting on religious practices in Rome, he said that the religious beliefs were (then as now, presumably) "considered by the people as equally true; by the philosopher as equally false; and *by the magistrate as equally useful*".[11] The magistracy's conservatism in regard to religion is traditional; it would use religious sentiment to keep the people in line. The conservatism of The Fraser Institute is "neo"; it would use religious sentiment to marshal opinion against wasteful government. The contrast and conflict in the meanings of charity in contemporary public discussions, then, is remarkable: the central case of charity in the Judaeo/Christian tradition, the love of God, is abused in the name of charity (poor relief) by the modern left and used (as an engine of moral sentiment) by the traditional and neo right. For the social scientist it is merely a delusion.

The main claim of this chapter is that this gap between what charity really is (meaning something like the religious view of it) and the way it is talked about in public policy settings presents problems for the formulation of public policy in respect of the charity sector. The mistaken camps divide *roughly* into the three identified: socialism, which emphasizes the normative concept "equality" and is concerned mainly about distributions; conservatism, which emphasizes the normative concept "liberty", or "property", and is concerned mainly with

[9] Consider another example. Think of the feelings of a donor who has financed the construction of a university library upon seeing the fruit of that generosity for the first time, a building full of books and attractive work spaces buzzing with scholarly activity. Among the donor's reflections undoubtedly will be awe at the sheer goodness of this achievement. It is not the books, spaces and building that inspire the awe, though; considered just as books and mortar, these are merely the material dimension of the good achieved. That good is fully and properly seen as the good of the persons at work in the library.

[10] Above n 2, xiii.

[11] E Gibbon, *The History of the Decline and Fall of the Roman Empire* (ed J B Bury, London, Methuen & Co, 1909) 31 (emphasis added).

the rights of owners; and social science, which in most phases emphasizes the explanatory concept, "self-interest", and is concerned mainly to reduce ethics and practical reasoning to an instrumental science.[12] In the first part of this chapter, I set out in the direction of a better definition of "charity" in philosophical and theological terms. The philosophical definition I suggest is a better platform from which to launch policy debates than what is currently available. In the second part I indicate briefly how the modern talk on charity has sought to distance itself from this reality in ways that I claim, but for reasons of space cannot prove, are bound to be harmful to public policy. The modern talk is divided into (A) law, (B) economics, (C) tax policy, and (D) current justifications for the welfare state. In these four topics I proceed by example only. An alternative method would be to investigate the underpinnings of each camp in detail, reconstructing the various theories of charity implicit in them, then critically evaluating those theories. Although an interesting project, it is beyond the scope of this chapter.

2. AN APPROACH TO THE DEFINITION OF CHARITY

A. Philosophical

1. *The OLRC Project on Charity Law*

Is it possible to write about charity in a way that is true to the Western tradition, but in secular terms, in the terms that ought to inform scholarly debate and that are acceptable in the voice of government? I dealt with this problem when working on the Ontario Law Reform Commission (OLRC) project on the law governing charities in Ontario.[13] I was to report to and write in the voice of a group of people, the Commission, who came from a variety of cultural and religious backgrounds: a secular Jew, a French-Canadian (lapsed) Catholic, a Protestant with no current church affiliation, a West-Indian Christian, a left-leaning academic, and two Irish-Catholics of uncertain current convictions. Of the writing available to inform our thinking, the strongest secular tradition was and remains economics. There was some political theory on nonprofits, charities, and civil society, a bit of business and tax literature, and a large body of mostly English writing on the legal regime governing charities in England. (This situation has changed dramatically in recent years.) None of this writing helped very much in identifying the basic policy perspective of government, since none of it

[12] Cf G Becker, *The Economic Approach to Human Behaviour* (Chicago, University of Chicago Press, 1976), 140: "All human behaviour can be viewed as involving participants who maximize their utility from a stable set of preferences and accumulate an optimal amount of information and other inputs in a variety of markets. If this is correct, the economic approach provides a unified framework for understanding behaviour that has long been sought and eluded Bentham, Comte, Marx and others."

[13] Ontario Law Reform Commission, *Report on the Law of Charity* (Toronto, Ontario Law Reform Commission, 1996) ("Report").

really talked about charity, at least in a way that was readily recognizable from the perspective of a common conception, in the Judeo/Christian tradition. The economic writing seemed entirely absorbed with making the sector fit into its model of analysis, a monolithic theory, as it were, casting about menacingly for applications. The legal writing, with many notable exceptions, likewise was content with working through the implications of *Pemsel*,[14] and the case law from *Pemsel*, even if, like much in the common law tradition, there was an incredible amount of incoherence built into the legal thinking. Notably, the standard line in response to a conflict arising between the common conception and the legal conception is to state flatly and dismissively that the two are distinct ideas. The political writing was too thin, since mainstream political science has not been until very recently too interested in topics outside of government and the state, and at the time we conducted the project was still wedded in one way or another to either methodological individualism or socialism, neither of which paid much interest to civil society, let alone nonprofits and charity.

The OLRC project was meant from the outset to be a comprehensive study of the law governing charity. It was therefore important to lay a proper foundation in terms of a definition of charity and in terms of theories of the sector that might inform government policy. It was clear from all the legal commentators, as it was clear from the length of the commentaries, that the issue of definition was the most vexed one. To define our jurisdiction—since the reference of the Attorney General to the Commission was for a project on "charities", not nonprofits—we adopted, provisionally, the *Pemsel* definition. The initial effort was then to work through what was in that definition—which is really a list—and its case law to see if something more coherent could be found. The significant boundary markers are well known: political purposes are not charitable; friendship societies and ethnic and cultural groups are under constant suspicion; play and recreation were outside the fortress in theory, but had been brought in selectively by legislative fiat; knowledge and aesthetics had to be packaged in a delivery mode—education—and could not yet stand on their own two feet. But case law was evolving on a number of fronts, both in Canada and across the Commonwealth, and questions were being asked about trends and prospects: Could environmental concerns be brought in? Abortion clinics? Ethnic and cultural friendship societies? These were some of the questions Canadian courts were asked to address.

The turmoil over charity was not a monopoly of the lawyers. The public commentators on the charity sector were also (and continue to be) divided into several camps. In an anti-charity camp, there are several groups: an anti-elite school of thought that rails against the privileges and the misdirected "philanthropy" of private foundations; the liberal left and segments of the liberal clergy who would prefer to enhance the social welfare efforts of the state at the expense of

[14] *Commissioners for Special Purposes of the Income Tax Act* v. *Pemsel* [1891] AC 531 ("*Pemsel*").

charity;[15] the beleaguered Canadian donor, wary of more fundraising scams; and intellectuals on the left and the right who regard the sector as ineffectual and therefore a waste of tax dollars. In the pro-charity camp, among others, there are: faith communities; the big charities—universities and hospitals; fundraisers; and a growing number of intellectuals in the civil society mode. The sector is divided in other ways as well: there is a clear enough distinction (conceptual and social) between religious charities and others, between social welfare charities and philanthropic charities (arts, sports, higher learning and research), and, within philanthropy, there is rivalry between arts groups and sports groups, between foundations and operating charities, and between private foundations and all the rest. The prospect of offering a definition of charity looked perilous and bleak. Surprisingly, it did not turn out that way.

Taking a few steps back and reflecting and abstracting from the turmoil, the OLRC Report suggests that the backbone of the definition is *doing good by others*, and an effort was made to craft a definition on this backbone which would validate as many of the points of view as possible, while providing a definition that was philosophically defensible and politically useful. This is what we proposed:[16]

> [T]he truly charitable act is the act whose form, actual effect, and motive are the provision of the means of pursuing a common or universal good to persons who are remote in affection and to whom no moral or legal obligation is owed.

To implement this definition we suggested that courts take the following approach:[17]

> In applying this definition to evaluate a project, we might proceed, first, by identifying the goods or intended goods; second, by asking whether the particular project is (really) a determination of one or more of the goods; third, by asking whether the project benefits only strangers; and fourth, rarely, by questioning whether the project is also motivated by the desire to be charitable.

There are a number of key ideas in these formulations which require further development. Before moving on to these, there are two points to notice. First, there is no mention of God in this definition, and therefore the definition remains secular; and, second, with this definition we are already in hot water with a central strain of liberal thought which categorically prohibits mention of the good of human beings and of motives.

2. *Five Key Ideas*

1) *The Notion of a* Common or Universal *Good*

By common or universal is meant shared, such that the goods are goods for each and every one of us, not that there is some overarching good of society or

[15] See for example, R Sirico "Ethics and the Budget Debate (Welfare Reform)", 157 *Forbes Magazine* 52.

[16] Report, above n 13, 152.

[17] *Ibid.*

a sub-group of society that is logically prior to, or morally superior to, or otherwise takes precedence over, the good of individuals. These goods are pursued individually and, because we are social by nature, in groups, in a multitude of ways, uncountable and not worth counting. In many circumstances social entities—the family, a club, a city, the state—pursue the common good as a group or entity such that there are characteristic patterns in the entity's behaviour and specific ethical norms governing its mode of cooperation. To mention an example that will become relevant in a moment, at the level of the political community or state, perhaps the "highest" level, there are reasonably clear norms which govern its use of coercion, establishing, in effect, the proper scope of its activity as an entity. Two further simple examples will illustrate.

(a) The bridge over the river facilitates the economic and social activity of each and every person that uses it. The users pursue their projects instantiating goods in a myriad of ways. The bridge is a common or public good in several senses. In the sense employed here, it is common or public because it is instrumental to these projects.

(b) Phyllis Lambert, a Montreal architect, fought long and hard to ensure the redevelopment of a downtown street which preserved and enhanced a prospect of Mount Royal; the real estate developers resisted her plan. In the end her idea prevailed. Both sides in the lengthy political debate had to, logically, argue on the basis of the common good. As a city, we had to proceed in one direction or the other, so the question at the centre of the debate, like all sound political dialogue, was: which vision in the circumstances best advances the common good, meaning the shared good of the citizens of the city in respect of the available opportunities concerning this street? There is no right answer to this question; we discuss, debate, we weigh facts, and we choose. In this way the "common good" is the foundation of all properly motivated political activity. (For this reason, when a politician declares herself to be in favour of the common good we become very suspicious, since we reason: of course she must be if she is a politician; therefore, what does she really mean?)

2) The Notion of Good

There is more concrete guidance in the notion of "the good of man". The argument here relies on a newly developed strain of Thomist natural law thinking.[18] It suggests that it is possible, and for the purposes of ethical and political theory necessary, to identify the self-evident good of human beings, meaning, simply, what it is possible and intelligibly worthwhile for us to do. According to one formulation of the answer to this question, the general determinations

[18] See J Finnis, *Natural Law and Natural Rights* (Oxford, Clarendon Press, 1980). See also G Grisez, *Beyond the New Morality? The Responsibilities of Freedom* 2nd edn (Notre Dame, University of Notre Dame Press, 1980), chap 4; R P George, *Making Men Moral* (Oxford, Clarendon Press, 1993); J Boyle, G Grisez and J Finnis, "Practical Principles, Moral Truth and Ultimate Ends", (1987) 32 *Am Juris* 99.

of the first principle of practical reason (that good is to be done; bad is to be avoided) are:[19]

> [L]ife, knowledge of truth and appreciation of beauty; satisfaction in playful activities and skillful performances; self-integration (harmony among the aspects of the self); practical reasonableness and authenticity (harmony among moral reflection, free choices, and their execution); justice and friendship (harmony among human persons); and religion (harmony between humankind and God).

These goods are our ultimate purposes; "they give our right-thinking actions their point, making them intelligible to ourselves and others".[20] They are the "basic forms of human flourishing to be pursued and realized" in all practical activity.[21] The Report goes into further detail as to the content of these goods, using Professor Finnis' slightly different version which lists life, knowledge, play (the Report adds work), aesthetic experience, friendship and justice, practical reasonableness and religion.

By "life", Finnis means "every aspect of vitality which puts a human being in good shape for self-determination".[22] Hospitals, medical schools, the work of surgeons and nurses, famine relief, soup kitchens, road safety laws, etc., all participate in the good of life. By "knowledge", Finnis means, simply, the good we achieve when we get "to the truth of the matter", or the good we identify when we speak of "knowledge for its own sake", or what we mean when we say, "It would be good to find out". Thus, for example, we consider the well-informed person, to that extent, to be well off, and not only for the profitable use he can make of his knowledge. Truth, in short, is self-evidently worth pursuing. By "play", Finnis means "performances which have no point beyond the performance itself, enjoyed for its own sake".[23] The performance may be "solitary or social, intellectual or physical, strenuous or relaxed, highly structured or relatively informal, conventional or *ad hoc*".[24] It is sufficient to explain the behaviour of people involved in a game to say, "They enjoy playing". The good of "aesthetic experience" points to the self-evident goodness, "the to-be-pursuedness" of beauty. The good of sociability or "friendship" can range from a minimum of peace and harmony among persons, to acting for the sake of one's friend. By "religion", Finnis means the "establishing and maintenance of a proper relationship between oneself and the divine",[25] the arrangement of all orders in an ultimate order of things. Secular humanism has brought with it scepticism over whether religion is a basic human good. Finnis argues that the sceptic must admit, at the very least, that whether in fact God exists or not, the

[19] W May, "Germain Grisez on Moral Principles and Moral Norms", in R P George (ed), *Natural Law and Moral Inquiry* (Washington DC, Georgetown University Press, 1998), 28.

[20] Report, above n 13, 148.

[21] *Ibid.*

[22] Finnis, above n 18, 86.

[23] *Ibid*, 87.

[24] *Ibid.*

[25] *Ibid*, 89.

question of God's existence is crucially important for everyone. Finally, there is "practical reasonableness" or reasonableness, the basic good of being able:[26]

> to bring one's own intelligence to bear effectively . . . on the problems of choosing one's actions and life-style and shaping one's own character . . . [T]his involves that one has a measure of effective freedom; . . . it [also] involves that one seeks to bring an intelligent and reasonable order into one's own action and habits and practical attitudes.

3) Means, Actual Effect and Projects

When these goods are implicated in a charitable act, they are never delivered as such to the beneficiary. A charitable act or project provides the means for this instantiation for the benefit of another. Aid for the poor is in a material form—money, shelter, schools, hospitals—never the good as such. The acts or projects, however, can vary in effectiveness or usefulness, and it therefore is relevant to ask of any purportedly charitable project, not only whether it seeks to instantiate a good for the benefit of another, but also whether it achieves or is likely to achieve its object. Some projects will fail this test because they are impractical.

4) Remote in Affection and Obligation

For the act to be charitable, the beneficiary of the charitable act must be a stranger, someone remote in affection and to whom no legal or moral obligation is owed. Benefits to one's family, although laudable, are moved by natural love and affection or by obligation. But the act of the Samaritan was charitable, like the life of Mother Teresa, because it was moved for the sake of the person as such.

5) Motive

This requirement means that what we really care about, at least from the moral point of view, is what moves the donor. An integral theory of charity is centered on what moves the donor to act for the good of the stranger. Given the difficulties evaluating motives, both practical, moral and charitable (it is too hard to tell, it is none of our business to judge the motives, and if it is properly motivated the donor will want to keep the whole thing quiet, anyway[27]), it makes sense for

[26] Finnis, above n 18, 88.

[27] Cf Maimonides' seventh degree in his "Eight Degrees of Charity":

The first and lowest degree is to give, but with reluctance or regret. This is the gift of the hand, but not of the heart.

The Second is to give cheerfully, but not proportionately to the distress of the sufferer.

The Third is to give cheerfully, and proportionately but not until solicited.

The Fourth is to give cheerfully, proportionately, and even unsolicited, but to *petit* in the poor man's hand, thereby exciting in the painful emotion of shame

The Fifth is to give charity in such a way that the distressed may receive the bounty, and know their benefactor, without their being known to him . . .

The Sixth which rises still higher, is to know the objects of our bounty but remain unknown to them . . .

The Seventh is still more meritorious, namely, to bestow charity in such a way that the benefactor may not know the relieved persons, nor they the names of their benefactors . . .

The Eighth and the most meritorious of all, is to anticipate charity by preventing poverty; namely,

the *application* of the public concept of charity in the law of trusts, or the law of charity generally, to avoid evaluations of motives. This reluctance, however, is not a denial of the centrality of motive to the public concept, nor an assertion that the public concept is of a different kind from the religious notion or philosophic notion. Rather it is an affirmation of these notions because it seeks to preserve them, while recognizing the limits of publicly enforced morality.

This proposition concerning the importance of motive is easily denied, and it seems that the essence of the socialist view is that it is not true. So it is worth examining in more detail whether the point is valid. Assume, for the purpose of brevity in this exercise, that applying the suggested definition will validate all true charitable acts. That is to say, assume that no charitable act will be inadvertently excluded if all we ever test for when evaluating an act or project is every aspect of the definition except motive. We focus on the "external" criteria only. This assumption is arguable, but a strong case in its defense can be made. The converse, however, is definitely not true. Focusing on the external elements of the act or project will undoubtedly validate acts and projects that are not truly charitable. Lawyers, among others, have long recognized this and have asserted that it is perfectly alright that the legal conception should thus derogate from the common conception. In law, the donor can truthfully testify "I am doing this [setting up this charitable trust] to spite my children" and the law of trusts will say "valid trust" nonetheless. The "external" focus thus validates everything that merely looks like true charity. But is it a simple derogation due to incompetence, deference or reluctance, as suggested in the previous paragraph, or is there a new concept operating here, a "public benefit" conception (to select an appropriate term)? Advocates of this alternative conception recommend we hive off the recipient's side of the equation; they seem to be saying: "Look, it's a hospital, a school, a university: who cares why he/she/they gave the money?"

The proper response to this has to start with the nature of state activity in general, then to consider its activity in the charity sector, in particular. In the liberal and natural law tradition there is a very strong principle that holds, in one formulation, that law—state coercion—cannot and should not be used to promote general virtue. Under this principle, the proper domain of the use of state force—the "common good of the state"—is justice and peace, temporal tranquillity, or, simply, order in the way citizens relate to each other *externally*. In exercising that force with the end of maintaining temporal tranquility in mind, however, the state still may hope and aim that its citizens will be moved by justice, not just by the threat of state coercion.[28] Thus, the proposition regarding

to assist the reduced fellow man, either by a considerable gift, or a sum of money, or by teaching him a trade, or by putting him in the way of business, so that he may earn an honest livelihood, and not be forced to the dreadful alternative of holding out his hand for charity.

(*Quaere*: Is eight the welfare state?)

[28] J Finnis, "Public Good: The Specifically Political Common Good in Aquinas" in George, above n 19, 174, 185.

state activity is: although it may legitimately want and encourage citizens to form just dispositions, it may not force them to do so. What is the reason for this deference? Why is the individual's true inner life that person's own responsibility? This is a difficult question to answer in secular terms. Many have tried. It is sufficient for present purposes just to accept it. It is noteworthy that the exact same valuation happens on the other side of the charity equation.

So here, in the central case of state activity, the use of coercive force, we see a virtue actualized at the level of the state, but in a form that is pared down to its external features. We also see that it is achieved without any denial of the essential connection between what the state is doing (external justice) and the core virtue (internal justice). To the contrary, the whole point is to affirm that essential connection.

A parallel phenomenon occurs in charity law. In the charity sector the modern state's main role is to protect the sector from fraud and to facilitate its activity by providing it with the necessary legal, administrative and social infrastructure, but otherwise, as with religion, to leave it be. (There is also the matter of the privileged tax treatment, which should be set to one side. The tax treatment is justified, it will be suggested, mainly for tax policy reasons, but also possibly as a tax expenditure.) Historically, the main prop in the legal infrastructure was the trust, and it is in trust law doctrine where we first encounter the point about the irrelevance of motive. The suggestion here is that this posture also flows from the state's general incompetence with respect to motive, not from a separate concept of public benefit. Thus, it is not the case that the community says "who cares?"; nor is it the case that the political community or state says "who cares?"; it is simply not a matter over which the state has jurisdiction.

A separate but related point flows out of this discussion. It has to do with the justifications, on this type of view, for the welfare state. The two main components of the welfare state requiring some sort of justification are the socialized provision of services (education and health) and the direct transfer of financial resources to needy fellow citizens. To justify the socialized provision of services properly would require a full consideration of just where the responsibility for the provision of the relevant service lies in the first place and whether, having identified the relevant entity, that entity has sufficient resources to provide it. Education, for example, is the primary responsibility of parents, but it may make sense to enter cooperative schemes involving the state or to delegate the responsibility in substantial measure to the state in light of the state's superior financial and social resources. On what basis could nonparents be made to contribute to this system? Whatever reasons one comes up with, they are bound to contain an element of coerced charity, as the Fraser Institute complains. It seems this coerced charity point, however, is especially strong in the case of wealth transfers. What are we to make of it? Historically, the fact is that in some measure, the wealth transfer system simply was *coordinated* charity. This is the social gospel understanding of the welfare state. Where there is substantial support for the tax system, or where there is at least substantial support for a wealth transfer system which operates through tax payers, as there was at the time when the welfare state was instituted, the dissenting element of the taxpayer class can be coerced under an interpretation of the above principles, as a matter of justice, since, given the relevant level of consensus to co-ordinate charity in the particular way chosen, opting out would be unjust, or tantamount to unjust, and therefore should come under the state's power. You can be made in some circumstances to do the charitable thing as a matter of justice, even if you do not want to. However, if the social consensus erodes—if the motive to support is diminished—then, the argument in favour of coercion is weakened proportionately.

3. *Some Conclusions*

On the basis of this notion of charity it is possible to suggest several principles for the development of public policy in the law of charity proper.

First, this definition suggests that charity and politics are different activities. The basic goods, the basic forms of human flourishing, provide the *what* of both charity and politics, and to some significant degree, both charity and politics are properly motivated by the desire to see the good properly instantiated. Yet politics is the activity in which the community, at its highest level the state, publicly deliberates in what under a particular range of circumstances the good consists—should we spend the budget surplus on transportation infrastructure, increased social welfare, or tax relief? Charity is actually doing good for strangers in the sense of providing the means for its delivery.[29]

Second, the definition is entirely formal. It requires application in concrete circumstances. Therefore, the content of the good or whether an act is charitable or not requires that close attention be paid to circumstances.

Third, each of the goods has its own peculiarity. None is reducible to another. They are incommensurable, cannot be compared. The uniqueness of each plays out in concrete circumstances in its own peculiar way.

Fourth, the uniqueness of religion, however, bears noting and comment. In its typically practised form, of course, there is no religion in general, only particular historically-conditioned faiths. In the forms in which it is found, moreover, those who provide the material support provide it to their own. Thus from a secular humanist perspective, if the existence of God is disavowed, and if the good of religion is thus denied, the material support of religion comes across as a sort of mutual benefit organization, where the members of the faith group pay for the provision to themselves of psychological comfort. This sceptical view contrasts remarkably with the way religion is generally regarded in the Western tradition, and to some extent within the law of charity.

Fifth and last, the definition makes reference to the fact that the giver can provide only the means of flourishing, not the goods themselves, so there is implicit

[29] For a different interpretation of the relationship between charity and politics, cf Alison Dunn's chapter in this collection (chap 3), and part 4 of Michael Chesterman's chapter (chap 9).

in the definition the idea that to be effective as charity the means provided must be addressed to a relative need. This suggests a basis in the application of the definition of a preference for the poor, those most deprived of means, and therefore, a preference in public policy in favour of charity in the more traditional sense of poor relief.

B. A Theological Perspective

1. The Language of Faith

The discussion up to this point emphasizes the importance of motives, the goods, and the person, and stresses that these elements are essential to a public concept. It asserts that state coercive force can never be used to coerce motives. At the least, therefore, we need a way to talk about the inner life that is outside the bounds of the state's coercive influence. Historically, this subject matter has been the jurisdiction of religion. In most faith traditions, the question of the inner life is a question of one's relationship with God. As suggested in the introduction, there may be ways to deal with this that are mainly secular. My claim is not that only properly religious people are moved for the sake of the good of another. But I would suggest that seeing that we ought to be moved for the sake of the good of another is essentially a realization that comes with faith, a sense that the "brotherhood of man" is real, not figurative.

The main public discourse on the inner life occurs in faith traditions, then, not in universities, courts, or legislatures. It is out of place in these settings, as is talk of one's family, for a variety of reasons. Yet if the definition of charity is correct, the discussion of charity in these settings should at least leave that space empty so that it may be filled up elsewhere; these discussions should not try to fill it up with concepts that seek to replace it or usurp it. In the remaining parts of the chapter, I will apply the natural law (and therefore secular) definition from the previous part to criticize the conversation in these settings for trying in effect to do just that. Mother Teresa's version of charity and Helen Prejean's version of charity, therefore, are rescued by that definition, not by anything that is said in this part. The only need for this detour is to show what might be said about the nature of the charitable disposition in a language that is adequate to the task.

I cannot hope to do justice to the topic given the centrality of charity in Western religious traditions. What is possible is a brief survey of two formulations, in slightly more depth than is permissible in the voice of government. I rely on the Thomist tradition, partly because it fits in easily with the definition just provided, and partly because it remains neutral to specific faith groups well into the explication. What is said in much of what follows is available, I think, to almost any person with religious convictions in at least the Judeo Christian tradition, but perhaps others as well. The important point throughout is the stress in this view of charity on the interior life of the giver, the heart of that person, and therefore the relationship between that person and God. This is the spiritual dimension of charity ignored by Hitchens, harvested by Gibbon and Fraser, and scientifically obliterated by the social scientist.

2. *The New Natural Law*

The best place to begin is with the revision of Thomist thought in the work of Grisez, Boyle, George and Finnis.[30] The first principle of practical reason, as suggested above, states the *what* of human flourishing, morality deals with the *how*, or the modes of moral responsibility controlling the pursuit of the good. As an example of such a rule, it would be a violation of morality to choose directly against one good in the pursuit of another: I am not permitted to run down pedestrians at a crosswalk on my way to play football. Grisez formulates the first principle of morality as follows:[31]

> In voluntarily acting for human goods and avoiding what is opposed to them, one ought to choose and otherwise will those and only those possibilities whose willing is compatible with a will toward integral human fulfillment.

This principle suggests an ideal, not a good, and therefore does not constitute a reason for action. By directing us to remain open to further goods and to avoid unnecessary limitations, this ideal acts to correct or rectify the will, encouraging us to choose well. The principle can be translated into more specific determinations of morality by identifying the ways that choosing and acting might fail to respect the ideal of integral human fulfillment. Grisez has identified eight modes of responsibility:[32]

> 1. *One should not be deterred by felt inertia from acting for intelligible goods.* This happens when one refrains from doing something worthwhile out of laziness, conquerable depression, or the like. . . .
> 2. *One should not be pressed by enthusiasm or impatience to act individualistically for intelligible goods.* This happens when one acts by oneself, although knowing that by cooperation with others the good would be more perfectly attained insofar as others could share in it. . . .
> 3. *One should not choose to satisfy an emotional desire except as part of one's pursuit and/or attainment of an intelligible good other than the satisfaction of the desire itself.* Violations occur when people act for no good reason, on account of impulse, craving, routine, or the continued lure of goals which no longer make sense. . . .
> 4. *One should not choose to act out of an emotional aversion except as part of one's avoidance of some intelligible evil other than the inner tension experienced in enduring that aversion.* This happens when one is deterred from reasonable action by feelings of repugnance, fear of pain, anxiety, and so forth. . . .
> 5. *One should not, in response to different feelings toward different persons, willingly proceed with a preference for anyone unless that preference is required by intelligible*

[30] Above, n 18.
[31] G Grisez, *Christian Moral Principles* (Chicago, Franciscan Herald Press, 1983), 184.
[32] *Ibid*, 225–6.

> *goods themselves*. This mode is violated when one's treatment of others is marked by partiality toward some (including partiality toward oneself). . . .
> 6. *One should not choose on the basis of emotions which bear upon empirical aspects of intelligible goods (or bads) in a way which interferes with a more perfect sharing in the good or avoidance of the bad*. This happens when people act for the conscious experience of a good rather than its fuller reality. . . .
> 7. *One should not be moved by hostility to freely accept or choose the destruction, damaging, or impeding of any intelligible human good*. Violations occur when negative feelings cause people to act destructively (including self-destructively). . . .
> 8. *One should not be moved by a stronger desire for one instance of an intelligible good to act for it by choosing to destroy, damage, or impede some other instance of an intelligible good*. This happens when one deliberately acts to bring about something bad, either for the sake of a good or to prevent something else bad.

One reasons from these to specific moral norms as follows, again quoting Grisez:[33]

> Since specific moral norms refer to kinds of actions and apply to them moral determinants, one obviously needs something common to kinds of action and to moral principles as the middle term of the reasoning by which a specific moral norm is drawn from a mode of responsibility. What is common to both are relationships of the will to basic human goods. The modes of responsibility indicate the moral exclusion of certain relationships, and various kinds of action are morally significant insofar as they involve such relationships. . . . Thus, a specific, negative moral norm can be derived as follows. First one considers how the voluntariness involved in a certain kind of action is related to basic human goods. Next one considers the moral determination which the modes of responsibility indicate for this relationship. From these two premises one deduces the negative moral determination of that kind of action. . . . A specific, affirmative moral norm logically depends on the affirmative first principle of morality, which directs the choice of those and only those possibilities whose willing is compatible with a will toward integral human fulfillment. Thus, a certain kind of act is morally good if it offers a way of voluntarily serving a human good and involves no voluntariness excluded by any of the modes of responsibility. Not all morally good acts are obligatory—for example, feeding the hungry is good yet not obligatory. The reason is that an act of this kind can have an alternative itself morally good. However, whenever a morally good kind of act is such that its alternative is excluded by one or more modes of responsibility, then that sort of act is obligatory.

The important thing to notice is that we have not yet, in this line of thought, encountered charity. It is not excluded, but it is not advised or required. All we have in this logic is a set of objects (the goods) which make acts intelligible, a basic principle of morality in the form of an ideal from which are derived specifications, all in the form of prohibitions, which must be observed in practical activity. These ideas constitute a natural law in the important sense that none of this system requires revelation to justify it. It is in the next step of the system, when religion is added, so to speak, that charity appears. In Grisez' formulation

[33] G Grisez, *Christian Moral Principles* (Chicago, Franciscan Herald Press, 1983), 255 (emphases omitted).

of the Thomist tradition, the first principle of Christian morality is the commandment to love: "As the Father has loved me, so I have loved you; abide in my love".[34] The relationship between natural law and Christian morality is stated by him as follows:[35]

> The first principle of all human morality is: In voluntarily acting for human goods and avoiding what is opposed to them, one ought to choose and otherwise will those and only those possibilities whose willing is compatible with a will toward integral human fulfillment. . . . Such fulfillment is more than an ideal; it is being accomplished in the fulfillment of all things in Jesus. . . . Thus, Christian love transforms the first principle of morality into a more definite norm: One ought to will those and only those possibilities which contribute to the integral human fulfillment being realized in the fulfillment of all things in Jesus.

And the determinations of this first principle of Christian morality, the "modes of Christian response", are stated in the beatitudes, which Grisez explicates as follows, the important one for our purposes being the fifth:[36]

> 1. *To expect and accept all good, including the good fruits of one's work, as God's gift*—for the "poor in spirit" understand that their achievements are only a share, given freely and generously by God, in his fullness. The virtuous disposition is humility; the vice is pride. The corresponding gift of the Spirit is fear of the Lord.
> 2. *To accept one's limited role in the Body of Christ and fulfill it*—for the "meek" understand that submissiveness to God's will involves no loss or delay to their personal fulfillment. The virtuous disposition is "Christian dedication," while lukewarmness and minimalism are opposed to it. The corresponding gift of the Holy Spirit is piety or godliness, an attitude of filial reverence and dutifulness toward God.
> 3. *To put aside or avoid everything which is not necessary or useful in the fulfillment of one's personal vocation*—for those who "mourn" (not only contrite sinners but all those who turn from transient goods to fulfillment in Jesus) understand that to be disposed to goodness itself frees one from the pursuit of particular, finite goods for their own sake. The virtuous disposition is detachment; worldliness and anxiety are opposed dispositions. The corresponding gift of the Spirit is knowledge, by which one discerns what belongs to faith and judges everything by its light.
> 4. *To endure fearlessly whatever is necessary or useful for the fulfillment of one's personal vocation*—for those who "hunger and thirst for righteousness" understand that they have nothing whatsoever to fear. The virtuous disposition is the faithfulness and heroism characteristic of the martyr, though required of all Christians, while weakness of faith and faintheartedness in the face of non-Christian standards are among the Christian vices. The corresponding gift of the Spirit is fortitude.
> 5. *To be merciful according to the universal and perfect measure of mercy which God has revealed in Jesus*—for those who "are merciful" understand that they are to be as disinterested and selfless as God is. The virtuous disposition is mercy, compassion, service to others on the model of Jesus, while the opposed vice is a legalistic attitude toward others. The corresponding gift of the Spirit is counsel. . . .

[34] John 15, 9.
[35] Above, n 31, 605 (emphasis omitted).
[36] *Ibid*, 654–5.

6. *To strive to conform one's whole self to living faith, and purge anything which does not meet this standard*—for the "pure of heart" understand that in this life charity requires continuous conversion. The virtuous disposition is single-minded devotion to God, including a sense of sin and continuing conversion, while the Christian vice is reflected in mediocrity and insincerity. The corresponding gift of the Spirit is understanding.
7. *To respond to evil with good, not with resistance, much less with destructive action*—for "peacemakers" understand that the effort to live according to divine love must be universally conciliatory. The virtuous disposition is the conciliatoriness which seeks the redemption of enemies; one opposed disposition is the tendency to shun evil instead of carrying on a redemptive ministry to those enslaved by it. The corresponding gift of the Spirit is wisdom, the power of putting in order as peacemakers do.
8. *To do no evil that good might come of it, but suffer evil together with Jesus in cooperation with God's redeeming love*—for "those persecuted for righteousness' sake" understand that one must undergo evil in order to bring the evildoer in touch with perfect goodness. The virtuous disposition is self-oblation, the Christian vice the fragile rectitude of the person who does not wish to sin but seeks fulfillment in this world. Since there are only seven gifts, Augustine assigns none here; however, one might say there is a corresponding gift, unique to each Christian and disposing him or her to offer God the unique gift of himself or herself.

Notice that all are addressed to the internal dispositions of character.

Joseph Pieper sets out the elements of the Thomist tradition in more conventional but less systematic terms in his book on faith, hope, and charity.[37] He argues in the following terms: In Thomist theology, God is the first lover. Thinking about God inevitably involves thinking about what the love of God must be like.[38] Human love) charity) is a participation in, and an imperfect reflection of, the divine love which God has for us. Love directed to another human is affirmative of that person's existence and essential goodness—"it's good that you exist." It reflects God's creative love, by whose favor all are kept in being.[39] This love can be expressed through ordinary, everyday charitable acts. There are those who due to ill fate, poverty or other circumstances feel less affirmed by society and in themselves, and may consequently become less capable of feeling the basic loving affirmation of God. These, in particular, are in need of charitable love. Benevolence is not yet love, but rather the sheer act of wishing someone well. The true act of *caritas* goes further, involving a full participation of mind, body and spirit.[40] Mother Teresa:[41] she was literally spurred upon seeing deathly sick people to help them get off the streets of Calcutta, where many others would be repulsed at the same sight. This could be interpreted as penetrating human insight, an affirmation of the essential dignity of

[37] J Pieper, *Faith, Hope, Love* (San Francisco, Ignatius Press, 1986).
[38] *Ibid*, 191.
[39] *Ibid*, 193.
[40] *Ibid*, 195.
[41] *Ibid*, 274.

these desolate persons which Mother Teresa keenly recognized despite their state. If so, this is an insight which few of us ever attain to such a degree. Alternatively, this insight may be explained as the result of grace. Love, whether seen in affirmation towards friends or charity towards strangers, is participation in the divine love; but God's love is universal, as compared to human love.[42] This is what distinguishes charity from affection: but for man's participation in the divine love, he would be incapable of turning to the "unattractive stranger" and affirming him.[43] This last point implies that charity is best understood and achieved in the context of a transcendental reality. In a secular society where God is minimized and the State becomes the supreme being, the value of charitable acts will become intrinsically diminished.

The discussion whether these ideas are valid and worth living by and if they are whether as individuals we live up to them is profoundly personal. They go to the very heart of the person, to the person's conscience. There can be no coercion here since it would be illegitimate and, in any event, impossible. Attitudes change from the inside out. The state might encourage the adoption of certain attitudes and society is certainly built on shared perspectives, but nowhere does the matter receive the treatment it requires except in the family and in religion. In these settings we publicly and explicitly deal with the shape of our souls; in both settings, the accountability is in a context of unconditional love. In these settings we are persons dealing with our natures in a context of love. The citizens and the subject of social science, by contrast, are individuals, with a territorial and temporal jurisdiction, and the normativity is in rights and utility.

If these ideas or something like them express a basic truth about charity, then public policy perspectives which explicitly or implicitly deny the truth are bound to go wrong. Explicit or implicit denial of truth should not, however, be confused with circumspection. We may and probably should remain silent on these highly personal matters in most public settings. But silence or circumspection is not denial. I am afraid that the views briefly described in the next part all assume, like Hitchens, Robinson, and the Fraser Institute, a fundamental denial.

3. MODERN APPROACHES THAT "USE" OR "ELIMINATE" CHARITY

A. Law

Recall the definition laid down in *Pemsel*: "trusts for the relief of poverty, advancement of education, advancement of religion, and other purposes beneficial to the community".[44]

Notice, initially, two things: (1) Why is the definition of "charity" in its legal sense tied to an organizational form and not to the central case, the charitable

[42] *Ibid*, 277.
[43] *Ibid*.
[44] Above, n 14, 583.

act? This is perhaps a minor problem, but notice that this forms part of a larger strategy of objectifying and absolutizing a peculiar "legal" view that renders motive *irrelevant*, and makes reference to the "common meaning" *irrelevant*;[45] it also, incidentally, renders it difficult to deal with matters of definition in non-trust contexts, such as with charitable corporations. (2) Notice also that the test in *Pemsel* is an odd collection of odd things. (a) Relief of poverty focuses on charity in the traditional narrow sense; the phrase identifies the project of providing material support to the poor to pursue the whole range of goods. But, as formulated it is too narrow to pick up all the senses of charity in the traditional narrow sense, such as cases where the beneficiaries are distressed or disadvantaged emotionally, physically, mentally or spiritually. (b) Education and religion name projects referencing, directly (religion) or indirectly (education), goods from the list of common goods.

So the list is a list of three types of project, but each type of project is defined using concepts of different types: the first (poor relief) is identified by the class of persons benefiting, the second, (education) is identified, directly by a project, education, and indirectly and incompletely, referencing the good of knowledge, and the third (religion), is identified directly by the good of religion. This strategy is not well-designed to pick up everything in the field, so the history of the case law is a history of trying to make things fit, often using the fourth catch-all "purposes beneficial to the public".

The *Pemsel* list, in short, is not based on a clear conception of charity, so much as on the experience of English courts with the conception of charity down to the date of the *Pemsel* decision (1891). In 1891, the *Pemsel* list picked up all the main projects, more or less, so it was, and is, useful *as* a rough guide. As a rough guide, however, it was bound to get many cases wrong. Here are some examples:

(1) Play is left off, so it has had to be included somewhat artificially in education, or by legislative fiat in various Commonwealth countries and in England.

(2) Aesthetic experience is left off so gifts to endow museums, art galleries, choirs, etc., have had to squeeze artificially into education.

(3) Knowledge is problematic under the list. Unless it is packaged as education, it seems to be excluded. This position creates problems for projects advancing fundamental research, libraries, and reading rooms. All of these advance knowledge, but not in any way that easily or conventionally fits under education.

(4) The *Pemsel* test has an additional requirement. The project must fit into one of the slots and it must be for the benefit of the public. This requirement is a poor articulation of the idea that the project must be effective in its advancement of the good and that the beneficiary must be a stranger. The law's current

[45] This point is pursued in Charles Mitchell's chapter in this collection at 201–2, where he challenges the orthodoxy that a body's purposes and activities may be clearly distinguished, and that only its purposes should be taken into account, when its entitlement to legal charitable status is assessed.

understanding of the public benefit requirement is peculiar and causes problems. I will end by mentioning only one, involving religion. In that context it has been interpreted to include the material and infrastructure support for worship, but, paradoxically, in *Gilmour* v. *Coats*[46] not worship itself!

There are a variety of deep-seated problems with the conceptualization that underlies the *Pemsel* list and these are compounded by the insistence of courts that this list constitutes the legal definition which is different from the real definition. To my mind, this is all bound to lead lawyers seriously astray in their discussions of technical legal charity to their detriment, the detriment of the law, and insofar as this intellectual system has social impact, on society. Much of what passes for intelligent legal analysis simply misses the point. Sometimes it is a case of silence and circumspection but I suspect that most of it is moved by the descendants of Hobbes, and the confrères of Gibbon, Hitchens and the Fraser Institute.

B. Economics

To deal with the economic perspective properly would require a fuller investigation of that discipline's philosophical foundation.[47] I cannot do that here, so I will merely suggest, rather briefly, some of the presuppositions and propositions from that perspective which I think render economics an even poorer guide than law to public policy on the sector.

There are three complaints against economics in particular. The first is the parsimony of its postulates.[48] By this is meant that the discipline casts a grid on the world that takes account of only one dimension of social reality. That grid is based on the postulate that people act rationally only when they act in their own self-interest. Albert O Hirschman has complained about this as follows:[49]

> Economics as a science of human behaviour has been grounded in a remarkably parsimonious postulate, that of the self-interested, isolated individual who chooses freely and rationally between alternative courses of action after computing their prospective costs and benefits.

And Thomas Schelling has noted likewise:[50]

> The human mind is something of an embarrassment to certain disciplines, notably economics . . . that have found the model of the rational consumer to be powerfully productive.

[46] [1949] AC 426.

[47] For an excellent treatment, however, see, D Hausman and M McPherson, *Economic Analysis and Moral Philosophy* (Cambridge, Cambridge University Press, 1996).

[48] Cf John Gardner's comments in this book at 23 and Sue Moody's discussion in 84 ff.

[49] A O Hirschman, "Against Patrimony: Three Ways of Complicating Some Categories of Economic Discourse", (1985) 1 *Economics and Philosophy* 7, 7.

[50] T Schelling, *Choice and Consequence*, (Cambridge, Mass, Harvard University Press, 1984).

Among the many modes of behaviour that this model excludes is love. Hirschman points to the fact that things like love and skill and civic spirit should not be modelled as a scarce resources, but as abilities or dispositions that grow or increase in value as they are used or practised. So any economics—any science of efficient resource use—in the charity sector or civil society in general would have to accommodate the different logics of these types of resources into its basic model. But this is something economics refuses to do. To the contrary, what one finds in much of the economic literature is a reluctance to see the sector in other than profit-maximizing terms. One economist thus praises the work of another on religion, as follows:[51]

> James is perhaps the only economist to have taken up the question of religions explicitly. Observing the significant role of religious founders in typical nonprofit industries such as health and education across countries, she introduced an ingenious argument: nonprofit organizations are chosen by religious entrepreneurs because "the objective is not to maximize profits, but to maximize faith or religious adherents".

The scholarly thing to do is to try unravel the philosophy that could issue a statement such as this, but, given time constraints, it really is not very different in logic or spirit from Hitchens' critique of Mother Teresa. Yes, we should be sufficiently sceptical of a religious claim, as of any other, yet one suspects that the practitioners who adopt the economic point of view have gone beyond religious scepticism to professing a faith of their own, founded on the impossibility of genuine religious conviction, or charity, or altruism.

The second is the insistence of the discipline on a negative definition of its object of study. Standard economic analysis of the sector provides only a negative definition of the sector. One major research paradigm puzzles over why the sector exists and investigates what it conceives to be the relevant two hypotheses: government failure and market failure.[52] In other words, the sector is defined as the residual left over after government and after market. One might just as well hypothesize as a research paradigm government and the market as "not altruism". The sector under this research paradigm is identified as the *nonprofit* sector, the essential characteristic being that, unlike the market sector, it does not operate for the benefit or profit of owners. Again, here, what the economic grid does not take into account is the possibility of *charity* or *altruism*.

The third complaint is the typical taxonomy of sector organizations according to two axes (four quadrants): (a) how it is financed—either commercially or by donation, and (b) how it is controlled—either by the persons who finance it or not. The specific altruistic or other purpose is missing here but this ought to be the central focus of lawmakers designing organizational laws. For example, organizational law should vary principally around the purpose of the organiza-

[51] H K Anheier, "Theories of the Nonprofit Sector: Three Issues", (1995) 24 (1) *Nonprofit and Voluntary Sector Quarterly* 15, 20.

[52] H Hansman, "Economic Theories of Nonprofit Organization", in W W Powell (ed), *The Nonprofit Sector: A Research Handbook* (New Haven, Yale University Press, 1987).

tion—charity, mutual benefit, religious or political advocacy—with the appropriate non-distribution or non-profit constraints being derived or being a function of this purpose.

C. Tax Policy

With respect to tax policy, the puzzle in the North American literature is to explain the tax exempt status of nonprofits in general and the tax deductibility or credibility of donations to charity.[53] Almost all views of this special treatment see it through the tax expenditure concept—it is a case of government largesse or government subsidy. One Canadian tax lawyer puts the point as follows:[54]

> The argument is that government has limited resources and that it is up to it as elected representatives of the people to allocate these resources according to some plan of priorities. To the extent that charities do what government would otherwise have to do, tax concessions to them can be justified. Otherwise, the activities, however estimable, should not be subsidized through the tax system.

The academic support for this position comes in three or four sophisticated varieties but all regard the exemption as a state subsidy. The state is on top, the sector is third, residual.

As to the favourable tax treatment of charities, it is not a subsidy at all, but a matter of a proper definition of the tax base and tax unit. Thus, donations are deductible (or creditable) because the proper base in an *income* tax is capacity to consume and removing income by making donations reduces that capacity. This line of argument explains the donation deduction or credit. If the donation earns income in the hands of the charitable organization that income ought to be exempt, because as a matter of theory we ought not to tax entities, except to prevent deferral opportunities, of which there are none in the case of charities, since there are no shareholders.

D. The Welfare State

Compare what is now happening with the state's social welfare activities. Individuals are no longer moved by any moral principle to pay taxes, only the sanction of getting caught. There is no altruism here, or I suspect elsewhere, in this type of right-wing view of the world, and there are consequently only two sectors, the individual (market), and government, which is residual. The egalitarian and socialist ideologies of the left are not persuasive against this view.

[53] For a good review, see J J Fishman and S Schwarz, *Nonprofit Organizations: Cases and Materials* (Westbury, NY, The Foundation Press Inc, 1995), chap 5.

[54] F L Woodman, "The Tax Treatment of Charities and Charitable Donations Since the Carter Commission: Past Reforms and Present Problems", (1988) 26 *Osgoode Hall LJ* 537, 571.

They offer an idea, but no motive, no reason to desire it. And the idea itself is probably flawed, and in any event has been the instrument of incredible harm. The selfish right wins by default since at least it appeals to a common desire.

As to the Welfare State, I think the answer must be that the aggressive right's point about waste and inefficacy is valid, but that as a matter of principle, "property" may be taken away—taxed—by society to support society's co-ordinated *charitable* efforts in government's social welfare programs. In other words, I would suggest that we need this public conception of charity, as much for the sake of government social welfare activities as for the sake of the sector itself.

4. CONCLUSION

Although it is possible to put some of the thesis of this chapter in purely secular terms, the initial formulation remains the most accurate.[55] Mother Teresa's concept of charity is essentially religious. Not only are her two elements diminished or distorted in legal and theoretical accounts of charity, in extreme versions, such as Hitchens' and that of the social sciences, their foundation is scorned. How strange it must seem to Gibbon's philosopher and magistrate that a person would give her whole life to *this* idea. This observation suggests, how-

[55] In *The Heart of Altruism: Perceptions of a Common Humanity* (Princeton, Princeton University Press, 1996), Kristen Monroe notes that Adam Smith in *The Theory of Moral Sentiments* (1759) postulated a sense of sympathy, some principle in man's "nature, which interests him in the fortune of others, and renders their happiness necessary to him, though he derives nothing from it except the pleasure of seeing it" many years before he postulated that it is "vain for man to expect the help of his brethren" in *The Wealth of Nations* (1776). Monroe suggests that the heart of altruism, what moves and therefore explains the actions of the rescuers and the heroes and heroines she interviewed for her study, is the perception that these people have of a "common humanity". She argues that their behaviours are "a reflection of the perceived relationship between the altruist and *all* other human beings"; that their perception of a shared humanity leads altruists to respond at great personal cost to the plight of others, by reflex, out of the sheer necessity of the circumstances. She suggests that none of the variants on the theme of self-interest suggested by economists and evolutionary biologists—goods altruism (altruists want honour, prestige, recognition), psychic benefits altruism (altruists want to "feel good") reciprocity (altruists desire a return of the favour), dual utility functions (altruists have a personal and a social utility function)—explain it. These explanatory models "fail abysmally" (159). Monroe concludes (236):

> . . . [a] study of altruism should remind us that squashing some behaviours into a self-interested paradigm robs them of their meaning. Love cannot be bought and still remain love. Nor can justice. The kind of religious belief that comes only because a clever rational actor deems it expedient to place a Pascal's wager is not really belief at all; it is mere expediency. So it is with altruism. If we subscribe uncritically to intellectual theories that reduce significant social phenomena—such as altruism, marriage and prejudice—to mere acts of rational calculus, we limit our understanding of human action.

The religious sentiment that is missing in legal and theoretical accounts—the love of persons and the advancement of their good through charitable acts—can be at least partially conveyed in more secular terms, as sympathy, altruism or a sense of a common humanity, as to the first element, and material and psychological well-being, as to the second. As Monroe suggests, especially with respect to the first, even these elements have been excluded from prevailing legal and theoretical accounts.

ever, the importance of posing the issue initially in religious terms: the modern failure to see through to the essence of charity is of a piece with the post-modern denial of the value of religion. Charity and religion are read out or read down *together* in modern accounts of charity. Certainly, there are very good reasons to remain silent or circumspect in regard to religious perspectives in public accounts of anything, including charity. As leading considerations, the following come readily to mind: ecumenism, the danger of chauvinism for one's own and the need for tolerance of another's, and the irrelevance of the big picture in the discussion of merely local issues. Religiously neutral language is useful and advisable in many public settings. But the Hitchens/social science/Gibbon/Fraser perspectives, at least in their extreme forms, are essentially atheistic. These extreme views intend to alter the meaning entirely by dissolving the foundation, severing the essential link with religion. After their modifications, we would come at best to be concerned for the poor not love them, to recognize their equality, not their dignity, to manage their poverty in socially adept ways, not risk encounters with them. Our hearts would be dead to them, as would their hearts for us. Mother Teresa's concept or Helen Prejean's concept, at least as public concepts, would be dead.

Thomas Hobbes was certainly not the first to encounter the difficulty of theoretical integrity, but his encounter with it is instructive for present purposes. In the rudiments of his system, society is resolved into its simple elements, individuals, and human nature is reduced to two desires, to "dominate" and to "avoid death". "Misery" awaits those who lose the "scramble" for possessions and power, "felicity" for those who win. In the war of all against all, the only virtues are "force" and "fraud". The social contract is entered as a matter of prudence to avoid death. Human beings pursue peace by agreeing to set aside arms and deathly competition in order to save their lives. They delegate to the state, "that mortal God", the exclusive authority to make law and enforce it. We obey the rules of society out of fear for the sanction of the sovereign and we do that primarily because we fear death. Hobbes makes several commitments which seem obviously false. 1) Society and the state are collapsed, since society is created in the one and same contract that creates the state. 2) Pre-contract human beings cannot bind themselves in a moral setting such as the one described by Hobbes, since the act of contracting presupposes some morality of contract, which is absent in his state of nature. These are the most obvious objections of the many to his essential claim that all of our shared rules arise by agreement. On the act of alms giving, Alasdair McIntyre relates the following story concerning Hobbes:[56]

> Outside of St Paul's Cathedral, an Anglican clergyman who had seen Hobbes give alms to a poor man tried to improve the occasion by asking of Hobbes (who was reputedly impious and atheistic) if he would have given the alms, had not Christ commanded it. Hobbes' reply was that he gave the alms because not only did it please the poor man, but it pleased him to see the poor man pleased.

[56] A MacIntyre, *A Short History of Ethics* (New York, Collier Books, 1966), 135.

McIntyre comments on the story as follows:[57]

> Thus Hobbes tries to exhibit his own behavior as consistent with his theory of motives, namely that human desires are such that they are all self-interested. The kind of lie told by Hobbes according to this anecdote is a kind of lie indulged in more often by philosophers than by other men, a lie told in the interests of saving the face of a theory. It remains a lie and a culpable lie, although one that Hobbes needed to tell. For the root of his error is here. Human nature and human motives are not and cannot be what he says they are.

McIntyre's observation alerts us to the fact that the problem we are dealing with is as old as liberal political theory itself. He also suggests the main theme of this chapter, that, at least initially, it is a problem of theory, a matter of the language proposed not being adequate to the reality it purports to capture.[58] Ultimately, to the extent that we believe what we say, as Hobbes in this case clearly did not, a poor theory is bound to issue in poor results. Hobbes' theory of individuals and society is not adequate to the task of describing his own act. Imagine the results if we used his account of individuals and society to generate public policy for the sector.

The equality of socialism, the liberty of conservatism, and the value neutrality of social science are all strands of a liberal theory of individuals and society which, in English political theory, is perhaps first clearly formulated by Hobbes. "Charity" presents a difficult topic in a political culture which places too much faith in these ideas for two sets of reasons. *First*, on the receiver's side, if it is true that charity is an act of one person for the good of another, then the public discourse on it will have to talk directly or obliquely about the good of man, something typically shunned by liberal theories. And government will have to choose among conceptions and instantiations of the good in order to act in this domain, as it does already in the definition of charity and in the policy consequences it attaches to that definition. Basic liberal concepts, such as equality and equal respect and dignity, on the socialist side and autonomy, choice, ownership, and rights, on the neo-conservative side, are not capable of accommodating the basic concepts of charity—persons, love, altruism, common humanity, and the good of man, etc. The options for the theorist in either camp are two: either sup-

[57] A MacIntyre, *A Short History of Ethics* (New York, Collier Books, 1966), 135.

[58] The distance between legal and theoretical accounts of charity and commonsense notions reflects a similar, but larger and more complex divide between modern ethical theory and everyday ethical thinking and practice, the "common morality" of Gibbon's people. In the common morality we find, in no particular order, the presence of shared narratives, a belief in the normativity of nature, an emphasis on virtuous conduct as well as on cost/benefit considerations of utilitarian thinking, the belief in the essential dignity of persons, the idea that rights in some fundamental respect are prior to social and political conventions and a belief in the an ultimate accountability for the persons we finally become. It would seem that the task of theoretical ethics should be to give some systematic account of these elements of common practice. Instead, with notable exceptions, we usually find theoretical systems built on one or two of the fragments. Again, this might be due to the need in certain contexts to abstract in order to enlighten, in which case one would expect a warning that one is dealing with a construct, a model, in which important features are omitted, on purpose, but only temporarily.

plement the particular liberal theory with another logic, perhaps resulting in a basic reordering of normative ideas; or, like Hobbes, read significant elements of the concept charity out of the theory altogether. The suggestion here is that the latter has been adopted as the dominant strategy to the detriment of discussion of public policy. *Second*, on the giver's side, there are two main points. (1) Not only will government and public discourse have to commit to the suspect activity of dealing with the good of man, it will have to occasionally address or deal with a giver's motivation. Unless the idea of liberty or property or rights is modified to accommodate this possibility, some of the discussion will necessarily be distorted. (2) We require a principled public basis to maintain the welfare state. Historically, at least in North America, the welfare state emerged due to the efforts of a coalition of two forces, socialism and the social gospel movement.[59] The social gospel movement promoted state welfare schemes on the basis that these were more effective means of pursuing charity in the traditional religious sense. If that basis of support is no longer available, once socialism is buried, the remains of the idea of charity—those elements that are logically compatible with liberalism, such as property and choice, the weakened giver's side deployed by the Fraser Institute—will be used to dismantle it.

[59] J Richards, *Retooling the Welfare State: What's Right, What's Wrong, What's to be Done?* (Toronto, C D Howe Institute, 1998).

3

Charity Law as a Political Option for the Poor

ALISON DUNN[1]

1. INTRODUCTION

IN CURRENT CHARITY law, and in the wider voluntary sector, there has been much debate over the extent to which charities may undertake political acts or become involved, generally or specifically, in the political process. The question concerning the involvement of charity in the political arena is one that has had a relatively short but involved history, with particular controversy spanning from the Charity Commission's inquiry into Oxfam's activities,[2] the increasing scrutiny of the nature and content of charity advertising,[3] to the debates over protection of donors and taxpayers, and claims for freedom of expression, freedom of association and basic human rights.[4] The arguments which have been advanced for the restriction on political activities by charities include the need for the judiciary to remain politically neutral; the inability of the Charity Commission or the judiciary to assess whether political activity will be for the

[1] This essay was first published by the Northern Ireland Legal Quarterly in 1999 and appears with their kind permission. The author is particularly grateful to John Gardner, for his assistance and for his comments on an earlier draft; to Roger Brownsword, Ilona Cheyne, Ian Dawson, Peter Luxton and Mia Murillo for their comments on an earlier draft; to Dylan Griffiths, Chris Hughes, Clare McGlynn, Richard Mullender and Peter Oliver for their suggestions of helpful material; and to Jonathan Garton and James Watson for their research assistance.

[2] S M St Clare Smith and Charity Commission, *OXFAM: Report of an inquiry submitted to the Charity Commissioners on 8 April 1991, including the response of the Charity Commissioners* (London, HMSO, 1991).

[3] For example, Christian Aid's advertising campaign to highlight suffering caused by Third World debt was held to breach Art 10 of the ITC Code as it was used to achieve political ends: *The Times*, 16 December 1997, 7. Earlier, in 1995, the Advertising Standards Authority upheld complaints against various charities concerning similar political and emotive advertisements: ASA, *Report No 53* (London, ASA, 1995).

[4] See, *inter alia*, E Burt, "Charities and Political Activity: Time to Rethink the Rules", (1998) 69 *Political Quarterly* 23; M Chesterman, *Charities, Trusts and Social Welfare* (London, Weidenfeld & Nicholson, 1979); L Chisholm, "Politics and Charity: A Proposal for Peaceful Co-existence", (1990) 58 *George Washington Law Review* 308; E Clark, "The Limitation on Political Purposes: A Discordant Note in the Law of Charities", (1960) 46 *Virginia Law Review* 439; C Rickett, "Charity and Politics", (1982) 10 *NZULR* 169; L Sheridan, "Charity Versus Politics", (1973) 2 *Anglo-American Law Review* 47; P 6 and A Randon, *Liberty, Charity and Politics: Non-Profit Law and Freedom of Speech* (Aldershot, Dartmouth, 1996).

public benefit, an essential requirement within charity law for an act to be charitable; the view that the functions of the legislature should not be usurped; and, more generally, the protection of donors to charities who may not wish their donations to be used for political purposes.[5]

It may be argued that the position has been clarified: that the guidance given by the Charity Commission[6] plus interpretative case law provide a reasonably comprehensive picture of the permissive political activities that charities may undertake. It is certainly true that charities are permitted to engage in a range of political activities, providing they remain ancillary to and in furtherance of the charity's main purpose.[7] But it is equally true that, despite the guidelines and their effect of fostering a healthy debate on charitable political activities, the legal and practical position is neither clear nor settled.[8] The extent to which charities are permitted to be political remains constrained. Boundaries per se may not be problematic where they are grounded on rational criteria, but in this context some of the limits upon charities are arbitrary, and quite often it proves to be not a charity's actual message which infringes the rules, but rather how it decides to convey that message. More seriously, the restrictions are arguably based upon unreasoned and misconstrued case law which may owe much to public policy but little to rigorous jurisprudential analysis.[9]

Beyond the policy of the law there remain serious practical issues which impress upon charities the (predominantly financial) problems inherent in their undertaking the political acts open to them under the law. Some charities, for

[5] *Charities: A Framework for the Future* Cm 694 (1989), chap 2; and see *inter alia,* the cases cited in n 9, below.

[6] Charity Commission, *Political Activities and Campaigning by Charities*, leaflet CC 9 (London, Stationery Office, 1997); Charity Commission, *Political Activities and Campaigning by Local Community Charities*, leaflet CC 9a (London, Stationery Office, 1997). For comment see A Dunn, "Charity Law—A Political Scandal?", [1996] 2 *Web JCLI.*

[7] Accordingly, charities may undertake a political activity, such as influencing government or public opinion, organising and presenting petitions, responding to proposed legislation or providing members with information to send to their Members of Parliament, where such activity furthers or is reasonably expected to further the charitable purposes of the charity, is within the powers of the charity trustees, is consistent with all the provisions of the Charity Commission's guidelines and the case put forward by the charity and its views are well-founded, reasoned and responsibly expressed (Charity Commission leaflet CC 9, above n 6, para 14, and Charity Commission leaflet CC 9a, above n 6, para 5).

[8] The paucity of cases has meant that few issues are clarified at judicial level (as is also the case with respect to the law relating to charitable status, for the reasons discussed by Charles Mitchell in this book, at 183). As testament to the prevailing uncertainty in understanding of the law, the Deakin Commission revealed that the question of the political activities of charities was an issue in frequent evidence before them years after the guidance by the Charity Commission was first produced: *Meeting the Challenge of Change, Voluntary Action into the 21st Century: Report of the Commission on the Future of the Voluntary Sector* (London, NCVO, 1996), vol 1, para 3.5.12.

[9] The case law developed in the early part of this century from a statement made by Lord Parker in *Bowman* v. *Secular Society Ltd* [1917] AC 406. Although strictly obiter, his view was endorsed in subsequent cases, and a general rule laid down in *National Anti-Vivisection Society* v. *IRC* [1948] AC 31. A more comprehensive prohibition was set out by Slade J in *McGovern* v. *A-G* [1982] Ch 321 and has been endorsed ever since (though cf *Public Trustee* v. *A-G of New South Wales* (1997) 42 NSWLR 600).

example, are restrained by their umbrella bodies, and there is evidence to suggest that corporate sponsors may have a role in limiting legitimate political activity.[10] Corporate donors often choose charities which give them a particular profile, for example, a caring or ecological face, and will not wish to be associated with a charity which undertakes overt political acts. Further, contracts to provide services often have the effect of preventing the charity speaking out. As Lord Astor of Hever recently commented in a House of Lords debate on the future of charities: "With so much of the charities' money coming from government sources, many charities lack genuine freedom of action."[11]

Moreover, the (largely twentieth century[12]) preoccupation of the law with charitable neutrality is misplaced given that charity works and exists on the periphery, dealing with partial circumstances. The modern law's concern with the extent to which charities may be political will always create tension where it fails to take into account an understanding of the nature of charity itself and an understanding of the basis of politics. This article undertakes such an examination and argues that there is much common ground between the political and charitable spheres, most particularly in that they are unified by their concern with public benefit, or the common good. The tensions in law between charity and politics are mirrored in the theology arena, and this article goes on to draw a comparison with the area of liberation theology which teaches that at its inception charity leads to a political option for the poor. Although criticised for being distortionary, exclusionary and for having false legitimacy, liberation theology has forced an institutional reconsideration of fundamental principles. A similar reconsideration needs to take place in law and this article concludes with some options for reform which may enable charity law to more fully reflect the nature of the arena it regulates.

2. CONSTRUING "POLITICS"

The consistent occurrence of political scandals has done much to encourage a conception of politics as self-serving and narcissistic, and this often accounts for the general uneasiness which surrounds the involvement of charity in the political sphere. Although regrettable, such instances make up no more than the outer layer of a much more complex notion.

"Politics" and "political activity" have both been variously defined, though unity can be found in an analysis of the different meanings. Modern definitions posit "political" as any act which is "of the state" and which relates to "the art

[10] S Beishon, "Homelessness and Company Giving", (1995) 16 *Policy Studies* 49.

[11] *Hansard, HL Debs*, 5th series, vol 586, cols 1213–1214, 4 March 1998.

[12] As Francis Gladstone rightly pointed out, many of the great nineteenth century reforming charities would clearly have infringed the present rules: *Charity, Law and Social Justice* (London, Bedford Square Press, 1982), chap 7. See also Lord Porter's dissenting judgment in *National Anti-Vivisection Society* v. *IRC*, cited above n 9.

and science of government".[13] In law too, definitions similar to the above abound, albeit that these definitions are not necessarily consistent, since interpretation has to be placed within the context and purpose of each particular jurisdiction.[14] Lord Diplock, for example, stated in *Tzu-Tsai Cheng* v. *Governor of Pentonville Prison*[15] in the context of the law of extradition, that:

> . . . politics are about government. "Political" as descriptive of an object to be achieved must, in my view, be confined to the object of overthrowing or changing the government of a state or inducing it to change its policy.

Similarly, in the context of charity law, Slade J's view in *McGovern* v. *A-G*[16] was that "political" pertained to furthering the interests of a particular political party, procuring changes in the laws of this country or of a foreign state, or procuring a reversal of government policy or decisions of governmental authorities in this or in a foreign country. More broadly, *R* v. *Radio Authority, ex parte Bull*,[17] a case concerning construction of the term "political" in the context of the Broadcasting Act 1980, endorsed the approach in *Tzu-Tsai Cheng* and *McGovern* and defined "political" as including an act which pertained to government policy, McCullough J stating at first instance that:[18]

> Once the matter has become the subject of government policy, or once the need for legislation about it is advocated, particularly if the matter has become contentious, then, as it seems to me, it is open . . . to treat it as "political".

Accordingly, "politics" may be allied with the actions of government, and concerns a process where the differing, often conflicting needs and interests of individuals, communities, or nations, are reconciled, accommodated or furthered. This may be achieved directly through legislation, or indirectly through the adoption of a range of policies or the pursuit of a fundamental ideology. Here politics has many layers of activity and complexity. On the one hand, as an aspect of government it is concerned with hard choices with regard to the distribution of scarce or limited resources, the extent and nature of protective action and the accommodation of one set of interests or needs with another.

[13] Typical of which is that to be found in the *Oxford English Dictionary*, sv "political".

[14] The context in which an act occurs can be very important to an analysis of its political nature. This is particularly so in current charity law where an ordinarily political act will not be considered political where it is ancillary to a charitable purpose, and vice versa. This point, emphasised in *McGovern* v. *A-G*, above n 9, was reiterated most recently in *R* v. *Radio Authority ex parte Bull* [1998] QB 294—particularly by Lord Woolf MR and Aldous LJ. See further text to nn 42 and 43 below, and see also Michael Chesterman's discussion in his contribution to this book at 261 ff.

[15] [1973] AC 931, 945.

[16] Above n 9, 340.

[17] [1996] QB 169 (DC); [1998] QB 294 (CA). In some circumstances a political activity can also be described as a business activity: *Commissioners of Customs & Excise* v. *British Field Sports Society* [1998] *The Times*, 4 February, in which the political campaigning, lobbying and related public relations activities of the British Field Sports Society were deemed to be business activities within the meaning of section 47(2)(a) Value Added Tax Act 1983.

[18] [1996] QB 169, 191.

However, supporting that level of activity is commonly perceived to be a process of consultation and deliberation which provides the impetus for political action and is the foundation of reasoned governmental decision-making.

These notions and the prevalent political debate thus directly associate politics with government and actions which are indeed "of the state". However, it would be a misconception to polarise the political to this institutional arena. Whilst taking care not to debase the notion entirely, it is clear that by delving within and beyond the art and science of government one finds that politics and its associated notions exhibit more fundamental qualities concerning the interrelationship between members of any given community and between communities. Thus, "politics" as a process of policy formulation and decision-making to reconcile the interests of the community does not simply exist on the macro—or governmental—scale. Politics equally forms part of the relations between individuals within the community, thus operating on a micro-level.[19] This can be seen in a quasi-institutional sense, such as within the world of commerce or business, the church or the family, but it similarly exists where any unit of persons becomes bound up as a social group.

Current trends in society and in social organisation indicate that political activity has become more vibrant and effective on this micro, or as Beck has termed it, "sub-political" level.[20] He argues not only that "the individual is returning to society", but that in fact "the political constellation of industrial society is becoming *unpolitical*, while what was unpolitical in industrialism is becoming *political*": that is, that the emphasis upon political activity as falling within the exclusive remit of government no longer holds true. The bolstering of micro-level politics has both vertical and horizontal causes. The process of consultation from the government downwards demands discussion with interested individuals and groups within society.[21] The promulgation of a healthy civil society[22] which this necessitates likewise has an effect upon the prevalence of groups who can capitalise upon explicit or implicit notions of citizenship.[23] In this horizontal context it can indeed be seen that "man moves man".[24]

[19] U Beck, *The Reinvention of Politics: Rethinking Modernity in the Global Social Order* (London, Polity Press, 1997), 99.

[20] *Ibid*, 98 and 99 (original italics). See also J Sachs, *The Politics of Hope* (London, Jonathan Cape, 1997), 137–8 and 237.

[21] B Crick, *In Defence of Politics* (4th edn, Harmondsworth, Penguin Books, 1993), 33. The role of the voluntary sector within the political arena has long been lauded as an essential prerequisite for a healthy civil and political society: see further text to nn 88–90 below.

[22] Civil society takes as its root the positive contribution that can be made by citizens as conscientious actors in the political process: see, for example, S Ndegwa, *The Two Faces of Civil Society: NGOs and Politics in Africa* (Connecticut, Kumarian Press, 1996); and the comments made by Baroness Pitkeathley in a recent House of Lords debate: *Hansard, HL Debs*, 5th series, vol 586, col 1256, 4 March 1998; and see also Lord Astor, col 1214; Baroness Young, col 1216; Baroness Linklater of Butterstone, col 1225.

[23] On an explicit level, citizenship is one of the key concepts within the European Union, though the EU notion of citizenship may be more exclusionary than the term would indicate, see I Ward, "(Pre)conceptions in European Law", (1996) 23 *Journal of Law and Society* 198.

[24] B de Jouvenal, *The Pure Theory of Politics* (Cambridge, Cambridge University Press, 1963), x, and generally 77ff. For an early examination of the concept of citizenship see A Ferguson, *An Essay*

Politics can then be defined as the act of reconciling and furthering interests within communities on both a micro or macro-level. Though it may appear that the meaning of politics differs across these two levels, in a pure sense they are unified by the purpose for which conciliation or advancement is sought. Whether one is concerned with the state or a nuclear unit, the aim of accommodating or promoting diverse interests is the achievement of a status quo which is of preponderant value to the unit, the community or to society as a whole.[25] At a more fundamental level, therefore, politics and political activity may be said to pertain to the promotion of a common good, or commonly held values, acting for the public benefit and transforming the parts of society which fall short of a shared social standard.[26]

3. CONSTRUING "CHARITY"

Much of what has been noted above about the realm and ambit of politics is also reflected in the charitable sphere, from difficulty over definition to its fundamental philosophy.

The very word "charity" is chameleon-like, having the tendency to take on different meanings according to both the circumstances in which it is used, and the person using it. "Charity" stems from the Latin term *"caritas"* connoting regard, esteem, affection or love.[27] According to Story:[28]

> Whatever is given for the love of God or the love of your neighbour, in the catholic and universal sense—given from these motives and to these ends—free from the stain or taint of every consideration that is personal, private or selfish, is a charity.

But it is clear that in this non-legal sense, the term charity has a number of varied connotations. The definition provided by the Oxford English Dictionary, for example, concentrates upon both charity's Christian and non-specifically

on the History of Civil Society (New Brunswick and London, Transaction Publishers, 1991 [1767]). A study into citizenship and civil society has more recently been launched by the Commonwealth Foundation. The project aims to identify ways in which citizenship and civil society can be strengthened and promoted. Consultation across the Commonwealth is currently in process.

25 On reconciliation, see R Hodder-Williams, *Judges and Politics in the Contemporary Age* (London, Bowedean Press, 1996), 36; B Crick, *In Defence of Politics*, above n 21, 21.

26 The last two speakers at the annual Arnold Goodman Charity Lectures, the President of the World Bank, Jim Wolfensohn, and the Cardinal Archbishop of Westminster, Basil Hume, developed this theme of good government: see 14th Arnold Goodman Lecture (London, Charities Aid Foundation, 1997) and "Searching for Purpose: God and The Future of our Society", 15th Arnold Goodman Lecture (London, Charities Aid Foundation, 1998). On the presence of common values in a democratic political system see further the comments of the Catholic Bishops' Conference of England and Wales in *The Common Good* (London, Catholic Bishops of England and Wales, 1996), para 34.

27 For an examination into the origin of the word "charity", see F Gladstone, above n 12, 9, and chap 1 generally.

28 J Story, *Commentaries on Equity Jurisprudence as Administered in England and America* (14th edn by W H Lyon, Boston, Little Brown & Co, 1918), vol 3, 175, n 3.

Christian aspects. With regard to the former, biblical connotations of charity relate to its intrinsic relationship with love.[29] Alternatively, "without any specially Christian connotations [charity is] love, kindness, affection, natural affection . . . especially with some notion of generous or spontaneous goodness", and more precisely it is "benevolence to one's neighbours, especially to the poor; [and] the practical benefices of which this manifests itself".[30]

Yet again, to others the spiritual and temporal aspects of the term cannot be separated, but intertwine. According to Loch:[31]

> In the word "charity" religious and social associations meet; and thus regarded the word means a disciplined and habitual mood in which the mind is considerate of the welfare of others individually and generally, and devises what is for their real good, and in which the intelligence and the will strive to fulfil the mind's purpose.

Indeed, in discussing charity, St Thomas Aquinas put forward not only seven spiritual deeds (to counsel, reprove, console, pardon, forbear, instruct or to pray) but also seven corporal deeds (to visit, quench, feed, ransom, cloth, harbour or bury) as instances of charitable acts.

Demonstrated within these definitions is the association of charity with the taking of an action and the achievement of a purpose. So too is this emphasis upon deed and objective carried through into charity law. The legal framework validates ad hoc acts which lead to the attainment of a specific and defined purpose, eschewing uncertain or ill-defined notions of benevolence.[32] One need only examine the contents of the Preamble to the Act of Charitable Uses 1601, which framed the development of the modern law of charity, with its emphasis upon amelioration and restoration to find a purposive approach carried through into charity law.[33] Further, in the context of charitable trusts for the advancement of religion, this purposive approach can be particularly noted through the emphasis of the law upon palpable deeds rather than ethereal acts of faith.[34]

[29] For example, the first letter of St Paul to the Corinthians verse 13 (if we have not love we are nothing); Leviticus 19:18, Matthew 22:39 and James 2:4–8 (call to love your neighbour as yourself); Luke 10:25–37 (parable of the Good Samaritan); Matthew 25:34–40 (provision of food and clothing for the hungry and naked stranger). For discussion of love and loyalty, and their relation with charity, see John Gardner's contribution to this book at 20–4, and David Stevens' contribution at 43–7.

[30] *Oxford English Dictionary*, sv "charity".

[31] C S Loch, *Charity and Social Life: A Short Study Of Religious and Social Thought In Relation to Charitable Methods and Institutions* (London, Macmillan & Co Ltd, 1910), 1.

[32] See *Chichester Diocesan Fund and Board of Finance (Inc)* v. *Simpson* [1944] AC 341.

[33] The Preamble provided a wide, although not comprehensive list of charitable purposes: "The relief of aged, impotent and poor people; the maintenance of sick and maimed soldiers and mariners, schools of learning, free schools and scholars in universities; the repair of bridges, ports, havens, causeways, churches, seabanks and highways; the education and preferment of orphans; the relief, stock or maintenance of houses of correction; the marriage of poor maids; the supportation, aid and help of young tradesmen, handicraftsmen and persons decayed; the relief or redemption of prisoners or captives; and the aid or ease of any poor inhabitants concerning payment of fifteens, setting out of soldiers and other taxes."

[34] *Gilmour* v. *Coats* [1949] AC 426; cf *Neville Estates Ltd* v. *Madden* [1962] Ch 832 and *Society of the Precious Blood* (1995) 3 Decisions of the Charity Commissioners 11.

However, the aims of charity, though now artificially demarcated into the relief of poverty, advancement of education, advancement of religion and other purposes beneficial to the community by Lord Macnaghten in *Commissioners for Special Purposes of Income Tax* v. *Pemsel*,[35] are more rudimentary. On one dimension, the purpose of charity may be said to be benevolence, that is the simple act of redressing need. This first dimension identifies charity with the poor. Poverty in this sense is construed widely and beyond financial restrictions to mean those within society who have a fundamental lack of opportunities and choices for action.[36] This powerlessness may exist, for example, in a person's or a community's material, cultural, educational, physical, mental or spiritual needs. The poor are thus "those without sufficient means to take part in the life of the community . . . excluded from the community, and ... denied the rights of membership".[37] In specifically directing attention to redressing need within society, acts of charity and the legal framework within which they operate exhibit a focus upon poverty. In providing opportunities and choices, this focus may be termed the provision of an "option for the poor".

But on a second dimension, the implementation of that benevolence and the act of redressing need reveal charity's more fundamental aims and nature. In its association between relieving and doing, or in Loch's words "striving to fulfil the mind's purpose",[38] charity necessitates a look beyond the immediate need to tackle the cause. At this level charity more specifically represents a "call to action", and is typified by innovation, effecting change, searching for solutions, pushing the boundaries, challenging existing order, being a "creative ferment in a free society",[39] giving a reason for hope and providing the opportunities and choices that the poor lack. The call to action which this second dimension involves is itself complex. It does not associate charity with the challenging of world order, but it does provide for a critical appraisal of society and of the elements within a community which cause or sustain a broad view of poverty.[40] The truly charitable act thus goes beyond the mere redressing of need to the

[35] [1891] AC 531, 583.

[36] Actionaid, *Bridging the Poverty Gap* (Somerset, Actionaid, 1993), 3. In *Re Coulthurst* [1951] Ch 661, 665–6, "poverty", under the specific heading "relief of poverty" in charity law, was defined as encompassing those people "going short". This definition appears to be restricted to financial matters. The EC working definition of poverty states that: "the poor shall be taken to mean persons, families and groups whose resources (material, cultural and social) are so limited as to exclude them from the minimum acceptable way of life in the member states in which they live", Bull EC 12–1984, pt 2.1.95.

[37] John Paul II, Encyclical letter: *Sollicitudo Rei Socialis* (On Social Concerns), 30 December 1987, para 74.

[38] Above, n 31, 1.

[39] *Hansard, HL Debs*, 5th series, vol 586, cols 1271–1272, 4 March 1998, Lord Dahrendorf; see too *Hansard, HL Debs*, 5th series, vol 576, col 315, 27 Nov 1996, Lord Dahrendorf.

[40] Charity's intrinsic connection with the political does not mean that an organisation has to undertake political or campaigning activities in order to be charitable. Rather, that within a charitable act lies the potential for a moral outpouring, whereby the understanding which charity gives of another's poverty can lead to a desire to redress not just the manifestations of that poverty, but also its causes. The moral purpose of charity is a call to action, but that call to action is enabling and not prescriptive. That is why charity may be described as a political *option* for the poor.

point where it is concerned by purpose or deed with transforming society. It is only when both dimensions are transcended that charity is fully formed.

4. IDENTIFYING COMMON GROUND

A distinction is often made in this debate between the end, or purpose of a charity and the means by which that end is achieved, as a way of differentiating charitable acts from political acts and justifying the legal restrictions placed upon charities.[41] The argument is that the charitable end or purpose determines what is the common good,[42] and that political activities are no more than one means by which the common good can be achieved. Because the distinction between ends and means argues that the charitable and the political are, in principle, different and concerned with separate issues—the former determining the common good, and the latter a tool to achieve that good—it follows upon this view that the charitable foundation of the common good does not intrinsically involve a political element. Crucially, this denies a role for the political purpose or substantial political act because, under the current law, a charity's purpose and the means used to achieve that purpose must be wholly and exclusively charitable. A purpose will be charitable and thereby concerned with the common good if it falls within Lord Macnaghten's four heads of charity, identified earlier.[43] A substantial political act or purpose cannot be an end in itself because it does not fall within one of Lord Macnaghten's categories and is not wholly and exclusively charitable. A political activity will be acceptable as a means to achieve a charitable end, but only if it falls within the ambit of an ancillary act. If the political act is and remains ancillary to the charitable purpose, as Slade J pointed out in *McGovern* v. *A-G*,[44] it will be deemed a charitable act in itself, but if it is not ancillary to the charitable purpose it will remain political in nature and thereby be unacceptable.

Though ostensibly plausible, these distinctions present a delineation of the two spheres of charity and politics in the starkest of terms and pay no credence to the fundamental nature of politics and charity. As noted in the preceding

41 The Ontario Law Reform Commission (OLRC), for example, argues that since charity is the good, and politics only a debate about the good, the two must be distinguished, albeit that they do agree that "politics is the process of a society's collaborative effort to make law, to come to some agreement or understanding on a particular determination of the good": *Report on the Law Of Charities* (Ontario, OLRC, 1996), chap 6.

42 The OLRC have argued that "the truly charitable act is the act whose form, actual effect and motive are the provision of the means of pursuing a common or universal good to persons who are remote in affections and to whom no moral or legal obligation is owed": above n 41, chap 6. The Commission drew upon the work of J Finnis, *Natural Law and Natural Rights* (Oxford, Clarendon Press, 1980), chap 4, to identify common or universal goods and to show how charity can provide for such goods: for discussion, see David Stevens' contribution to this book at 32–5.

43 Text to n 35, above.

44 Above, n 9, 341. See also the discussion of the same issue by the Court of Appeal in *R* v. *Radio Authority, ex parte Bull*, above, n 17.

parts, the charitable and the political are unified at a fundamental level by their association with the promotion of a common good—a public benefit—and thus providing the poor with choices and opportunities.[45] What is deemed a "good" and charitable to achieve in one community will in fact be determined within the community's prevailing social context. The prevailing social context is, in turn, partly or wholly determined by cultural and political considerations or assumptions either on a micro or macro-level. Whether these political considerations reflect no more than the historical location and development of a particular community, or whether they more properly represent the prevailing philosophy of a governing régime, they are nevertheless inherently used to define the good which it is deemed by society as charitable to pursue.

Whilst there is much to commend their congruency, this is not to argue that every political purpose or activity will be consistent with a charitable purpose or activity. Clearly, the charitable and the political are not wholly synonymous. There are many different political ideologies, and not all ideologies will be compatible with charity or share the same construct of the common good. Even some dimensions of accepted ideologies may raise concern as being for the public benefit. In this respect the challenge for the legal framework is to work with an interpretation of the common good, or public benefit, which capitalises upon the ground between the two spheres, but which does not debase the notion of charity to an unacceptable political realm. Propaganda or partisan political activities must surely fail a test of common good where they are neither, in Story's view of charity, "free from the stain or taint of every consideration that is personal, private or selfish",[46] nor, as Loch stated, widely "considerate of the welfare of others".[47] The problem of where the line should be drawn between palatable and unpalatable politics is presently obviated by the law's restriction on charities undertaking substantial political activities and the blanket restriction on political purposes. It is true that the political and non-political boundary will not necessarily become less problematic if rendered less arbitrary. But just as Clark noted that the "need for information and ideas is not diminished because the issue is controversial",[48] so too the expediency for the law to finely balance legitimate interests is not diminished simply because it is difficult to draw boundaries, particularly if the boundary presently so drawn represents an artificial severing of political considerations from charity's core.

[45] The Government in introducing its "compact" with the voluntary sector identified the common ground between the political arena and the wider voluntary sector on the basis of their shared "aspirations", these being, "the pursuit of inclusiveness, dedication to public life, and support for the development of healthy communities": *Compact on Relations Between Government and the Voluntary and Community Sector in England* Cm 4100 (1998), foreword.

[46] Above, n 28, vol 3, 175, n 3.

[47] Above, n 31, 1.

[48] Above, n 4, 458. For a similar argument see J Waldron, "Religious Contributions in Public Deliberation", (1993) 30 *San Diego Law Review* 817, 841–2.

5. THE THEOLOGY DEBATE

The dimensions of charity identified above can be explored more fully by making a comparison of the charity and politics debate with a similar debate in the theological arena. The sphere of theology and politics is particularly relevant in this context, not simply because of the Christian association of charity with love, but also because at a fundamental level it resonates with the problems encountered in the charitable sphere. Moreover, in terms of development, theology is more advanced, and the process of analysis and rationalisation it has undertaken may illuminate the debate in the context of charity, and help formulate a more feasible framework for the development of charity law.

6. LIBERATION THEOLOGY AS A COMPARABLE MODEL FOR CHARITY

The dynamic relationship of politics with hermeneutics developed through a particular Catholic movement termed "liberation theology".[49] In short, liberation theology emphasises social, economic, political, racial, environmental, military and spiritual liberation.[50] Liberation theology's meaning and purpose can be found in the fact that "it is the articulated cry of the oppressed", "puts on agenda for discussion questions that concern all human beings", "denounces the causes that produce oppression and inspires an outpouring of generosity destined to overcome destructive relationships and build freedom for everyone", and "sets out to be the servant of faith that works through charity inspired by hope".[51]

Liberation theology's primary tenets were developed, among others, by the Peruvian theologian Gustavo Gutiérrez in the late 1960s.[52] It was formally determined by the Latin American Bishops at Medellín, Columbia in 1968 and ratified eleven years later at the conference in Puebla. In a statement issued by the Bishops at Medellín, the essence of liberation theology and its association with the poor was laid down as an obligation:[53]

[49] For a good introduction see J A Kirk, *Liberation Theology: An Evangelical View from the Third World* (Basingstoke, Marshall, Morgan & Scott, 1979).

[50] E Norwood Evans, "Liberation theology, empowerment theory and social work practice with the oppressed", (1992) 35 *International Social Work* 135, 139. The theological themes are discussed by L Boff and C Boff, *Introducing Liberation Theology* (Kent, Burns & Oates, 1987), 49–63. See also G Gutiérrez, *A Theology of Liberation: History, Politics and Salvation* (London, SCM Press Ltd, 1971), xiii, arguing that liberation theology is essentially "a theological reflection born of the experience of shared efforts to abolish the current unjust situation and to build a different society, freer and more human" which gives a "reason for our hope from within a commitment that seeks to become more radical, total, and efficacious".

[51] Boff and Boff, above n 50, 88–9.

[52] His main thesis is contained in *A Theology of Liberation: History, Politics and Salvation* (London, SCM Press Ltd, 1971).

[53] Bishops of Latin America, *Poverty of the Church*, Medellín document, 6 September 1968, paras 9–10.

> to sharpen the awareness of our duty of solidarity with the poor to which charity leads us. This solidarity means that we make ours their problems and their struggles, that we know how to speak with them.

Moreover, that our charitable relationship with the poor:

> has to be concretised in criticism of injustice and oppression, in the struggle against the intolerable situation which a poor person often has to tolerate, in the willingness to dialogue with the groups responsible for the situation in order to make them understand their obligations.

Within the concept of liberation theology there are two themes, both of which are directly comparable with the dimensions of charity already identified. In the first instance liberation theology teaches that charity leads to solidarity with the "poor". John Paul II stated in his encyclical letter *Sollicitudo Rei Socialis* (On Social Concerns) that solidarity:[54]

> is not a feeling of vague compassion or shallow distress at the misfortunes of so many people, both near and far. On the contrary it is a firm and persevering determination to commit oneself to the common good; that is to say, to the good of all and of each individual.

In the context of solidarity charity means "being-for-others",[55] identifying with their poverty and seeking redress of that poverty. This was expressed earlier as the first dimension of charity—providing an "option for the poor". But in the context of liberation theology, charity in a one dimensional sense is inadequate. A further step is required. As has been argued:[56]

> in the social dimension, loving means collaborating in the formation of new structures, supporting those that represent an advance in the campaign for a better quality of life, and political commitment in favour of an option for solidarity with the poor.

Thus it is only when charity goes to the essential quality of solidarity that it becomes complete. Within liberation theology, solidarity demands the criticism of injustice and oppression and dialogue to effect change. In fact, solidarity or charity—"being-for-others"—means nothing unless it is coupled with attempts to mediate or change an unjust or intolerable situation. This leads to the second theme of liberation theology, termed "subsidiarity":[57] the call to action.

Gutiérrez described liberation theology as "a political hermeneutics of the Gospel",[58] and the theme of subsidiarity as a tenet of liberation theology is concerned with the questioning of the situation of the poor in order to challenge and change the circumstances which lead to poverty. The notion of "subsidiarity" is becoming increasingly common. It is one of the concepts that lies at the heart of

[54] Above, n 37, para 38.4.
[55] Phrase taken from Boff and Boff, above n 50, 62.
[56] Boff and Boff, above n 50, 62.
[57] For a discussion of subsidiarity see A Duff (ed), *Subsidiarity Within the European Community* (London, Federal Trust for Education and Research, 1993); Ward, above n 23.
[58] Above, n 52, 13.

post-Maastricht European law,[59] though its ambit is neither fully drawn out, nor sufficiently hemmed in. As Peterson[60] has argued, it stands as a concept which is able to support competing ideologies rather than accommodating different views. In whatever sense subsidiarity is eventually interpreted, on a basic level it involves the premise that power and contribution to decision-making should be delegated downwards from the political and governmental institutions to the people. Indeed, it can be seen as supporting "a dispersal of authority as close to the grass roots as good government allows … [preferring] local over central decision making".[61]

Subsidiarity is more than just a theory, indeed its existence and gradual dissemination explains Beck's identification of a change in the construct of the political arena of post-industrial society and consequently the increase in micro-level political activity.[62] Moreover, as a tenet of liberation theology it leads to a further correlation with the charitable and political arenas. That connection relates directly to their wider schematic purpose for action. At the heart of the Latin American Bishops' Medellín statement is the broad purpose of bringing the poor out of their poverty into participation for the benefit not just of the individual poor, but of the community as a whole.[63] Not only does liberation theology exhibit the two themes of an option for the poor and a call to action but, like charity and like politics overall, in transforming society it has as its aim the achievement of public benefit through the pursuit of a common good, a shared social purpose, a shared social value.

7. CRITICISMS OF LIBERATION THEOLOGY AND THEIR PARALLEL IN CHARITY LAW

The connection of theology with politics was the cause of much debate and criticism both within and without the Vatican.[64] The core criticisms centred upon the problems of distortion, legitimacy and exclusion.

59 See Art 5 European Community Treaty (now Art 10 of the consolidated Treaty).

60 He identifies three competing constructs of subsidiarity: the wide view based on Catholic social teaching which dictates that "small social groups should be autonomous and sovereign in a pluralist society, yet united in a common morality which stress duty and harmony . . . assisted in their activities by the state which neither substitutes for social groups nor is it shackled by their demands, but which serves the public good and provides legal order"; secondly, the more rigid federalist view of Germanic origin which defines the respective powers, duties and roles of different levels of government; thirdly, the "British conservative ideology" which sees subsidiarity as a means by which supranational powers can be limited. He argues for a broad definition: J Peterson, "Subsidiarity: A Definition to Suit Any Vision?", (1994) 47 *Parliamentary Affairs* 116, 118–19 and 128–30. See also A Teasdale, "Subsidiarity in Post-Maastricht Europe", (1993) 64 *Political Quarterly* 187.

61 Catholic Bishops' Conference of England and Wales, *The Common Good*, above n 26, para 52.

62 See text to nn 19–23, above.

63 See, for example, the Medellín document, *Justice*, 6 September 1968, para 16.

64 In particular by Cardinal Ratzinger on behalf of the Congregation for the Doctrine of the Faith. These objections are considered in greater detail in P Berryman, *Liberation Theology: Essential Facts about the Revolutionary Movement in Latin America and Beyond* (London, I B Tauris & Co Ltd, 1987), chap 12.

To take the first criticism, that of distortion, there existed the fear of the impact which liberation theology's twin notions of solidarity and subsidiarity could have directly upon either the church and its members or upon the political process. This manifested itself particularly in an institutional anxiety over the development of a predominantly Marxist theme, and the fear that actions taken by liberation theology's actors for the poor and to relieve poverty would become simply a secular philosophy.[65] Secondly, the Church recoiled from embracing liberation theology on the basis that controversial political acts undertaken by church representatives in pursuit of, say, opposing oppressive régimes, could be popularly perceived to be legitimised by the Church from the fact that the actors' actions fell within the auspices of a recognised institution. This criticism further introduces its corollary that sustained controversial politicking would bring opprobrium or disgrace upon the Church as the institution represented by the liberation theology actors. Thirdly, liberation theology was criticised as being exclusionary; first, per se, because it concerned a Christian notion, and secondly because it could lead to the dogmatic insistence upon the application of Christian or politico-Christian doctrine in all or in inappropriate circumstances.[66]

Significantly, the criticisms raised did not seek to deny the political nature of charity as expressed in a theological framework. Rather, they demonstrated a wariness over the extent of the consequences of the association. These criticisms and their concern with external consequences rather than challenging inherent characteristics, find their parallel in the arguments which traditionally censure the association of charity with politics in law.

In the context of the criticism of distortion, for example, the boundaries within the legal framework reflect a general apprehension over the consequences of a clear political role for charities. Aside from the perceived distortion of charity's good name and the alienation of donors,[67] an option for the poor and a call to action by charities may lead, it is thought, to a distortion of the political process through the promotion of biased or unbalanced information and policies, the use of undue or emotive public pressure rather than reasoned argument, or through an overt emphasis upon a single issue which may have the effect of diverting political debate from the main issues of the day. Anxiety over this form of distortion of the political process either by charities directly, or indirectly by taxpayers' subsidy of charitable activity, has been highlighted by the Charity Commission and the Government.[68] With regard to the latter's view, it

[65] That is, redemption through temporal actions rather than through recourse to God.

[66] In fact this has proved not to be the case in comparisons of liberation theology working in different social and cultural environments. See, for example, the observations of F Wilfred in the context of the inter-faith Indian experience of liberation theology: "Action Groups and the Struggle for Justice in India: Ecclesiological Implications", (1987) 39 *Ecumenical Review* 291.

[67] This was one of the contentions employed by the Government in their White Paper, above n 5, to argue against allowing charities to campaign or act politically in any manner other than that which was ancillary to and in furtherance of their main charitable purpose.

[68] The Government's view in its White Paper was that the taxation subsidy given to charities meant that taxpayers were subsidising political activities, and that it "would be wrong if taxpayers . . . were to find themselves unwittingly distorting the democratic process by subsidising bodies

represents a wider concern with independence and autonomy, particularly in the electoral process.[69] This concern has some foundation given the wide support and trust reposed in charities and the subsequent political muscle that they and their supporters could flex.

With regard to legitimacy, in charity law there is concern that since charities are legitimised through their charitable status generally and their taxation concessions specifically, any political actions undertaken will be automatically endorsed, or perceived to be endorsed, precisely because they take place within the auspices of a recognised legal framework. Similarly, that sustained controversial political acts will only serve to bring opprobrium or disgrace upon that framework, and de facto upon the actors within it, including any non-politically acting charities.

Finally, predominant political action by charities may lead to exclusion through partisan political influence or bias, or through the imposition of fundamental political dogma under the guise of charitable works. The law is vigilant to prevent political propaganda masquerading as charitable purposes and particular attention is paid to those purposes which seek to fall within the head of advancement of education, an area most susceptible to manipulation.[70] This concern with the consequences of accepting partisan political purposes within the definition of charity is the kernel of the law's objection against greater latitude for charities to campaign or otherwise act politically. It lies at the heart of the Government's refusal to reconsider reform of the definition of charity, since in their view the present law provides an "indispensable safeguard" to donors, taxpayers and the public generally.[71]

The criticisms of distortion, legitimacy and exclusion do not go to the base or the essence of either liberation theology or charity and do not represent a

whose true purpose was to campaign not so much for their beneficiaries as for some political end", above n 5, para 2.41. The Charity Commission's emphasis upon not distorting the political process and upon presenting well founded and reasoned material can be found throughout their guidelines on the political and campaigning activities of charities cited in n 6 above.

[69] The problem of the distorting effect upon the democratic process of the pursuit of single issues by interested groups was emphasised by the Government in their submission to the European Court of Human Rights in *Bowman* v. *UK* (1998) 26 EHRR 1, in which Bowman successfully challenged the Representation of the People Act 1983, s 75, on the basis that it concerned a breach of freedom of expression under Article 10 of the European Convention on Human Rights. In his dissenting opinion, Judge Sir John Freedland re-emphasised the distortion point. He stated at para 13: "the role played by single issue pressure groups in influencing and mobilising public opinion in modern democracies is, as the Government acknowledged, an important one. But a factor of which the State may legitimately take account in determining the regulation of the electoral process is the extent to which limits of the funding of single-issue campaigns at parliamentary election may be needed in order to counter the risk of excessive diversion of the main electoral debate."

[70] See *Re Hopkinson* [1949] 1 All ER 346, 350 (Vaisey J); *McGovern* v. *A-G*, n 9 above; *Southwood* v. *A-G* [1998/99] ITELR 119; and the Charity Commission Guidelines, above n 6, paras 45, 52, and 54; cf *Re The Trustees of the Arthur McDougall Fund* [1956] 3 All ER 867; *Re Koeppler's WT* [1986] Ch 423; *Re Scowcroft* [1898] 2 Ch 638.

[71] *Charities: A Framework for the Future*, above n 5, para 2.41.

mphasis upon not distorting the political process and upon presenting well founded and reasoned material can be found throughout their guidelines on the political and campaigning activities of charities, above n 6.

challenge to their prevailing principles. Rather, they focus upon external considerations which are the perceived and preconceived consequences of undue political action. Solidarity, an option for the poor, and subsidiarity, a call to action, mean pushing the boundaries of a system, but nevertheless working within that system to change, strengthen or alter its direction.[72] Distortion, legitimacy and exclusion are objections which would be raised in any system which sought but had not completely implemented a strong civil society. In such a system there is an onus upon government to govern responsibly.[73] This does not simply mean fairly and justiciably, it also means having the strength not only to encourage pluralism and diversity, but also to avoid distortion and exclusion in the face of strong pressure, to foster consultation and collaboration and to provide a framework which respects true legitimacy.

8. THE WAY FORWARD

Despite the criticisms of liberation theology for pushing the boundaries of the system, its value lies in the fact that it forced an institutional reconsideration of the position to which faith leads. The Church's response to the challenge of liberation theology stands as a prime example of the benefit which can be derived from analysing the foundation of an area. It has allowed the political nature of charity to be harnessed with theological teaching in a manner which is acceptable in the current global and ecclesiastical climate.

Although initial attempts were made to deny the political manifestations of faith in action, in fact by challenging liberation theology the Church was led to focus its attention on the foundation of faith and the call of the Gospels. This reappraisal in turn led to a renewed institutional emphasis upon the Church's social teaching through which it highlighted the need for an active "preferential option for the poor".[74] This institutionally organised focus upon poverty takes as its root the community's individual and collective obligation to pull the poor out of their condition of poverty by means of spiritual and temporal acts. It places an emphasis upon working within a system to bring about change. In the context of the present discussion, the significant feature of the Church's renewed emphasis upon social teaching and its preferential option for the poor is that it not only more fully reflects the Gospels' call to action, but that it also differs little from the original vision of liberation theology which was first

[72] So too in the context of liberation theology, a theology which Gutiérrez termed "the activity of 'peacemakers' ", in *A Theology of Liberation: History, Politics and Salvation*, above n 52.

[73] According to Tony Blair's vision for the development of a "third way" in politics, "a key challenge of progressive politics is to use the State as an enabling force, protecting effective communities and voluntary organisations and encouraging their growth to tackle new needs, in partnership as appropriate", *The Third Way: New Politics for the New Century* (London, Fabian Society, 1998), 4.

[74] See most recently John Paul II's Apostolic Letter: *Tertio Mellenio Adveniente* (As the Third Millennium Draws Near), 14 November 1994, paras 50–51.

rejected as politically unacceptable. The crucial distinction is that the moves to put faith in action with regard to the poor are now sanctioned and regulated by the Church.[75]

The framework of charity law needs to undertake a similar rationalisation in order to more fully reflect the arena which it regulates. Without an examination of the foundations of charity the restrictions currently in place will be found wanting where they fail to accommodate the inherent nature of charity. As highlighted earlier, at a fundamental level the charitable and the political arenas are unified by their association with the promotion of a common good, a public benefit. Recognising this connection would do much to obviate the difficulty presented by the principal arguments advanced for prohibiting charities from undertaking substantial political activities or purposes: that is, that the judiciary cannot be the arbiter of whether a political activity satisfies the requirement in charity law for a purpose to be for the public benefit;[76] and that, in any event, the judiciary must remain politically neutral and not become embroiled in debates over the legitimacy of diverse political purposes.[77] These arguments pertain to points concerning justiciability and seek to place charity law beyond the reach of partiality by distancing the decision-making process from controversial issues which would reflect upon the legal framework and the legitimacy of the separation of powers.

Justiciability is an important issue and one should not seek to place within legal consideration issues which are beyond the scope of the judiciary. However, aside from side-stepping the fundamental nature of charity, these arguments in fact obscure the environment within which decisions in charity law are taken. First, in the context of political activities used to achieve a charitable purpose, the charitable purpose itself will have already passed the test of public benefit when the organisation in question applied for charitable status, since it is at the point of registration that the organisation's express objects clause is subject to scrutiny. Public benefit is considered in the context of assessing if the purpose in the objects clause is charitable, not in the context of how that purpose is achieved.

Secondly, with regard to political purposes and public benefit, public benefit as construed in charity law is a tangible benefit afforded to a cross-section of society which is not numerically negligible.[78] So construed, such a test has the

[75] See, for example, Paul VI's Apostolic Exhortation: *Evangelii Nuntiandii* (On Evangelisation in the Modern World), 8 December 1975, paras 25–39. Catholic social teaching has long lauded the use of "intermediate groups" within a democracy to effect change and to help man reach his full potential, seeing such groups as "the indispensable means to safeguard the dignity of human person and freedom while leaving intact a sense of responsibility": John XXIII's Encyclical letter: *Pacem Terris* (Peace on Earth), April 1963, para 24; see also para 35. So too, has there been a strong emphasis upon civil society and upon each person becoming "the artisans of their own destiny": Paul VI's Encyclical letter: *Populorum Progressio* (On the Development of Peoples), 26 March 1967, para 65.

[76] An argument once described as "a strain on credulity": Sheridan, above n 4, 58.

[77] *Bowman* v. *Secular Society Ltd*, above n 9; *National Anti-Vivisection Society* v. *IRC*, above n 9.

[78] See *Verge* v. *Somerville* [1924] AC 496, 499 (Lord Westbury); *Oppenheim* v. *Tobacco Securities Trust Co* [1951] AC 297, 306 (Lord Simonds); *Gilmour* v. *Coats*, above n 34, 446; *Dingle* v. *Turner* [1972] AC 601.

capacity to be applied irrespective of the colour or nature of the purpose. Concern may, of course, be expressed as to the dilemma caused to the judiciary in assessing the benefit afforded to a cross-section of society by politically opposed right-wing or left-wing purposes. But the key to the public benefit test is not the approach or ideology taken to the purpose, but whether the purpose per se provides a benefit. By way of comparison, if, as is the case, the tenor of spiritual belief is irrelevant to the public benefit test for charitable purposes falling within the head of religion,[79] so likewise should it be for the tenor of political belief. Further, in the context of charitable status, the restriction against unacceptable political activities currently de facto implied into each charitable purpose means that the judiciary are already in the process of accepting that a charity's express object clause is limited, and limited so to exclude what the law presently deems to be inappropriate activities. This decision is in itself politically charged.[80]

Moving forward from a consideration of charity's inherent nature, how the association between the charitable and the political is to be harnessed is open for debate, but represents the challenge to contemporary charity law. Sheridan's view is that the law should take into account political considerations by returning specifically to the spirit and intendment of the Preamble to the 1601 Act of Charitable Uses.[81] The spirit of that Act, however, was bound up with Elizabethan reform and seventeenth century social concerns. What is more pertinently required is a move forward which would enable charity law to transparently reflect the essence of charity within the context of the current social and political climate. The American position[82] of permitting charities to be politically active but with a prescription upon the funds and general resources that can be so dedicated is a quantitatively artificial solution which would not meet this challenge of transparency. Neither would the setting up of a separate body to make decisions upon charitable status,[83] since the problems of partisan politics, or construing the public benefit would be simply transferred between bodies. The view that the market should be allowed to decide whether or not to support charities who actively enter into the political arena is attractive,[84] but

[79] As Cross J stated in *Neville Estates Ltd* v. *Madden* [1962] Ch 832, 853, "As between different religions the law stands neutral". Consider also *Thornton* v. *Howe* (1862) 31 Beav 14; *Varsani* v. *Jesani* [1998] 3 All ER 273; *Re South Place Ethical Society* [1980] 1 WLR 1565. And cf Rob Atkinson's discussion in this book at 147 ff, of the sectarian state's handling of doctrinal disputes between members of religious sects.

[80] See Rickett, above n 4, 170. It remains true that in certain areas the judiciary have not shied away from the political ramifications of their decision-making. Consider in this respect the judiciary's revolutionary approach to tax avoidance schemes in *Ramsay* v. *IRC* [1982] AC 300, which came as a significant departure from the more lenient approach previously adopted in *IRC* v. *Duke of Westminster* [1936] AC 1. On the significance of the judicial change see Lord Diplock in *IRC* v. *Burmah Oil* [1982] STC 30, 32.

[81] Above, n 4.

[82] See B Hopkins, *Charity, Advocacy and The Law* (New York, Wiley & Sons, 1992).

[83] A view put forward by J Hackney, "The Politics of Chancery", (1981) 34 *CLP* 113, 127–8.

[84] See, for example, the arguments of A Sprince, "Political Activity by Charitable Organisations: An English Model with More to Learn than to Teach?", (1997) 11 *Trust Law International* 35.

holds some reservations for protecting against the dissemination of propaganda or unpalatable political acts under charity's badge of credibility.

Charity's nemesis is the taxation advantages through which it is privileged. Any re-examination of charity law must take into account charity's privileged financial status, given that it is fiscal policy which lies at the heart of current charity regulation. One option could be to sever the fiscal line wholly, another to place an additional tax upon political activities so defined.[85] A third view could be to grade taxation privileges according to the nature and extent of the political activities undertaken.[86] The question of the taxation advantages of charities is a particularly thorny issue, and one which demands detailed attention in all respects of charitable activity, from main charitable purposes to subsidiary activities, such as charity trading. Though a key issue, altering the fiscal privileges in respect of political activities would not be feasible in practice without a commitment to wholesale reconsideration of the taxation structure.

Perhaps the most preferable way forward would be to permit certain categories of charities more latitude in respect of political considerations. There are a number of ways in which this could be implemented, albeit that some means would be more feasible than others. It could be achieved outright by permitting only those charities which fall within a particular category to undertake substantial political activities or purposes, or, less artificially, it could be achieved through permitting greater political latitude for those charities whose purposes specifically aim to provide opportunities and choices for the poor. This latter method, however, may lead to problems of arbitrariness and would question the criteria involved in decision-making.

A third approach to this proposal could be to isolate those charities involved in partnership with, and in receipt of funding from central or local government, since it is arguable that only those charities truly independent of government that should have the freedom to engage in political activities. One advantage of this proposal is that it would exclude charities which may have political backing from unfairly influencing their members, the wider public or distorting the political process. However, it would present an unwarranted dilemma for the many charities which wish to partake in the political arena but who, in the present highly competitive market economy, rely upon government contracts for their continued existence.[87] Further, this approach would seem to be at odds with the Government's more recent moves to create a "compact" with the wider voluntary sector.[88] The role of the voluntary sector within the political arena has long been lauded as an essential prerequisite for a healthy civil and political

[85] See 6 and Randon, above n 4.

[86] HRH Prince Phillip put forward a similar view for an overall redefinition of charity in giving the 1994 Arnold Goodman Charity Lecture: 11th Arnold Goodman Lecture (London, Charities Aid Foundation, 1994).

[87] See further B Knight, *Voluntary Action* (London, Centris, 1993).

[88] *Compact on Relations between Government and the Voluntary and Community Sector in England* Cm 4100 (1998). See also T Blair, *The Third Way*, above n 73.

society,[89] and the Government's compact has emphasised the unique contribution to a socially inclusive democratic society which is made by voluntary groups through their role in working with and on behalf of the vulnerable or disadvantaged.[90] It would not be consonant with this approach to artificially exclude those charities in partnership with government from a political role when other voluntary groups in similar partnerships are not so limited. Further, as noted earlier,[91] distortion of the political process by charities campaigning whilst acting in partnership with government should not be sustainable in a strong civil society.

A fourth alternative is that the proposal for allowing only a certain category of charities to act politically could be more sensitively achieved through reconstructing the test for public benefit as it applies across Lord Macnaghten's four heads of charity.[92] Lord Cross in *Dingle* v. *Turner*[93] long favoured a qualitative approach to charity law which assessed purposes by fact and degree. A similar approach which qualitatively assessed tangible benefit to a sufficient cross-section of the public, with a concentration upon the substance of the purpose rather than its form or method, could be utilised here. Political purposes which offered tangible benefit to the common good would not be debarred because of their apparent colour, but would not be admitted without evidence of their essentially charitable nature. This latter method would be advantageous in the context of ensuring that those political activities which militate against a socially constructed common good, such as partisan policies or terrorist acts, remain outside and are not embraced within charity's ambit.

9. CONCLUSION

Allowing charities more latitude in the political arena will not obviate the many substantial difficulties involved in creating a workable framework for regulation. Indeed, rendering the distinction between the political and non-political sphere less arbitrary will, if anything, place greater emphasis upon the requirement for a strictly accountable system. What is at stake is the question of policy. In the end the choice is whether protection of the democratic process is placed higher than the ability of all interested groups to contribute to that process. If

[89] For example, the Wolfenden Report in the late 1970s, in calling for decentralisation of power and greater involvement for the individual in decision-making, expressed the view that there was room for a number of methods to relieve need within society, such as an informal system of social help through a network of friends and family, a commercial system of private education, health care and pensions, the statutory system of welfare provision and the voluntary system: *The Future of Voluntary Organisations: Report of the Wolfenden Committee* (London, Croom Helm, 1978), 22.

[90] Above n 88, paras 5–7.

[91] Text to nn 72 and 73, above.

[92] The notion of "public benefit" is discussed generally in Patrick Ford's contribution to this book (chap 8).

[93] Above n 78. See also Lord Porter's dissenting judgment in *National Anti-Vivisection Society* v. *IRC*, above n 9.

on public policy grounds the status quo of the current law is to be ultimately enforced, it is vital that a whole or partial restriction against political involvement should be in place only in the face of a full and frank analysis of charity's foundation, rather than simply upon fears of where an overt political connection may lead. A self-critical reconsideration of the foundations of charity and of charity law is necessary if its legal framework is to be both respectable and successful.

4

Self-Giving in "Charity": The Role of Law

SUSAN R MOODY[1]

1. INTRODUCTION

THE CURRENT DEFINITION of "charity" in English law is the result of prolonged and sometimes tortuous interpretation and reinterpretation, primarily of case law[2] but stemming initially from statute.[3] In spite of the artificial and even archaic ways in which English courts have restricted or extended the meaning of "charity" there appear to be three key indicators upon which all commentators agree: (1) that a body claiming charitable status must have as its object a "charitable" purpose or purposes; (2) that it must apply its charitable income to further its charitable purpose or purposes, with the result that any profits accrue for the benefit of the charity and not for the individuals who manage or control that charity or for shareholders; and (3) that such a body must operate independently and not so as to further the interests of individual members, commercial interests or party political concerns.[4] Underpinning these essential criteria is the requirement that charities should operate for "public benefit" (although the degree to which all bodies which currently have charitable status meet this requirement has been questioned[5]). "In order for the space for voluntary activity to be as substantial as possible, society must esteem both the values associated with these contributions and what is achieved through them—the public benefit."[6] This "public benefit" requirement is in effect the

[1] I am grateful to John Gardner for bringing to my attention the contemporary literature on self-ownership and to other speakers and participants in the Foundations of Charity Colloquium for their suggestions. I acknowledge the assistance of the British Academy in financing my participation at the Annual Conference of the Association for Research on Nonprofit Organisations and Voluntary Action in Washington DC in November 1999, where this paper was discussed.

[2] See, for instance, *Commissioners for Special Purposes of the Income Tax* v. *Pemsel* [1891] AC 531.

[3] Preamble to the Charitable Uses Act 1601.

[4] For a description from the former head of the Charity Commission see R Fries, "Charity and the Charity Commission", (1999) 2(1) *International Journal of Not-for-Profit Law* 1 (www.icnl.org journal/vol2iss1/rfries.htm).

[5] See, for instance, the criticisms of charitable status for independent schools and private hospitals in M Chesterman, *Charities, Trusts and Social Welfare* (London, Weidenfeld and Nicolson, 1979) and also his comments in this collection at 253–61.

[6] N Deakin, *Meeting the Challenge of Change, Report of the Commission on the Future of the Voluntary Sector* (London, NCVO, 1996), section 2, para 1.3.35.

quid pro quo for the particularly privileged place which charities enjoy in contemporary society. It recognises the financial benefits of tax concessions to charities[7] as well as the more intangible but nonetheless advantageous position which charities occupy in the public mind, encouraging donations and personal involvement in the work of charitable bodies. It is claimed that "charity law would never have developed into the sophisticated system which now obtains in England and Wales were it not for an additional public policy objective: the desirability of encouraging citizens to undertake—voluntarily—financial and other obligations towards the rest of society".[8]

The charitable purposes outlined in the Preamble to the Statute of Uses and adopted into English case law by *Pemsel* have been the subject of considerable criticism. One commentator has described them as "a ragbag of purposes"[9] and has questioned the wisdom of continuing "to define a charitable purpose in so abstruse a way".[10] The Charity Commissioners are currently in consultation with the sector about a reworking of the current definition to include certain activities which appear currently to be ineligible, such as economic regeneration and employment opportunities.[11] Several other chapters in this book deal specifically with the issue of charitable purposes. My particular focus is rather on the second and third essential elements in "charity", the requirement of non-profit distribution, and the need to preserve independence. My analysis therefore extends far beyond the mere relinquishment of profit to incorporate what I believe is and ought to be a *sine qua non* of charitable status, the giving of oneself freely and without material reward, which I call voluntarism.

The second element is usually dealt with in monetary terms only, focusing on "trading" and other commercial activities by which profit could be generated. Charities can of course make a profit through charging for their charitable activities, for example charitable housing associations which receive income from rents, and increasingly do so. The key issue is the disposition of such profits, which must not be applied for the benefit of members, so that there can be no parallel with the shareholders in a "for-profit" company. This requirement implicitly carries with it the necessity for accountability and transparency in the financial dealings and management of the charity, to ensure that profits are being ploughed back into the charity rather than to individual beneficiaries. It also demands that those concerned in the running of the charity, apart from

[7] In the form of relief from income tax, corporation tax, capital gains tax, inheritance tax, and stamp duty, reductions in Council tax and business rates, and, in certain circumstances, exemption from VAT.

[8] F Quint, "The Rationale for Charity Law", (1993/4) 2 (3) *Charity Law and Practice Review* 211, 214.

[9] E Cairns, *Charities: Law and Practice* (3rd edn, London, Sweet & Maxwell, 1997), 2.

[10] *Ibid*, 1.

[11] See Charity Commission, *The Review of the Register of Charities*, leaflet RR 1 (London, Charity Commission, 1999); *Promotion of Urban and Rural Regeneration*, leaflet RR 2 (London, Charity Commission, 1999), *Charities for the Relief of Unemployment*, leaflet RR 3 (London, Charity Commission, 1999). For general discussion, see Charles Mitchell's chapter in this collection (chap 7).

salaried employees, should not benefit in any tangible way from their involvement with the charity.

The third element is mainly concerned with governance issues, both within the charity and in relation to external bodies. The importance of maintaining the independence of the charity requires, I contend, that management personnel must include a majority of members (charitable trustees) who are not primarily answerable to external bodies. The notion of the voluntary charitable trustee is essential in order on the one hand to maintain a clear distinction between self-interest and the interests of the charitable trust and on the other to ensure that charities are run to further their charitable aims and not predominantly to serve the interests of external bodies. The essential criteria for charitable trustees of non-remuneration and of independence together underline the importance of voluntarism in the definition of charity.

Further, the significant contribution which volunteers make to the provision of services by many charities, although not a prerequisite of charitable status, nevertheless merits greater recognition by the law. A more focussed, protective legal approach to the role and status of volunteers could assist by indirectly encouraging and enhancing voluntarism.

In addition to this "practical project", which seeks to establish that voluntarism is both an essential part of the legal definition of "charity" and an aspect of national life which the law should seek to foster, I have also sought in the "theoretical project" to draw on a variety of jurisprudential perspectives to justify my belief that "charity" requires some element of voluntarism and that bodies claiming charitable status should not be granted that privilege unless they can demonstrate an element of "self-giving". I consider four very different perspectives: self-giving as freedom, represented by libertarianism, particularly in the work of John Locke; self-giving as moral obligation, derived from a reworking of Kantian philosophy; self-giving as central to the notion of civil society; and self-giving as mutual exchange, drawing on communitarianism.

2. BACKGROUND

Before presenting these arguments, however, two preliminary issues need to be considered.

First, the scope and nature of "self-giving" deserve some attention to illustrate the extent to which involvement in voluntary work continues to be an integral part of British society. While such a description cannot, of itself provide a justification for requiring self-giving as an essential element in "charity", nevertheless it underlines the central role played by volunteering in national life and suggests that the significance of this contribution in both economic, political and social terms needs to be clearly understood.

Secondly, counter-arguments to those presented here usually seek to demolish the concept of altruism, by focusing on self-interest as the sole impetus for social action. It is important to take such arguments seriously, particularly since they exert such a very strong influence on economic theory, which itself has a significant impact on political, social and social-psychological ideas, and, to an increasing extent, on legal theory. However, my intention is to counter this view of human action as solely self-centred, firstly by considering the current importance of volunteering in United Kingdom society and secondly by critically analysing some of the literature on the pursuit of self-interest.

A. Volunteering in National Life

Millions of people give their time, energy and skills every day not just to their family, kin and close neighbours (which is really a matter of obligations derived originally from necessity) but to strangers. The most recent National Survey of Volunteering noted that just under 50% of the adult population took part in voluntary activity at least once in 1997.[12] The survey defined volunteering broadly as "any activity which involves spending time, unpaid, doing something which aims to benefit someone (individuals or groups) other than, or in addition to, close relatives, or to benefit the environment".[13] The same study concluded that 22 million people in Britain regularly take part in formal voluntary activity, representing a collective 88 million hours per week. An earlier study, which focused on volunteering in health and welfare services only, estimated that one in twenty people volunteer regularly for such activity.[14] In relation to charities in England and Wales it has been estimated that 750,000 people act as charitable trustees.[15]

Volunteering makes a significant contribution to the economy, with recent European research estimating that most organisations using volunteers benefited significantly from their "investment" in volunteers (that is, expenditure incurred in using volunteers, such as training and supervision costs). The study estimated that organisations got back between three and eight times their initial investment through unpaid work carried out by volunteers.[16] In Britain voluntary work has been estimated to represent £25 billion of unpaid work.[17] The human resource of the UK voluntary sector is derived mainly from volunteer labour, with 3 million unpaid workers contributing the equivalent of almost 1.6 million full-time jobs or £12 million.[18] In addition to these direct financial ben-

[12] J Davis Smith, *The 1997 National Survey of Volunteering* (London, National Centre for Volunteering, 1998).

[13] *Ibid*, 1.

[14] M Knapp, "Are Voluntary Organisations Really more Effective?", in D Billis and M Harris (eds), *Voluntary Agencies: Challenges of Organisation and Management* (London, Macmillan, 1996) 166.

[15] K Ford, *On Trust: Trustee Training and Support Needs* (London, NCVO, 1992).

[16] K Gaskin, *Valuing Volunteers in Europe: A Comparative Study of the Volunteer Investment and Value Audit* (London, Institute for Volunteering Research, 1999).

[17] Volunteer Centre UK, *The Economic Value of Volunteering*, Volunteering Research Bulletin (Berkhamstead, Volunteer Centre, 1995).

[18] L Hems and A Passey, *The UK Voluntary Sector Almanac 1998–9* (London, NCVO, 1999).

efits it has been suggested that volunteering contributes to skills development producing a more competent and better equipped pool of labour.[19]

This method of assessing value deals only with those aspects of volunteer involvement which are easy to quantify and does not cover the more intangible benefits to volunteers, service-users and society at large of volunteering. For instance, it has been suggested that volunteering, particularly by young people, might be a substitute for forms of anti-social behaviour which are costly to society and damaging to the young people concerned. This thinking has certainly influenced the establishment of *Millennium Volunteers*, through which it is claimed "young people will experience the benefits of volunteering in terms of personal development, confidence and skills".[20] Writers have also encompassed volunteering within the notion of the "active citizen", with research indicating that those involved in voluntary activity are also more likely to be politically active at community level.[21] Social inclusion of marginal groups is fostered, it has been claimed, by volunteering, both for members of these groups and for those who engage with them in voluntary work.[22] Volunteering offers opportunities for all to take part in activities which reduce social distance and enhance individual confidence and perceptions of belonging.[23] It must, of course, also be accepted that volunteers are not "without cost" and that volunteering may not always be the most cost-effective way of providing a service.[24] Nevertheless, a clear understanding of the cost implications of voluntarism (in terms of recruitment, training, support, supervision and payment of expenses) and a discriminating approach to the use of volunteers should not detract from the contribution made by volunteering.

These findings about the positive contribution of volunteering could be dismissed as simply demonstrating the application of self-interest. The reasons for volunteering, cynics may assert, are either based on the realisation that such activity will improve the volunteer's employment and life prospects or because the alternative is even less palatable (as with the more "coercive" schemes where volunteering is required of recipients who wish to continue to receive welfare benefits). However, research does not bear out this conclusion. Virtually all

[19] See, for instance, G Elam and A Thomas, *Stepping Stones to Employment: Part Time Work and Voluntary Activities Whilst Claiming Out-of-Work Social Security Benefits*, DSS Research Report No 71 (London, TSO, 1997); J Davis Smith, "Volunteering for Employment: An Examination of the Link between Volunteering and Employability", paper presented at the Third International Conference of the International Society for Third Sector Research held in Geneva, 8–11 July 1998.

[20] Department for Education and Employment, *Millennium Volunteers: Setting the Framework* (London, DFEE, 1998).

[21] P Dekker and A van den Broek, "Civil Society in Comparative Perspective: Involvement in Voluntary Associations in North America and Western Europe", (1998) 9 (1) *Voluntas* 11.

[22] Volunteer Development Scotland, *Response to the Scottish Office Consultation Paper on Social Exclusion* (Stirling, VDS, 1998).

[23] B Hedley and J Davis Smith, *Volunteering and Society: Principles and Practice* (London, Bedford Square Press, 1992).

[24] M Knapp, *Time is Money: The Crisis of Volunteering in Britain Today*, Voluntary Action Research Paper No 3 (Berkhamstead, Volunteer Centre UK, 1990).

volunteers when asked about their motivations and the benefits they derived from volunteering included a desire to help others and a satisfaction in so doing.[25] While their motivations were seldom unidimensional this should not detract from the importance they placed on self-giving as essentially altruistic.

The public have a fairly well-developed sense of what is a volunteer and appear to welcome volunteering. In the 1997 survey of volunteering nine out of ten respondents agreed with the notion that a society with volunteers is a caring society. At the same time the public definition of volunteering requires that the benefits which the individual derives from volunteering must be outweighed by the cost, i.e. a "net-cost" approach, although defining costs and benefits may be very complex.[26]

B. The Pursuit of Self-Interest

The importance of volunteering in economic and social terms may provide a valuable functional explanation for such activities. It does not, however, deal with the moral justifications for self-giving and does not locate volunteering within certain philosophical perspectives. And yet such a fundamental aspect of human behaviour requires to be analysed at a deeper level, so that its significance can be properly understood.[27]

Altruistic self-giving is apparently an anomaly in today's world, according to economists,[28] some contemporary social theorists and sociobiologists.[29] Economic models of volunteering include a variety of tangible and intangible donor benefits obtained from the act of volunteering: "job training, signalling job skills, information acquisition, association with other volunteers, power to direct non-profit allocations in favoured directions, prestige".[30] According to Weisbrod, an economist with a special interest in nonprofit activity, people behave rationally in pursuit of their individual objectives of utility maximisation and adopt a "rational choice" approach to every aspect of their lives.[31] Recent research by a zoologist, reported in the journal, *Nature*, concludes that apparently altruistic behaviour is in fact based on self-interest because people's "value" in the eyes of others is enhanced when they are known to be helping others.[32]

Even if such altruism exists, other critics say, it is in fact a cover for a demeaning form of patronage: "it excuses the vanity of donors, makes recipients of

[25] Davis Smith, above n 12; Dekker and van den Broek, above n 21.

[26] R Cnaan, F Handy, M Wadsworth, "Defining Who is a Volunteer: Conceptual and Empirical Considerations", (1996) 25(3) *Nonprofit and Voluntary Sector Quarterly* 364.

[27] For a further critique of economics as a guide to public policy on the voluntary sector, see David Stevens' discussion in this book at 49–51.

[28] B Weisbrod, *The NonProfit Economy* (Cambridge, Mass, Harvard University Press, 1988).

[29] M Novak, Review Article, (1998) 395 *Nature* 760.

[30] R Steinberg, "Overall Evaluation of Economic Theories", (1997) 8(2) *Voluntas* 179.

[31] Weisbrod, above n 28.

[32] Novak, above n 29.

charity even more uncomfortable and mutely beholden, and distorts many descriptions of charity".[33] Simmel claims that altruistic giving can create a relationship of "bondage" because the initial giver will always be on higher moral ground than the recipient.[34]

In an unpublished paper O'Regan explores the literature on volunteers' motivations and the dominant view among contemporary economists and psychologists that self-interest is the main determinant of human behaviour.[35] He notes there is considerable interest in this area with one literature review identifying over one thousand studies on helping behaviour.[36] An acceptance of volunteering as directed at achieving the good of the "other" strikes at the heart of much contemporary psychological and social psychological theory: "not only does it contradict the common assumption in psychology that all motivation is ultimately directed towards the egoist goal of increasing our own welfare, but it also contradicts the underlying assumption that all human nature is fundamentally self-serving".[37] It is particularly at odds with traditional evolutionary biology, O'Regan claims, which places a premium on individual survival.

However, in spite of these formidable critics of altruism O'Regan demonstrates that there are alternative approaches in both the psychological and the economic field. For instance, the evolutionary biologists Buck and Ginsburg emphasise that natural selection involves communication between genes and that these systems "form the basis of all social behaviours, including empathic emotions and altruism".[38] Kristen Monroe, in her critique of the economic approach to human behaviour, presents a contrary view to the rational choice model, based on her empirical study of philanthropists, heroes and altruists. In her interviews with them, these people did not see themselves as atomistic, self-interested individuals. Rather their actions were based wholly or partly on a sense of shared humanity. "Altruists share a view of the world in which all people are one. This world view appears to bond them to all humanity in an affective manner that encourages altruistic treatment."[39] They did not see themselves as fundamentally different from those they were helping, they took positive action in situations where others retreated and they reaffirmed their identity through such activities. If this understanding of altruistic behaviour is applied to voluntarism it emphasises the essentially social, non-judgmental nature of the

[33] R Mullin, *Present Alms: On the Corruption of Philanthropy* (Birmingham, Phlogiston, 1980), 29.

[34] G Simmel, *The Sociology of Georg Simmel* (trans K Wolff) (New York, Free Press, 1950).

[35] A O'Regan, "In Search of the Voluntary Actor: A Critical Review of the Literature", paper given at the Annual Conference of the Association for Research on Nonprofit Organisations and Voluntary Action in Washington DC 4–6 November 1999.

[36] J Dovidio et al, "The Arousal: Cost-Reward Model and the Process of Intervention: A Review of the Evidence", in M Clark (ed), *Prosocial Behaviour* (London, Sage, 1991).

[37] *Ibid*, 80.

[38] R Buck and B Ginsburg, "Spontaneous Communication and Altruism: The Communicative Gene Hypothesis", in M Clark (ed), *Prosocial Behaviour* (London, Sage, 1991), 171.

[39] K Monroe, *The Heart of Altruism: Perceptions of a Common Humanity* (New Jersey, Princeton University Press, 1996), 198.

enterprise, which is about communication and empathy rather than "do-gooding" and superiority.

The contribution of voluntary work, as one form of altruism, is not simply an economic one. By its very nature it gives the lie to "*homo economicus*" whose every action is motivated by self-interest alone. But what is the role of law and of the State in supporting and encouraging voluntarism? In particular does the law relating to charities take sufficient account of voluntarism? In the remainder of this chapter I will consider four different philosophical approaches to self-giving through volunteering and explore their implications for the law and legal regulation of charities. I do not advocate one particular school of philosophy as offering the most appropriate justification for self-giving; nor do I try and resolve the inevitable conflicts between different approaches. In general terms, the four philosophical understandings have little in common, except that they derive from a secular and not a religious view of the world. What is remarkable, I believe, is that they all share a clear commitment to voluntarism, in spite of the major schisms between them. Nor is it my intention to provide a legal blueprint for the implementation of each approach or to produce an overarching legal framework encompassing the four schools. My much more modest aim in the practical project is to sketch in ways in which the law relating to charities currently fosters voluntarism and to suggest new ways in which self-giving might be further embedded in the legal definition of charity.

3. SELF-GIVING AS FREEDOM

A. Locke and Self-Ownership

The central importance of property rights in John Locke's political philosophy is often construed solely as a matter of rights in things. His view that the social contract is designed primarily to protect property rights and that free subjects have a right to accumulate wealth and to inherit wealth are central to his concept of freedom. However, Locke also speaks about property in ourselves: "man . . . hath by nature a power . . . to preserve his property, that is his life, liberty and estate".[40] Indeed he sees property in ourselves as the cornerstone of all other property rights. "Man (by being master of himself, and proprietor of his own person and the actions of labour of it) had still in himself the great foundation of property."[41] (He was of course writing at a time when many people did not enjoy such rights over their own person, because of slavery. While rejecting the idea of "chattel slavery", Locke nevertheless argued that people could become slaves.)

[40] J Locke, *Two Treatises of Government*, in M Salvadori (ed), *Locke and Liberty* (Liverpool and London, Charles Birchall & Sons, 1960), 162.

[41] J Locke, *The Second Treatise on Government*, in D Wootton (ed), *John Locke: Political Writings* (London, Penguin, 1993), para 44.

At the same time, Locke's belief in the importance of self-ownership does not lead him to the conclusion that human beings should be merely self-interested. In a rather eloquent passage from a letter to his friend Tom he speaks of the importance which people should attach to the interests of others: "let us make it our interest to . . . be useful to our fellows" and justifies this by suggesting that, while it may not entirely "secure us from error [it] will keep us from losing ourselves" since "if we walk directly straight we shall not be altogether in a maze".[42] Indeed he also speaks out strongly against the "economic fallacy" which we have already identified, that the nature of human existence is based solely on self-interest. "Many of the most important virtues consist simply in doing good to others at our own expense."[43]

He goes further and maintains that it is neither obligatory nor is it even permissible for human beings always to do what gives them individually the highest return. First, it makes a nonsense of history and morality if altruism is to be regarded as foolish and positively wicked. "If the logic of virtue is to be identical with that of profit, and if the measure of justice is to be self-interest, what is this than to throw open the door to every species of villany?"[44] Second, in a more pragmatic sense private interests cannot be pursued unstintingly without causing suffering, that is:"anyone who grows rich does so at the expense of someone else".[45] Further, the prioritising of self-interest will have disastrous consequences for all citizens since: "what reason is left for the fulfillment of promises, what protection for the interests of society, what sense of community and common purpose between men, when equity and justice are the same as self-interest?"[46] However, if the contrary approach is adopted everyone benefits because people are no longer in conflict with one another and it becomes possible to develop the essential bond of trust which binds members of a free society together. Self-interest, then, becomes the consequence and not the cause of our actions;"a moral action [may be] self-interested, but only because it is right".[47]

The notion of "self-ownership" which is particularly relevant to this paper envisages that all men (and it was men in Locke's civil society although he came close to justifying equal treatment for women also) are born with a title to freedom, become free at maturity and cannot lose that freedom except by their own actions: "every man has a property in his own person: this nobody has any right to but himself".[48] The choice to give up freedom can only be exercised by a free person and is therefore the hallmark of self-ownership. This, combined with the benefits which each person derives from the pursuit of the common interest instead of individual self-interest, is the distinguishing characteristic of the liberal State. "The only way, whereby any one divests himself of his natural liberty,

[42] J Locke, *Letter to Tom*, in Wootton, above n 41, 40.
[43] J Locke, *Essays on the Law of Nature*, No. VIII, in Wootton, above n 41, 176.
[44] *Ibid*, 181.
[45] *Ibid*.
[46] *Ibid*, 182.
[47] *Ibid*, 183.
[48] J Locke, *The Second Treatise on Government*, in Wootton, above n 41, para 27.

and puts on the bonds of civil society, is by agreeing with other men to join and unite into a community."[49] However, at an individual level also such relinquishing of self-ownership may be necessary and beneficial to a free society, by underlining the shared commitment each to all and by emphasising the "property in self" enjoyed by every citizen. So in effect the value which the restrictions placed by all free people on their actions represent at a collective level is strengthened and reflected at an individual level by self-giving to others.

As Cohen has demonstrated in his collection of essays on various aspects of self-ownership,[50] the concept has a long history. The idea was further developed and used in the movements against slavery and serfdom (although Locke's own views about slavery were somewhat ambivalent). Cohen defines self-ownership as "the fullest right a person (logically) can have over herself provided that each other person also has just such a right".[51] It has been resurrected within the last twenty years by neo-liberals to justify non-payment of taxes[52] and in what Harris has called "the bodily-use freedom principle".[53] Modern theorists have endorsed Locke's view of self-ownership as "a primordial property right in the self which then grounds all other property rights".[54]

The idea is not without its difficulties. As one commentator has noted "talk of property in persons might strike some modern ears as an artificial and unwarranted extension of the concept of property".[55] Kantian philosophers have fiercely opposed the notion as leading to objectification and the commodification of the self. From a feminist viewpoint, Ngaire Naffine critiques the self-owning individual as male only and considers that his property-in-self requires the dispossession of woman, certainly in the sphere of conjugal relations.[56] The concept may only be useful if it is confined to the public economic sphere, according to others. In addition, critics of the notion, such as Cohen, have sought to demonstrate that the logical implication of the self-ownership thesis is the reinforcement of individual inequality and the unequal distribution of resources.

Cohen's arguments have been met by counterclaims that there is no necessary relationship between self-ownership and inequality, and that such a stark opposition does not represent either Locke's concept of self-ownership or his idea of justice.[57] And self-ownership is not simply the province of the libertarian. As

[49] J Locke, *Two Treatises of Government*, in Salvadori, above n 40, 166.

[50] G A Cohen, *Self-Ownership, Freedom and Equality* (Cambridge, Cambridge University Press, 1995).

[51] *Ibid*, 213.

[52] R Nozick, *Anarchy, State and Utopia* (New York, Basic Books, 1974).

[53] J W Harris, "Who Owns my Body?" (1996) 16 *OJLS* 55, 55.

[54] J Frow, "Elvis: Fame, the Commodity Form and the Form of the Person", (1995) 7 *Cardozo Studies in Law and Literature* 131, 149.

[55] M Otsuka, "Self-Ownership and Equality: A Lockean Reconciliation", (1996) 27 *Philosophy and Public Affairs* 65, 69.

[56] N Naffine, "The Legal Structure of Self-Ownership: Or the Self-Possessed Man and the Woman Possessed", (1998) 25(2) *Journal of Law and Society* 193.

[57] Otsuka, above n 55.

Cohen also shows, in Marx's good society a person is the proprietor of his or her own labour-capacity and so the free development of each is the condition of the free development of all.[58] Here self-ownership implies liberation from the coercive demands of the employer but also, and perhaps more importantly, freedom to think beyond work.

Either from the Right or the Left of the political spectrum, then, it is possible to see self-giving as the ultimate expression of freedom. What I have not got I cannot give away but what I have I can. So self-giving becomes a secular expression of the Christian paradox that he who loses his life shall save it[59]—the ultimate sign of control over one's destiny.

B. Legal Implications Of Self-Giving As Freedom

How can self-ownership be expressed within the domain of charity law? In what ways can the law uphold and encourage the value of self-giving, where the donor receives no financial reward? English and Scots charity law have been doing this for centuries, ever since the requirement that the control of charities should lie with independent non-salaried people who do not depend for their livelihood on the charity nor derive other tangible personal benefits from such involvement. This is in part a purely pragmatic rule to avoid conflicts of interest but it also has a deeper significance. "[T]he essence of charitable service in the capacity of trustee is to act without gratuity . . . this is the only branch of British law which has placed at its very heart a moral quality; that is, the duty and characteristic of altruism in the charity sector".[60]

The concept of the independent trustee is, of course, a cornerstone of trust law generally. In English law it stems from the equitable rules that a trustee must act gratuitously and must not profit from the trust. The ban on remuneration was first established in the case of *Robinson* v. *Pett* which states that "a trustee . . . shall have no allowance for his care and trouble: the reason which seems to be, for that on these pretenses, if allowed, the trust estate might be loaded, and rendered of little value".[61] In Scotland, the doctrine that a trustee must act gratuitously has also been strictly applied and *Robinson* v. *Pett* referred to approvingly (see, for instance, *Lord Gray and Others*[62]). "The rule depends on the fact that the right to payment would involve a possible conflict of duty and personal interest . . . if [a trustee] be allowed to perform the duties connected with the [trust] and to claim compensation for his services, his interest would then be

58 Cohen, above n 50.

59 Luke 17, 33.

60 Lord Phillips of Sudbury speaking in the debate on the Second Reading of the Trustee Bill 2000: *Hansard, HL Debs*, 5th series, vol 612, col 387, 14 April 2000.

61 (1734) 3 P Wms 249, 251.

62 (1856) 19 D 1, 5.

opposed to his duty, and, as a matter of prudence, the Court does not allow the . . . trustee to place himself in that position."[63]

This "voluntary principle" "has helped to shape the ethos of the charitable sector. . . . [it] ensures that those with the role of governing a charity carry it out free from any conflict with their personal interests; instead they can focus exclusively on the best interests of the charity".[64] The rule that a trustee cannot be *auctor in rem suam* is also of some antiquity and prohibits trustees from using the trust to advance their private interests.[65] In England any profits acquired by trustees or any financial benefit gained from their position as trustees is held in the form of a constructive trust for the charity.[66] These rules are narrowly construed so that even where a truster or settlor includes a charging clause in the trust deed the Court will give it the most restrictive interpretation possible.[67] There are some exceptions to this general rule. For example, small local charities which may have difficulties in obtaining goods and services otherwise may be permitted to appoint suppliers as trustees and pay them, provided certain safeguards are met.[68] In addition, where a solicitor-trustee is concerned with court proceedings on behalf of the trust he or she may claim for services provided.[69]

The Charity Commission was at one time very unwilling to register a body which had a charging clause in its founding document although recently the Commissioners have taken a more liberal approach.[70] Their current guidance offered to bodies which seek charitable status and also want to pay some or all of their trustees states that there remains a presumption against remuneration but that charities may be permitted to do so provided remuneration can be shown to be reasonable and necessary and in the best interests of the charity.[71] Where an existing charity without a charging clause wishes to pay trustees it may be allowed to do so if this is necessary "for the good administration of the charity". Factors to be taken into account by the Charity Commission include the size of the charity, the nature of its activities, the degree of involvement in the day to day running of the charity required of the trustees, the specialist nature of the skills required and the cost of obtaining those skills by employing others.[72] Safeguards will be built into such arrangements for charging, such as

[63] A Mackenzie Stuart, *The Law of Trusts* (Edinburgh, W Green, 1932), 168.

[64] Charity Commission, *Trustee Remuneration—Consultation Document* (London, Charity Commission, 1999), 3.

[65] For a historical overview in Scotland, see *Aberdeen Town Council* v. *Aberdeen University* (1876) 3 R 1087.

[66] *Keech* v. *Sandford* (1726) Sel Cas Ch 61.

[67] "Truster" is the Scottish equivalent of the English term "settlor", meaning the person who sets up a trust.

[68] See [1970] Ch Com Rep 33, paras 92 and 93.

[69] Known as the Rule in *Cradock* v. *Piper* (1850) 1 Mac & G 664.

[70] *Smallpiece* v. *A.G.* (unreported); see Charity Commission, above n 64, 17.

[71] (1994) 2 *Decisions of the Charity Commissioners* 14.

[72] See Charity Commission, *Remuneration of Charity Trustees*, leaflet CC 11 (London, Charity Commission, 1999); J Warburton and D Morris (eds), *Tudor on Charities* 8th edn (London, Butterworths, 1995), 255.

the exclusion of the trustee from relevant decision-making, and by ensuring that no more than one or two trustees are paid. Issues about accountability, supervision and evaluation are central to the satisfactory implementation of charging by trustees.

However, this strict approach to the issue of remuneration of trustees has been questioned. For instance, McCall considers that "there is in a proper case no objection to the charging of remuneration" and claims that trustees "face many . . . obligations and responsibilities, heavy enough to ensure that the trustee who treats his office as one of honour will fail to do the job properly".[73] Much of his justification for paying trustees, however, is based on the fact that they may incur personal liability for the debts of the charity, without any fraud or negligence on their part, as for example in relation to contractual obligations entered into by the charity. This legitimate concern could in part be met by making a charitable trust a company limited by guarantee. A more fundamental issue raised by McCall is the danger that charitable trustees are mainly "well-intentioned and comfortably placed amateurs . . . who may be no match for a misplaced professionalism elsewhere in the chain of command".[74] Although in theory charitable trustees are not permitted to delegate their responsibilities for managing the charity in practice this happens all too frequently. At best, they are likely to be directed by the charity's employees; at worst they may fail to uncover fraud and misconduct on the part of the executive arm. However, under existing law there is no reason why consultants should not be paid to assist trustees in a new or complex area of their work. In addition, the growth of employer-sponsored volunteering has led to a greater willingness to allow employees time to undertake voluntary activity, including the role of charitable trustee. Most fundamentally, McCall overlooks the significance of self-giving, both for the giver and in the view of the wider public. The Commission into the Future of the Voluntary Sector in England did not recommend paying trustees and did not conclude that non-remuneration was a negative factor in recruiting trustees.[75]

The principle of non-remuneration is also questioned in the Law Commission's Report on *Trustees' Powers and Duties*.[76] The Report recommends that a trustee acting in a professional capacity for a private trust should have a general statutory right to receive reasonable remuneration for any services provided to the trust, if each of the other trustees agrees to this in writing. The Law Commission asks whether a distinction should be made between private and public trusts in relation to remuneration of trustees. It notes that there is a need to encourage people with the best skills to act as charitable trustees and that where such people are professionals with financial expertise they cannot be

[73] C McCall, "Remuneration of Charity Trustees", (1992/3) 1(3) *Charity Law and Practice Review* 191, 196–7.

[74] *Ibid*, 198.

[75] Deakin, above n 6.

[76] Law Commission, *Trustees' Powers and Duties* (Law Com No 260, 1999).

expected to act on an unpaid basis. The assumption that most charities require some financial expertise is, of course, a sound one but it is a rather imaginative leap to presume that a) such services cannot be provided by paid staff, accountants or auditors who are not trustees and b) that financial advisers would not be willing to give their time unpaid. It also seems somewhat patronising to other skilled trustees to focus solely on financial skills. The other justification for remuneration, according to the Law Commission, is that it might be more expensive to employ an outside agent to provide the service than to permit a trustee to charge for his or her services. The Report does not refer to the difficulties which other trustees may experience in monitoring and controlling the performance of a fellow trustee, in contrast with an outside expert. However, the Law Commission also recognises that charities are in a different position from private trusts and that a universal power to pay professional trustees might dilute altruism and undermine public confidence in charities. The Report notes the reluctance of the courts and the Charity Commission to sanction charging clauses in charitable trust deeds.[77]

This trend in favour of payments for trustees is also seen among some experts on charity management, who point to the problems which currently beset voluntary charitable trustees and, indeed, question whether they can survive as "charity leaders", the role which the Charity Commission sees them fulfilling. Harrow and Palmer, for example,[78] consider that trustees are not willing to adopt the entrepreneurial role which is required of them but instead retreat into a "holding" position where they try and retain the traditional stewardship image of the charitable trustee. Harrow and Palmer see this as particularly dangerous in the face of increased external monitoring of charities, challenges from salaried managers as leaders, and public concern about trustees' responsibilities and accountability. However, they do not consider that paying trustees directly will of itself enable charities to find the right people and get rid of unsatisfactory trustees. Their main concern appears to be that we know little about the different management styles adopted by trustees, that further research and evaluation of this is required and that we should not adopt a homogenous view of the charitable trustee.

The role of the charitable trustee is clearly a key one in the pursuit of "charity". The principle of non-remuneration not only offers safeguards against fraud and misconduct but underlines the importance of voluntarism as a positive contribution to national life. Payment of trustees might well reduce the pool of eligible people and simply provide alternative careers for lawyers, accountants and management consultants. The development of two classes of trustees, one "professional and paid" the other "amateur and unpaid" could create major schisms within charitable trusts and might cause considerable resentment among those "amateurs" who have given and will continue to give their time

[77] These proposals are currently before Parliament in the form of the Trustee Bill 2000.

[78] J Harrow and P Palmer, "Reassessing Charity Trusteeship in Britain? Towards Conservatism, Not Change", (1998) 9(2) *Voluntas* 171.

and skills freely.[79] "Charity" requires distinctive features in order to justify itself, features which distinguish it from the public and the commercial sector. The non-remuneration of trustees offers one such clear and tangible distinction.

4. SELF-GIVING AS A MORAL OBLIGATION

A. Kant and Altruism

The idea of self-ownership offers one way of understanding and promoting voluntarism. However, the value of self-giving is also a central part of very different philosophical traditions which may in other respects be fundamentally at odds with Lockean ethics.

For instance, Kant would have found the notion of self-ownership abhorrent, suggesting as it appears to do that human beings can be owned, even by themselves. Such a commodification of the free individual runs counter, in a Kantian understanding of morality, to upholding respect for the dignity of individual human beings. Nevertheless, self-giving as moral obligation is a key aspect of Kant's philosophy, which can best be understood in today's vocabulary through the word altruism.

Some useful work has been done by moral philosophers on the idea of altruism. A thoughtful paper by Çlohesy, for instance, notes that "altruism is a suspect and controversial category in both the social sciences and philosophy".[80] He looks in particular at the work of Weisbrod and "public choice theory" which claims that the third sector is simply an economic alternative to both the private commercial sector (the market) and the public sector (the state).[81] Here, while altruism may exist in name, it is in fact just a way of expressing egoism or "increasing utility maximisation", in economic jargon. Clohesy, however, draws on the opposing view that altruism is "the definitional fulcrum of [third sector organisations'] normative ethics".[82] Simply translated, an organisation is defined as part of the third sector if it is has an altruistic purpose. Given the breadth and variety of such organisations altruism becomes crucial as the only element which is common to all.

Accepting this argument does not mean that we have to reject the possibility that self-interest may also be present; rather we reject the notion that unselfish

[79] Lord Phillips of Sudbury described this distinction as "invidious" and "wholly inappropriate with regard to charities" during the Second Reading of the Trustee Bill 2000: *Hansard, HL Debs*, 5th series vol 612, col 386, 14 April 2000.

[80] W W Clohesy, "Altruism and the Endurance of the Good", paper given at the Third Annual Conference of the International Society for Third Sector Research, Geneva, 8–11 July 1998, 1.

[81] B Weisbrod, "Towards a Theory of the Voluntary Non-Profit Sector in a Three Sector Economy", in D L Gies, J S Ott, and J M Shafritz (eds), *The Nonprofit Organisations: Essential Readings* (Belmont, Ca, Wadsworth Publishing, 1990).

[82] H Rubin, "Dimensions of Institutional Ethics : A Framework for Interpreting the Ethical Context of the Nonprofit Sector", in Gies et al, above n 81, 215.

acts are impossible. Clohesy explores this idea further with reference to Kantianism. He notes Kant's emphasis on respect for people as moral beings, that moral agents should strive to create a "realm of ends" and that actions should meet the test of universality. While Kantian philosophy is often portrayed as offering a rather cold-blooded, anti-emotional morality Kant did recognise the importance of feeling in encouraging people to behave morally. Feelings of sympathy and love spur us on to do moral acts; they "provide an important counterweight to the self-regarding inclinations that we tend to allow to tempt us to take moral holidays".[83] Self-giving assists us to develop an understanding for and an empathy with others which provides reinforcement for moral behaviour. In addition, the emphasis that the Categorical Imperative places on upholding respect for the dignity of persons ensures that we have a positive duty not only of benevolence but also beneficence, although the precise form this should take will depend on individual circumstances.[84]

Perhaps the most vital part of Clohesy's argument for the purposes of this paper is his rediscovery of "universal altruism", as defined by Philip Selznick, which ensures that we do not restrict our altruistic behaviour to an "in-group" of family or friends.[85] While Kant acknowledged that we might well find it easier to help those closest to us and that we are not bound literally to love strangers as much as we love ourselves, the "law of love" requires us to act beneficently towards strangers. This is not because we have a personal concern for their happiness but rather because such action upholds the dignity and respect which we should have for all people. Altruistic actions increase our understanding of the value of human beings and are the antithesis of the exploitation of others as means to our own self-serving ends which Kant condemned so strongly. Charity may begin at home but it cannot end there, if we are to define it in the sense of a moral obligation. It is this element which finds its fullest expression in the work of charities.

Clohesy also draws on Hannah Arendt's idea of public action[86] to locate the third sector as part of the "public good". This enables him to break the unilateral nature of the giving relationship which left such a bitter taste for recipients and helped to coin the phrase "cold as charity". Embedded in this concept are solidarity, equity and partnership because in providing services for someone the danger of creating a distance between donor and recipient must be faced and, it is hoped, overcome. In any case, Kantian ethics would bar the use of self-giving simply as a means to boost our self-esteem or value in the eyes of others, since

[83] H E Allison, *Kant's Theory of Freedom* (Cambridge, Cambridge University Press, 1990), 67.

[84] For further development of this argument, see R J Sullivan, *An Introduction to Kant's Ethics* (Cambridge, Cambridge University Press, 1994), 79 ff.

[85] P Selznick, "Personhood and Moral Obligation", in A Etzioni (ed), *New Communitarian Thinking: Persons, Virtues, Institutions, and Communities* (Charlottesville and London, University Press of Virginia, 1995).

[86] H Arendt, *Between Past and Future: Eight Exercises in Political Thought* (London, Penguin 1968). Arendt believes that it is only through exposure to the experience and attitudes of others that we can be liberated from our own private interests.

that would be to use the recipients as the means of achieving our end of self-aggrandisement. For Kant beneficence must be an end in itself.

B. Legal Implications Of Self-Giving As Moral Obligation

From a perspective which views self-giving as a moral obligation it is important that such beneficence should be managed in ways which demonstrate its moral character and encourage others to do the same. While mixed motivations on the part of those giving themselves are permissible, at the core must be a sense of altruism. In addition, transparency and accountability become particularly important as the proof of the fulfilment of this moral obligation. To assist in this, the practice of self-giving should be open to scrutiny and effective ways need to be found to monitor and evaluate voluntarism.

It is unlikely that legal intervention alone will be either the sufficient or the most desirable means to achieve such ends. However, the law can assist by opening the work of charities to public scrutiny. Indeed, the purpose of the earliest forms of regulation of charities was to ensure that the truster's or settlor's "charity" was applied appropriately and was not simply a ruse to circumvent restrictions on alienation of property. Today, the public has access to charities' accounts, their founding documents and other information.[87] While a balance must be struck, particularly in the case of smaller charities, between accountability and an unduly heavy administrative burden, it is essential that "charity" be open to such public inspection.

This is particularly important at a time when there appears to be concern among some members of the public about the *bona fides* of charities and the degree to which charitable income is spent on administration rather than directly on the objects of the charity.[88] In a national survey conducted by the Henley Centre in 1996 charities scored lower than schools, the National Health Service, the BBC, the Police, the Royal Mail and the Armed Forces in relation to the confidence which the public had in their efficiency and ability to deliver services.[89] A later survey carried out by the same researchers tapped the degree to which the public trusted charities, that is the degree to which the public thought charities were "honest and fair".[90] Here the results were more positive, with 56% saying they trusted charities. Nevertheless, other institutions fared a great deal better, including school teachers (74%), the police (67%) and the BBC (59%).

[87] Charities Act 1993, s 47(1) (annual report and other material held by the Charity Commission); s 47(2) (accounts). Law Reform (Miscellaneous Provisions) (Scotland) Act 1990, s 1(4) (explanatory document); s.5(7) (accounts).

[88] See, for instance, D Leat, "Funding Matters", in J Davis Smith, C Rochester and R Hedley (eds), *An Introduction to the Voluntary Sector* (London, Routledge, 1995).

[89] Henley Centre/Gallup Poll, *Planning for Social Change 1993/4 and 1995/6* (London, Henley Centre, 1997).

[90] *Ibid.*

A key issue in these surveys of public attitudes to charities appears to be the values which are seen to be embedded in the notion of "charity". The public expect charities to adopt an altruistic set of values and to emphasise commitment to a cause.[91] Accountability is seen as central in demonstrating the implementation of these values but accountability is also fraught with difficulties. First, charities have expanded both the range and spread of their work and are increasingly taking over functions which were once the prerogative of state services. It is therefore much more likely that a wider section of the public will come into contact with or have a direct interest in the work of charities. Second, there has been a decline in the trust which the public place in institutions generally, and this is bound to be reflected in their view of charities.[92] Third, the fundraising activities of charities have become much more commercialised and aggressive, and this has not always been welcomed by the public.[93] Fourth, charities have become much more streamlined and professional generally and this has had a significant impact on the way they are viewed by outsiders. Fifth, charities are now extremely diverse in terms of their objects, method and scale of operation, geographical location and the degree to which their work can be understood and evaluated by outsiders. They may be answerable to a variety of bodies, including the Charity Commission, Companies House, funding agencies, local and central government and umbrella organisations. There may be a great deal of information available in the public domain about certain charities, particularly where they are involved in fundraising on a large scale, and very little about others, for example grant-making trusts. Underlying these public concerns about accountability is a sense that charities may be losing the essential ingredient which makes them different from the state and the market, namely voluntarism, both in the form of financial giving and self-giving.

In addition, if we are to take seriously Kant's concern about using people as means to an end, we should take particular care to avoid such abuses in relation to volunteers. Employees now enjoy considerable protection from exploitative employers, which places restrictions on employers' freedom of action. Health and safety legislation from the mid-nineteenth century onwards, for instance, acknowledged the dangers which employees face and sought to curb the excesses of employers. These protections have been enhanced by European legislation, such as the Working Time Directive, maternity and paternity provisions, Equal Pay and Equal Treatment Directives. While some would say that we now have an over-regulated workforce, few would wish to return to the *laissez faire* days of unfettered power to the employers.

However, the situation is very different for volunteers. One charity law expert has noted: "because of the trust concept, the system [of charity law] con-

[91] See, for instance, K Gaskin and N Fenton, *Blurred Vision: Public Trust in Charities: Report submitted to the National Council for Voluntary Organisations* (London, NCVO, 1997).

[92] See F Fukuyama, *Trust: The Social Virtues and the Creation of Prosperity* (London, Penguin, 1995).

[93] See Leat, above n 88.

centrates far more on preserving money and property than on protecting people's time and effort".[94] Unlike employees, volunteers enjoy no particular status and are largely ignored in legal regulation. Indeed the very term volunteer is not one which is of much significance in law. Voluntary workers are specifically referred to in two legal contexts only: benefits legislation and the National Minimum Wage Act 1998. In both instances reference is made only to distinguish them from paid workers. The same is true of case law where voluntary workers are defined negatively, that is in contrast to paid workers. The result of this failure to acknowledge the particular position of volunteers is, I consider, disadvantageous for voluntary workers.

The possibility of exploitation and abuse of volunteers is not recognised, or where it is, remedies have to be sought through the general law of tort. The kinds of protection, from race, sex and disability discrimination, for instance, which paid workers enjoy are not available currently to volunteers. While it would be unsatisfactory simply to give voluntary workers the same status as paid workers—and most volunteers would not wish for this—there is a need for voluntary organisations, especially charities which benefit from their own special status, to be more transparent in their dealings with their volunteers. A clear understanding of rights and responsibilities on both sides is an essential pre-requisite for a relationship of dignity and respect between charity and volunteer. A failure to do so which is based on a fear of turning volunteers into paid workers is misplaced. It should be possible for charities to differentiate clearly between the two while alerting volunteers to their position and offering clear guidance on their rights and responsibilities.[95]

5. SELF-GIVING IN CIVIL SOCIETY

A. Ferguson and Civil Society

Both Locke's and Kant's philosophies are rooted in an understanding of moral responsibility which focuses on the individual human person rather than on collective human interaction. The notion of civil society, however, brings with it a social dimension which is lacking in the perspectives already considered. While it has experienced renewed vigour over the last ten years, which have seen its espousal by philosophers and politicians of very different persuasions,[96] its origins go back several centuries and can be traced to, amongst others, the Scottish philosopher, Adam Ferguson, one of the leading figures of the Scottish

[94] Quint, above n 8, 216.

[95] For further consideration, see D Morris, "Volunteering: a Nice Little Job for a Woman?", in A Morris and T O'Donnell (eds), *Feminist Perspectives on Employment Law* (London, Cavendish, 1999). See also S R Moody, "Policing the Voluntary Sector: Legal Issues and Volunteer Vetting", in A Dunn (ed), *The Voluntary Sector, the State and the Law* (Oxford, Hart Publishing, 2000).

[96] See, for example, W Hutton, *The State We're In* (London, Cape, 1995); and see too the discussion in Alison Dunn's chapter in this book at 61–2.

Enlightenment, whose writings did so much to develop the concept.[97] Ferguson combines an interest in human nature, clearly distinguishing it from the situation of other animals, with an acknowledgement that human beings have always lived socially: "we can learn nothing of his nature from the analogy of other animals. If we would know him, we must attend to himself, to the course of his life, and the tenor of his conduct. With him the society appears to be as old as the individual, and the use of the tongue as universal as that of the hand or the foot."[98] Unlike Kant and Locke, Ferguson takes great account of the non-rational in influencing human behaviour at individual and societal levels. He also celebrates the value of living in society as more than mere protection against enemy outsiders:[99]

> Mere acquaintance and habitude nourish affection, and the experience of society brings every passion of the human mind upon its side. Its triumphs and prosperities, its calamities and distresses, bring a variety and force of emotion, which can only have place in the company of our fellow-creatures. It is here that man is made to forget his weakness, his cares of safety, and his subsistence; and to act from those passions which make him discover his force. . . . That condition is surely favourable to the nature of any being . . . we have reason to consider his union with his species as the noblest part of his fortune.

The main purpose of civil society, a society within which strong links between free individuals are fostered, is not protection from without or control from within but the happiness of individuals. Happiness, however, cannot be achieved by individual pursuit of self-interest; rather self-giving is an essential component of it, "it should be the happiness of man, to make his social dispositions the ruling springs of his occupations . . . courage, and a heart devoted to the good of mankind, are the constituents of human felicity".[100] This sense of the social, which is realised through benevolent actions, is threatened when the conduct of nations makes the accumulation of national wealth rather than the inculcation of public spirit the overriding priority: "we would have nations, like a company of merchants, think of nothing but the increase of their stock; assemble to deliberate on profit and loss; and like them too, entrust their protection to a force which they do not possess in themselves".[101]

Today the idea of civil society has been resurrected and has achieved particular significance in a reworking of the democratic ideal.[102] Civil society is still understood in the sense that Ferguson and others gave it in the eighteenth cen-

[97] A Ferguson, *An Essay on the History of Civil Society* [1767] (New Brunswick, Transaction Publishers, 1991).

[98] *Ibid*, 6.

[99] *Ibid*, 18–19.

[100] *Ibid*, 54–5.

[101] *Ibid*, 145.

[102] See, for example, J Keane (ed), *Civil Society and the State: New European Perspectives* (London and New York, Verso, 1993). See too Mark Freedland's discussion in this book at 117–21, where he considers the dynamic of change in the modes in which the relations between the state and the voluntary sector are conducted in the United Kingdom.

tury but it also today has a more concrete meaning. It represents those institutions and agencies which belong neither to the fully public (the state) nor the entirely private (the market) sectors. This includes but is broader than the voluntary sector, encompassing also religious groups, extended family networks and other formal and informal social groupings. One writer has described it as "invisible networks of small groups submerged in everyday life".[103] The presence of a vibrant and diverse third force is regarded by many political analysts as essential to a balanced and harmonious society.[104] It also encompasses a moral dimension, within which a co-operative, inclusive and altruistic approach to others is fostered, and is "not simply a neutral area of exchange".[105] In the development of democratic institutions and ideologies in the countries of Eastern Europe post-communism special emphasis has been placed on strengthening civil society.[106] Resources have been channelled by, for instance, the British government through the Charities Aid Foundation and by the European Union into establishing third sector organisations in Eastern Europe.

According to Dekker and van den Broek "voluntary organisations and volunteering appear to be core elements of civil society everywhere . . . *voluntariness* [is] . . . the guiding principle of civil society and *associations* [are] . . . its dominant collective actors".[107] The third sector stands between states and markets, acting as both a buffer and a positive contributor in its own right.[108] It helps to increase social capital and extend the activities of citizens not just in the social but also in the political and even the economic spheres, as the work of Dekker and others demonstrates. In Britain charities form a key part of civil society and make a significant contribution to self-giving through volunteering. A key element in their intrinsic value is their location in the "third" sector, separate from the state and the market. It is not fanciful to suggest that the preservation of "charity's" independence both from the state and from the market is an essential prerequisite of a healthy democracy.

B. Legal Implications Of Self-Giving As The Hallmark Of Civil Society

The essence of civil society in practical terms lies in the independence of civil society institutions from manipulation by the market on the one hand and government interference on the other. This is also a key aspect of voluntarism,

[103] *Ibid.*, 12.

[104] See, for instance, A Seligman *The Idea of Civil Society* (New York, Free Press, 1992).

[105] *Ibid*, 31.

[106] See G Hegyesi, "The Revival of the Nonprofit Sector in Hungary", and A Kapiszewski, "The Independent Sector in Poland: Past and Present", both in K D McCarthy, V A Hodginson, R D Sumarivalla and Associates (eds), *The Nonprofit Sector in the Global Community: Voices from Many Nations* (San Francisco, Jossey Bass, 1992).

[107] Dekker and van den Broek, above n 21, 12–13 (emphasis added).

[108] R Wuthnow (ed), *Between States and Markets: The Voluntary Sector in Comparative Perspective* (Princeton, New Jersey, Princeton University Press, 1991).

ensuring that self-giving is conducted under conditions of optimum autonomy. However, the independence of the third sector generally, and of charities in particular, is under threat, both from commercial pressures and from state intervention.

Voluntary sector organisations are increasingly exposed to "commercial take-over" in a variety of ways. To achieve maximum efficiency and to be cost-effective they are encouraged to adopt a business orientation to their work. The advent of a "best value" culture has put pressure on service providing agencies to become mini-businesses. A reading of the mission statements and business plans of such organisations reveals a vocabulary of "customers' outputs", "targets", "performance indicators", and "value-for-money". Increasingly, the staff in charities are highly professionalised and apply current concepts and practices borrowed from business management.[109] This has undoubtedly been beneficial in terms of improvements in financial and administrative systems and a more streamlined approach to the work of charities. However, there is a danger that the altruistic ethos of the voluntary sector will be eroded and that organisations which adopt the management methods and language of business will become just that. In particular the valuable contribution made by volunteers may be ignored if it does not fit within the commercially-driven framework.

Research on the impact of contracting on the role, status and participation of volunteers suggests that increased reliance on service contracts as their main source of income (as opposed to grants) has led to significant changes within charities, both in the skills required of voluntary management and in the workload and responsibility falling on volunteer service providers.[110] An empirical analysis of the impact of contracts on volunteers concludes that the role of service volunteers has become increasingly formalised as a result of the development of contracts, their role has become more tightly specified and there is increased supervision and performance review.[111] Nevertheless the authors state that volunteers remain "(almost) invisible in contract specifications" and that many volunteers are unaware of the shift to contracts and have not been consulted. The study goes so far as to suggest that this may have been deliberate in some cases, so as to ensure that volunteers remain ignorant of the contractual obligations taken on by the charity for which they are working. While the authors note that some volunteers welcomed the increased formality which contracting brought—clear delineation of role, higher standards, improvement of the service—others felt de-motivated by the changes. A recent study of the impact of the "contract culture" on charities notes that few contracts made any reference to volunteers, despite the fact that many of the charities in the research

[109] For an analysis of parallel developments in the United States not-for-profit sector, see S R Smith and M Lipsky, *Nonprofits for Hire: The Welfare State in the Age of Contracting* (Cambridge, Mass, Harvard University Press, 1993).

[110] J Lewis, "Voluntary Organisations in 'New Partnership' with Local Authorities: The Anatomy of a Contract", (1994) 28 *Social Policy and Administration* 206.

[111] L Russell and D Scott, *Very Active Citizens?* (Manchester, University of Manchester, 1997), 42.

sample relied very heavily on voluntary work.[112] Occasionally volunteers were simply subsumed under the heading "staff", ignoring the key differences between paid workers and volunteers and neglecting the "specific responsibilities [which volunteers represent] for charities . . . to ensure that they are properly recruited, vetted, supervised, supported, trained, and most importantly, available".[113]

These difficulties are not unique to the United Kingdom. Experienced analysts of the third sector have noted the crisis faced by American nonprofit organisations as they try and "hold the center".[114] According to Lester Salamon, for example: "[T]he nonprofit sector is . . . being hoisted by its own mythology. Having failed to explain adequately to the American people what its role should be in a mature welfare state, the sector has been thrown back on the defensive by revelations that it is not operating in the way its own mythology would suggest."[115] Nevertheless, he sees the voluntary sector as *the* crucial component of civil society, and recommends a process of "renewal".[116] According to Salamon, nonprofit organisations should enter into partnerships with the state and with capital in a more robust fashion. However, as other writers have shown, the buzz word "partnership" all too frequently masks an unequal power relationship in which the state is the more powerful partner. In an interesting critique of Salamon's argument Jennifer Wolch points up the importance of citizen participation but also notes that an undifferentiated approach to citizen participation is no longer tenable, given the fragmented nature of the postmodern world.[117] Instead, she argues, citizenship becomes a social production, in flux and open to multiple influences. Such complexity requires volunteering to respond in an inclusive dynamic way to the needs and wishes of potential "active citizens" and to move away from Lady Bountiful to a vision which can encompass cultural diversity, devolved power and what Wolch calls "voices from the periphery".[118]

Co-optation by the state is the other potential threat to the independence of the voluntary sector. Yet at the same time the relationship between the two sectors must inevitably be a close one, given the important role now played by voluntary organisations in the provision of state funded services and the desire of the present government to encourage citizen participation in voluntary effort.[119]

112 D Morris, *Charities and the Contract Culture: Partners or Contractors?* (Liverpool, Charity Law Unit, Liverpool University, 1999).

113 *Ibid*, 24.

114 See, for instance, L M Salamon, "The Nonprofit Sector at a Crossroads: The Case of America", (1999) 10(1) *Voluntas* 5; L M Salamon, *Holding the Center: America's Nonprofit Sector at a Crossroads* (New York, Nathan Cummings Foundation, 1997).

115 Salamon (1999), above n 114, 15.

116 See J Gardner, *Self-Renewal: The Individual and the Innovative Society* (New York, Norton, 1981).

117 J Wolch, "Decentring America's Nonprofit Sector: Reflections on Salamon's Crises Analysis", (1999) 10(1) *Voluntas* 25.

118 *Ibid*, 30.

119 See, for instance, the focus on "active communities", as in *Active Communities: Supporting Active Communities in Scotland: A Draft Strategy for Volunteering and Community Action* (Edinburgh, Scottish Executive, 2000).

In the United Kingdom there is considerable interest on the part of academics, the voluntary sector and, more recently, the Charity Commission in the notion of "partnership" between the state and voluntary organisations and its practical implementation. Nicholas Deakin, in his key review of the voluntary sector, emphasised the importance of independence from the state, but also acknowledged the value of partnership.[120] The four Voluntary Sector Compacts which central government has agreed with voluntary and community organisations in England, Northern Ireland, Scotland and Wales respectively are intended to provide a framework for positive partnerships. The English Compact, for instance, contains undertakings both "to recognise and support the independence of the Sector . . . to determine and manage its own affairs" and "to work in partnership [with the voluntary and community sector] for the betterment of society".[121] Codes of Good Practice, including one on Partnership Working, are the next step in implementing the compacts.

However, research suggests that the state continues to be the dominant partner in partnerships with the third sector. Jane Lewis points out that "the notion of partnership between the sectors has been reworked time and again during the 20th century" and that the rhetoric of partnership does not necessarily produce genuine co-operation and a balance of power between the state and the voluntary sector.[122] In addition, partnerships may be exclusive, insular and unaccountable to any external body. There is the danger that they deal only with the major, established and "safe" players, excluding particularly the smaller, innovative projects working with marginalised groups, and may especally disadvantage black and ethnic minority communities.[123] Indeed, this cautious approach to partnership is echoed in the Scottish Good Practice Guide on Partnership Working, which notes that "there is a marked concern in the [voluntary] sector that independence of voluntary sector partners can be seriously compromised by partnership working and to allow them to withdraw if this is the case without losing face or compromising integrity".[124]

In a recent Discussion Document, *The Independence of Charities from the State*, the Charity Commission considers the legal position of English and Welsh charities in relation to their links with the British State. As the Registrar of Charities the Commission in this document is primarily concerned with the initial eligibility of an applicant for charitable status but some of the discussion in this document deals with the possibility of the loss of charitable status because

[120] Deakin, above n 6.

[121] *Compact: Getting it Right Together: Compact on Relations between Government and the Voluntary and Community Sector in England*, Cm 4100 (London, Home Office, 1998), para 4.

[122] J Lewis, "Reviewing the Relationship between the Voluntary Sector and the State in Britain in the 1990s", (1999) 10(3) *Voluntas* 255, 264.

[123] M Taylor, *The Best of Both Worlds: The Voluntary Sector and Local Government* (York, Joseph Rowntree Foundation, 1997).

[124] *The Scottish Compact: Good Practice Guides Consultation Document* (Edinburgh, Scottish Executive, 2000), para 4.2.

of an established charity's subsequent conduct.[125] The Commission asserts that "in order to be a charity, an organisation must be independent"[126] so that in terms of registration "a body created for the purpose of doing whatever was necessary to discharge [a] public authority's statutory responsibilities would not be a charity".[127] Nevertheless, the document notes that "a very considerable degree of involvement, amounting, indeed, to substantial control, on the part of the State is not seen as inconsistent, as the law stands, with an institution being a charity for the purposes of the Act [i.e. section 96(1) of the Charities Act 1993]".[128] Essentially, charitable status will only be lost where control by a public body (or by any outside body) is so extensive as to oust the jurisdiction of the High Court.[129] This very high threshold permits public bodies to exercise extensive control over charities and, while it is clearly a correct statement of the current legal position, can legitimately be questioned as providing inadequate protection against undue governmental interference in the affairs of charities.

The Discussion Document looks particularly at the role of public bodies in the governance of charities. According to its interpretation of legal and equitable principles the State must exercise its powers over the governance of charities "in a fiduciary way" so that decisions are always taken which are in the best interests of the charity.[130] The appointment of trustees is such a power, which falls to many local authorities and, occasionally, to other public bodies. It is a general rule that those with the power to appoint trustees should select the people best equipped to play that role and that conflicts of interest should be avoided.[131] Public bodies should not, therefore, appoint their own members or employees as trustees of charitable trusts which have a contractual relationship with the appointing body. As the Charity Commission points out, public bodies would not expect to make appointments to the boards of companies with which they contract and in this regard charities should be treated no differently from other contractors. (There is also the danger that public bodies which have the power to make appointments may thereby become shadow directors of charitable companies.) In addition, the Charity Commission advises that charitable trustees must retain their discretion to select the beneficiaries and determine the precise nature of the service to be provided to such beneficiaries. Finally, the Charity Commission's Guidelines stipulate that trustees must be free to make their own decisions on matters outside the funding arrangement.

[125] The document could be criticised, however, for failing to identify all the possible post-registration difficulties: see F Quint, "Local Authorities and Charities: II Appointments" (1991) 155 LGR 942 and J Garton, "Charities and the State" (2000) 14 TruLI 93.

[126] Charity Commission, *Review of the Register: The Independence of Charities from the State: Discussion Document* (London, Charity Commission, 1999), para 7.

[127] *Ibid*, para 18.

[128] *Ibid*, para 21.

[129] See *Construction Industry Training Board* v. *Attorney General* [1973] 1 Ch 173.

[130] Charity Commission, above n 126, para 23. The founding document of a charity may permit a departure from this general principle. However, if the purposes of the charity are compromised by such a departure the charity may endanger its charitable status.

[131] *Re Skeats' Settlement* (1889) 42 Ch D 522.

In spite of concern about preserving the independence of charities the Charity Commission does not consider that the establishment of a charity through the initiative of a public body represents a threat to the independence of the charitable sector, provided that the governance rules outlined above are met. This may be regarded as an acceptance of the *status quo* rather than a principled approach to the dangers posed by political interference. Nowhere in the Discussion Document, for instance, does the Commission distinguish between the state as an enduring part of the body politic and the "current administration", which will inevitably adopt a particular party political line. This is surely a crucial distinction. The priorities set by local authorities, for instance, will vary depending on their political complexion and may also shift with changes in the approach taken by central government. Timetabling of goal achievement may be geared towards the next election rather than more realistic time frames.

It may also be argued that the power of appointment, regardless of the degree of independence of the trustees so selected, gives public bodies an inappropriate and unnecessary degree of control over charities. While it is perfectly legitimate for charities to be accountable for the public money they receive, to be transparent in their operations and to apply high standards of efficiency and effectiveness in the provision of services this, it may be argued, can best be achieved without giving public bodies rights of appointment. On the one hand, carefully negotiated contractual arrangements can put in place service requirements; on the other, satisfactory internal governance can be established through the application of the Nolan principles. Much work has already been done in this area, for example in the joint Code of Practice agreed between the National Council for Voluntary Organisations and the Local Government Association.[132]

Charitable self-giving as an expression of civil society, then, offers a sphere of operation to the citizen which should be relatively autonomous from the demands of the state on the one hand and the market on the other. The law can assist by providing a fairer contractual framework in which service provision arrangements can be negotiated, and by clarifying the status and legal responsibilities owed to and from volunteers. In addition, the law should seek to help redress the power imbalances between public bodies and charities by encouraging and protecting independent governance.

6. SELF-GIVING AS MUTUAL EXCHANGE

A. The Communitarian Ideal

The difficulty with the philosophical approaches already outlined is that they "treat human society as a matter of fact".[133] They ignore the transformative,

[132] NCVO/LGA, *Are You Sitting Comfortably?* (London, LGA, 1998).
[133] J MacMurray, *Persons in Relation* (London, Faber and Faber, 1995 [1961]), 129.

mediating effects of human interaction and the fact that society is only realisable because individuals make it so. While they acknowledge the moral identity of the self they ignore the contingent nature of society which is itself "a moral entity [with] its basis . . . in the universal and necessary intention to maintain the personal relation which makes the human individual and his life a common life".[134] Such an intention can only be fulfilled through action which reflects "loyalty and keeping faith".[135] And for such a society to truly be a community it must not attract loyalty and fealty because of fear. Acting out of obligation, then, whether moral or legal, is hollow and does not produce the kind of society, "community", which most people wish for. Rather, the personal relations between people provide the cement which binds them together. The communitarian ideal "represents a gain in understanding over those ontologies/epistemologies which give priority to a disengaged subject, standing over against an external world".[136] In the absence of small-scale homogenous groups and extended families forms of personal interaction which are not based on financial imperatives offer a way of enhancing community. Some writers have claimed that heterogeneity encourages voluntary action so that a more diverse population and varied communities result in more voluntary association.[137] Whatever the truth of this assertion self-giving and voluntary association have a much deeper and more profound role to play in social interaction. According to Anne De La Patrie, for Westerners living in the modern world "'constitutive communities' answer the question 'who are you?' . . . provide a largely background way of meaningful thinking, acting and judging . . . [and prevent us from] being thrown in to a state of severe disorientation where one is unable to take a stand on many things of significance".[138]

Communitarianism lends itself to the notion of self-giving provided it is seen as reciprocal and a way of enhancing "social capital".[139] Thus the essentially product driven idea of exchange which reduces people to commodities must be replaced in "charity" with an idea of sharing at a deeper level. Henry Tam, for instance, speaks of the need to establish democratic mechanisms through co-operative enquiry and open participation.[140] He pinpoints particularly the third sector as a site for such developments, through community groups which acknowledge the importance of listening to different and sometime opposing viewpoints. He recommends the establishment of "community audit teams" to

[134] *Ibid*, 128.

[135] *Ibid*.

[136] D Bell, *Communitarianism and its Critics* (Oxford, Clarendon Press, 1993), 93.

[137] VA Hodgkinson and K D McCarthy, "The Voluntary Sector in International Perspective: An Overview", in V A Hodgkinson, K D McCarthy, R D Sumariwalla and Associates (eds), *The Nonprofit Sector in the Global Community: Voices from Many Nations* (San Francisco, California, Jossey-Bass, 1992).

[138] Bell, above n 136, 103.

[139] See A Etzioni (ed), *New Communitarian Thinking: Persons, Virtues, Institutions and Communities* (Charlottesville and London, University Press of Virginia, 1995).

[140] H Tam, *Communitarianism: a New Agenda for Politics and Citizenship* (London, Macmillan, 1998).

ensure democratic organisational development, effective communication and external partnerships. So charity in a communitarian context becomes a form of exchange, a mutual responsibility for the Other.[141]

It would be wrong to assume, however, that this is an entirely new way of interpreting voluntarism. Thus Carl Milofsky traces the development of voluntary associations, as seen by such diverse theorists as Marx, de Tocqueville, Durkheim, Toennies and Simmel, back to their community origins, and notes the importance historically of third sector ties with local communities.[142] William Beveridge, who made a key contribution to the development of charities in the post-War period through his report *Voluntary Action,* identified the two key impulses for voluntary action as philanthropy and mutual aid.[143] This "discourse on citizenship"[144] is also pointed up by the Deakin Report nearly fifty years later which urges government to acknowledge the distinctiveness of the voluntary sector and its contribution to community development.[145]

But the thrust of this argument is far more radical in its implications for charity. It offers a fundamental reordering of the usual uni-linear relationship which is traditionally seen as charitable giving, moving solely from the giver to the recipient. Instead it emphasises the reciprocal nature of charity, more akin to a circular than a linear relationship, through which each person can both give and receive, and where the straight lines and distinct roles become increasingly blurred.

B. The Legal Implications Of Self-Giving As Mutual Exchange

If self-giving is to be perceived as mutual exchange charities may need to rethink a wide range of issues concerning user involvement, inclusiveness and reciprocity. This in turn will have implications for the ways in which the law regulates voluntarism.

Self-help organisations have traditionally been excluded from charitable status because the courts have been unable to see benefit to the wider public in their operations. This produces some anomalous and, it is submitted, unjust results. A self-help group for sufferers from a particular disease is not entitled to charitable status whereas the provision of private health care or private education is included under the umbrella of "charity". A community newspaper which

141 For an interesting and varied critique of communitarianism and the third sector see A Wagner, R Bauer, J van Til and C Ranci, "Reviews of Etzioni (ed.), *New Communitarian Thinking*" (1997) 8(1) *Voluntas* 64. See too Rob Atkinson's comments in this book at 141–5.

142 C. Milofsky, "Neighbourhood-based Organisations : A Market Analogy", in W W Powell (ed), *The Nonprofit Sector: a Research Handbook* (New Haven, Connecticut, Yale University Press, 1987).

143 W Beveridge, *Voluntary Action: A Report on Methods of Social Advance* (London, HMSO, 1948).

144 See Lewis, above n 122.

145 Deakin, above n 6.

serves a housing estate will not be registered whereas a church newsletter is likely to be given charitable status. A very wide variety of organisations are thereby deprived of the valuable benefits of registration.

Clearly there are issues about conflicts of interest and organisations which are entirely self-serving. A charity which is run solely to benefit a very narrow and self-selected group of members may conceivably offer no "public benefit". Nevertheless, the provision of mutual aid in an open and transparent way which is inclusive must surely bring benefits to the wider community. If "charity" is to move on from a unilateral relationship between a clearly identified giver and a needy beneficiary to the process of mutual exchange and reciprocity envisaged by communitarianism the current definition of charitable purposes may need to be recast.

Even where charitable status has been obtained there may be difficulties about the involvement of users in the work of the charity. Many charities which provide services are wary of such involvement. Some fear user take-over, some feel that users will not have the skills required to assist in running the charity, and others are concerned about governance issues and the possibility of conflicts of interest arising. In a research study on user involvement Robson, Locke and Dawson suggest that a "confused picture" emerges.[146] Voluntary organisations generally fail to articulate a clear strategy and either introduce changes piecemeal or pay lip service to user involvement. In essence the study identifies two distinct but sometimes overlapping concerns, namely that services should be responsive to users' needs and that the organisation itself should include consumer representation. Issues about governance are important here, and the research illustrates the difficulties which arise from ambivalence, when voluntary organisations both want and mistrust user involvement in decision-making. In addition, uncertainties over user involvement seem to highlight a failure on the part of charities to "explore assumptions about voluntary organisations, their ownership and values".[147] A traditional approach to charity governance adopts a rational, neutral model, in which trustees are somewhat detached from the emotional heat generated by close involvement and where a balance of self-regulation (through adherence to constitutions and codes of practice) and external regulation (by the Charity Commission and other bodies) ensures appropriate accountability. User involvement may, Robson *et al* claim, precipitate charities into a more democratic arena where stakeholders quite unashamedly declare and fight for their sectional interests. They advocate that charities should consider very carefully the key issue of "ownership" of the organisation since this should help to clarify who should have control over activities and decision-making. Finally they question the "relevance of the

[146] P Robson, M Locke, J Dawson, *Consumerism or Democracy? User Involvement in the Control of Voluntary Organisations* (Bristol, Policy Press, 1997), 13.

[147] *Ibid*, 15.

trustee/beneficiary split in the charity model for organisations which are based on mutual help or empowerment".[148]

The degree to which users can be involved in the work of a charity without threatening its charitable status has come under the scrutiny of the Charity Commission.[149] While the Commission welcomes user involvement it considers that the appointment of users as trustees "needs to be introduced with care to avoid any problems with conflicts of interest".[150] The guidance acknowledges that users may bring particular strengths to the role of trustee, such as first-hand experience of the service and an understanding of the "user perspective". Users acting as trustees can combat the elitist, unrepresentative nature of some charitable boards, open charities up to local communities and possibly to new sources of funding and help to empower users generally. At the same time charities may need to change aspects of their arrangements (such as the time and place of meetings) to accommodate users and, as with all new trustees, will be required to explain the role of trustee and provide training. There is no such thing, according to this guidance, as "single interest" trustees, so that user trustees must not regard themselves as simply speaking on behalf of users. Clearly, the possibility of conflicts of interest, either direct or indirect, arising for user trustees must be anticipated, and acknowledged when they occur. Practical steps can be taken, such as asking all trustees to declare an interest (perhaps through a register of interests), requiring individual trustees to withdraw when decisions are being made which will directly benefit them or their relatives and disclosing material benefits in the charity's annual accounts. The founding document must also not bar such appointments and where user trustees are anticipated should build in safeguards to address conflict of interest situations.

The appointment of users as trustees should be encouraged as part of a more open, reciprocal approach to "charity". All too often, the decision-making bodies of service-providing and grant-making charities are constituted by the "Us" of middle-class, elderly, white, men with no direct experience of the "Them" who receive the service or financial assistance. It should be possible to allow for proper management of conflicts of interest, in the same way as the Nolan Principles have dealt with such matters in the public sphere. In addition, more imaginative ways should be sought of obtaining the involvement of service users and former users of the service in the management of charities. Some charities involved with service users who have learning disabilities, for instance, team them up with trustees so that they can work together on key issues. Where user groups are excluded from being trustees because of their age (that is, people under 18) advisory boards would enable such users to have a voice. In certain circumstances user involvement as trustees may be regarded as so vital to the

[148] *Ibid.*

[149] Charity Commission, *Users on Board—Beneficiaries Who Become Trustees*, leaflet CC 24 (London, Charity Commission, 2000).

[150] *Ibid*, para 8.

effective running of the charity that a waiver may be sought from the Charity Commission or the Lord Advocate to permit people who otherwise would be disqualified, for instance in a charity designed to assist those whose poverty stems from bankruptcy. If communitarian values are to inform the work of charities then reciprocity and mutual exchange must be fostered.

7. CONCLUSIONS

Self-giving is clearly central to a variety of philosophical interpretations of "charity", including libertarianism, Kantianism, ideas derived from the notion of civil society and communitarianism. While the law can only be an enabler of voluntarism (since any coercive approach would threaten the essence of self giving) it can uphold this essential element of charity in a variety of ways. The non-remuneration of charitable trustees, for instance, should continue to be protected by legal safeguards, in order to encourage altruism. Consideration should be given to the legal position of volunteers and how volunteering can be accorded appropriate status and protection from exploitation. The very real difficulties identified in research findings on the contract culture and its impact on volunteering and the voluntary ethos need to be addressed by the law. A reappraisal of the legal status of volunteers and the central role they play in many service contracts could make a significant contribution by introducing greater clarity and by acknowledging, in a concrete and practical way, the importance of volunteering in civil society. The importance of retaining the independence of charity from the state should be recognised through a strengthening of governance rules and practices. Finally, reciprocity and mutual exchange could be fostered through greater attention to user representation in charities in a variety of ways, including user trustees. All these steps would assist in placing self-giving at the core of "charity", where it should belong.

5

Charity Law and the Public/Private Distinction

MARK FREEDLAND[1]

1. INTRODUCTION

THE PURPOSE OF this chapter is to consider how the public/private distinction applies to charity, or, more precisely, to the law of charity. It will be argued that the public/private distinction is extremely difficult to apply to the law of charity, much more so than appears to be the case upon a superficial examination. In order to do this in a way which is satisfactory and coherent, we have to re-examine the public/private distinction itself. This turns out to mean that we should regard the distinction as multi-partite, and as multi-dimensional, although that is not the way the distinction has hitherto tended to be regarded. So the law of charity will be found to be a proving ground for an attempt to conceptualise the public/private distinction in a particular, perhaps novel, set of ways. This in turn will permit us to take an unusual perspective upon the notion of "public benefit" as an essential component of the English legal definition of "charity".

Before embarking upon that discussion, there is a major preliminary issue which we need to address, namely whether it is useful to be concerning ourselves with the public/private distinction in the first place. Why, in other words, should we regard the application of the public/private distinction to the law of charity as an interesting question, discussion of which might add to our understanding of the law of charity or the law in general? This might indeed be regarded as a positively perverse line of discussion to pursue, in the face of arguments to the effect that the public/private distinction is an unsatisfactory one, the role and impact of which we should be seeking to minimise in our thinking about our legal system. The latest in a distinguished line of such arguments[2] is that advanced by Dawn Oliver in her recently published treatise entitled *Common*

[1] In developing the theme of this chapter, I have benefited particularly from discussions with David Faulkner and Richard Fries, and more generally from the exchange of ideas between the participants in the St John's College Oxford Seminars on "Public Services—Developing Approaches to Governance and Professionalism", which took place from April to June 1999.

[2] Compare, for instance, C Harlow, "'Public' and 'Private' Law: Definition without Distinction", (1980) 43 *Modern Law Review* 241.

Values and the Public-Private Divide.[3] Is this the moment to be dwelling upon an increasingly questioned dichotomy?

I suggest that Dawn Oliver's arguments, properly understood, should not be seen as a deterrent from the discussion which will be undertaken in this chapter; indeed that in a certain sense they actually add point to that discussion. The main thrust of her argument is that the sort of control of abuse of power which is exerted through judicial review cannot satisfactorily be confined to a supposedly "public" sphere and excluded from a supposedly "private" sphere. She develops this theme mainly by showing that public law and private law are both actuated by an underlying set of common values. These are essentially democratic values, or values associated with citizenship, by reference to which both public power and private power should be controlled. She regards the procedural distinctions which are made between the public law process and the private law process as inimical to the implementation of those core values. She would like to see the procedural fence which has been erected by the jurisprudence of *O'Reilly* v. *Mackman*[4] largely or entirely demolished.

It seems to me to be consistent with an acceptance of most or all of her set of arguments to believe that the public/private distinction will retain its significance for some while to come, and that in the immediate and medium term future, judicial review would be apt to lose its vitality if the judges and their critics could not perceive it to be anchored in some notion, however inclusively defined or applied, of controlling the abuse of specifically *public* power. In that, perhaps interim, situation, it becomes especially important to have considered whether the control of the abuse of public power is being conducted on a sufficiently broad front; whether, in other words, the public sphere is being sufficiently generously interpreted.

In Dawn Oliver's set of arguments, this need is acknowledged, to the extent that she identifies a number of strands of democratic theory which interweave to create the texture of public law. They represent the formulation, in public law terms, of a set of values which, at a higher level of generality, become common with those of private law. But before that higher level of generality is reached, these formulations do have a specifically public character, and as such help to sketch out the special concerns of public law. Two such strands are those of "considerate altruism", and "participative communitarianism".[5] For Dawn Oliver, these are values which public law ought to and does pursue, and I think she would want to see public law boldly go wherever those values are at stake and in jeopardy to the abuse of power.

Now, to return to our primary subject-matter, it is quite striking to what an extent those values of "considerate altruism" and "participative communitarianism" pervade, and even in a certain sense define, the law of charity, mainly in

[3] London, Butterworths, 1999.

[4] [1983] AC 236.

[5] Above, n 3, at 2–9, esp 5–7. Cf Sue Moody's discussion in this book at 104–6.

the form of the idea of "public benefit". Yet this continuity between public law and the law of charity is not acknowledged in our exposition or understanding of either public law or charity law. I suggest that this makes it extremely important to consider how the public/private distinction applies and should apply to the law of charity; and I hope to have shown how that view actually derives support from, rather than encounters opposition from, Dawn Oliver's set of arguments about common values across the public/private divide.

When, thus encouraged, we begin to apply the public/private distinction to the law of charity, the position appears to be a straightforward one. In English law (to which all that is said in this chapter relates, unless otherwise stated[6]), the law of charity is seen as part of the law of trusts, and the law of trusts is seen as an aspect of the law of equity, and, as such, part of private law.[7] It is established that charitable trusts have to be "for the public benefit", but that is not seen as jeopardising their private law nature. The law of charitable trusts, in particular that relating to the powers and duties of trustees, is expounded, and taught in law schools, as a set of variations upon a theme of the general law of trusts.

However, the more one considers this question, the more doubts begin to accumulate about the allocation of the law of charity purely and simply to the private law category. Charitable trusts used to be primarily known as "public trusts", and contrasted as such with what we still call "private trusts". Quite a lot of the pre-history and early history of what we now regard as public law is to be found in cases concerned with the judicial control of the actions and decisions of trustees of charitable trusts, or of the corporators of charitable corporations—such as charity hospitals, or Oxford or Cambridge colleges.[8] This incidentally reminds us that the law of charity does not consist entirely in the regulation of charitable *trusts*, for it also consists in part in the regulation of charitable *corporations*. Those corporations do not necessarily hold their property and assets as trustees in the technical sense of that term, just as private corporations do not necessarily hold as trustees.

[6] It is particularly important to note that under the law of Scotland private bodies can be subject to judicial review proceedings more extensively than under the law of England, the public/private distinction being less clear-cut—and that several of the leading Scottish cases regarded as exemplifying this point concern charities—see The Hon Lord Clyde, "The Nature of the Supervisory Jurisdiction and the Public Private Distinction in Scots Administrative Law", in W Finnie, C Himsworth and N Walker (eds), *Edinburgh Essays in Public Law* (Edinburgh, Edinburgh University Press, 1991), 281–93.

[7] This seems to be the clear assumption of the leading treatises on the law of charity; cf H Picarda, *Law and Practice relating to Charities* (3rd edn, London, Sweet and Maxwell, 1999), chap 1; D G Cracknell et al, *Charities: The Law and Practice* (London, Longman Law, Tax and Finance, 1994), chap 1; J Warburton and D Morris (eds) *Tudor on Charities* (8th edn, London, Butterworths, 1995), esp chap 3.

[8] See especially the long line of cases on the jurisdiction of university and college Visitors, culminating in recent times in *R* v. *Lord President of the Privy Council ex parte Page* [1993] ICR 114, but going back to *Appleford's Case* (1672) 1 Mod Rep 82 and, the locus classicus, *Philips* v. *Bury* (1694) Holt KB 715. See P M Smith, "The Jurisdiction of the University Visitor: How Exclusive Is Exclusive?" (1993/4) 2(2) *Charity Law and Practice Review* 103.

Once it has been realised that the law of charity is not necessarily and totally bound up with the law of trusts, the assumption that it is simply a branch of private law starts to look questionable, at least at the margins. If a charity may be a corporation or legal body, why might not that be a *public* body, or at least a body wielding *public power*, so that it might be amenable to judicial review (and might now be a "public authority" within the meaning of that term as it is used in the Human Rights Act 1998[9])? In any event, is it not the case that, even within the law of trusts, the control of the ways in which charitable trustees use their powers and discretions displays more and more similarity with the techniques and reasoning of public law? Is it not the case also that the actions or decisions of some, at least, of the charitable corporations which exist have, to an extent, continued to be subject to judicial review in the modern era?

This brings us to a point where the ground which we had regarded as safe and stable really does start to move and crumble beneath our feet. For, if charities really are creatures of private law, though they are defined in terms of "public benefit", and are in certain situations regulated as, or in much the same way as, public bodies, then how robust and coherent is the public/private distinction which seems capable of giving rise to such dubious categorisations? In this essay, the suggestion will be advanced that the law of charity does in some ways cast doubt upon the public/private distinction in the form in which we are accustomed to draw it.

2. THE PUBLIC/PRIVATE DISTINCTION RE-EXAMINED

Although in this essay the law of charity is the lens through which the public/private distinction is scrutinised, we shall begin our argument by looking afresh at the public/private distinction in general, and shall only later revert to the specific context of charity law. However, to embark upon the endeavour of considering how the public/private distinction applies and should apply to charities, immediately reminds us of what is probably the central difficulty about that distinction. There are two principal methods of identifying the different spheres of application of public law and private law; one is according to the nature of the person or body whose activities are in question, and the other is according to the nature of the activities, or functions, themselves. Neither method is wholly satisfactory, as the case of charities and their activities will serve to illustrate.

Thus, if we consider first the method of distinguishing by reference to the nature of the person or body, we immediately realise that this cannot provide a complete method of classification, since we cannot satisfactorily assign human persons to the public category (though we can think of them as "private persons"). If we speak of the Home Secretary, or of a senior civil servant in the Home Department, as public persons, we really mean that they are persons

[9] Section 6(3)(b).

holding public offices or discharging public functions. Even if that kind of classifying can be regarded as meaningful, it would still be somewhat anomalous to describe the trustees of charitable trusts as public persons or the holders of public offices. Yet if we are obliged to regard them as private persons even when they are acting in the capacity of charitable trustees, we beg the very question we are trying to resolve, namely whether their function is as a public or a private person.

Moreover, even as between legal persons, that is to say bodies, companies or corporations, it is very difficult to enforce at the margins the distinction between those which are public and those which are private. We would accept that a city council is a public body, but that a limited company whose shares are traded on the Stock Exchange is (despite its description as a *public* limited company!) a private corporation. However, we might be hard put to it to specify the criterion for those classifications. Is it that of ownership (by the community at large, by individual persons), or that of the nature of their functions (administrative or entrepreneurial)? In the absence of consensus about those criteria, how should we classify a charitable corporation, for instance a university college or a research foundation? These are crucial and unavoidable questions for any legal system which maintains a distinction between its public law aspect and its private law aspect.

Where there exists a set of legal categories, but a deep lack of agreement about what constitutes a coherent set of criteria for applying it to factual situations, the indications are that the set of categories itself needs to be reconsidered. It is not proposed in this essay to take on the large and enticing question of whether it is satisfactory to think about legal systems or any particular legal system as having simply a public law aspect and private law aspect. Although I think the argument, which some people advance, in favour of distinguishing a third, intermediate, body of law of public services, is a serious one, I prefer for present purposes to concentrate upon the difficulty of identifying the public sphere and private sphere to which public law and private law respectively apply.

For I wish to argue that even if the dual category system of public law and private law can be regarded as coherent, we cannot satisfactorily use a simple pair of categories to establish their different spheres of application. By relying on a simple pair of categories for this purpose, we run the obvious risk that the classification process becomes a circular or self-referential one; public law applies in the public sphere, private law applies in the private sphere, and the law and the sphere define each other. We might hope to escape that from that kind of autopoiesis if, independently of the legal system, there existed in society a simple clear delineation between the public domain and the private domain; but there does not. Thus, there is no simple way to assign the activity which we describe as "charity" to the public or the private spheres of society.

My argument is that we should try to make the great escape from autopoiesis, in relation to the public/private distinction, by analysing the respective spheres of application in a more complex and discriminating way than we have generally tended to do. If the task is that of applying the public/private distinction to the range of political, inter-personal and economic activities and relations which make up society, that task has generally been performed by means of an analysis which treats those activities and relations in a way which is both *bi-polar* and *one-dimensional*. The activities and relationships in question are assumed to lie along a notional line which has the public at one end and the private at the other end, and it is assumed that we can, with sufficient care and ingenuity, find an appropriate point on that line at which to divide the two spheres.

We might do better to employ an analysis which is *multi-polar* and *multi-dimensional*. Such an analysis would be multi-polar in the sense that it would identify more than two types of activities or relations; in fact, I argue for a division into the four types of:

I. governmental (or regulatory),
II. communal (or social-service),
III. commercial (or entrepreneurial), or
IV. domestic (or personal).

It is not claimed that every possible kind of activity or relation can satisfactorily be grouped in this way, but simply that this is a good way of classifying those types of activities or relations which are normally in question when the public/private distinction is being drawn. The categories are reasonably self-explanatory, with the exception of II, which refers to activities or relations concerned with the provision of services viewed as a communal responsibility.

My suggested analysis would also be multi-dimensional, in the sense that it would distinguish not only between *types* of activities or relations but also between *modes of conducting* those activities or relations. Again I argue for a four-fold division into the modes of:

A. political (or representative),
B. official (or functionary),
C. contractual (or agreement-based), or
D. voluntary (or autonomous).

Again, this is by no means a complete taxonomy of all the modes of social or economic action, but simply a good way of refining the analysis of the sort of activities and relations which need to be subjected to the public/private distinction. These "modes" of action are differentiated according to the different kinds of obligation or legitimation which motivate the conduct of the activities or relations in question. Again, the categories should be fairly self-explanatory, with the exception of B, which refers to the mode of acting upon powers conferred, and duties imposed, by an *institutional framework*.

It might be thought that this scheme is no more than a straightforward elaboration of the public/private distinction, indeed even that it is a gratuitous over-elaboration of that distinction. It will be argued, to the contrary, that the elaboration brings its own added value to the analysis. On the face of it, the scheme of analysis, proposed above, appears to be a simple and direct expansion of the public/private distinction. It looks as if heads I to IV correspond respectively to heads A to D, and as if the resulting combinations IA and IIB between them constitute the "public" category, while IIIC and IVD between them constitute the "private" category. The scheme seems to represent a symmetrical unpacking of the original, dual, and linear, classification system.

If this were the end of the matter, the scheme of analysis presented above would not make any significant contribution to our understanding of how to apply the public/private distinction. What may give it some extra analytical force is the fact that heads I to IV actually have a very complex relationship with heads A to D. The different kinds of action or relation combine in many different ways with the different modes of action. Most of the sixteen theoretically possible combinations occur in reality. Their incidence varies according to the different ways in which societies organise themselves in different places and at different historical times.

It will quickly be perceived, not only that "asymmetrical" combinations between types and modes are possible, but also that it is those "asymmetrical" combinations which are likely to present the interesting complications in, and possible refinements of, the simple public/private classification system. It is not proposed to argue out all the combinations in the present essay. It is readily admitted that the whole scheme must be regarded as a tentative or speculative one in the absence of that comprehensive argumentation. In the present context, the aim is to do no more than apply the scheme to the development of the social practice, and the law, of charity. However, even by doing no more than that, we may hope to show why the area of "charity" represents such an illustratively difficult testing ground for the public/private distinction as a whole.

3. THE DISTINCTION APPLIED TO CHARITY

To apply the public/private distinction, and the scheme for understanding it which was presented above, to the law and practice of charity is to realise how essentially dynamic or protean that distinction is. At least three kinds of change may operate to re-balance the way that the public/private distinction is drawn; these kinds of change vary in the extent to which they are obvious or manifest. We shall attempt to describe them in, as it were, descending order of obviousness, generally taking charity as our illustrative case.

The first, and most obvious, kind of change is that whereby the legal categories of public law and private law are themselves modified or re-drawn vis-à-vis each other. In this regard, it is important to bear it in mind that the very separation of public law from private law as a distinct category is a relatively recent development in English law, and is in itself an enormous re-drawing of legal conceptual boundaries. It is interesting to note how, as this evolution occurs, the law of charity is placed increasingly firmly in the private law sector, despite the historical designation of charitable trusts as public trusts, to which we referred earlier.

The second kind of change in the way that the public/private distinction operates is perhaps less visible from the perspective of legal doctrine than is a reworking of the legal categories, but is nevertheless at least as important in its effects. This type of change consists of a re-assignment of activities or relations between the four different types which we have identified—not as a matter of legal categorisation, but as a matter of social, political or economic development, which as such may well affect the legal analysis, but does so indirectly, rather than directly as the previous kind of change did.

The dynamics of this kind of change are extremely interesting, and relevant to the way that charity law has developed in relation to the public/private distinction. For a long historical period, the tendency was for the first two categories (I and II) to expand at the expense of the second two categories (III and IV), which implied a degree of transfer of activities and relations from the private sphere to the public sphere. In the United Kingdom this dynamic was an accelerating one for much of the twentieth century, which intensified during the "welfare state" period of 1945 to 1980. Indeed, the very notion of the "welfare state" signifies an enlargement of the activities which are regarded as the direct responsibilities of the political state, and so undertaken as communal or even as governmental ones.

In many of the fields in which charities operate, that set of developments created a deep ambiguity as to when and how far the activities or relations in question were to be regarded as public ones or private ones. We could say that this created at some points a kind of antithesis between the welfare state and the world of "charity", which added to the sense that "charity" was the essentially *private* counterpart to welfare provision by *public* authorities. In fact, in some ways this made "charity" seem a rather suspect way of meeting responsibilities now interpreted as essentially public ones, either because private bountifulness appeared, in this context, as unduly patronising, or because it seemed a relatively arbitrary and sectional way of distributing social goods increasingly viewed as, in their nature, public goods.

This dynamic was effectively halted, we may even say partially reversed, by the policies and measures of British governments from 1979 onwards.[10] There has been a "privatisation" of many activities and relations in a broad sense as well as in a narrowly technical sense. At the time of writing, the predictions or hopes of those who saw that reversal as a transient phenomenon, itself likely to be reversed when Conservative governments were succeeded by a Labour government, seem to many people to be in the course of being falsified or disappointed. This may, for reasons which will appear shortly, somewhat understate

[10] See J Lewis, "Reviewing the Relationship between the Voluntary Sector and the State in Britain in the 1990s", (1999) 10(3) *Voluntas* 255; also, Michael Chesterman's discussion in this book at 251–2.

the differences between the politics of the 1980s and those of the 1990s, but it certainly marks out a broad contrast between both those decades and the ones that had preceded them.

We might expect that this would bring about a corresponding change in the antithesis between "charity" and the public state, in the form of a revived sense of private charity as an essential *complement* to the public state rather than as a less satisfactory way of doing the work of the public state. There is indeed to some degree an effect of that kind. Society probably, and governments certainly, seem readier to regard the relief of visible destitution, homelessness, and personal suffering, as more properly the role of private charity than of the public state, as compared with the collective mentality of a quarter of a century before. Moreover, in a rather complex way, the National Lottery has operated to re-privatise benevolence and the public support of "good causes", both at a national level and at more localised levels.

However, such an analysis, if treated as a complete one, would, in the terms we used earlier, be rather one-dimensional, and would fail to capture the full inwardness of the dynamics affecting the public/private distinction, both generally and as far as charity is concerned. In order to make the analysis a fully-rounded one, we need to take account of what is probably the least obvious but most significant set of category shifts affecting the public/private distinction, namely a dynamic of change in the *modes* by which activities or relations are conducted.

That is to say, an even stronger contrast between the mentality of the welfare state and that of the neo-liberal post-welfare state is to be found in their respective approaches to the *modes* of conduct of social and economic relations than in their ways of classifying the *types* of those relations. For if there has been, since around 1980, a slightly wavering tendency to shift those relations from the "public" types I and II to the "private" types III and IV, there has been a consistent and perhaps even strengthening tendency to shift the modes of conducting those relations towards the *contractual* mode C. Thus far, a New Labour government seems perhaps slightly less bent, than its Conservative predecessors, upon privatising the types of social and economic activity earlier recognised as public ones especially during the welfare state era, but seems to be at least equally intent upon contractualising the mode of conduct of those activities.

This trend could be illustrated by referring, for instance, to the way in which the Private Finance Initiative, originated under a Conservative government, has been enthusiastically built upon by the succeeding New Labour government after 1997. However, our present concern is with the manifestations of this trend in relation to the law and practice of charity. In that context, contractualisation presents itself in a variety of ways. Firstly, there has long been the possibility, now somewhat more actualised than it previously was, that the fiscal advantages accorded to charities would place them in a kind of contractual relationship with government, whereby they could be required to work for, or to "earn", those fiscal benefits. Secondly, at the level of political discourse, that relationship has been in a loose sense contractualised in the form of the Compact on Relations between Government and the Voluntary and Community Sector in England made in 1998, which, although it disclaims the status of a legally binding document, is expressed to "set out the key principles and undertakings which should underpin the relationship between Government and the voluntary and community sector".[11]

But it is probably the third sense of contractualisation which is the most significant one. In the very extensive programme and practice of contracting out a wide range of social and communal services, central government chooses, and local authorities are expected, to regard charities and other voluntary sector institutions as appropriate contracting parties, or "partners" as the current rhetoric would have it. These various forms of transformation of the mode of conduct of communal activities by charities have had a very significant bearing upon the way that the public/private distinction applies to the law and practice of charity, as I will seek to explain and explore in the remainder of this section of this essay and in the next section.[12]

The most obvious or immediate effect of the contractualisation of a significant proportion of "charitable" activity is to render that activity intractably equivocal in terms of the public/private distinction. That comes about in the following way. For much of their history, charities seemed to belong more to the private domain than to the public one because of the way in which people regarded or classified both the type of activity in which they engaged, and the mode in which they conducted that activity. That is to say, the activities or relations were regarded to a significant extent as private ones, as being an extension of the domestic type—education, religion, and the relief of poverty all have that aspect to them in the sense that they can be regarded as primarily a matter of *family* responsibility. The mode of conduct of those activities was also seen as private in nature, as being voluntary in character, and thus expressing the freedom of choice or autonomy of citizens as private individuals. Respecting the wishes of the founder of a charity, or of the donor to a charity, represents a profound deference to the private will.

The more recent configuration, which contractualisation embodies, is very different in character, and much harder to relate to the public/private distinction. On the one hand, much of the activity of charities is identified as being communal in the sense that it is a matter of public responsibility. This is confirmed by the contractual framework; public authorities appear as parties to contracts with charities, whether in the broader or in the technical sense, because they are responsible for providing, ensuring, or supervising the activity in question. On the other hand, the contractual mode is one of the defining modes of the private sphere, namely that of competitive, primarily financial,

[11] *Compact: Getting it Right Together: Compact on Relations between Government and the Voluntary and Community Sector in England*, Cm 1400 (London, Home Office, 1998).

[12] See, for instance, D Morris, *Charities and the Contract Culture : Partners or Contractors?* (Liverpool, Charity Law Unit, Liverpool University, 1999).

efficiency. The rhetoric is that of "value for money", in its own way at least as "private" a notion as that of the individual will, especially as the model for it, in current discourse, is overwhelmingly that of the successful business enterprise. The charity thus becomes the private (in the sense of quasi-commercial) agent for the carrying out of a public purpose. This defies the application of the public/private distinction. Some of these difficulties can be better understood by considering how the "public benefit" test of charitable status has been affected by contractualisation, to which question we now turn our attention.

4. THE DISTINCTION AS APPLIED THROUGH THE "PUBLIC BENEFIT" REQUIREMENT FOR CHARITABLE STATUS

We could say that charity law has sought to reflect the equivocality of charity, in terms of the public/private distinction, by generally subjecting it to a private law regime but by imposing the requirement of "public benefit" as a condition of access to the special effects and advantages of charitable status. In this part of this essay, it is argued that contractualisation certainly affects, and probably disturbs, the delicate balance which is sought to be maintained by means of the "public benefit" test.

The formulation of the public benefit test is complex, multi-faceted, and few would regard it as wholly coherent or satisfactory. The requirement of public benefit amounts to a loose, and at times rather indirect, insistence upon the qualities of non-sectionality, altruism, and non-politicality in the way that the objects of a charity are formulated and, to a lesser extent, pursued in practice. There are great problems about whether that set of commitments is discharged by a body of doctrine which is much criticised in many ways, for example for the way in which it allows a rather token notion of "relief of poverty" to substitute for, or even be deemed to fulfil, the public benefit requirement.

Those problems need not, however, occupy our main attention, because our present concern is with the ways in which the analysis of non-sectionality, altruism, and non-politicality is altered or distorted by the shift from a voluntary mode to a contractual mode of conducting or regarding "charitable" activity. These alterations or distortions can be perhaps be understood as the replacement of a notably pluralistic approach to the idea of "public benefit" by an approach which is at once more statist and more commercial in character.

Let us firstly look at the development of the idea of non-politicality. This requirement has generally been regarded as one which was necessary in order to legitimate the privileges or advantages of charitable status, but which should be lightly applied in order to respect the voluntarist character of charitable activity. In a contractualist framework, the public state is likely to lay claim to the right to make a more exacting selection of its contractual partners. Indeed, the government of the day may demand that the contractual partners subscribe closely to its own precepts and policies for the conduct of the activity in question. In the early 1990s, the suggestion emerged that charities could be divided into, on the one hand, contractors with public authorities for the provision of communal services, who would continue to enjoy the benefits of charitable status, and, on the other hand, campaigning charities who would, as such, lose those benefits.[13] Although no less a person than the Prime Minister of the day disclaimed the suggestion that this idea represented government policy, one cannot avoid the sense that this notion still manifests itself as an inherent consequence of the contractualist approach.

If the contractualist framework tends to edge charity into a more de-politicised corner (in the sense that it tends to reduce its political independence), it also in some ways weakens the requirements of non-sectionality and altruism which the notion of "public benefit" demands (admittedly in a rather pragmatical and unsystematic way). The pursuit of competitive or business-like efficiency, which typically attends the contractual mode of performance of communal services, is often seen to sustain an allocation of social goods according to the means and expectations, rather than the absolute needs, of the recipients. Those administering the public state may devoutly wish to contract for the provision of uniformly excellent social and communal services to all its citizens, but may find that the business-like mentality in which that contractual process is conducted produces its own particular kind of obliviousness to various kinds of social and economic exclusiveness or even exclusion.

However, none of this critique of the effects of contractualism should be allowed to obscure the problems of arriving at a coherent notion of "public benefit" in the context of a more straightforwardly voluntarist mode of conducting charitable activity. Nor does this critique suggest its own solutions to the problems, which it identifies and highlights, about the application of the public/private distinction in the charitable sphere and more generally. In a brief conclusion to this essay, an agenda for further discussion of those outstanding issues will be tentatively suggested.

8. CONCLUSION: CIVIL SOCIETY AND THE PUBLIC/PRIVATE DISTINCTION

In the foregoing sections, arguments have been advanced which indicate that it is difficult, to the point of outright impossibility, to apply a mutually exclusive classification, as between the public and the private spheres, to various areas of social, political and economic activity of which the area of "charity" provides a good example. Hence it is equally difficult, by means of such a process of classification, to arrive at a clear specification of exclusive spheres of application for public law and private law.

It should not, however, be concluded, or even argued, from this that the very distinctions between the public and the private domains, and correspondingly

[13] B Knight, *Voluntary Action* (London, Centris, 1993).

between public and private law, are false ones. The point is rather that public law and private law provide us with two distinct types of legal regulation, or two distinct sets of starting points for thinking about what it means to put in place and to maintain the Rule of Law. There are some areas of social and economic life where both perspectives are applicable, and where it may be appropriate to draw upon both sets of inspiration in order to arrive at the best overall system of legal regulation.

It has, in effect, been argued in this essay that charity is such an area. I have attempted to show how the variety of ways of understanding what types of activity or relations are comprehended within the notion of charity, coupled with the variety of modes by which such activity or relations may be conducted, identify this as a realm which is contested not merely as between the public and the private spheres, but also as between different modes in which its activity or relations may be conducted.

Analyses of the law of charity frequently produce, with varying degrees of vehemence, the conclusion that it is a body of law which is not intellectually or practically coherent, and that it could not be made so within its existing terms of reference. It might be thought that the present argument seeks to reinforce that view by means of a critique based upon the public/private distinction and the difficulty of applying it to the law of charity.

However, I do not in fact advance so negative a view. Somewhat to the contrary, I am inclined to argue that the law of charity provides a not wholly unsatisfactory attempt to find some firm ground between the exclusively public and the exclusively private domains of law and of social and economic activity. This is an inherently difficult thing to do; it is part of a larger problem of establishing a coherent basis for the law of civil society in general.

The solution or set of solutions to that larger problem would have to consist of arriving at an understanding of how public law and private law might severally and jointly contribute to the regulation of the interplay between many kinds of values and expectations. The law of charity has to do that, essentially, in relation to what are, today, regarded as mainly communal activities or relations to be conducted either in voluntary or in contractual mode. The law of civil society has to comprehend a number of other combinations of types of activity with modes of conducting them. The law of charity is a good place to start to think about that set of problems, though it certainly could not represent the endpoint of such thinking if a useful set of results is to be reached.

6

Problems with Presbyterians: Prolegomena to a Theory of Voluntary Associations and the Liberal State

ROB ATKINSON[1]

AN ANTHOLOGY OF ANTIQUE EPIGRAPHS, COMPRISING A BRIEF BUT COMPREHENSIVE HISTORY OF THE PROBLEM WITH PRESBYTERIANS (AND ITS SOLUTION)

Render therefore unto Caesar the things which are Caesar's, and unto God the things which are God's.

Joshua ben Joseph, also known as Jesus of Nazareth[2]

If it were a matter of wrongdoing or vicious crime, I should have reason to bear with you, O Jews; but since it is a matter of questions about words and names and your own law, see to it yourselves; I refuse to be a judge of these things.

Gallio, Roman Imperial Proconsul of Achaia.[3]

I am standing before Caesar's tribunal, where I ought to be tried; to the Jews I have done no wrong. . . . [I]f there is nothing in their charges against me, no one can give me up to them. I appeal to Caesar.

Saul of Tarsus, also known as the Apostle Paul[4]

I am speaking all the while of private individuals. For if there are now any magistrates of the people, appointed to restrain the wilfulness of kings (as in the ancient times the ephors were set against the Spartan kings, or the tribunes of the people against the Roman consuls, or the demarchs against the senate of the Athenians; and perhaps, as things now are, such power as the three estates exercise in every realm when they hold their chief assemblies), I am so far from forbidding them to withstand, in accordance

[1] Participants at that Foundations of Charity colloquium, particularly its organizers, John Gardner and Margaret Bolton, offered many helpful comments on the paper from which this chapter is derived, as did members of the New York Nonprofit forum. Kristen Decker, Wesley Haber, Kristie Hatcher-Bolin, and Philip Fowler provided invaluable research assistance. A grant from the Florida State University College of Law supported my research.

[2] Matthew 22:21.

[3] Acts 18:14–15.

[4] Acts 25:10–12.

with their duty, the fierce licentiousness of kings, that, if they wink at kings who violently fall upon and assault the common lowly folk, I declare that their dissimulation involves nefarious perfidy, because they dishonestly betray the freedom of the people, of which they know that they have been appointed protectors by God's ordinance.

John Calvin[5]

We Noblemen, Barons, Knights, Gentlemen, Citizens, Burgesses, Ministers of the Gospel, and Commons of all sorts in the kingdoms of Scotland, England, and Ireland, by the providence of GOD, living under one King, and being of one reformed Religion, Having before our eyes the glory of GOD, and the advancement of the Kingdom of our Lord and Saviour Jesus Christ, the Honour and Happinesse of the Kings Majesty and his Posterity, and the true publick Liberty, Safety, and Peace of the Kingdoms, wherein every ones private condition is included. . . . after mature deliberation, resolved and determined to enter into a mutuall and solemn League and Covenant: wherein we all subscribe, and each one of us for himself . . . do Swear.

Preamble, the Solemn League and Covenant[6]

The Solemn League and Covenant
Now brings a smile, now brings a tear.
But sacred Freedom, too, was theirs:
If thou'rt a slave, indulge thy sneer.

Robert Burns[7]

New presbyter is but *old priest* writ large.

John Milton[8]

The light which we have gained was given us, not to be ever staring on, but by it to discover onward things more remote from our knowledge. It is not the unfrocking of a priest, the unmitering of a bishop, and the removing him off the Presbyterian shoulders, that will make us a happy nation. No, if other things as great in the church, and in the rule of life both economical and political, be not looked into and reformed, we have looked so long upon the blaze that Zwinglius and Calvin hath beaconed up to us, that we are stark blind.

John Milton[9]

Is it therefore infallibly agreeable to the Word of God, all that *you* say? I beseech you, in the bowels of Christ, think it possible you may be mistaken.

Oliver Cromwell[10]

[5] John Calvin, *Institutes of the Christian Religion*, book 4, chap 20, para 31 (ed J T McNeill and trans F L Battles) in *The Library of Christian Classics* vol 21 (Philadelphia, The Westminster Press, 1960), 1519.

[6] In J K Hewison, *The Covenanters: A History of the Church in Scotland from the Reformation to the Revolution* (Glasgow, John Smith, 1908), vol 1, appendix 2, 479.

[7] Robert Burns, "The Solemn League and Covenant", in *Poems and Songs of Robert Burns* (James Barke ed, London, Collins, 1955) 361.

[8] John Milton, "On the New Forcers of Conscience in Parliament", in *The Complete Poetical Works of John Milton* (Douglas Bush ed, Boston, Houghton Mifflin, 1965) 176.

[9] John Milton, "*Areopagitica*: A Speech for the Liberty of Unlicensed Printing to the Parliament of England", in *The Five-Foot Shelf of Books: The Harvard Classics*, vol 3 (New York, Collier, 1909), 221.

[10] Letter to the General Assembly of the Kirk of Scotland, 3 August 1650: *Oliver Cromwell's Letters and Speeches*, Part V, (Thomas Carlyle ed, London, Ward Lock & Co, 1888), 168–69 (original emphasis).

I was a good Christian; born and bred in the bosom of the infallible Presbyterian church. How then could I unite with this wild idolator in worshipping his piece of wood? But what is worship? thought I. Do you suppose, now, that the magnanimous God of heaven and earth—pagans and all included—can possibly be jealous of an insignificant bit of blackened wood? Impossible! But what is worship?—to do the will of God—*that* is worship. And what is the will of God?—to do to my fellow man what I would have my fellow man do to me—*that* is the will of God. Now, Queequeg is my fellow man. And what do I wish that this Queequeg would do to me? Why, unite with me in my particular Presbyterian form of worship. Consequently, I must unite with him in his; ergo, I must turn idolator. So I kindled the shavings; helped prop up his innocent little idol; offered him burnt biscuit with Queequeg; salaamed before him twice or thrice; kissed his nose; and that done, we undressed and went to bed, at peace with our own consciences and all the world. But we did not go to sleep without some little chat.

Hermann Melville[11]

Many more words I had with him; but people coming in, I drew a little back. As I was turning, he caught me by the hand, and with tears in his eyes said, "Come again to my house; for if thou and I were but an hour of a day together, we should be nearer one to the other"; adding that he wished me no more ill than he did to his own soul.

George Fox[12]

1. INTRODUCTION

THE PRINCIPAL THEME of my chapter is state intervention in the internal affairs of voluntary associations to resolve disputes among their members. I share the widely held belief that such interventions pose a serious threat not only to the very existence of voluntary associations, but also to the legitimacy of the liberal state itself. On the other hand, I believe that such interventions can be structured and restricted in ways that are both appropriate for the liberal state and consistent with the desirable degree of autonomy of voluntary associations. State intervention into disputes within such associations is fraught with risks on both sides, but those dangers can be contained and even turned to mutual advantage.

This thesis is subject to two important qualifications: first, not all voluntary associations warrant the same degree of autonomy in resolving their internal disputes, and, second, not all visions of the liberal state accord the same voluntary associations the same degree of autonomy. With respect to the first qualification, part 2 first distinguishes voluntary associations from the governmental sector on the one hand and the for-profit sector on the other, then classifies voluntary associations according to their relative difference from the other two sectors. The voluntary associations that are most distinctive, in terms of their

[11] Hermann Melville, *Moby-Dick* (New York, Alfred A Knopf, Everyman's Library, 1988), 73.

[12] George Fox, *An Autobiography* (R M Jones ed, London, Headley Bros, 1912), 214–15 (speaking of a visit to the Lord Protector Oliver Cromwell at Hampton Court).

purpose and their members' interactions, pose the most problems for the liberal state.

To clarify the second qualification, part 3 distinguishes among three different visions of the liberal state in its relations with voluntary associations. These are libertarian liberalism on the right, with its minimalist state; communitarian liberalism on the left, with its maximalist state; and sectarian liberalism, more or less in the middle. This last, I shall argue, avoids serious deficiencies of the other two and offers the greatest promise of giving voluntary organizations their due measure of autonomy. This is principally because sectarian liberalism alone adequately acknowledges that voluntary organizations provide two critical elements of human flourishing that the liberal state cannot provide: intimate friendship and fundamental beliefs about human excellence.

Part 4 applies the sectarian version of liberalism to what part 2 identifies as the most difficult problem voluntary associations pose for the liberal state. These are doctrinal disputes within what I will call sects, associations of intimately related members devoted to a fundamental system of normative belief or, in a word, a faith. Taking as examples famous Presbyterian schisms in the United Kingdom and the United States, I argue that both the United Kingdom's traditional implied trust doctrine and the United States' alternative implied consent doctrine are deeply flawed. In their place, I recommend a principled version of the British Parliament's very practical solution in the Free Church of Scotland appeal: split the baby, over each faction's loud objections that its body is one, indivisible—and theirs alone.

Against the background of these rather unseemly squabbles, part 5 looks for a sect to complement the sectarian state. This will be a sect that is tolerant toward outsiders, loving in the relations among its members, and clear on how the state is to handle appeals from its internal decisions without having to delve into matters of esoteric doctrine. That ideal complement is best described as a Religious Society of Friends of Truth. As we shall see in detail a bit later, each element of this name is important. But you may already have recognized that this is the formal name of those whom outsiders more frequently call the Quakers. I should, accordingly, hasten to point out that I am not now, nor have I ever been, a member of that Society. Rather, to quote Melville's Ishmael, "I was . . . born and bred in the bosom of the infallible Presbyterian church."[13]

That familiarity aside, there are several reasons why the history of Presbyterianism offers useful insights into the relations between voluntary organizations and the state. As we have already seen, schisms within Presbyterian churches allow us to compare the approaches of the highest courts in the United Kingdom and the United States. These prominent Presbyterian cases in our respective countries provide a vehicle not only to raise fundamental problems about the relationship between voluntary associations and the liberal state, but also to examine different resolutions in what we all tend to think of as essentially similar liberal polities.

[13] Above, n 11.

More fundamentally, the history of Presbyterianism reminds us of the scope of the trilateral relations between voluntary associations, the liberal state, and the market economy. In both time and space, Presbyterianism extends beyond the liberal state. We are accustomed, especially in a geographically large nation like the United States, to think of voluntary associations within the bounds of the state, though occasionally operating elsewhere, in the way of overseas relief organizations like CARE and Oxfam. The history of Presbyterianism reminds us that voluntary associations don't just operate overseas; some are truly international.

In historical terms, too, Presbyterianism transcends the liberal state. In essentially its present form, Presbyterianism flourished when the seeds of liberal political institutions in the English-speaking world, for all its precocious parliamentarianism, were barely recognizable. Indeed, in important respects, the liberal state is a response to the problems of religious strife that the Reformation unleashed on European civilization in the sixteenth and seventeenth centuries,[14] strife that has continued unabated until little better than yesterday in Ulster. Early in its history, in Presbyterianism's first generation, the international Calvinist movement was the original exporter of revolution, the prototypes of modern radical political parties. What Bolshevik Moscow was early in the twentieth century and Jacobin Paris was in the late eighteenth, so Calvinist Geneva was in the mid sixteenth. And the origin of Presbyterianism in the theology of John Calvin stands near the beginning of the modern market economy as well. Calvinism was arguably the first ideology sympathetic with capitalism, not just grudgingly tolerant of it.

In the course of its long history, Presbyterianism has held radically different views on the relation of the church and the state. The Scottish Covenants called, perhaps too insistently, for reform of state as well as church. The call came before the foundation of the liberal state, in terms and tones hardly compatible with such a state. Burns may have been right that, "sacred Freedom, too, was theirs,"[15] but they were none too eager to extent its benefits to others. Yet Presbyterianism in America, and to a very large extent in Britain as well, has abandoned its former insistence on religious establishment and state-enforced orthodoxy.

This evolution, furthermore, is but one instance of a fundamental tension within Presbyterianism, a tension found, though often to a much lesser extent, in other sects as well. This is the tension between the sect's dynamic and static tendencies, its internal conflict between fidelity to its past and the need to accommodate itself to the future. As we shall see in part 4, this is a tension that ultimately must be worked out within the organization itself, though the state may well ensure that it is worked out through the structures and procedures agreed to by the disputing factions.

[14] See J Rawls, *Political Liberalism* (New York, Columbia University Press, 1993), xxiv.
[15] Above, n 7.

2. SECTORAL GEOGRAPHY

To appreciate the role of the liberal state in regulating the internal affairs of voluntary associations, we must first sketch the place of both in the modern three sector economy. This includes, in addition to the public and nonprofit sectors, the for-profit, commercial sector.[16] In this section we will examine each of these three sectors in terms of two critical factors, mode of inclusion and fundamental purpose.

This examination will reveal, at a high but nevertheless useful level of generality, that the nonprofit sector resembles each of the other sectors with respect to one of these factors and differs with respect to the other factor. Voluntary associations, like the public sector, are nonprofit, but, unlike the public sector, inclusion in them is voluntary. With respect to the commercial sector, the reverse is true. The mode of inclusion in voluntary associations, as in organizations in the commercial sector, is voluntary, but voluntary associations, unlike commercial organizations, are not for profit.

A. The Governmental Sector

1. *Distinguishing Factors*

a) Mode of Inclusion

The governmental sector consists of the modern territorial state and its various political subdivisions and subordinate institutions. The mode of inclusion in the state is essentially involuntary. Citizenship, the general term for membership in the modern state, liberal or otherwise, is a matter of birth (either inside the country or to parents who are themselves its citizens) not choice. Whatever the merits of social compact theory as an account of the origins or legitimacy of the state, the fact remains that, as a practical matter, we as individuals do not make our states, or even merely find them: we find ourselves being made in them. As the laws of Athens long ago told Socrates, a state that is minimally liberal lets us leave it if we can find another state to take us in.[17] But in modern times this is a very costly alternative and, even if citizens can ultimately opt out, the fact remains that they do not initially opt in. We are born in, and getting out is not easy.

b) Fundamental Purpose

The purpose of the state, of course, has been much debated, at least since Plato's *Republic* and Aristotle's *Politics*. We have already narrowed the scope of that discussion for our purposes to the liberal state, but even here there is notoriously

[16] See J van Til, *Mapping the Third Sector: Voluntarism in a Changing Social Economy* (New York, Foundation Center, 1988), 71.

[17] Plato, *Crito* (F J Church trans, 1956), 61–2.

great diversity of opinion. I want to focus first on areas of agreement, reserving for later divergences within the liberal school.

For the tightest and yet I think most telling summary of the general liberal position, I will borrow, if you will forgive me, from Thomas Jefferson's Declaration of Independence: the role of the state is to preserve and promote the fundamental human rights of life, liberty, and the pursuit of happiness.[18] The first right, life, implies a minimal requirement of all governments, ensuring the kind of public order that is prerequisite to preserving the basis of any human end, human existence itself. The latter two rights, liberty and the pursuit of happiness, are more complex, more peculiar to liberalism, and more problematic.

In the liberal vision, liberty is generally thought of as essentially individual, and essentially negative: liberal liberty is an endowment of each human being, and that liberty is primarily the absence of interference.[19] Except as necessary to preserve the life and liberty of others, each citizen should be allowed the maximum latitude to pursue his or her own vision of happiness. Thus in classical liberalism the second basic right, liberty, is intimately linked with the third, the pursuit of happiness.

Taken together, they imply that the liberal state's role in promoting welfare is not to provide a collective vision of human flourishing, but to allow each citizen to pursue his or her own private vision, alone or with others of like mind. Any more positive statement of the liberal vision of human flourishing must be strictly formal and content-free: the human happiness the liberal state is to promote is the freedom of each citizen to pursue his or her own vision.

2. IMPLICATIONS FOR INTERNAL OPERATION

The governmental sector's essentially involuntary mode of inclusion and liberalism's commitment to fostering pursuit of individual life-plans significantly influence its mode of internal organization. Since inclusion is automatic and emigration difficult, allowing members to participate in governance, particularly the choice of substantive policy, becomes imperative. In the now-classic expression of Hirschman, meaningful "voice" is the answer to the absence of easy "exit."[20] That participation should be not only meaningful, but on an equal

[18] By taking these principles as shared by all liberals, and by limiting my discussion to an intramural liberal one, I avoid the need to examine the basis for these principles. My own view, elaborated elsewhere, is that the ultimate basis of such principles can be nothing more than the shared commitments of those who espouse them, and need not be more. See R Atkinson, "Beyond the New Role Morality for Lawyers", (1992) 51 *Maryland LR* 853 (suggesting a fideist ethic founded on metaethical skepticism).

[19] J Rawls, *A Theory of Justice* (Cambridge, Mass, Harvard University Press, 1971), 202: "A general description of liberty, then, has the following form: this or that person (or persons) is free (or not free) from this or that constraint (or set of constraints) to do (or not to do) so and so." See also I Berlin, *Two Concepts of Liberty* (Oxford, Clarendon Press, 1958) (distinguishing negative liberty of the liberal tradition from positive liberty).

[20] A O Hirschman, *Exit, Voice, and Loyalty: Responses to Decline in Firms, Organizations, and States* (Cambridge, Mass, Harvard UP, 1970), 96–8.

footing, follows both from the liberal state's neutrality toward ultimate ends and from its individualistic attitude toward liberty.

This egalitarian individualism implies not only an equal right to participate in the making of law, but also equal treatment under the laws once made. Finally, respect for the autonomy of individuals requires that the obligations and prohibitions of law be stated in clear, objective terms and applied in consistent, regular procedures by unbiased tribunals. Without these basic "rule of law" principles, individuals cannot know the legal limits of their liberty and thus cannot effectively exercise their basic rights of self determination.[21]

B. The For-Profit Sector

1. *Distinguishing Factors*

In contrast to the governmental sector, the commercial or for-profit sector is, for all its internal complexity, marvelously simple with respect to the two factors we are considering here, mode of inclusion and fundamental purpose. Commercial organizations are voluntarily formed for the purpose of making money; they produce and distribute goods and services for profit. Their essential constituents are voluntary investors, joined together in a common for-profit enterprise.

2. *Implications for State Intergention*

From these central features—voluntary participation and profit motivation—logically flows virtually everything about for-profits' internal ogranization and the state's role in their internal affairs. Since commercial associations are voluntary, the liberal state can allow wide variety in the terms and conditions of participation in them. Thus we have not only joint ventures, partnerships, and corporations, but also a myriad of subspecies and hybrids, and an almost infinite range of possible allocations of decision-making authority, operational control, profits, and risks. Indeed, to lower the cost of forming such associations, and thus to make them more profitable to their participants, the liberal state can and does provide statutory "form contracts" with boiler-plate provisions already in place.

The principal role of government, in dealing with internal disputes in such associations, is to make sure that the parties get what they bargained for, to enforce the contractual or quasi-contractual arrangements they made among themselves. There are, of course, problems with even that agreement-enforcing role: sometimes the participants will not have anticipated a particular problem; sometimes their intentions on a particular point will be unclear. In all such

[21] See Rawls, above n 19, section 38, "The Rule of Law" (relationship between liberalism and the rule of law); L Fuller, *The Morality of Law* rev'd edn (New Haven, Yale UP, 1969), 33–94 (normative prerequisites of the rule of law)..

instances, however, the organization's essential profit-making function, and the participants' presumptive profit-making motivation, will provide a powerful interpretive touchstone.

At the most basic level, the very language in which these arrangements are written will be the lingua franca of the market-place. Beyond that, any ambiguities in particular arrangements among constituents, or between constituents and the organization, can be tested against the basic criterion of profit. Any position of the association that cannot be defended in terms of maximum stake-holder profit, long term or short, is deeply dubious; any interpretation of the terms of a particular stake-holder's participation inconsistent with that stake-holder's seeking maximum personal gain is highly unlikely. These canons of interpretation will not always give a single certain answer, since there are presumably many plausible ways to design, produce, and distribute a better mouse-trap. But these canons certainly narrow the scope of acceptable answers, for in the commercial sector "better" will always mean more profitable, and each participant in a commercial association will presumably want more of that profit for him or herself.

C. The Non-Profit Sector

1. Distinguishing Factors

The mode of inclusion in nonprofit organizations is essentially voluntary; indeed, what economists and tax theorists call nonprofit organizations are what I, following political theorists, have been calling voluntary associations.[22] Economists, contrasting this third sector principally with the commercial sector, distinguish nonprofits from their for-profit counterparts; political theorists, thinking principally in terms of the state, focus on the voluntary mode of inclusion in third-sector organizations. But there the simplicity ends: "voluntary" in this context needs important qualification, and nonprofit purposes are almost infinitely plural.

a) Mode of Inclusion

The voluntariness of voluntary organizations is not so absolute as it might at first appear. Entry is not always as consciously willing, nor exit as easy, as the blanket term "voluntary" implies. As a matter of law if not of definition, voluntary associations cannot compel anyone to become or remain a member. In that respect, they are distinct from nation-states. And yet, as the example of Presbyterianism in Scotland should remind us, there is an interesting intermediate

[22] *Nomos* (i.e. Yearbook of the American Society for Political and Legal Philosophy) vol II (J R Pennock and J W Chapman eds, New York, Atherton Press, 1969): *Voluntary Associations*, ix: "Political philosophers are inclined to use 'voluntary association' to cover all those private activities that enter into the composition and operation of a plural society."

case: the national or established church. Of course today, in the United Kingdom as in other liberal states, essentially full citizenship is possible without being a member of any church, established or otherwise. But virtually the opposite was almost universally true in the two centuries after the Reformation. Indeed, with respect to non-Christians, full citizenship required membership in the established church in Western Europe from the time of the Emperor Constantine's adoption of Christianity as the religion of the Empire.

Partly as a result of this history, partly as a result of their present practice, even many non-established churches committed to the disestablishment of all churches retain vestiges of involuntary inclusion. Take, again, the example of Presbyterianism. In the ancient rite of infant baptism, adult members of the church place their infant children into a kind of provisional church membership, to be consummated as full membership when they become old enough to decide such matters for themselves.[23] It hardly need be said that infant baptism is not a uniquely Presbyterian rite. Indeed, in the Lutheran, Anglican, and Roman Catholic communions, the connection between infant baptism and adult membership is even clearer. The consummation of the former in the latter is formally known as confirmation, reflecting the belief that it is not a mere joining afresh, but the mature affirmation of a relationship that began in infancy.

The provisional church membership of infants is obviously not voluntarily assumed on their part. Yet, for our purposes, it is important to note that the later, adult induction is not entirely unconditioned, even if it is legally unconstrained. For one thing, confirmees are traditionally very young; the tender years that may have amounted to full adulthood in medieval Europe would hardly support a binding commercial contract, much less the right to cast a ballot, anywhere in the western world today.

And, of course, between baptism and confirmation, much may be committed to Providence, but little is left to chance. In the traditional Presbyterian baptism, both the child's parents and the parents' local congregation solemnly pledge to "raise up the child in the way which is right, that when it is old, it will not depart from it." Thus, when a child of practicing Presbyterian parents assumes full membership, he or she is the product of thoroughly Presbyterian catechizing. The lad or lass's will may be unconstrained, but it will not be unshaped, and the shaping may well last a lifetime. That, of course, is the purpose, though the effects can sometimes be peculiar. Thus, as C S Lewis wrote of his Oxford mentor, "An Ulster Scot may come to disbelieve in God, but not to wear his weekday clothes on the Sabbath."[24] In a way that liberal political theory sometimes fails fully to appreciate, voluntary organizations are thus our creators as well as our creatures; it is not always easy to tell which is the chicken and which the egg.

[23] See Westminster Confession of Faith, chap 28, "Of Baptism," esp para IV: "Not only those that do actually profess faith in and obedience unto Christ, but also the infants of one, or both, believing parents, are to be baptized"; see also John Calvin, *Institutes of the Christian Religion* (above, n 5), book 4, chap 16, "Infant Baptism Best Accords with Christ's Institution and the Nature of the Sign."

[24] C S Lewis, *Surprised by Joy: The Shape of My Early Life* (London, Geoffrey Books, 1955), 133.

b) Fundamental Purpose

If the mode of inclusion in third sector organizations is thus less simple than the term "voluntary association" implies, the identification of purpose in the term "nonprofit organization" is, if anything, even less helpful. Though the latter term may serve nicely to establish a border with the for-profit sector, it raises without answering a critical question within the third sector itself: "If not for profit, for what?"

The law, traditionally, has given not one answer, but two, thus dividing the nonprofit world into two hemispheres. Some nonprofits are said to exist principally for the benefit of their members; others, for the benefit of the public. In American tax law parlance, the former are "mutual benefit organizations"; the latter "public service organizations," or charities.[25] For tax purposes, these two distinctions may well suffice. But, alas, we shall have to draw further distinctions within the nonprofit sector to determine the appropriate degree of governmental intrusion and, conversely, organizational autonomy as to internal disputes.

2. *Implications for State Intervention*

To further distinguish among voluntary associations, we must again consider modes of inclusion and fundamental purposes. Here, however, we must refine these factors to admit gradations: previously, they told us simply that voluntary associations in general differ from organizations in the other sectors; now we need to know how and to what extent particular kinds of voluntary associations differ from the other two sectors.

a) Distinctiveness of Purpose

With respect to the organization's fundamental purposes, we can distinguish three tiers of nonprofit distinctiveness, three levels of remove from the purposes of governmental and for-profit organizations. The first, least distinctive level is in the goods and services the organizations provide. The traditional theory of charity has long sought to find the essence of charity in either "especially good" goods charities provide, or in "especially deserving" people to whom they provide them. On this view, charities either provide "especially good" goods, even if only to ordinary people, or they assist especially deserving people, even if only by supplying mundane goods.

But traditional theory never got very clear on what the criteria of goodness and deservedness were,[26] and modern economic theory, with its agnosticism on both points, has largely by-passed the quest. The most we can say with respect to most so-called charitable goods and services is that charities may provide them in a way that is somehow different from both for-profit firms and the state,

[25] Boris Bittker and George Rahdert, "The Exemption of Nonprofit Organizations from Federal Income Taxation", (1976) 85 *Yale LJ* 299, 302.

[26] However, cf David Stevens' discussion in this book at 33–42.

more efficiently or more altruistically, for example. Thus the first level of distinctiveness is not what voluntary organizations provide, but how.

There are, however, two desirable[27] things that neither government nor for-profit firms can provide at all well, owing to features of the products on the one hand and the providers on the other. The provision of these two things marks our second and third levels of distinctiveness. The first of these is fellowship, being together with other people in a mutually meaningful way. Though fellowship is obviously deeply desired by most human beings, the very oddness of thinking of it as a "thing" produced or consumed points to the difficulty of acquiring it in the market. Friends are notoriously not for sale; indeed, the more intimate the relationship, the more dubiously we regard its for-profit provision. Our deep desire for fellowship combines with these profound reservations about its commercialization to make prostitution the oldest, but also the least honored, profession.

And if fellowship by its nature is not readily bought and sold, neither is it easily requisitioned. The welfare state may care for your physical needs from cradle to grave, but it will never be your friend in anything but a loosely metaphorical way. The state itself is simply not a human person. And, given its obligation to act legally and democratically, by both objective and egalitarian criteria, the state will have a hard time providing fellowship chosen in the idiosyncratic, ad hoc way we all go about meeting our mates, whether they be spouses or drinking companions. The municipal government may well provide your neighborhood with a soccer field, but you'll want to choose your own goalie, not to mention manager, by processes that are probably distinctly lacking in bureaucratic nicety.

Beyond fellowship, there is a third thing that both the liberal state and for-profit firms are even less capable of providing, again, on account of both its nature and theirs; this, accordingly, gives us our third, most distinctive tier of nonprofit organizations. This quintessentially nonprofit product is "ideology" or "faith," a system of ultimate value and moral meaning.

For-profit firms cannot provide such systems of belief well because they have many features of a classic public good.[28] In particular, those who produce them

[27] "Desirable" is an admittedly slippery modifier, merging as it does the descriptive, "what is desired," and the prescriptive, "what should be desired." See, e.g., John Stuart Mill, *Utilitarianism* (1861, Oscar Priest ed, 1957), 44–5 (equating the normatively desirable with the descriptively desired). For my purposes, the descriptive meaning will suffice; as a matter of fact, most people, most of the time, really do desire the two desiderata I identify. But I think the prescriptive meaning, at least in a weak sense, is also relevant; people who are committed to classically liberal values will find themselves necessarily committed to these two values. I call this a weak prescriptive sense because, of course, one need not be committed to liberalism at all. Thus the obligation to desire these two values liberalism entails is hypothetical, not categorical; even if, as I believe, they are necessary means to liberal ends, they are not necessarily good in themselves. See Immanuel Kant, *Foundations of the Metaphysics of Morals* (1785, Lewis White Beck trans. 1959), 31–34 (distinguishing hypothetical from categorical imperatives).

[28] See M Seidenfeld, *Microeconomic Predicates to Law and Economics* (Cincinnati, Anderson Publishing, 1996), 66 (defining public goods); H Hansmann, "The Role of Nonprofit Enterprise" (1980) 89 *Yale LJ* 835, 848–51 (identifying the advantages of nonprofit organizations in the provision of public goods).

have difficulty excluding from their enjoyment those who do not pay for them. For the liberal state, the problem is even more serious. The liberal state is fundamentally committed to neutrality on precisely this point; its essential function, protecting (and perhaps enhancing) individuals' liberty to pursue their own ultimate ends, is at best in extreme tension with proffering ultimate ends of its own. This is near the core of the disestablishment clause of the American constitution. Religion is the traditional source of ultimate moral meaning, and the American federal government was forbidden at its inception from favoring one religion over others. Religious organizations, by contrast, are historically at the center of the nonprofit sector. As the case of Calvinism indicates, they provide distinctive world views with a zeal that sometimes becomes a literal vengeance.

b) Degree of Intimacy of Inclusion

In initially distinguishing between voluntary associations and governmental and for-profit organizations, we focused on mode of inclusion as an external matter, how one becomes a member of the organization. Here we need to focus on mode of inclusion as an internal matter, how members of the organization interact once inside, among themselves.[29] The critical factor is the members' degree of "intimacy" or "fellowship" or "mutuality" or "associativeness." As with voluntary associations' purposes in the last subsection, I want to identify three tiers or levels. This closely parallel Aristotle's analysis of *philia*, which is usually, if somewhat imperfectly, translated as "friendship."[30]

The first, and lowest, level of associativeness is purely functional, what is needed to get the organization's job done. At this level, the organization exists only to do a job better than its constituents can do on their own. As Aristotle puts it, "If they are friends for utility's sake, each likes the other not for what he is but only for some benefit he can supply."[31] These benefits are the advantages of firms and vertical integration generally. This is the level of associativeness captured in common wisdom like "two heads are better than one" and "many hands make light work."

Associativeness reaches its second level when it becomes not so much a means to an end, a better way to get a common job done, as an end in itself. Here the

[29] See G Alexander, "Dilemmas of Group Autonomy: Residential Associations and Community", (1989) 75 *Cornell LJ* 1, 26 (noting that communitarians, in contrast to libertarians, "focus not only on the basis of membership, but also on the character and quality of relationships among members of groups").

[30] Aristotle, *Nichomachean Ethics* (Wheelwright trans, Cambridge, Cambridge University Press, 1909), book 8, "Friendship". Cf P Wheelwright, *Aristotle* (New York, Odyssey Press, 1981), 236, n 1 ("*Philia* (connected with the verb *philein*, to love) is a stronger word, connoting a greater degree of emotional content, than the word friendship, which however is its closest approximation in English") with Aristotle, *Nichomachean Ethics* (Martin Oswald trans, New York, Macmillan Publishing Co, 1962), 214, n 1 (the connotations of *philia* are considerably wider than those of "friendship"). Alexander, above n 29, 26, describes a spectrum of intra-group intimacy that runs from "mere aggregations of self-seeking individuals" to "communities . . . drawn together by shared visions that constitute for each [member] their personal identity".

[31] *Nicomachean Ethics*, above n 30, book 8, section3; see also Alexander, above n 29, 26 (describing minimally integrated groups the members of which come together "exclusively through contract" and solely "for instrumental purposes").

"going," not the "getting there," becomes paramount. This is the level of associativeness characteristic of social clubs and amateur sports organizations. In the latter, it is not so much whether you win or lose, or even how you play the game, as who you play the game with, and whether you have a good time. Similarly, in social clubs, what matters is less the fineness of the cuisine (or the liqueur or the cigars) than the company of those with whom you mutually enjoy that fineness.

The third level of associativeness—and this is pure Aristotle now—is friendship proper. It is marked by what his mentor once removed, Socrates, called concern for one another's souls. In the Greek philosophical tradition that runs from Socrates through Plato and Aristotle and on down to us, friendship proper is the mutual pursuit of human excellence, or virtue. In the parallel and overlapping Judaeo-Christian religious tradition, it is salvation, membership in the body of those restored to fullest fellowship with each other and with God Himself. In that tradition, paradise was walking with God in a garden in the cool of the evening,[32] and the father of the faithful, Abraham, is called "the friend of God."[33] This is not altogether lost in what our Shorter Catechism teaches us Presbyterians as children, though it does seem something of an afterthought: "Man's chief end is to glorify God, and to enjoy him forever."[34]

To summarize, then, voluntary associations can be classified by their degree of distinctiveness from governmental and for-profit organizations. Two factors are relevant here, one substantive, the other formal. As to the first, the question is how distinctive are their purposes; as to the second, how intimately associated are their constituents. The more distinctive the nonprofit purpose, the less likely that modes of judicial intrusion appropriate in the other sectors will be appropriate for nonprofits and, conversely, the more likely that the voluntary association will warrant special treatment. Similarly, the more intimate the relations, the less helpful analogies to the other sectors will be, and the more appropriate will be some special dispensation. The hardest internal disputes for courts to resolve, accordingly, will be those where the organization's purpose is most distinctive, and where its constituents' relations among themselves are most intimate.

But to identify which kinds of nonprofits will present courts with the most difficult internal disputes, and to trace the source of that difficulty to the two related factors of distinctiveness of purpose and degree of intimacy, is still to leave open the largest question. Assuming that, in these cases, analogies to other sectors are less directly helpful, and thus that some special regime of judicial intervention may be necessary, it remains to be said what that regime should be. Here our analysis must turn from the descriptive to the normative, from the way things are to the way they should be. On this critical point, the proper mode of governmental intervention into voluntary associations' internal disputes, different schools of liberalism diverge, as we shall see in the next part.

[32] Genesis 3:8 (original fellowship disrupted by sin).

[33] James 2:23.

[34] Westminster Shorter Catechism, Answer 1.

3. DIVERGENCES IN LIBERAL THEORIES OF THE STATE

From the basic points of agreement we sketched above in part 2, liberal opinion refracts widely across the familiar left-to-right spectrum. In this section we need to identify three critical bands of this spectrum,[35] then to see how each colors the state's approach to internal disputes within voluntary associations.

A. Three Liberal Positions

1. *Libertarian Liberalism*

On the right of the spectrum is liberalism's libertarian band, with its vision of the minimalist, night-watchman state. That vision is, on the one hand, profoundly confident of the private, contractual orderings of the capitalist market, and, on the other hand, profoundly skeptical of the public, regulatory orderings of the state. At its most skeptical and reductive, this view sees government as a kind of corrupt market of rent-seeking vote-traders intent upon reaping politically what they have not sown economically.[36]

2. *Communitarian Liberalism*

At the left end of the spectrum is liberalism's communitarian band, with its competing vision of the interventionist, welfare state. In contrast to the libertarian viewpoint, the communitarian perspective sees much to fear in the individualistic transactions of the market, and much to gain from the collective decisions of a democratic polity. At its most skeptical and reductive, this view sees private property as a form of state power delegated to some citizens to exercise over others without the usual public safeguards.

3. *Sectarian Liberalism*

Between these poles, obviously stereotyped for heuristic purposes, lies a broad middle ground, with room for a wide range of liberal positions. I want to outline here, and elaborate incrementally below, one such position, which I will call

[35] The points at which libertarians on the right and communitarians on the left lapse out of liberalism is much debated. Cf P Pettit, *Republicanism: A Theory of Freedom and Government* (Oxford, Clarendon Press, 1997), 7–10 (distinguishing republicans from populists and communitarians on the left, and liberals, including "left-of-center liberals" and libertarians, on the right); Alexander, above n 29, 47–8: "Modern communitarian theory aims at developing an alternative to both atomistic individualism and classical communitarism," avoiding the former's methodological and normative individualism and the latter's "collapsing the self into the other".

[36] See also Alexander, above n 29, 19–21 (describing a "public choice/pluralist" theory of groups derived from neo-classical economic theory and interest-group political theory).

"sectarian."[37] This position stands roughly half-way between communitarian and libertarian liberals with respect to both government and the market. (The political spectrum metaphor has a serendipitous aspect here: if communitarians on the left are a scary "red" and libertarians on the right a chilly "blue," my sectarians in the middle should be a reassuringly cool "green".) Sectarian liberalism fears the abuse of both public and private power, yet it is confident that both the state and the market can contribute to human welfare. Not surprisingly, therefore, sectarian liberalism places its greatest confidence in neither the private, for-profit sector nor the public, governmental sector, but in the sector that stands roughly between them as a kind of hybrid: the voluntary, nonprofit sector.

B. The Three Liberal Positions and Voluntary Associations

Against this background of their general features, we can now appreciate the position of each branch of liberalism toward nonprofits and their internal disputes. Here again, the sectarian position is the middle ground, and I think the better view, the view most consistent with liberalism's own commitments and most conducive to the kind of voluntary associations that liberalism itself needs to foster.

1. Libertarianism

Libertarianism tends to assimilate voluntary associations to the market, focussing on their voluntary mode of inclusion, the feature that they share with for-profit organizations. Viewing all private organizations, nonprofit and for-profit alike, as aggregates of individuals, libertarianism tends to overlook the relatively greater importance of the group with respect to some kinds of non-profits, particularly those that, like Presbyterianism, are as much the creators as the creatures of their members. The reductio ad absurdum of libertarianism's individualist, voluntarist assumption is in this paradoxical aphorism: "Abraham Lincoln was born in a log cabin he built with his own hands."

As libertarianism assimilates voluntary associations to for-profit firms, so it tends to see the government's role in internal affairs in minimalist terms, in the nonprofit sector as in the for-profit. In both sectors, this produces a paradox: in seeking to protect individuals from public power in the form of the state, it exposes them to private power in the form of nonprofit and for-profit organizations. By refusing to acknowledge the power of groups to shape individuals, and the greater sophistication that groups may bring to their dealings with individuals, libertarianism inadvertently abandons the individuals it purports to protect to private organizations that, if not monitored by the state, begin to exercise

[37] I use the term "sectarian" with a bow to the flourishing of religious and political movements under the remarkably tolerant policies of the Puritan Commonwealth and Cromwell's Protectorate.

unreviewable, state-like powers over their members. From its commendably liberal normative commitment to individual autonomy and freedon of choice, it tends to draw the dubious descriptive conclusion that individuals are already autonomous, their choices in dealing with other private parties invariably free. To the extent that libertarianism assumes, rather than ensures, that aggregations of individuals are freely entered into, on terms genuinely reflecting the agreement of each, it abandons its own principles.

The value-agnosticism of classical liberal economics, a principal source of libertarianism, tends to blind its adherents to the distinctions among voluntary associations identified in part 2. Assuming that the only evaluative criteria are those of individuals in the market, libertarianism tends to treat all voluntary groups as essentially fungible, distinguishable only by their ability to attract members. This is a serious oversight. It is one thing to assume, as liberals must, that the state has to be neutral on the relative merits of, say, Presbyterianism and Judaism; it is quite another to ignore, as liberalism should not, the structural and functional differences between a church or synagogue and a polo or pinochle club.

In its tendency to conflate these latter differences, libertarianism fails to appreciate appropriately the importance of sects to both the liberal polity and the capitalist economy. The nightwatchman state may not produce its own nightwatchman statesmen; business enterprise may not produce business-like entrepreneurs. What the governmental and for-profit sectors respectively need to operate as libertarians suggest may be exogenous to these sectors, precisely because it is indigenous to the voluntary, nonprofit sector.

2. *Communitarianism*

If libertarianism's over-emphasis on the individual paradoxically ends up enlisting the state on the side of the group at the individual's expense, communitarianism errs in almost precisely the opposite direction: focusing on the importance of the group, it tends to undermine the group by allowing excessive individual member appeal to the supposedly common values of the political community, enforced by the state. We need to unpack this paradox: how does emphasis on "groupness" undermine the group at the behest of its members?

The critical catalyst in this odd transmutation is communitarianism's confidence in the inclusive political community and its principal agency, the state. Communitarianism, as its name implies, centrally acknowledges the importance of groups to human flourishing. Indeed, in some of its forms, it so subordinates the individual to the group as to cease to be recognizable as a form of liberalism;[38] those forms, furthermore, tend to be intensely hostile to groups less inclu-

[38] See J W Torke, "What Price Belonging: An Essay on Groups, Community, and the Constitution", (19990) 24 *Indiana LR* 1, 22–4 (describing this tendency in communitarianism as "the ghost of Robespierre"); N Rosenblum, *Another Liberalism: Romanticism and the Reconstruction of Liberal Thought* (Cambridge, Mass, Harvard UP, 1987), 153 (citing "examples of all-consuming public spirit such as ancient Greek citizenship or revolutionary republicanism with its Jacobin fervor").

sive than the entire political community. Liberal communitarianism, by contrast, affirms liberalism's normative insistence on the value of individual autonomy, but maintains, as a descriptive matter, that individual self-realization requires a significant degree of initial socialization and continuing sociability.

In this essentially descriptive respect, communitarianism improves significantly on the individualistic picture of the relationships between groups and their members that libertarianism presents. It acknowledges that we belong to the voluntary associations we choose, but also insists that, to a greater or lesser extent, our range of choice is influenced by associations that we did not voluntarily choose.[39] Communitarians recognize, in other words, the power of children's catechisms; they affirm, with America's First Lady, that "It Takes a Village."[40]

Their village, however, is a carefully chosen, and extremely pregnant and powerful, symbol. Villages, of course, are involuntary, political communities, territorial sub-states. Yet they symbolize an intense degree of belonging, for which communitarians deeply long; in the communitarian heart, if not on our common maps, these are places called "Hope". They embody *gemeinschaft* rather than *gesellshaft*; they elevate community over contract, love over law. And they are inclusive: everybody belongs; everyone has a proper place. Most importantly, everybody believes. Village values are communal values, shaped by the traditions of common life and unconsciously shared by all.

What I have sketched is, of course, a parody, a theoretician's Potemkin village. Real villages tend to run long in the workday and short in the consumer goods department. They're more about ploughing ankle-deep in the mud than playing barefoot around the May-pole; they're more accurately depicted in Monty Python's Holy Grail than in William Morris tapestries. Once real villagers have seen the modern liberal city, they are notoriously loath to return to the rural commune, however pleasingly pastoral it appears in the pastels of its mostly urban admirers.

Communitarian liberals, to their credit, are well aware of all this. What they seek is the best of both worlds, a way to combine the supposed virtues of traditional village life with the advantages of the modern, industrial state. Here they encounter two basic problems: community size and normative skepticism. The first is a practical matter: how to create a meaningful community on the scale of a modern nation-state. The second is a matter of principle: how to find moral norms that legitimately bind dissenters? In the solution of each problem, voluntary associations play a crucial role. That role, on the other hand, largely determines the role of the state in their internal affairs.

The problem of size tellingly bedevilled the debates about the American constitution: if republican institutions require the face-to-face fraternity found in

[39] See Alexander, above n 29, 41: "What binds the group together is a shared characteristic that is unchosen, or is chosen only in a weak sense, such as cultural identity."

[40] Hillary Rodham Clinton, *It Takes a Village and Other Lessons Children Teach Us* (New York, Simon & Schuster, 1995).

classical Athens and Rome and in Renaissance Italy, and to some extent even in Enlightenment Holland and Switzerland, how could a republican government work on a continental scale? In part, the American answer was to opt for a federal republic, a kind of big republic of little republics, more or less consciously on the Swiss and Dutch models. But, in larger part, the answer, in America and elsewhere in the West, has been to deny in effect the fraternity premise: in modern America, as in the modern United Kingdom, liberal institutions exist despite the radical erosion of all but the thinnest sense of fraternity among citizens. It has proved possible, perhaps all too easy, for citizens to love the liberal nation, even to die and kill on its behalf, without loving, or even knowing, their neighbors across the street, much less across the country.

But communitarian liberals dislike this loss of social solidarity, both as bad in itself and as the source of numerous social woes, particularly the widening gap between rich and poor, the decline of public institutions, and even the decay of basic civility. They see its tragedies in the triumph of libertarian political movements, Reaganism in America, Thatcherism in the United Kingdom. Most significantly, for our purposes, they see nonprofit organizations as one step toward bridging the gaps between citizens, of providing the meaningful interpersonal links that, as we have seen, may lie beyond the capacity of the state itself.

Yet here communitarian liberals encounter their second problem, which is a problem of principle. What they admire about villages is not only their emotional closeness, their richness and depth of social relations, but also their shared value systems, their members' union in common purpose as well as mutual affection. But if they admire the formal unity of these traditional belief-systems, they abominate, in at least equal measure, their typical content: xenophobia, frequently to the point of violent antisemitism; homophobia; and paternalism. As antidotes to these, of course, communitarian liberals, like even the most libertarian of liberals, would substitute the essentially negative liberal virtues of tolerance and individual liberty of conscience, through the instrumentalities of the liberal state.

But communitarian liberals want more, a new, better system of positive public values to replace the old, benighted values of the village and to supplement the new but formal and negative values of the liberarian liberals' nightwatchman state. Here liberalism's essential value-skepticism poses a very serious problem: the liberal state, as we have seen, is deeply committed to neutrality toward different substantive visions of human flourishing. In particular, all liberals, including communitarian liberals, are loath to enforce matters of faith, fundamental beliefs about the ends of human existence, on dissenters.

Faced with this serious substantive problem, communitarian liberals explicitly propose a procedural solution that depends on an implicit and dubious descriptive assumption. The procedural solution is dialogue, or, as it is more frequently called, deliberation. Communitarian liberals concede that citizens cannot, consistently with liberalism's normative agnosticism, be forced to adopt a shared set of substantive values. But communitarian liberals insist that, consistently with liberalism's commitment to democratic process, citizens can be required to talk with each other about such values. And the liberal state can legitimately encourage the kinds of procedural virtues that will make these deliberations genuine, mutually respectful conversations, not just window-dressings for the behind-the-scenes horse-trading of pluralist politics-as-usual.

For all this to produce a set of shared substantive values, however, communitarians must make two truly heroic empirical assumptions: that reasonable people can be made to take such conversations seriously and, even more heroically, that, at the end of such conversations, reasonable people will tend to agree, thus converging through deliberative processes on a shared substantive agenda and value system. Even in outline, the red and scary side of all this should be apparent: if the much-sought-after agreement is not forthcoming, it will be tempting to think, not that it was too much to hope that reasonable people would ultimately agree, but that those who are holding out are not being reasonable. Since "being reasonable" can be characterized as a procedural requirement, those who fail to meet it can be punished for their deficiency, arguably in accord with liberal principles. Perhaps, indeed, the unreasonable can be said to have forfeited their place, political or otherwise, in the Republic of Conversation-Tending-Toward-Virtue.

In its search for a common substantive value system, communitarian liberalism is thus at risk of lapsing leftward, out of liberalism altogether and into various forms of radical communitarianism, Jacobinism and Bolshevism at the worst. Even if liberal communitarians' reddish vision never darkens into revolutionary terror, it may well shade into something very like the rosy monotony of a continuous PTA meeting. At its best, liberal communitarian's insistence on continual dialogue calls to mind Oscar Wilde's objection to his friends' Fabian socialism: "It takes too many evenings."[41]

These problems with communitarian liberalism, from the truly terrible to the merely mind-numbing, have been widely bemoaned, and need not further detain us. What we need to focus on here are the implications of the communitarian liberals' vision for voluntary associations. As we have seen, communitarians expect that such organizations will help their state deal with its size problem; membership in voluntary associations will increase, in a large territorial state, the opportunities for face-to-face communication among citizens, since members of each separate voluntary group are also citizens of the common republic.

Beyond that, voluntary associations can function as "schools for citizenship," accustoming their members to conduct their intra-group affairs in the deliberative way that communitarians hope will come to characterize their dealings as citizens with those outside their respective groups in the polity as a whole. Moreover, at a substantive level, just as deliberation among citizens is expected to produce shared values, so might deliberation among members of voluntary

[41] O Wilde, *The Soul of Man under Socialism and Other Essays* (New York, Harper and Row, 1970).

groups. Indeed, by combining these substantive and procedural aspects, one can imagine the communitarian liberal state as a new kind of confederation. As opposed to the classical confederation of smaller political sub-divisions, the state of states in which sterile social relations reproduce themselves on a larger scale, this new confederation would be a group of groups, in which the close, fraternal relations of small groups leaven relations among citizens of the entire polity.

For all this to work, however, two doubtful conditions must be met. First, groups need to reflect the same deliberative values that communitarians are looking to export from them into the polity as a whole. Second, groups need to produce substantive value-systems consistent with those of the larger, political dialogue. On communitarianism's empirical assumptions, to quote the ironic title of a Flannery O'Connor short story, "Everything that Rises Must Converge."

This produces parallel substantive and procedural pressures from the communitarian liberal state into the internal affairs of voluntary associations. Both non-deliberative procedures and substantively illiberal outcomes will be suspect. Since communitarianism is more attuned than libertarianism to the ways in which individual member's involvement may not be fully voluntary, the communitarian liberal state will be able to correct real instances of group overreaching. But, since that state is anything but indifferent to both the process and the product of internal group decision-making, it will be tempted to fault even those internal arrangements that reflect fully voluntary assent of group members. Communitarian liberalism has an obviously deep need for these matters to go right, for reasons we have already seen; it also has a less obviously principled basis for correcting them when they do not, to which we must now turn.

Voluntary associations, as we have seen, are to serve the communitarian liberal's vision of the state by engaging in dialogue, both internally among their members and externally with other groups. Given the empirical reality that members do not enter all such groups entirely freely, and the further fact that exit is not always practically easy, communitarian liberals tend to insist that members enjoy "voice" within their organizations as well as the possibility of "exit" from them. "Voice" is, of course, the principal formal aspect of communitarian liberals' "deliberative democracy". To refuse to engage in it is, as we have seen, a substantial lapse of citizenly virtue. Accordingly, communitarian liberals, consistently with their own principles, need not be shy about forcing sects to justify their positions in public forums. Indeed, they see law suits by individual members as an entirely appropriate means of achieving this obligatory dialogue.

This dialogue, moreover, will have for communitarian liberals an aspect it lacks for libertarians. Individual member appeals from internal group decisions to the state need not rest only on the group's violation of its side of any deals with its members. Members can also argue that the results of such deals frustrate substantive state policy unrelated to the keeping of individual bargains.

This opens the group to charges that its structure, process, or substantive ends are not consistent with emerging or established community-wide ends.[42]

We have already seen how libertarianism's overweening confidence in the reality, not just the ideal, of individual autonomy leads it to oppose judicial review even of internal group deals that the weaker, individual parties may well not have meaningfully agreed to. Thus, paradoxically, libertarian liberalism favors the group over the individual. Here we have the opposite paradox: communitarian liberalism favors the individual over the group. This is because its overweening confidence in the creation of shared public values permits the individual member to invoke those values to overturn internal group arrangements that the individual clearly understood and intended. Thus each wing of liberalism, communitarian on the left and libertarian on the right, reasons from a dubious descriptive assumption to a normative conclusion in considerable tension with its fundamental normative commitment. To avoid the dilemma of these paradoxes, we need a model that is more descriptively accurate and more normatively modest.

3. *Sectarianism*

My own preferred model, sectarian liberalism, is best seen as a middle way between libertarianism and communitarianism, both descriptively and normatively. On the descriptive side, sectarianism simply removes the more optimistic assumptions of both the right and the left. Unlike libertarianism to the right, sectarianism does not assume that individuals join groups entirely freely, or that they stand on a footing entirely equal to that of the groups to which they belong. Rather, it recognizes real constraints on individual choice, short of outright coercion, and it acknowledges the importance of information asymmetries and other market failures and structural features that permit groups to take advantage of individual members. In particular, it sees a tendency of group power to concentrate toward the top, and it recognizes the practical difficulty of "exiting" even from groups that are legally and nominally voluntary.

On the other (left) hand, sectarianism rejects the communitarian assumption that mutually respectful dialogue among citizens will produce substantive agreement as to common ends, either within groups or within the larger state. In its more pluralistic moods, sectarianism accepts the possibility of multiple, equally valid visions of human flourishing.[43] In its more pessimistic moods, sectarianism affirms the irreducible reality of radical evil in the world: some, with

[42] Alexander, above n 29, 23 ("moral communitarians understand each person's identity to be connected, in some sense, not only with one or more discrete groups, but with society as a whole"); *id*, 52–3 (insisting that ideal of shared group values must, in communitarian theory, be a universal ideal); *id*, 55–6 ("Through the dialogic process of adjudication, courts can serve as a bridge between communities and society, preventing the former from lapsing into a solipsistic perspective that would pervert the ideal of community and, at the same time, inhibiting sheer majoritarianism from denying a community's opportunity to formulate a conception of the good").

[43] e.g. K Sullivan, "Rainbow Republicanism," (1988) 97 *Yale LJ* 1713.

open eyes, will forever oppose human flourishing. But in both moods, the pluralistic and the pessimistic, sectarianism recognizes the grave danger of empowering the state to police fundamental beliefs.

Even the element of skepticism is not, however, born of a cranky or doctrinaire cynicism, but of a chastened realism. The real history of voluntary associations and the liberal state not only counsels caution, but also offers hope. To say, against the libertarian assumption, that dealings between groups and their members are not *always* free and equal is not to say that they are *never* free or equal; many, manifestly, are often both. And to doubt, over against the communitarians, that all reasonable people can be expected to converge through dialogue on shared ends is not to say that none will. Many, again, manifestly have. Similarly, to despair of fraternity in matters of politics is not to lapse into social atomism at every level. Intensely close personal ties of mutual respect and even affection were not lost above the level of family and friendship with the passing of the traditional village; these intimate ties live on in contemporary voluntary groups. Finally, to dispute that voluntary associations can be expected to act as "schools" for liberal virtues is not to deny that the liberal state has very real need of them, to produce not only liberal visions of the good, but also good liberal citizens.

As what *can* be always conditions what *ought* to be, so these cautiously optimistic, or reluctantly pessimistic, descriptive views circumscribe sectarianism's normative outlook. In a sense, sectarianism shares the dreams of its brethren on both the left and the right, but believes they can only be realized, or safely sought, on a smaller scale. With libertarians, we affirm that individuals should be able to seek their own ends through voluntary associations of like-minded individuals, and that the state should require that those commitments be honored, in the nonprofit sector as in the market. But we also believe that the state will have, alas, to police these deals to ensure that their basic premise is met: that they are voluntary and knowing.

With communitarians, we affirm the value of deep affectionate ties between individual human beings; we seek fraternity, not just liberty and equality. But we deny that fraternity can be acheived any more successfully in the agora of politics than in the marketplace of economics. Accordingly, we seek it among members of voluntary groups. In part, to be sure, we seek it there because we have never found it elsewhere; in larger part, however, we seek it in such groups because we and others have often found it there before.

Similarly we, like communitarians, seek shared visions of human flourishing, and we seek those visions through dialogue with others. But we seek those visions as individuals and as members of particular groups of like-minded individuals, not as political liberals, and thus not at the level of the entire political community. That is the ultimate meaning of sectarianism: it is not to despair of finding meaning in life, or even of sharing that meaning with others; it is merely to doubt that all will ever agree to share it, and thus that the state has any right to impose it.

What the state may do—indeed, for sectarians, must do—is almost exactly the opposite. Minimally, it must abjure the imposition of value systems of its own, and it must prevent any group from imposing its system on any other group or individual. Optimally, it should take affirmative steps to ensure that all citizens really have the kind of autonomy that libertarianism tends to assume so that they can engage in the kind of dialogical choosing and shaping of value systems that sectarianism and communitarianism affirm.

4. DISPUTES OVER SECTS' DOCTRINES IN THE SECTARIAN STATE'S COURTS

To appreciate the full implications of the last part, we would have to integrate it with part 2. We would need, in other words, to apply the perspectives of all three schools of liberalism—libertarian, communitarian, and sectarian—to each of the various kinds voluntary organizations we identified in part 2 according to the distinctiveness of their purpose and the degree of intimacy experienced by their members. But even that would seriously over-simplify, for the internal disputes that arise in voluntary organizations are themselves multifaceted. Even at a very high level of generality, they can be seen to cover substance, jurisdiction, and procedure. Yet to try to address all this complexity—to try to apply the perspectives of all three schools of liberalism to the full range of voluntary organizations as to even the most generalized categorization of their problems—would take us well beyond our present scope.

Accordingly, I propose to take the perspective of a single liberal school, sectarianism, and apply it to a single kind of organization, sects, with respect to a single kind of problem, disputes about fundamental organizational purpose. This particular narrowing of focus has several advantages. First, sectarianism is, at least in this context, the least explored version of liberalism and, as we saw in part 3, it stands as something of a mediating position between the other two alternatives. Second, sects—voluntary associations the principal purpose of which is to create and sustain moral worlds—are arguably the most distinct of voluntary associations, from both government on the one hand and for-profit firms on the other. Moreover, as we saw in part 2, sects may involve the most intense forms of integration among their members. For both of these reasons, as we shall see more fully in this part, disputes over sectarian doctrine produce the hardest cases for civil courts to adjudicate. After examining these hardest cases, we may reasonably hope to interpolate answers to easier issues in less distinctive voluntary organizations. In that sense, this narrower focus should provide what our title promises: an appropriate prolegomena for broader inquiries.

We will take as our principal examples schisms within Presbyterian denominations in the United Kingdom and the United States. We shall identify deep flaws in the traditional approach of the United Kingdom courts, which looks for the faction loyal to the sect's original doctrine.[44] The principal flaw does not, however, lie quite where American courts have said, in the United Kingdom's courts' "little delicacy in grappling with the most abstruse problems of theological controversy".[45] The real reason lies closer to that articulated by English pluralists early in this century: ecclesiastical doctrine almost inevitably evolves in all but the most static of sects.[46] But the result of the pluralists' observation is not necessarily what they anticipated, victory for the church as an organic, evolving body over those of its members who insist on clinging to its past. On balance, by far the better approach, from the perspective of sectarian liberalism, is a Solomonic middle ground. This is the approach taken both by the United Kingdom Parliament in the watershed Free Church of Scotland Appeals[47] and by the English Court of Appeal in a recent schism in a Hindu sect.[48] Without declaring which faction is the true church, this mediating approach simply lets the two parties go their separate ways, each asserting its own version of truth and taking along the property it could have reasonably expected to retain.

A. Members' Challenges to the Sect's Doctrinal Change

In the classic departure-from-doctrine case, an allegedly orthodox party asserts that another faction has fundamentally departed from the sect's original purpose, and dissents from this doctrinal change. For all their variety, such disputes generally follow an identifiable declension into substantive, jurisdictional, and procedural issues. It will be useful to outline these issues here, then turn to the details of each in separate subsections. In the discussion which follows, I shall generally refer to the allegedly orthodox faction as "dissenters", and to the allegedly heterodox faction as "the sect". This terminology reflects the fact that in many cases of this kind, one faction dissents from an alleged deviation by those who purport to speak for the sect. But it obscures the fact that the dissidents' central position is that they themselves are not dissidents, but the true sect. We must thus bear in mind that who is really heterodox, and who really deserves to be called the true sect, is very much the issue in question.

[44] Cf *Jones* v. *Wolf* 443 US 595 (1979), 599, n 1 (Blackmun J): "This [implied trust theory] is sometimes referred to as the "English approach" to resolving property disputes in hierarchical churches."

[45] *Watson* v. *Jones* 80 US 679 (1871), 727–28 (Miller J) (citing the United Kingdom approach as appropriate only for a state with an established church).

[46] J N Figgis, *Churches in the Modern State* 2nd edn (Longman, Green and Co, London, 1914); H Laski, "Notes on the Strict Interpretation of Ecclesiastical Trusts", (1916) 36 *Canadian LT* 190; H Laski, "The Personality of Associations", (1916) 29 *Harvard LR* 404, 418–29. It is important to distinguish these English pluralists from their ideologically distant cousins of the same name, the American "interest group" pluralists. See Note, *Developments in the Law: Judicial Control of Actions of Private Associations*, (1963) 76 *Harvard LR* 983, 987, n 9: "Pluralism in this country took the form of an empirical methodology for studying the political process."

[47] Churches (Scotland) Act 1905.

[48] *Varsani* v. *Jesani* [1999] Ch 219.

In the most straightforward mode, the question is whether the sect has, as alleged, departed from its fundamental doctrine. In this substantive mode, the sect can respond in either of two ways. First, it can deny any such departure. Its current doctrinal position, it will insist, is consistent with its original position, properly understood. This approach essentially concedes that the issue is substantive, but denies the charge itself, that a substantive change has occurred. Alternatively, the sect may admit the change in doctrine, but assert that fundamental doctrine is subject to change. It will, in effect, be arguing that the sect's fundamental doctrines are amendable, and that the allegedly improper departure is in fact just such a proper amendment.

Either side may attempt to pre-empt these substantive issues with a jurisdictional challenge. The dissenters may argue that the substantive decision, either as to compliance with doctrine or permitted change in doctrine, was not made at the proper level within the organization; typically, the dissenters will argue that the decision is one for a subordinate body, like the local congregation, not for the sect as a whole. On the other hand, the sect will typically insist that the decision was indeed made at the proper level, and that such decisions are not subject to review outside the organization itself.

Finally, either faction may charge that the decision, wherever made, violated the sect's prescribed procedures for making such decisions. These procedural irregularities will be said to have vitiated the substantive decision. Here, too, it is possible to raise a jurisdictional response, arguing that procedural issues are themselves within the purview of some internal body, not subject to external, judicial review.

Judicial intervention at any step in the process can resolve the dispute favorably to either the dissenters or the sect. Substantive resolutions are particularly thorny. But each step poses problems, as we shall see in the following subsections.

1. *Substantive Issues and the (English) Implied Trust Theory*

The substantive approach to doctrinal disputes, and the problems it poses, are nicely illustrated in the Free Church of Scotland Appeals.[49] To understand this case, a Holmesian page of history is essential. The congregations that formed the Free Church withdrew from the established Church of Scotland in 1843. A principal issue in this Great Disruption was the role of the state in ecclesiastical affairs. Even after its secession, the Free Church continued to espouse establishmentarian. Although no longer itself part of the established church, it avowed the propriety of an established church and officially looked forward to the day when the Church of Scotland would return to the principles that only it, the Free Church, had faithfully followed. The Free Church, in other words, was a disestablished church that believed it should be the established church.

At the turn of the last century, the Free Church's national body approved, by a wide margin, a union with the United Presbyterian Church, itself the product

[49] *General Assembly of Free Church of Scotland* v. *Overtoun* [1904] AC 515.

of earlier secessions from the established Church of Scotland. The United Presbyterians, unlike the Free Church, had officially disavowed establishmentarianism in favor of its antithesis, voluntaryism. The United Presbyterians, in other words, were a disestablished church that believed no church should be established. As a condition of the two denominations' union, the Free Church agreed to a loosening of the new, consolidated denomination's commitment to the establishment principle. Establishmentarianism thus became, in effect, an optional belief in the new body.

A relatively small minority of the Free Church—hence the "Wee Frees"—objected to the union on the ground that this compromise on the establishment principle departed from an essential doctrine of the Free Church. The House of Lords, in a divided opinion, agreed with the dissenters, awarding all the property of the pre-union Free Church to the minority, establishmentarian faction. Parliament soon reversed this decision, ordering a division of the Free Church's property between the two factions;[50] what we must look at now is the reasoning of the majority of the law lords.

The majority of the law lords took a substantive approach to the problem. In their view, those who originally contributed to the Free Church gave on the implicit condition that the new body would continue to promote the doctrines on which it was founded. These, by everyone's admission, included the establishment principle. Accordingly, any substantial departure from that doctrine constituted a breach of trust, in effect an abandonment of the church's property to the loyal faction.

This approach, generally called the implied trust theory, has enjoyed wide popularity with courts in both the United Kingdom and the United States. Four critical steps in applying this reasoning need careful analysis. First, the court must determine the sect's original beliefs, as the touchstone for the alleged departure. Second, the court must determine whether, and to what extent, the sect has departed from the baseline of its original doctrinal position. Third, if it finds an essential doctrinal change, it must find whether that change was impermissible. And, finally, if it finds the change impermissible, it must decide its consequences in the case at hand.

a) Determining the Sect's Original Doctrine

In the Free Church appeal, the first of these determinations did not come up on the point of the establishment doctrine, because the majority faction admitted its abandonment of that doctrine. It did come up, however, with respect to alleged deviations from the church's original doctrine of predestination. The dispute on this point was mooted by the court's finding of a fatal departure on the establishment point. For our purposes, however, it is interesting to see how the debate on the predestination point might have gone, and why the establishment point did not go the same way.

[50] Churches (Scotland) Act 1905.

The establishment principle, as compared to predestination, is a marvel of simplicity: either the state gives official preference to one religion, or it doesn't. Though establishment admits of degrees—one church only, one church whose members enjoy special political privileges, one church that is more or less heavily subsidized—its core meaning, and the meaning of its gradations and permutations, are fairly clear. This is at least in part because ecclesiastical establishment is a political reality, a fact of this world, whatever its political or theological merits.

Predestination, by contrast, is notoriously other worldly. It occurs, by definition, in the eternal counsels of God's own mind, and its actual effects in the world are known only to Him – indeed, to tighten the epistemological circle still further, He Himself is known only by those to whom He has chosen to reveal Himself. The mechanism of predestination is admittedly mysterious, even to its most avid proponents; Calvin himself cautioned repeatedly against presuming to understand too much too well.

To capture these difficulties better, consider an easier case than either establishmentarianism or predestination. In voluntary organizations that are not very distinct in their purposes from either governmental or for-profit firms, disputes over fundamental purpose are fairly easy to resolve, in principle if not always in practice. Take, for example, a charity that has been running a hospital for many years, but whose board decides to sell the hospital and use the proceeds to establish and operate local clinics. If a dissident director were to challenge this decision as an improper departure from the organization's purpose, the majority could respond that the original purpose was health care generally, not specifically the operation of a hospital, and that the shift from one mode of health care delivery to another was well within the scope of the original purpose.

Which side had the better argument would very much turn on the facts, which could clearly favor one side or the other, or could be quite murky. The organizational document's language on fundamental purposes, and on changing those purposes, would be crucial, and that language could be more or less clear. But, whatever the facts, no great problems of principle need arise. Indeed, such cases would look very much like similar cases involving for-profit firms making the same shift, except that the easy metric of greatest profit would be lacking. This is because, in both the for-profit and non-profit world, the term "running a hospital" has a clearer referent than "believing in predestination" or even "being establishmentarian".

b) Determining the Degree of the Departure from Essential Doctrine

Even if the court can find a departure from doctrine, it must further determine if the doctrine is essential; if, that is, the departure is too great. "Essential" here could mean any one of three related things: what the founders explicitly said was essential, what the founders can be inferred to have believed was essential, and what in some non-subjective sense is really essential.

The law lords had little trouble with this phase of the Free Church case. In the majority's view, the founders had been clear, and indeed pretty explicit, about the importance of the establishment principle. It is important to note more generally, however, that this need not be the case. Just as the sect's original doctrinal position could be quite murky, so can its position on which original beliefs are essential. The latter, indeed, is if anything more likely. Even if the founders are quite explicit in expressing what they believe, they may well be completely silent as to whether that belief could ever legitimately be revised. This would force the court to fall back to the second position on essential doctrine, what the sect can be inferred to have believed, a much more practically difficult inquiry.

That would still leave the third view on essential doctrine, but that is not a way that courts of the liberal state will see as open to them. Courts could, in principle, test the competing faction's understanding of a doctrine like predestination against the "real" meaning of that concept. In other words, rather than looking for what true Presbyterians mean by predestination, the court could adjudge as true Presbyterians those who hold the true understanding of predestination. The precedents on which the House of Lords majority relied carefully abjured this third approach, insisting that courts were only to find what the sect had originally believed, not what was true.[51] To do otherwise would be to abandon the liberal state's agnosticism about matters of faith. On the facts before it, however, the Lord's majority, without too much difficulty, got past the first two substantive issues: that establishmentarianism was an essential doctrine of the Free Church at its founding, and that the Free Church majority had abandoned that doctrine.

c) Determining Whether the Sect's Departure from Essential Doctrine Was Impermissible

But they tripped up badly on the third element of the implied trust analysis: the determination of whether departure from the essential doctrine in question is impermissible. Here the House of Lords majority ran afoul of a hidden, or at least overlooked, paradox. Stated most baldly, it is this: an arguably essential doctrine of historical Presbyterianism is that its essential doctrine is not static. The Calvinist tradition, in which Scottish Presbyterianism stands, does not see the church as having been reformed once and for all. Rather, if the church is to be true to its essence, on this view, it must constantly be in the process of being reformed. Thus "reformed," a word that has come to be synonymous with, if not preferable to "Calvinistic," has both a static, or historical, element and a dynamic, or progressive, element. The Reformed Church is the church founded by the Genevan reformers and their allies; these Reformers conceived of their church as reforming—purifying—itself throughout its entire history. The Westminster Confession of Faith, the reformed creed to which the Free Church subscribed, carefully acknowledged this dynamic aspect.

[51] *Craigdallie* v. *Aiken* (1813) 1 Dow PC 1; 3 ER 601.

The tension between these two aspects, the static and the dynamic, was the crux of the Free Church of Scotland appeals. The dissenters could not, consistently with an historically Reformed or Calvinistic understanding of the church, maintain that the Westminster Standards were inerrant. This opened the door for the sect to assert, as in effect it did, that its abandonment of the establishment principle, and, indeed, of the original Westminster position on predestination, were proper reforms, the very kind of reforms the original Reformers, in their own day, had urged upon the Roman Church.

Had it squarely faced this paradox, the court would have found itself in an impossible bind. Courts can, albeit sometimes with difficulty, determine how Presbyterians have struck the balance between stasis and dynamism in the past. As we have seen, they can determine what Presbyterians have held to be the essential articles of their faith, pointing, for example, to their great creedal statements like the Westminster Confession. In this they would use the same methods as intellectual historians and theologians, Presbyterian and otherwise.

But courts cannot do the same prospectively; they cannot say which changes to the Reformed creeds, all of which anticipate doctrinal change, will be doctrinally sound.[52] To do so would be to set themselves up as the ultimate arbiter, not of what Presbyterians have believed, or even believe now, but should believe. For what Presbyterians have traditionally believed they should believe is what is true, the revealed will of God for His own glory and the good of humanity. This, of course, is exactly the kind of fundamental moral issue on which the liberal state cannot, if true to itself, take a position.

Nor is this tension between static and dynamic tendencies peculiar to Presbyterianism. Rather, as the English pluralists pointed out, it is present in all churches and, I would suggest, the same is true of all organizations that promote fundamental value systems. Thus, as to the very kind of issue most important to such organizations, the implied trust theory is fundamentally unworkable.

d) Consequences of the Sect's Improper Departure from Its Essential Doctrine

There remains, however, the fourth issue, the consequences of the sect's improper change in an essential doctrine. In the Free Church appeal, this issue came down to what to do with the sect's property. As we have seen, the court, having found that the sect had departed from an essential doctrine, determined that the property belonged to the dissenters, who were in effect held to be the true church. The pluralists, who saw the paradox of essential doctrinal evolution, apparently thought the opposite result appropriate: the property should have belonged to the sect, the progressive faction. Yet this assumes that that faction itself was the ultimate arbiter of "true" Presbyterianism. That, we shall see

[52] Courts in liberal states with written constitutions face an analogous limitation. Even if, as in the United States, courts can declare legislative acts to be in violation of the fundamental law, they cannot do the same to properly enacted amendments to that law. The very point of constitutional amendments is to make constitutional in the future what was not constitutional in the past.

in the next subsection, is quite close to the United States Supreme Court's implied consent theory. But it was not the view of Parliament, which ordered the property divided on equitable principles between the two factions. Parliament's position made eminent political sense; we shall see in a bit that it may also—though probably accidentally—have been the most principled approach for the liberal state. First, however, we must examine jurisdictional moves, which promise to remove substantive doctrinal disputes from the courts altogether.

2. *Jurisdictional Issues and the (American) Implied Consent Theory*

These unavoidable problems with substantive resolutions in sectarian disputes understandably press civil courts toward formal solutions as a way of cutting the Gordian knots of sectarian doctrine. Though this preference is demonstrably more consistent with the limitations of the liberal state, it is not without problems of its own. Problems with formalist solutions are nicely illustrated by what might be called the American alternative for dealing with sects, the implied consent theory. The United States Supreme Court first articulated this theory in a case involving this country's greatest Presbyterian schism, the split between the denomination's northern and southern branches over slavery at the time of America's Civil War.[53]

At the broadest level of generality, this approach is elegantly liberal: let the organization choose its own formal means of internal dispute resolution, to which the state, on contractarian principles, will defer. This approach works relatively well in the case of two classic ecclesiastical forms, the congregational and the episcopal. In the former, the local congregation has final say in all matters; in the latter, final authority rests with the church hierarchy. Even these pure paradigms can present problems, however. And Presbyterianism, which is something of a hybrid form, raises even greater difficulties.

For one thing, "pure" models themselves are seldom entirely pure. Rather, in sects with a generally congregational form, some matters may be committed to higher church authorities; management of denomination-wide colleges and seminaries, for example. Conversely, in sects with a generally hierarchical form, matters like local relief work may be committed to congregational decision.

This hybridized form, lying between the pure paradigms of congregationalism and episcopacy, is very much the model of Presbyterianism. In its leading case dealing with that hybrid form, the US Supreme Court announced its deeply dubious doctrine of "implied consent". Under that doctrine, any congregation belonging to a hierarchical denomination is deemed to have submitted ultimate authority on all issues to the denominational hierarchy.

There are two related problems here. First, the assumption of complete local subordination may run counter to the actual arrangements within the sect itself. As we have seen, some matters may be reserved to the local body, some to the

[53] *Watson* v. *Jones* 80 US 679 (1871).

larger. To be sure, these arrangements may be vexingly difficult for a civil court to unravel. But to cut the Gordian knot with a counter-factual presumption systematically favoring one side—and often the better-informed, stronger side at that—is a dubious means of doing the job. Second, the parties may never have been clear on a particular question, like the disposition of congregational property in the event of a schism. In such a case, it is hardly appropriate to assume, without more, that the locals intended to empower the nationals.

If the implied consent rule is a dubious inference of the parties' intent, it is an even more dubious as a default rule designed to implement public policy toward sects. Indeed, in the case of sectarian liberalism, very much the opposite seems to be appropriate default rule for one of the more common and vexing problems, control of local congregation's property in the event of a fundamental disagreement between the local congregation and higher denominational authorities. To state the matter affirmatively, the policies underlying sectarian liberalism counsel in favor of a presumption of local control.

The principal reasons for this presumption are the various factors contributing, all else being equal, to concentration of power at upper levels of the denominational hierarchy. To paraphrase Milton,[54] it is not so much that presbyters will become priests, as that permanent denominational bureaucrats install themselves as de facto papal curias. To British audiences (and American watchers of public television), this might be called the "Yes, Minister" problem; to those versed in Weberian sociology, it is the "iron law of oligarchy". The history of American protestantism is replete with repetitions of the Wee Frees' case: denominational initiatives opposed by substantial majorities within local congregations which congregations are themselves minorities in the church at large. And often, as in the case of the Wee Frees, these are more remote, rural congregations, the very constituents likely to suffer from information asymmetries.

3. *The Secession Alternative: Parliament's Solomonic Solution*

In this situation, the British Parliament hit upon a brilliantly Solomonic, baby-splitting solution, the Churches (Scotland) Act 1905: let the locals secede, taking their congregational property with them. Curiously, this solution almost precisely parallels that proposed in the governmental sector by my illustrious co-religionist and compatriot, John Caldwell Calhoun, another Scots-Irish Presbyterian from South Carolina. In Calhoun's theory of nullification, any action of the federal union deemed by one of its constituent states to violate the union's fundamental law must be treated as an amendment of that law, and thus must be passed by the appropriate amendment process. If the amendment passes over the state's objection, the state has a final recourse: secession from the union into its own original, independent sovereignty.

As a theory of American Constitutional law, Calhoun's model may be deeply flawed (though I doubt it); as a matter of fact, it lost on the battlefield, not in the

[54] See text to n 8, above.

courtroom. But many of its problems as a political structure do not apply in the realm of voluntary associations. For one thing, fissiparity is more acceptable here, both as a matter of history and as a matter of principle. Virtually all sects are traceable back to some larger whole, and the whole notion of voluntary organization implies freedom to leave as well as to enter the common enterprise. What is being cut in the Solomonic approach is hardly a human baby nor, at least for the last half-millenium, a single body of believers, even within the Christian faith. (A faith which, after all, began as a dissident Jewish sect.)

For another, many voluntary organizations, especially religious denominations, have federal structures, as we have seen. The local levels of these structures, congregations, often exhibit a degree of integration lacking in Calhoun's ostensibly sovereign American states. The face-to-face, town-meeting mode of transacting institutional business at the congregational level gives them a measure of organic integrity arguably lacking in the mostly territorial definitions of Calhoun's proffered political sub-units, the American states.

Finally, strengthening potentially dissident constituencies within large denominations may well be in the long-run best interest of the denominations themselves. This is nicely illustrated in Hirschman's analysis of the way organization managers, be they for-profit, nonprofit, or governmental, respond to constituent complaints.[55] In situations where "exit," severing ties with the organization, is very costly to a constituency, they are likely to remain affiliated and register their perceptions of organizational decline through "voice," more or less direct communications with management. But management, at least in the short run, has perverse incentives not to encourage or heed constituent voice, even at the cost of long-term institutional decline. Moreover, voice tends to be less effective at getting management's attention when it is not accompanied by credible threats of exit.

Religious organizations, according to Hirschman, typically exhibit high exit costs. Allowing congregations to leave with their local property intact would significantly lower those costs. Consistently with Hirschman's analysis, this lowering of exit costs would improve congregations position vis-à-vis the hierarchy. Beyond that, it might also benefit the denomination as a whole. By forcing the hierarchy to attend more to constituent voicing of perceived institutional decline, increased opportunity for exit might well help avert such decline. That, in turn, might well make congregations less, rather than more, likely to secede. If so, the ultimate beneficiaries would be both the sect and the congregation; the only losers, current management, and only in terms of short-run interests.

The elegance of Parliament's Solomonic solution, whether explicitly adopted by a sect itself or used by the civil courts as a default rule, is subject to frustration by clever procedural moves on the part of higher denominational authorities. Accordingly, as we shall see in the next section, the sectarian state must also develop a sophisticated approach to procedural issues as well.

[55] Above, n 20.

4. *Procedural Issues*

Even if the alleged change is found to be substantively proper (or unreviewable) and made at the appropriate level within the organization, there is a final set of hurdles. As we have seen, either the sect or the dissenters may charge that the decision was not made in accord with the sect's internal procedures. Procedural irregularities will be said to have vitiated the decision. With respect to fundamental doctrinal matters, procedural problems take three basic forms: attacks on the decision-making body's credentials, attacks on the process by which that body decided the matter before them, and assertions that a body within the sect has unreviewable authority to decide these and other procedural issues. We need to examine each of these avenues of attack in turn.

a) Credentials Challenges

Dissidents can argue, and have argued, that the decision they oppose, though made at the proper organizational level, was nevertheless made by individuals who had obtained their positions improperly.[56] To anti-popes, popes are always anti-popes; for the faithful, and for the courts, the problem is to tell which is which. Assuming the selection criteria are clear, the courts of a sectarian liberal state should be able to grant a limited hearing to such charges. Thus, for example, if the national governing body is, by the denomination's internal rules, to be elected by majority vote, and the dissidents allege fraud in the counting of ballots, courts could and should hear the charge, just as they would hear analogous charges about electoral irregularities in a political subdivision or for-profit corporation. To refuse to hear such cases would both deny the dissidents the benefit of their bargain with the organization and reward egregious misconduct on the part of the organization's management. Management, on the other hand, should have available the standard equitable defenses of laches and estoppel.

Credentials challenges can come from the other side as well. Suppose, for example, that local congregations have the authority by majority vote, either as a matter of denominational rules or local law, to withdraw from the denomination and take with them all property vested in the local congregation. Yet suppose, further, that final decisions in all other matters, including determination of membership in good standing, rest with the denominational hierarchy. The hierarchy could obviously undermine any local vote to secede by expelling the dissident majority or otherwise ruling those members ineligible to vote, thus leaving the loyalist rump in control of the congregation's property.[57] To protect the jurisdictional arrangement as to secession, courts must thus be able to police such procedural manipulations of members' credentials.

[56] See e.g. *Serbian Eastern Orthodox Diocese* v. *Melivojevich* 426 US 696 (1976); *Kedroff* v. *St Nicholas Cathedral*, 344 US 94 (1952).

[57] This was essentially the case in the US Supreme Court's latest Presbyterian case, *Jones* v. *Wolf* 443 US 595 (1979), 606 (Blackmun J).

b) Procedural Challenges Proper

More common than these credentials challenges will be challenges to the process by which the doctrinal change itself is made. These processes will often be straightforward. The sect's internal documents might provide, for example, for a majority vote by a designated body in a properly announced meeting conducted according to standard parliamentary procedures. Here again, the courts can review alleged procedural irregularities very much as they would in examining the pedigree of a legislative enactment or a corporate policy decision.

Sometimes, however, sects may officially proceed in ways that are not easily reviewed by liberal courts. The organization's foundational documents may, for example, direct that matters of basic doctrine be dealt with "prayerfully," "with the guidance of God," or "in a spirit of love." At the extreme, the sect may consciously eschew secular, liberal modes of group decision-making, as we shall see in the case of the Quaker meetings. Thus, in matters of process as in matters of substance, liberal courts may find themselves at the edge of Professor Chafee's "Dismal Swamp of obscure rules and doctrines".[58]

Faced with this prospect, liberal courts would best be served by the sect itself providing an alternative, secular set of standards. Thus, for example, the sect's internal rules could provide that, in the event that its esoteric, internal procedures fail on a point like the entitlement to local congregations' property, a specified set of secular standards be applied.[59] These could be very hierarchy-favorable—for example, letting the bishop decide unilaterally—or very congregation-favorable—for example, resting control with the majority of members on the roll at the time the dispute arose. In applying the sect's own secular default rules, the courts' principal concern, as always, would be to ensure fairness to the parties with the weaker bargaining position.

If the sect provides no such secular default rules, the courts will have to proceed as closely as possible to the way they would in other cases where the parties' intent is unclear. In the first instance, this would mean trying to infer the party's likely intent. Beyond that, the court will have to adopt default rules that best advance the general position of sects in a liberal state. In that regard, a preference for local voice, amplified by a presumed right to secede with congregational property, seems appropriate.

c) Jurisdiction to Resolve Procedural Issues

There is a final procedural problem that liberal courts must address. We have already seen how jurisdictional claims inside the sect can pre-empt substantive challenges to doctrinal disputes in the civil courts. Either faction can assert that the sect's fundamental rules unreviewably commit the substantive appropriateness of doctrinal change to a particular body within the sect. A structurally

[58] Z Chafee, Jr, "The Internal Affairs of Associations Not for Profit", 43 *Harvard LR* 993, 1024 (1930).

[59] The United States Supreme Court explicitly asked for such anticipatory help from churches in *Jones* v. *Wolf*, above n 46.

parallel claim can be made about procedure as well. It can be argued that all procedural issues, including charges of procedural irregularity, are committed by the sect's own rules to final review by an internal body.

It is extremely important to notice that the similarity of these jurisdictional claims, the one as to substantive issues, the other as to procedure, is structural only. The courts must treat them almost entirely differently. With respect to the substance of doctrinal disputes, as we have seen, the civil courts cannot, by their very nature, have any direct role. Issues of substance must be resolved within the sect, whether or not the sect's internal rules so provide, because the liberal state cannot take positions on the rightness of fundamental views of human flourishing.

With respect to the process by which doctrinal disputes are resolved, however, the civil courts can, and should, have a much larger role. Though they cannot say, even as a matter of default, what any of their citizens should believe, they can say whether those citizens have gotten the process they agreed to, at least if that process has not been specified in esoteric terms. Moreover, even when the specified process is esoteric, courts can police whether particular constituencies of the sect willingly and knowingly submitted to such procedures.

Such submission should, of course, be allowed, as part of the citizen's right to join groups and freely determine the terms of membership in them. But the courts of the sectarian state should, on the other hand, be very wary of such claims, and should be open to challenges by the weaker party that esoteric procedures were not freely and knowingly adopted. To do otherwise would be to succumb to the libertarian tendency to assume, rather than ensure, that such individual concessions are what they purport to be, and thus to ignore the systemic biases in favor of institutions over against individuals.

B. Sect Charges of Member's Deviation on Essential Doctrine

So far in this part, we have focused on dissident challenges to changes in the sect's fundamental doctrines. As we have already seen, these disputes can, and often do, have another side: the sect may claim that it is not they, but the dissident members, who are falling into apostacy. In concluding our discussion of doctrinal disputes, we should, accordingly, examine the other side of the coin.

Sects, like voluntary organizations generally, must have the power to determine their own membership; the freedom to associate, as the United States Supreme Court has pointed out, necessarily includes the freedom not to associate.[60] Especially in the case of sects, the criteria of membership will be difficult to state in legally intelligible terms. This is partly because, as we have seen, the courts of the liberal state are inherently unfit to determine matters of fundamental doctrine, the substantive basis for sect membership. Who is a true Presbyterian is a question only Presbyterians can answer. The sectarian state is

[60] *Roberts* v. *United States Jaycees* 468 US 609 (1983), 623 (Brennan J).

also unfit to resolve membership issues because the characteristics necessary for intimate association with other members of such a group, the formal aspect of sect membership, are hard to specify in objective terms. Stated most Socratically—and also most problematically—how could a sectarian court determine whether someone evinced an adequate concern for the souls of fellow sect members?

Accordingly, the substantive bases for expulsion from a sect are ultimately not susceptible to judicial review. With respect to process, once again, the courts can and should insist that the member be given what the organization has promised. Ultimately, however, expulsions will come down to the merits, and on the merits the organization must have final say. Even if a member successfully challenges the process of his or her expulsion, the most that the courts can ensure is that the organization proceeds according to form in re-hearing the case.

The real problems with expulsions from sects have to do with ancillary effects, which are in effect penalties beyond the expulsion itself. In principle, an individual member, upon joining a sect, might agree to subject himself or herself to a very wide range of extremely severe penalties for doctrinal deviation. Beyond some point, these would become external, rather than internal, matters; the liberal state will not let prospective heretics bindingly agree in advance to being burned at the stake, branded with a scarlet "H," or relegated to slavery in the temple precincts.

But, short of these extremes, new members might agree to harsh penalties upon excommunication. They might, for example, agree to forfeit large initiation fees or capital contributions to the organization. Again, consistently with its policy of free association, and, even more basically, freedom of contract, the sectarian liberal state should stand ready to enforce these commitments at the behest of the organization against the individual. But, mindful of the relative bargaining advantages of the organization, the courts should also ensure that not a single extra ounce of flesh or drop of blood is extracted. In particular, the state should be careful to ensure that stigmatizing of the excommunicant outside the organization does not exceed ordinary civil restrictions on defamation, in the absence of very clear waivers.

The bottom line is this: a member's appeal to the state can very well be the basis for loss of membership rights in a sect, but membership in a sect can never be the basis for the member's loss of the right to appeal to the state. The former is an internal matter, properly committed to the sect and its members for their own determination. But the latter is an inherently external matter; the liberal state cannot allow its citizens, even with their full and knowing assent, to anticipatorily bind themselves not to appeal to its courts. In the liberal state, the right to protect one's rights must be an inalienable right; any citizen may at any time decline to exercise that right, but none may ever lose it, voluntarily or otherwise. This degree of subservience to the will of others is perhaps the one form of happiness that the liberal state cannot consistently allow its citizens to pursue. The liberal state may have to tolerate masochism, but it cannot countenance slavery.

C. Summary

The sectarian liberal state, by its own terms, must give to its citizens the maximum latitude in forming and operating sects, voluntary associations with the central purpose of promoting visions of human flourishing. On the other hand, it must stand ready to see that its citizens get what they bargain for. When it comes to doctrinal matters, this produces a deep tension: sects and their members can mutually commit themselves to any vision of human flourishing they care to adopt, but the sectarian state cannot police compliance with any such commitments. In that respect, the law lords fundamentally erred in the Free Church of Scotland appeal.

Yet this does not mean, as the English pluralists and some American courts have inferred, that the courts of the sectarian state can have no proper role in such matters. If they cannot examine the substance of such commitments, they can nevertheless ensure that such commitments are made and changed by the properly designated and constituted internal organs, by the agreed internal procedures. Sometimes, to be sure, even these formal matters will be worded in unreviewable terms; sometimes, they will not have been addressed at all.

In such cases, the courts should be very careful to insist that any departure from liberal processes be very clear. This is especially true of the ultimate liberal process, judicial review of disputes among citizens over basic civil rights like property. In fashioning default rules, the courts must be aware of both the disadvantages of individuals in dealing with groups and the particular virtues of voluntary associations. These considerations counsel strongly in favour of the Parliamentary resolution of the Wee Frees' case.

5. LIBERAL SECTS

From the sectarian perspective, as we have seen, the liberal state cannot provide all that its vision of human flourishing requires, nor can the market wholly make up the deficit. These missing elements are fraternity, close personal ties between biologically unrelated individuals, and faith; broadly speaking, fundamental commitments about the ultimate meaning and purpose of human life.

What the liberal state needs, accordingly, is a complement on the nonprofit side. That counterpart, predictably, would have complementary views about the internal affairs of sects and about the state's intervention into those affairs. This section first outlines the likely contours of any such liberal sect, then focuses on the one that best complements sectarian liberalism. Finally, it considers the attitude of liberal sects, particularly this latter, ideal model, toward internal governance and state intervention.

Before turning to these particular aspects of liberal sects, a few general words about their relation to the sectarian liberal state are in order. The liberal sect would not aspire to be either a microcosm or a private sector twin of the liberal state. Its geographic scope, as we have seen, might even transcend that of the modern state. This is implicit in one of its two critical provisions, which is a faith or, literally, a world-view. The other critical provision, fellowship, similarly implies a significant difference from the liberal state at its local levels of organization. For these would be domains, for want of a better word, of love, not law.

If the liberal sect is not, for these reasons, the twin of the liberal state, neither would it be the state's spouse. The liberal sect would not accept, much less seek, special favors or privileged status from the liberal state. Rather, its only demand on the state would be that the state itself be liberal, which, as we have seen, implies official agnosticism toward competing world-views. But this demand does have one positive implication that, if met, will put the liberal state at odds with some illiberal sects. That implication, which we will take up in detail at the very end of this section, is that the liberal state will guarantee each of its citizens a liberal education. This guarantee will offend the most illiberal of sects, for it will empower their members to seek and assess alternative worldviews, and hence to find new spiritual homes. In summary, if we may continue the analogy to personal relations, the liberal sect would be to the liberal state neither sibling nor spouse, but friend; as such, it would simply insist that the liberal state be true to its ownmost self.

A. Liberal Sects in General

From the critical needs for human flourishing that the liberal state cannot supply, we can extrapolate the basics of the kind of group that would be its charitable complement. Indeed, to paraphrase Voltaire, if such groups didn't exist already, we could easily invent them: they would be Religious Societies of Friends of Truth. Each element in this description warrants attention.

Friendship, understood in the classical, Aristotelian sense, would be the members' basic form of interaction. They would structure and conduct their intramural affairs as befits those who have the deepest concern for each others' souls. To produce and sustain the kind of world view that liberalism lacks, they would have to transcend the geographical and temporal limits of individual friendships; they would have to be a Society of Friends. Moreover, they would have to share more than just the formal ties of friendly intimacy; they would have to share a common substantive vision, a common view of what the good life is: in a word, a faith.

In that sense, their society would be religious, though not necessarily in the traditional sense of having an other-worldly dimension or even a belief in God. Rather, it would be religious in the broader and more modern sense captured in the theologian Paul Tillich's understanding of faith: that with which one is most fundamentally concerned, the core of human commitment. Religion in this sense is any search for fundamental moral meaning. In a religious society, accordingly, members share a common world-view, or ethos.

And that understanding of religion, finally, gives the sense of "truth" relevant to such organizations. They would seek truth not necessarily as a matter of objective, propositional knowledge to be found "out there" in the mind of God, the order of the universe, or the nature of human beings. Rather, the truth they seek could also be moral truth, as understood by American pragmatism, English analytic philosophy, and Continental existentialism. Minimally, such truth must be a viable way of living a human life in the world; optimally, it must be a way that free people would freely choose. As such, its proof would be in those who choose it, and in how they live. Truth in that sense, as fundamental moral meaning, is, of course, the one thing the liberal state, consistently with its own self-understanding, cannot provide.

At our present level of abstraction, we can say little about the content of any such group's particular substantive commitments. We can, however, make one important observation about the way in which these fundamental commitments are likely to be held. The beliefs of any sect that lasts for long will have both a dynamic and a static aspect. Such a sect need not adopt so radically dynamic a principle as Calvinism's "the church is constantly reforming itself." But even the most conservative of faiths must confront new situations to which the faith must be applied, even if the faith itself is never to change.

The obverse, the necessity of a static aspect, a retrospective perspective, is more obvious. Even in the most radically self-reforming of creeds, there must be a creed to reform, some beliefs that have been held by the community in the past, even if the community holds that those beliefs are to be held up to constant re-examination in the future. Even to proclaim, as some sects are wont to do, that they have no creed is, paradoxically, to announce at least a minimalist creed; their members are at least united in a common commitment, essentially negative though it may be.

The interaction of these two aspects, the static and the dynamic, means that sects will have a tradition, a shared history, however short, through which their community has developed. In the course of this history, much may have been abandoned, much preserved. Indeed, no single original belief may remain, even as, in the life-cycle of a biological organism, no cell present at its birth may remain at its death.

This process depends on the possibility that the friendships in a society of friends can transcend time, can extend beyond the lives of individual members alive at any particular time. Living members stand in a kind of dialogue with the ideas of those past, and expect those who come after them to take their own ideas seriously. They recognize that those who have previously belonged to their sect have a special claim on their attention: if these predecessors' faith is to survive, it will mostly be through their successors' efforts; on the other hand, the latters' very ability to engage in this dialogue is a bequest from the former.

Just as each sect must have a creed, with dynamic and static aspects, so it must have a policy, explicit or implicit, toward those outside the creed. For groups that are most complementary to sectarian liberalism, this policy will be universalistic; the group will see outsiders as potential insiders. This is not to say that all such groups need actively proselytize; it is only to say that they will make some provision for outsiders to receive their message as true. Thus, for example, contemporary Anabaptists, who see themselves as essentially separate from society, make provision for outsiders to come in, albeit unbidden. Those who erect cities on hills for the instruction of the world generally assume that, however far below them the world may be, someone down there may see their light and, if successful in the climb, seek admittance at the gate.

This universalist perspective is important for sectarian liberalism because it assures that such groups will, at least minimally, engage in dialogue with others. They will be willing to try to explain their way, their "truth," to others in language the others can understand. In this way, they will thus contribute, at least when asked, to the dialogue about the meaning of life that the sectarian state most cherishes.

To better grasp this universalistic perspective and its significance for sectarian liberalism, consider what it would mean for an organization to lack it. Such a group would have to assume that no outsiders would be either willing or able to join. Its new members would presumably have to be the children of former members. Yet, if they alone were able to become members, there would have to be something very special about either their heredity or their environment. If the distinction were deemed hereditary, the group would have to be profoundly racist. Such groups could contribute to liberal society's dialogue about the meaning of life only in a negative way, by implicitly calling the legitimacy of that dialogue's universality into question. If the distinction were deemed environmental, the group would hardly seem voluntary. Such groups would seriously detract from liberal dialogue by rendering certain citizens, the children of its members, unable to enter that dialogue meaningfully.

To achieve a scope beyond the strictly local, and certainly to attain an international reach, the society of friends would have to have a federal structure. Within this structure, procedure would be governed by the aim of Aristotelian friendship, collaborative improvement of each others' souls. Love, not law, would be the regulatory ideal. Members would treat each other, not as the anonymous, abstract, and atomistic rights-bearers of liberal law, but as beloved fellow members with known needs, abilities, failures, and limitations. Policy decisions would have to be made deliberatively, as civic republicans understand that term.

This leaves room, of course, for immense institutional latitude. To borrow a metric calibrated in the Anglican Communion, such societies could range beyond the extremely High Church at the top right through the Oxford Movement to reunion with Rome in its post-Pius IX, papo-centric form. And it could run, in the other direction, below the Lowest Church evangelicals right out of the Establishment, into the most sectarian of sects, the Quakers. For purposes of our discussion, I want to move in this latter direction.

B. The Model Liberal Sect: An Ideal Society of Friends

If, as I believe, the Cromwellian commonwealth was the prototypical sectarian state, the early Quakers were its nearly ideal complement. Indeed, Quakerism was born in the very era in which sectarianism flourished in England, the time of the Puritan Revolution. Quakers were, in a sense, the most Puritanical of Puritans, and the most sectarian of sects. Out-purifying the Puritans, they reduced their worship essentially to purification itself, to a regular, meditative conversation about how to live well.

In practice if not entirely in principle, the leaders of the Commonwealth and the Quakers each seemed to realize this about the other. Cromwell accommodated, as much as his more orthodox subordinates would allow, the peculiar religious and even civil practices of the Quakers. Perhaps most importantly, he stayed in direct personal dialogue with their leaders. Indeed, according to the most prominent of these, George Fox, the Lord Protector said, "Come again to my house, for if thou and I were but an hour together we should be nearer one another."[61] Perhaps, of course, his comment was facetious, or even apocryphal; I rather suspect, however, that it was far-sighted.

In the remainder of this section, I want to sketch out the ideal Society of Friends' position on two related matters: its own handling of internal disputes, and the intervention of the state in those disputes. Both discussions will borrow heavily from the historical practice of the Quakers, particularly in their encounters with the liberal state. It should be borne in mind, however, that my ideal Society of Friends bears about the same relation to the historical Quakers as my sectarian liberal state does to existing liberal states.

1. *Internal Organization and Dispute Resolution*

The fraternal, friendly mode of decision-making is the essence of the traditional Quaker voteless "business" meeting.[62] Its process is deeply deliberative, not parliamentary. Efficiency is subordinate to rightness of outcome, and rightness of outcome, in turn, depends on "gathering the sense of the meeting." All members are encouraged to speak their minds, but only with a mind toward finding a position in which the meeting can unite. Individual members don't "stand against the sense of the meeting" unless deeply persuaded otherwise. On the

[61] George Fox, *An Autobiography*, above n 12.

[62] This description of the Quaker business meeting is drawn from H H Brinton, *Guide to Quaker Practice* (Wallingford, Pennysylvania, Pendle Hill, 1955), 30–6. See also M J Sheeran, *Beyond Majority Rule: Voteless Decisions in the Religious Society of Friends* (Philadelphia, Philadelphia Yearly Meeting of the Religious Society of Friends, 1983).

other hand, the group defers as far as possible to strongly felt minority and even individual views. The individual does not have a formal veto, but his or her voice is more than just a single vote, an increment toward a majority; the majority may indeed rule, but not before all dissent is respectfully heard.

The federal body will be a bottom-up rather than top-down hierarchy. Local bodies will send representatives to the higher bodies, where they will receive each other as friends of friends. Its meetings will, to the maximum extent possible among people who know each other less well, mirror the deliberative methodology of local meetings. But, since this reflection will be imperfect, higher levels must be viewed with a measure of suspicion. Matters of common interest may be delegated to them, but local meetings should remain the fundamental unit of organization.

Despite their commitment to harmony, the friends will occasionally reach an impasse at each level of organization. They will not be able to reach agreement and the dispute will be fundamental, in the sense that some will feel they must pursue a particular course, and some will feel equally strongly that they cannot. Such impasses should be extremely rare. But when they occur, secession will be an option, at all organizational levels, from the local to the international. This will always be viewed, on both sides, as tragic, without triumphalism.

The disagreeing groups will always strive to overcome it, and to continue cooperation on as many fronts as possible. Those who stay will do all they can to help those who leave, including offering them an equitable share of common goods. That share may well be more than a pro rata share, given the likely start-up costs of striking out on their own. The departing, for their part, will take no more than they need, particularly in view of the needs of those who remain behind, which may well increase with their departure. Indeed, the spirit on both sides will be as distinctly communistic at the point of their separation as at all other points of their common life: from each according to ability; to each according to need. Though they may well doubt that this is a viable basis on which to run a state, they will remember that it has often, and with considerable success, formed the basis of religious societies of friends. Finally, both parties will stay in dialogue, remembering the fullness of their former communion and earnestly seeking its early and complete restoration, consistent with the good conscience of all.

The same attitude would prevail in individual disciplinary actions within the society. Such actions would begin in informal and reflective consideration of the "unfriendly" conduct. If several friends concur in their informal assessments that something is amiss, they should, after discussing it among themselves, approach the offending member about the problem. At that point, they may become convinced that they have been mistaken, or the offender may accept their admonition to reform, or they all may reach an accommodation somewhere in the middle. If the problem is not resolved at that informal level, it may have to be brought to the attention of the full local fellowship. Here again, the offending friend should be given full opportunity to discuss the problem, and all feasible means of resolution should be open for consideration. Only as a last resort should the fellowship apply the final and ultimate sanction, expulsion from the meeting's membership.

The expelling meeting will always experience this as a tragic loss. Expulsion's purpose will always be twofold: restorative, as a final effort to bring the erring member back into fellowship, and protective of the sect, as a way of minimizing further harm. To these ends it may in a sense be punitive, but it will never be retributive or vengeful. Indeed, it will always be provisional; always done with the hope, if not expectation, of eventual return to the fold.

2. *Attitude Towards State Intervention*

Against this background of how the ideal sect, the model society of friends, would run their affairs internally, we can sketch their attitude toward state intervention into sects' affairs, first their own, then those of sects generally. With respect to the state's intervention into its own internal problems, the friends' position would be one of deep sadness, but not of total renunciation. Because of their basic commitment to amicable resolution of internal disputes, the friends would see any invocation of the state's authority as a failure, never more than a second-best solution to working things out among themselves. Friends would go to the state against each other only as a last resort; invoking the coercive power of the state would signal a fundamental breach of fellowship.

On the other hand, if litigation represents a fundamental breach of fellowship, then lawsuits almost automatically turn internal affairs into external affairs. Anyone who persists in suing the fellowship, after it has made appropriately generous offers of settlement, may have to be regarded as having renounced the fellowship, and thus as being no longer a friend, but an outsider (subject, of course, to the conditions, outlined above, on the restorative aspect of the society's internal discipline). Similarly, someone against whom the society can protect itself only by invoking the power of the state will almost certainly, by the same acts that gave rise to a civil cause of action, also have warranted severe internal discipline, ultimately resulting in expulsion.

Take, for example, the case of a local society's treasurer suspected of embezzling its funds. After confirming, through its normal internal procedures, that the embezzlement has indeed occurred, the society would try not only to have the funds returned, but also to have the embezzler him or herself restored to full, honest fellowship. But if the embezzler were unrepentant, the society might feel compelled to expel him or her. Even so, if the amount taken were relatively small, the society might choose, in light of a wide range of factors, including possible later reconciliation, not to sue to get the funds back. But if the amount taken were relatively large—large enough, say, to threaten the society's continued mission, or an aspect of its mission that serves especially needy individuals—the society might, quite consistently with its own principles, feel compelled to sue for their recovery. This would be simply an instantiation of the Pauline principle: concede as much as possible to those of tender conscience; yield nothing to those who would trammel your liberty for unworthy ends.

All this presupposes that the individual has voluntarily assumed the obligation to submit to the organization's final say, and understands what that say involves. Indeed, in order for the organization to hold a member accountable for a fundamental breach of fellowship in going to court, it must have made that principle clear as a matter of acceptance into membership, in terms of universal intelligibility. This is critically important because, if the sect has been faithful to its own principles in thus informing its members of the scope of the jurisdiction they are submitting themselves to, it will, in the eyes of the sectarian state, be entitled to great deference in its decision-making.

There remains, however, a final complexity: disputes that are not between a single member and the group, but between factions within the group, each claiming to be the true group. For reasons we have seen in connection with the Free Church appeals, the state cannot be expected to make this determination on substantive grounds. For its part, the ideal liberal sect would not believe that the state could or should attempt this. The decision, accordingly, will have to rest on formal grounds, jurisdictional and procedural.

Yet, in the case of our ideal society of friends, this, too, will pose problems. Their internal problems, as we have seen, will only come into court if their internal dispute resolution system has radically failed. Yet this internal process will in its very nature not be readily replicable or reviewable by a civil court. Its essence, as we have seen, is intimate, not abstract; particular, not general; in a word, loving, not lawful. By the friends' own admission, then, the state cannot possibly solve their problem their way.

The members, anticipating this impasse, will have two choices. They can either adopt legalistic procedures as a default mode from their preferred mode of dispute resolution, or they can let the liberal state muddle through as best it can, applying its own default rules. Under the former approach, they could adopt either a majority rule default mode, or vest final decision, in cases of radical disputes, in a single officer or body of officers, themselves deciding by a prescribed, legally reviewable procedure. Any such default system should be triggered by a legally cognizable event, perhaps the filing of lawsuit by one faction against another.

Under the second, default approach, the members would place the state in the awkward position of having to break their deadlock for them, under policy considerations that are probably not entirely theirs. The liberal state would have difficulty, both in theory and in practice, inferring the default rule that best promotes the internal goals of the sect. It would, presumably, have to fall back to rules that are either most conducive to the health of sects in general, most in accord with the likely wishes of sect members in general, or most consistent with the values of the liberal state. The latter two, at least, would usually point to majoritarian modes of decision and equitable divisions of property according to source. As the Free Church appeal makes clear, these two principles are not entirely consistent, but they can usually be reconciled.

Faced with these alternatives—choosing for itself a legal mode of dispute resolution or leaving that choice to the state—the ideal friendly society should choose the former. It would, presumably, try to establish that result closest to that which its own principles would produce: free departure of dissenters with need-based division of the assets of the formerly united society. It should be borne in mind that either side could, of course, be more generous to the other than the law requires and would, indeed, be required by its own principles at least to consider precisely that.

With respect to state intervention generally, the friendly society would be egalitarian. It would want no special treatment itself, but it would want like groups to be treated alike. Thus it would want the state to treat all sects, whether traditionally religious or not, according to the same principles, principles that take into account the special features of such organizations that we have already identified. Conversely, it would recognize the legitimacy of treating different kinds of organizations differently, and would thus accede to different treatment of voluntary groups that were less distinctive from governmental organizations on the one hand or for-profits on the other. From the friendly perspective, accordingly, pinochle clubs need not be treated for all purposes as if they were the legal equivalent of Presbyterian Churches, or of any other sect. As Blake put it, "One Law for the Lion and Ox is Oppression."[63]

The basic rule of intervention would derive from the essential voluntariness of sects. Individuals would be held to those commitments they had voluntarily made to the sects they join, whether those commitments are substantive, jurisdictional, or procedural. But, owing to the various asymmetries we have seen that stack the deck against the individual, the Society of Friends would accept as appropriate a fairly high standard of proving that those commitments had been made by a fully informed, fully mature individual. The Society of Friends would further accept that these commitments would have to be worded in the common language, the language of both outsiders and the law courts.

Any particular liberal sect has two basic motives for desiring the state's neutrality toward sects in general. One is essentially negative and skeptical; the other more positive and optimistic. On the negative side, sects might well be skeptical that, even if theirs is the one true way, the state will not have the capacity to recognize it as such. Unless the state itself is purged of unbelievers, these unbelievers are by definition not likely to be persuaded by the group's particular vision, and the hope of achieving such a purge has to be balanced against the fear of being persecuted. Something like this seems to have been the position of liberals all over Europe at the end of the exhausting religious wars of the mid-seventeenth century.

There is, however, a more positive perspective, the perspective likely to be taken by sects more compatible with the liberal state, particularly the ideal Society of Friends. These sects would see equality of treatment before the law as

[63] "The Marriage of Heaven and Hell", plate 24, in *Blake: Complete Writings* (G Keynes ed, Oxford, OUP, 1979), 158.

a positive good, as a condition of creating the "marketplace of ideas" in which their own version of the truth can be expected to win—or lose—on its merits alone. This, of course, is the thesis of Milton's classic plea for tolerance in *Areopagitica*,[64] a plea from the perspective of the ecclesiastical independents to the state, beseeching the state to be liberal.

3. *From Intervening in Internal Disputes to Advancing Common Ends*

This last, positive aspect implies a single but essential affirmative role for the liberal state in matters of belief: the state must ensure that its citizens are truly free, in the sense of being able freely to choose among the alternative ways of human flourishing offered by competing, legally co-equal sects. The state, in other words, must provide its citizens with an education that equips them to participate not only in a market economy and a liberal polity, but also in a religious plurality. Thus the liberal state may—indeed must—provide each individual citizen with a sense of history, a vantage-point from which to see the range of ways of being in the world, of being considered an excellent human being among one's peers. Optimally, such an education will show a wide range of ways, especially of those ways that have proved themselves by their ability to attract members without coercion. Minimally, it must show that there is not a single way. And, preferably, it should show that some groups' ways are destructive of freedom, and that members caught in such groups can escape, and have escaped, into freer and more fulfilling affiliations. The liberal state, from the perspective of liberal sects, is thus fundamentally obliged to provide a liberal—a liberating—education.

The Society of Friends will hope that liberal education will enable those who are not its members to join them in extra-mural dialogue, as Paul did the Athenians, even if they never actually join as members. Indeed, the Society would hope, not just to convert outsiders to its way, but also to learn from them, to join them in the search for a way of life consistent with, but more inclusive than, what had previously been theirs alone. For the failure of others to join freely may suggest, as nothing else can, that their own joining was not entirely free, and perhaps not entirely wise.

At the same time, the Society of Friends, like all liberal sects, would realize a painful paradox of liberal education: some traditional ways of life are very much endangered by it.[65] Sects that maintain that unthinking obedience to

[64] Above, n 9.

[65] As the United States Supreme Court has observed, "In short, high school attendance with teachers who are not of the Amish faith—and may even be hostile to it—interposes a serious barrier to the integration of the Amish child into the Amish religious community." *Wisconsin* v. *Yoder* 406 US 205 (1972), 211–12 (Burger CJ). To their credit, the more critical proponents of communitarianism are troubled by this dilemma. See R M Unger, *Knowledge and Politics* (New York, Free Press, 1984), 287: "The fourth major tension [within communitarian politics] opposes the demands of group cohesion to the ideal of a critical education that instructs in the past and present beliefs and creations of mankind in their richest and fullest variety."

authority constituted by others is the appropriate mode for at least some of their members will hardly find that liberal education enhances their position; sects that believe in limiting their members' exposure to alien ideas will find this principle very much at odds with a fundamental policy of the sectarian liberal state. Stated most starkly, freeing people to make their own choices is radically at odds with the goals of both authoritarian and obscurantist sects. Conversely, the ways of such sects radically challenge both sectarian liberal states and liberal sects.

This places the sectarian state in a paradoxical position: it cannot, on liberal principles, forbid the teaching of authoritarian or obscurantist principles; yet it must, on sectarian principles, give all its citizens the kind of education that minimizes their susceptibility to these same authoritarian and obscurantist principles. In the case of children of the members of such illiberal sects, this poses a truly tragic choice between the wishes of parents and the interests of their children. Even states that aspire to be most liberal have not always chosen the way that liberal sects and sectarian liberals must see as wise: freeing all children to make their own ultimate moral choices in light of a wide range of options, even if this enlightened freedom forever precludes choosing their parents' state of ignorant belief or blind obedience.[66]

Liberal sects would have to realize, of course, that their own children's beliefs are at risk in liberal education. Making such an education the right of all citizens allows liberal sects to reach outsiders, but only at the risk of exposing its own. But the cost of averting that risk is too great: from the perspective of liberal sects, it is nothing other that the precluding of true faith itself. As Milton said in the *Areopagitica*, "A man may be a heretic in the truth; if he believes things only because his pastor says so, or the Assembly so determines, without knowing other reasons, though his belief be true, yet the very truth he holds, becomes his heresy."[67]

Liberal education offers not only to eliminate this "heresy in the truth," but also to produce its necessary positive concommitant. At least in the tradition of the English sectarians, knowing the most tempting vices is a necessary condition to achieving the truest virtue. To quote Milton again: "Since therefore the knowledge and survey of vice is in this world so necessary to the constituting of human virtue, and the scanning of error to the confirmation of truth, how can we more safely, and with less danger scout into the regions of sin and falsity than by reading all manner of tracts, and hearing all manner of reason?"[68]

This faith, in practice, led Melville's Ishmael, though thoroughly Presbyterian, to bow with Queequeg in his idolatry, and, far more importantly, to converse with him on equal and intimate terms about every aspect of their lives.[69] And this faith, in principle, led Milton to challenge his own sect, the Puritans, to transcend themselves:[70]

[66] See *Wisconsin* v. *Yoder* 406 US 205 (1972) (affirming the right of Amish parents to terminate the formal education of their children beyond the age of fourteen).

[67] Above, n 9, 217.

[68] *Ibid*, 202.

[69] See text to n 11, above.

[70] Above, n 9, 221.

> The light which we have gained was given us, not to be ever staring on, but by it to discover onward things more remote from our knowledge. It is not the unfrocking of a priest, the unmitering of a bishop, and the removing him off the Presbyterian shoulders, that will make us a happy nation. No, if other things as great in the church, and in the rule of life both economical and political, be not looked into and reformed, we have looked so long upon the blaze that Zwinglius and Calvin hath beaconed up to us, that we are stark blind.

Amen.

It is in that spirit—a spirit no less universal for being quintessentially English, and no less liberal for being explicitly sectarian—that I offer my observations and welcome your comments. May our "little chat" go on—as Ishmael's and Queequeg's did, and as Cromwell's and Fox's would have, but for the Protector's tragically untimely death—until we become good Friends.

6. CONCLUSION (OR ANTI-CLIMAX)

In my title, I promised something of a theory of voluntary organizations and the liberal state. In my introduction, however, I narrowed our focus to state intervention in the internal affairs of voluntary associations, and, in part 4, I further narrowed our scope to the hardest cases for internal intervention, doctrinal disputes within intimately associated sects. I promised that understanding the proper role of the sectarian state in these hardest cases would permit us to interpolate back into easier cases. Here now—beyond the end of my paper proper—I have to confess that that project is beyond us.

But I can scope out how that project might, consistently with what we have seen in this present paper, proceed. Recall what made our hard cases hard. They arose in the class of nonprofit sector groups least like groups in the other two sectors, the for-profit and the governmental. Both the purpose of these groups, pursuing fundamental views of human flourishing, and their mode of organization, members' loving mutual concern for each other's fullest well-being, require the liberal state to give them the maximum degree of autonomy consistent with the liberal state's protection of the freedom of its individual citizens. In considering nonprofit groups that are less distinct in either or both of these respects, purpose and form, I suspect that we will find the need for deference correspondingly smaller, and the state's interest in protecting its citizens correspondingly greater.

Something of this pattern can be seen in the way contemporary American courts approach such groups. To the extent that groups are engaging in ordinary market transactions, the production and sale of goods and services, the state tends to subject them to the same laws as their counterparts in the for-profit sector. On the other hand, to the extent that groups resemble public-sector organizations, either because they perform quasi-governmental functions, as do some bar associations, or because membership is mandatory, as it is in some trade unions, the courts apply standards analogous to those applicable to governmental units. My tentative thesis—which will have to await another day's proof—is that this pattern is generally consistent with the principles of sectarian liberalism we have identified.

That still leaves us, however, with fully half of our territory unexplored. We have said little, so far, about the state's role in the external, as opposed to internal, affairs of voluntary organizations. At the outset, we defined, in somewhat formal and conclusory terms, internal affairs as those of principal concern to the group and, correspondingly, external affairs are those of principal concern to the state. Now we are in a better position to understand and justify the content of those definitions. Internal affairs are those that are most distinctive to the nonprofit sector, developing world-views and forming associations with friends. In these matters the state, if it is to be a liberal state, must tread with extreme caution and maximum deference.

This understanding of internal affairs should shed useful light on the other side. External affairs of nonprofits would seem to those that most affect either the market or some governmental function. Guaranteeing a competitive market economy and a democratic, rule-of-law polity are essential functions of the liberal state; when voluntary associations enter these realms, they must properly accede to the state's sovereignty and play by its rules.

By focussing on sects' internal affairs, understood in this light, we can thus see how to proceed with an analysis of the internal affairs of other voluntary organizations. Similarly, with this understanding of what internal affairs of voluntary organizations are, we can proceed to explore the proper role of the state in their external affairs. If I am right, this chapter will have been, as advertised, a proper prolegomena to a more fully developed theory of voluntary organizations and the liberal state. If I am wrong, I hope it will nevertheless be the occasion for a friendly exchange of views. That is the least one can hope for—and perhaps also the most.

7

Reviewing the Register

CHARLES MITCHELL[1]

1. INTRODUCTION

THE CHARITY COMMISSIONERS of England and Wales are currently undertaking a Review of the Register of Charities which they maintain, to consider:[2]

> whether those organizations which currently benefit from charitable status should continue to do so and whether there is scope to develop further the boundaries of charitable status . . . by the flexible use of [the Commissioners' powers] to apply and interpret the law.

My intention in this chapter is to discuss why the Commissioners decided to undertake this Review, how they have gone about it, and what progress they have made to date. I also propose to explore some of the implications of the Review for the way in which charitable status is determined under English law. I hope that this discussion will be of particular interest not only to those immediately affected by the Commissioners' activities—i.e. voluntary organizations in England and Wales, their users, and other supporters of their activities—but also to those participants in the voluntary sectors of other countries which have set up regulatory bodies similar in nature to the Charity Commission—for example, Singapore[3]—or which are contemplating doing so—for example, Canada[4] and Scotland.[5]

[1] Some of the material in this chapter has previously been published in an article, "Redefining Charity in English Law", (1999) 13 *Tru LI* 21, and is reproduced here with the kind permission of the editor of that journal.

[2] Charity Commission, *The Review of the Register of Charities*, leaflet RR 1 (Charity Commission, London, 1999), para 2.

[3] Under the Singapore Charities Act 1994.

[4] Broadbent Panel on Accountability and Governance in the Voluntary Sector, *Final Report: Building on Strength: Improving Governance and Accountability in Canada's Voluntary Sector* (Ottawa, Voluntary Sector Roundtable, 1999) (www.ccp.ca/information/documents/cp141.html), part 7 ("A New Voluntary Sector Commission"), esp 56: "the model we have proposed bears a resemblance to the Charity Commission of England and Wales". The Broadbent proposals are supported in A Drache QC, "The English Charity Commission Concept in the Canadian Context" (www.icnl.org/library/namerica/canadarep1.htm), but attacked in B April, J Clemens, and J Francis, "Preserving Independence: Does the Canadian Voluntary Sector Need a Voluntary Sector Commission?", Fraser Institute Public Policy Source Paper no 31 (Vancouver, Fraser Institute, 1999) (www.fraserinstitute.ca/publications/pps/31.html).

[5] On the present, rather fragmented, regulatory set-up in Scotland, see C R Barker, "The

In part 2, I shall describe the Charity Commissioners' status and responsibilities, explain the significance of registered charity status for voluntary bodies in England and Wales, and describe the ways in which the Commissioners have dealt with applications for registration, and so moved the law of charitable status forward, since they were first charged with maintaining a Register of Charities by the Charities Act 1960. In part 3, I shall consider why the Commissioners undertook the present Review of the Register, and describe what has emerged from the review process to date; I shall also examine some of the assumptions which seem to have informed the Commissioners' approach to the review process, although it is not my intention to assess their specific recommendations. Finally, in part 4, I shall suggest that the Commissioners' method of approach to the Review represents an interesting new departure for the way in which charitable status is determined under English law, but that it also requires us to revisit some tricky questions relating to the Commissioners' accountability as rule-makers.

2. THE CHARITY COMMISSION AND THE REGISTER OF CHARITIES

A. The Charity Commission

The Charity Commission is a non-ministerial Government Department, which was first established in its present form by the Charitable Trusts Act 1853,[6] and which now functions in accordance with the terms of the Charities Act 1993. It is broadly charged with overseeing the activities of all the registered charities in England and Wales. These currently number around 180,000, and their estimated total annual income is around £22.4 billion.[7] The Commission's budgeted expenditure for 1999/2000 is £21 million, and it has a staff of around 540.[8] It is overseen by two full-time, and three part-time Charity Commissioners, who

Regulation of Charities in Scotland", in A Dunn (ed), *The Voluntary Sector, the State and the Law* (Oxford, Hart Publishing Ltd, 2000) 87; also, Patrick Ford's comments in this book at 212–3. Proposals to institute a Scottish Registrar of Charities analogous to the Charity Commission are made in: the Commission on the Future of the Voluntary Sector in Scotland ("Kemp Commission"), *Report: Head and Heart* (Edinburgh, SCVO, 1997), paras 1.7.3 and 7.16.4; Scottish Executive Central Research Unit, *Scottish Charity Legislation: An Evaluation* (Edinburgh, Scottish Executive, 2000), chap 7; Scottish Charity Law Review Commission ("McFadden Commission"), *Consultation Document* (www.charityreview.com/docs/scl.htm), paras 2.1–2.4. By the end of August 2000, the majority of respondents to the latter document who chose to comment on this proposal were in favour: Jean McFadden, addressing the SCVO conference, "Modern Charity—Beginning at Home?", (Edinburgh, 7 September 2000).

[6] Discussed in R Tompson, *The Charity Commission and the Age of Reform* (London, Routledge & Kegan Paul Ltd, 1979), chap 9. At 212, Tompson comments that although the Board of Commissioners created by the 1853 Act was initially "innocuous . . . permanently understaffed, ignored, and isolated", it "proceeded to chip away at its task while it dutifully evolved a bureaucratic barony", and in due course "would become, by bureaucratic osmosis, much more than its blueprint implied".

[7] *Home Office Annual Report 1999–2000*, Cm 4605 (London, Stationery Office, 2000), 113.

[8] *Ibid*, 118.

are "answerable to the courts for their legal decisions and their interpretation of charity law, and to the Home Secretary and Parliament for the effective performance of the Commission as a Government department";[9] they must also account to the Treasury for the way in which they spend the Commission's budget, in accordance with the terms of the Commission's Public Service Agreement,[10] and their administrative competence is subject to review by the Parliamentary Ombudsman in the event that allegations of maladministration by the Commissioners and their staff are referred to him.[11]

Prior to the Charities Act 1960, the Charity Commissioners, like judges, were appointed by Royal Warrant for life *si bene gesserunt*,[12] a reflection of the fact that they were understood to act in a quasi-judicial capacity when exercising such comparatively limited powers as they possessed to intervene in a charity's affairs. Under the 1960 Act and successive legislation, however, they have been appointed by the Home Secretary and have been "deemed for all purposes to be employed in the civil service of the Crown".[13] Paradoxically, at the same time that the 1960 Act changed their status to render them less independent of the executive, it also considerably extended the scope of their quasi-judicial authority—by empowering them to make charitable schemes, for example, and more significantly for present purposes, by empowering them to determine charitable status pursuant to their task of maintaining the new Register of Charities.[14] The objection was accordingly raised to the Charities Bill 1960 in the course of the Parliamentary debate, that its cumulative effect would be that the Commissioners' "judicial status is to be destroyed, yet their judicial functions are to remain."[15] However, the Government responded to this by stressing that the Home Secretary would have no power to interfere in the Commissioners' day to day decisions, and that he would:[16]

[9] Charity Commission, *Charities and the Charity Commission*, leaflet CC 2 (London, Charity Commission, 1999), para 4. The Home Secretary and his junior ministers table the Commissioners' Annual Report in Parliament each year and answer Parliamentary questions relating to the Commisisioners' performance of their regulatory functions: see e.g. *Hansard, HC Debs*, 6th series, vol 344, cols 382–4, 9 Feb 2000 (P Boateng MP).

[10] *Home Office Annual Report 1999–2000*, above n 7, 113: the Commissioners report progress on meeting their PSA targets to the Treasury on a quarterly basis.

[11] As in e.g. *Case No C 1188/96*, reported in the Parliamentary Commissioner for Administration, *Sixth Report for the Session 1998–9* (upholding a complaint by a charity trustee that delays by the Charity Commission had led to a loss of earnings); *Case No A 14 00*, reported in the Parliamentary Commissioner for Administration, *Fourth Report for the Session 1999–2000* (partially upholding a complaint by the friend of a former charity trustee that the Charity Commission had refused to supply her with correspondence and other information relating to the charity) (both reports are available online at www.ombudsman.org.uk). The Parliamentary Commissioner Act 1967, s 12(3) prevents the ombudsman from questioning the merits of a discretionary decision taken by a body within his jurisdiction where no maladministration has occurred, and s 5(2) stipulates that the Ombudsman shall not normally investigate any matter in respect of which the aggrieved person has or had a remedy by way of proceedings in any court of law.

[12] i.e. "subject to good behaviour".

[13] See now the Charities Act 1993, Sched 1, para 1(3).

[14] This is discussed further in section B of this part, below.

[15] *Hansard, HC Debs*, 5th series, vol 622, col 479, 28 April 1960 (G Page MP).

[16] *Ibid*, col 480 (Sir J Simon).

> not be responsible [to Parliament] for their decisions in relation to particular charities, because it is their discretion and not his. In so far as they are answerable for the exercise of their discretion, they are answerable to the courts, because an appeal lies from their decisions to the courts and not to the Home Secretary.

The Charity Commissioners have themselves stuck to this line ever since, repeatedly stating that they are "independent of the political process",[17] because the Commission is "an extension of the High Court rather than of the executive",[18] and the Commissioners' "interpretation of the law in terms of what is a charity and what is not . . . and [their] regulation of charities [are] pro-judicial function[s]."[19] Whether matters have worked out quite so neatly in practice is a question to which I shall return below, in part 3, section A.

The Charity Commissioners have a range of responsibilities. One is to maintain the Register of Charities. This is discussed further below, in section B. The Commissioners are also charged with ensuring that registered charities are administered efficiently and honestly, by policing their activities and by providing them with such advice as they may need. Those registered charities with an annual income or expenditure of more than £10,000 must submit annual accounts and returns to the Commissioners,[20] who also have wide powers to institute inquiries into the administration of particular charities[21] and to require that people furnish them with information relevant to these inquiries.[22] In the event that they discover misconduct or mismanagement in a charity's administration, they can suspend and/or remove any of the charity's officers and appoint new ones as necessary.[23] With the agreement of the Attorney-General, they may also exercise the same powers with respect to the taking of legal proceedings with reference to charities as are exercisable by him *ex officio*, e.g. in order to enforce trust obligations against defaulting charity trustees.[24] They are further empowered to establish schemes for the administration of charities

[17] R Fries, "Charity and the Charity Commission", (1999) 2(1) *International Journal of Not-for-Profit Law* 1 (www.icnl.org/journal/vol2iss1/rfries.htm), 1.

[18] Select Committee on Public Accounts, *16th Report for 1987–1988 Session: Monitoring and Control of Charities in England and Wales, Minutes of Evidence*, 2 (D A Peach).

[19] Select Committee on Public Accounts, *7th Report for 1990–1991 Session: Monitoring and Control of Charities in England and Wales, Minutes of Evidence*, 4 (R Guthrie).

[20] Charities Act 1993, part VI.

[21] *Ibid*, s 8, discussed in A-M Piper, "Under Investigation", (2000) 144 *Sol Jo (Spring Charities and Appeals Supp)* 36. At 38, she states that "in our experience, the Commission is not always consistent in its approach to handling s 8 inquiries and it is difficult, therefore, to advise charities with any degree of certainty as to how long an inquiry will last".

[22] *Ibid*, s 9. Under s 11, it is an offence punishable by a fine or up to two years' imprisonment, either knowingly or recklessly to supply the Commissioners with false or misleading information, or wilfully to alter, suppress, conceal or destroy documents the production of which is required by the 1993 Act. For the purposes of the Public Disclosure Act 1998, the Charity Commission is the appropriate regulatory body to which "workers" for a charity can make appropriate disclosures on matters relating to the proper administration of the charity and the funds it receives or holds for charitable purposes. However, the Act does not apply to voluntary workers, as opposed to those with a contract of employment, and so does not extend to charity trustees and charity volunteers.

[23] *Ibid*, s 18.

[24] *Ibid*, s 32.

where it becomes necessary to apply their funds cy-près, or to adjust their mode of administration for some other reason.[25]

Until recently, very few members of the Commissioners' staff were employed on investigatory work—in 1986, 9 out of 330[26]—and in 1987, the Commissioners stated that they could not undertake the routine examination of charity accounts without substantial additional resources.[27] Further resources were subsequently made available, and the number of staff employed on investigatory work is now around 80.[28] Recurring problems in the administration of charities which have led to investigation by the Commissioners are the manipulation of charities by the trustees for their own benefit, conflicts of interest, aggressive fund-raising methods, absorption of funds into unjustified administration costs, domination of charities by particular trustees, and over-rapid expansion.[29]

In their role of "friend" rather than "enforcer", the Commissioners may give any charitable trustee an opinion or advice on any matter affecting the performance of her duties, and a charitable trustee acting on such advice is deemed to have acted in accordance with the terms of the trust.[30] But the Commissioners will not advise on policy matters or on legal questions concerning the charity's relationship with third parties.[31] In practice, they most commonly advise charities on how to simplify their administration, alter their trusts, amend their governing documents, transfer property, and appoint new trustees.[32]

The point has often been made, that the Commissioners' "supervisory and investigative role . . . does not sit too comfortably alongside their role as "friend", exemplified by providing advice to charities".[33] The Deakin Commission, for example, expressed concern that it has not always been made clear to charities when they are issued guidelines of best practice by the Commissioners that the Commissioners are acting in their advisory rather than their regulatory role, and that these guidelines are not prescriptive and should not necessarily be

[25] *Ibid*, s 13.

[26] Charity Commission, *Annual Report for 1986*, para 84.

[27] Charity Commission, *Annual Report for 1987*, para 29. See too the Select Committee on Public Accounts, *16th Report for 1987–1988*, *Minutes of Evidence*, passim.

[28] Much of this work is now undertaken by staff outside the Charity Commission's Monitoring and Investigations Divisions, making it difficult to quantify the amount of staff time spent on it, but according to a recent estimate, the amount of Commission staff time devoted to investigatory work has "effectively doubled" since 1990, when 40.5 staff were employed in these divisions: Piper, above n 21, 38.

[29] Charity Commission, *Annual Report for 1995*, para 51; *Annual Report for 1996*, paras 192–206.

[30] Charities Act 1993, s 29. The Commissioners owe no duty of care to the potential objects of a charity when giving such advice: *Mills* v. *Winchester Diocesan Board of Finance* [1989] Ch 428. When giving their advice, they must satisfy themselves that the action proposed is within the trustee's powers, and the trustee must supply them with sufficient information for them to make an informed decision on this point: Charity Commission, *Annual Report for 1991*, para 33; *Morley* v. *Mutual Security Bank & Trust Co Ltd* [1991] 3 All ER 198.

[31] Charity Commission, *Annual Report for 1982*, paras 24–26.

[32] Charity Commission, *Annual Report for 1996*, paras 123–5.

[33] G Moffatt, *Trusts Law: Text and Materials* 2nd edn (London, Butterworths, 1994), 709.

followed in every situation.[34] Critics from the Right have also made the more general argument, that the overlap between the Commissioners' roles as "friend" and "enforcer" has created unavoidable conflicts of interest, and that the Commissioners' natural sympathies for those working in the charity sector have led them to become a "fairly good friend to the sector and a very poor enforcer of legislative requirements".[35] A former Chief Charity Commissioner has replied to criticisms of this sort that "although combining the "policing" with the "friend" roles requires sensitivity, there is no conflict between them",[36] and he has stressed that:[37]

> although reasonably described as a regulator, the Commission's supervisory responsibilities have an essentially constructive bias. Even the investigatory function is remedial: to put things to rights, not to impose sanctions.

No doubt this defence of the Commissioners' performance of their investigatory and advisory functions will be found most persuasive by those who believe that the charity sector requires a light regulatory touch.[38] This is a controversial issue because not everyone agrees how big and how intrusive the state ought to be, both as a matter of general administrative policy, and more specifically as a matter going to the relations between the state and the voluntary sector.[39] As is discussed further below, in part 3, section A, the Commissioners have come under repeated fire from the Parliamentary Select Committee of Public Accounts, for failing to regulate the charity sector to a degree which the Committee thinks appropriate. Yet many within the sector would argue that a heavy regulatory hand is precisely what it does not need, and that bossing charities about and holding them to account if they fail to meet required standards

[34] Commission on the Future of the Voluntary Sector ("Deakin Commission"), *Report: Meeting the Challenge of Change—Voluntary Action in the 21st Century* (London, NCVO, 1996) ("Deakin Report"), paras 3.16.1–3.16.10. The Commissioners have accepted this criticism, and have stated that henceforth their leaflets will distinguish clearly between statements of law, policy, and advice: Charity Commission, *Annual Report for 1996*, para 126.

[35] April et al, above n 4, part 6. See too *Hansard, HC Debs*, 6th series, vol 153, col 176, 16 May 1989 (M Latham MP, describing the Commissioners as "extraordinarily complacent and passive, and [in need of] a jolly good boot up the backside"); vol 193, cols 576 ff, 20 June 1991 (Sir G Gardiner MP, complaining of the Commissioners' continuing failure to restrain the repeated infringements of the ban on political activities by Oxfam which are referred to elsewhere in this book, by Alison Dunn at 57, n 2 and text, and by Michael Chesterman at 267, n 95).

[36] Fries, above n 17, 6.

[37] *Ibid*, 5. See too Charity Commission, *The Hallmarks of a Well-Run Charity*, leaflet CC 60 (London, Charity Commission, 1999), para 3: "Our task is to supervise charities actively, on behalf of the public . . . It is not just a question of taking corrective action after something has gone wrong. We prefer to work in partnership with charities to make sure that problems do not arise in the first place."

[38] Cf Select Committee of Public Accounts, *16th Report for the 1987–1988 Session*, *Minutes of Evidence*, 9–10 (D A Peach): "Sir Gordon Downey and his colleagues [at the National Audit Office] . . . say "Here is a £10 billion a year industry. Should it not be controlled closely and supervised day by day like a Government department or quango." I am simply saying . . . that one is dealing with the voluntary world and there will inevitably be a spectrum of competence and efficiency across the range of charities; and provided the trustees behave with propriety in carrying out their trusts, then their independence must be respected."

[39] As discussed by Rob Atkinson in this book at 138–47.

of managerial competence will stifle their independence, creativity, and diversity—the very things, in short, which make the voluntary sector valuable to society at large.[40]

Thus, for example, Lord Dahrendorf has argued that:[41]

> [the] whole point of voluntary and charitable activity is that it can be idiosyncratic in purpose, amateurish in organization, prone to make mistakes, and even fail in its objectives . . . Government in general should let the associations of voluntary action get on with their jobs even if some of their funding is taxpayers' money.

In a similar vein, Sheridan has written that:[42]

> people engaged in voluntary work or supporting it financially can prize their independence fiercely, resent interference and lose heart if subjected to control. There is no point in increasing the purity of charity administration if one of the by-products is the drying up of the springs of generosity.

And Quint has argued that:[43]

> it is of vital importance to the health of the charity sector and of charity law that its development should be protected from Government or other "official" interference, since a flourishing and pluralistic charity sector is one of the signs that the essential freedoms of the individual are in good shape.

Perhaps the last word in this section should go to Chesterman, however, who has offered the more cautious assessment that:[44]

> resistance by charities and their supporters to *any* form of state supervision has always been based on this assumption that "the springs of charity will dry up". The enactment, for example, of the Charitable Trusts Acts 1853–60, which nowadays seem tentative and innocuous, was strenuously resisted on this ground. It therefore cannot be predicted with total confidence that further extensions of state power, in the overall interests of state welfare, will necessarily have such an effect.

B. The Register of Charities

Since the enactment of the Charities Act 1960, most—though by no means all—voluntary organizations who possess charitable status have been required to apply to the Charity Commissioners for entry onto the Register of Charities.[45]

[40] Compare Sue Moody's comments in this book at 99–104, where she considers the pressures on voluntary activists to become more "professional", a theme which is also considered by Michael Chesterman in this book at 251–2, and in J Lewis, "Reviewing the Relationship between the Voluntary Sector and the State in Britain in the 1990s", (1999) 10(3) *Voluntas* 255.

[41] *Hansard, HL Debs*, 5th series, vol 576, cols 315–16, 27 Nov 1996.

[42] L A Sheridan, "The Movement for Charity Reform", [1976] *Malayan LJ* lii, lxiii.

[43] F Quint,"The Rationale for Charity Law", (1994) 2 *Charity Law and Practice Rev* 211, 216.

[44] M Chesterman, *Charities, Trusts and Social Welfare* (London, Weidenfeld and Nicolson, 1979), 406.

[45] See now Charities Act 1993, s 3. Charities which are excepted from this requirement are specified in s 3(2). The Commissioners' internal operational guidance notes to their staff on exempt charities were recently posted on their website (www.charity-commission.gov.uk), as was a consultation document: *Charity Registration: When Should It Be Voluntary?*

In theory, the effect of a decision by the Commissioners to register an institution is not to establish its possession of legal charitable status, but merely to confirm it,[46] and it does not necessarily follow from the fact that the Commissioners have refused to register a body that it is not legally charitable.[47] However, registration leads to a conclusive statutory presumption that the institution in question is or was legally charitable at any time while it is or was registered,[48] and in practice "a body refused registration as a charity will be hard put to it to prove, for example to the Inland Revenue authorities, that it is nevertheless charitable".[49] Moreover, the courts have always treated the Commissioners' registration decisions as accurate statements of the law of charitable status, with the result that those who wish to challenge them must discharge the burden of proving that they are inconsistent with some other binding authority, whether statutory or judicial. Perhaps surprisingly, the Commissioners' quasi-judicial power to determine charitable status "is nowhere made explicit"[50] in the 1960 Act or in subsequent legislation, but it was clearly contemplated by those who enacted the 1960 Act that the Commissioners would be "exercising a judicial discretion" when considering applications for entry onto the Register,[51] and consistently with this,[52] the 1960 Act and succeeding legislation have all provided for appeals to the High Court from the Commissioners' decisions. The Charities Act 1993, ss 4(2) and (3) now respectively provide that "any person who is or may be affected by the registration of an institution as a charity" may appeal from the Commissioners' decision to register it as such, and that the "persons who are or claim to be the charity trustees of the institution" may appeal from the Commissioners' decision not to enter it onto the Register.[53]

[46] *Charities: A Framework for the Future* Cm 694 (1989), para 3.3; Select Committee on Public Accounts, *7th Report for 1990–1991 Session*, *Minutes of Evidence*, 13 (R Guthrie).

[47] *Over Seventies Housing Assoc* v. *Westminster CC* [1974] RA 247; *IRC* v. *Oldham Training and Enterprise Council* [1996] STC 1218. See too Select Committee for Public Accounts, *7th Report for 1990–1991 Session*, *Minutes of Evidence*, 14 (R Guthrie).

[48] Charities Act 1993, s 4(1). The courts are bound by this provision when considering the validity of a gift to a charity which has attained or subsequently attains registration: *Re Murawski's WT* [1971] 1 WLR 707. It also binds rating authorities: *Wynn* v. *Skegness UDC* [1967] 1 WLR 52. But tax relief may be disallowed to registered charities if they spend their money on non-charitable purposes: *IRC* v. *Educational Grants Assoc Ltd* [1967] Ch 123.

[49] Sheridan, above n 42, lix.

[50] Drache, above n 4, 3.

[51] *Hansard, HC Debs*, 5th series, vol 622, col 480, 28 April 1960 (Sir J Simon MP). See too cols 412–13 (R A Butler MP), describing the Commission as a "quasi-judicial body" when performing this function.

[52] Cf Charity Commission, *Annual Report for 1966*, para 29.

[53] Until the Commissioners' decisions are successfully challenged by the appeal procedures provided by this section, they are lawful, and cannot be challenged by some other means, e.g. in an action for libel or civil conspiracy: *Gaisance* v. *Fries*, unreported, CA, 22nd July 1998; *Gaisance* v. *Charity Commission*, unreported, CA, 15th April 1999. It has not been tested in the English courts whether a challenge by way of judicial review proceedings would be debarred for the same reason. To the extent that the Commissioners act as an extension of the High Court when interpreting the law of charitable status in connection with a registration application, one would not have expected their decisions to be amenable to judicial review in any case, but there are administrative aspects to their handling of applications which might perhaps be reviewable: cf *Alliance for Life* v. *Minister of National Revenue* (1999) 174 DLR (4th) 442, 484–7 (Stone JA).

Having said this, however, it must immediately be added that very few appeals from the Commissioners' decisions have ever reached the courts.[54] The Commissioners for Inland Revenue and for Customs and Excise are routinely consulted for their views on proposed new charitable purposes as part of the Charity Commissioners' decision-making process,[55] and even if they and the Charity Commissioners were to disagree about a proposed new charitable purpose, the revenue authorities would not challenge a decision to register a particular body unless they calculated that the loss in foregone tax that it threatened would exceed the cost of mounting a legal challenge.[56] Legal aid is not available to the officers of voluntary organizations wishing to appeal from decisions that their organizations are not legally charitable, and few such organizations have large resources at the time when they first apply for recognition as charities, or the inclination to spend their money (or to be seen spending their money) on the legal costs of mounting a challenge to such decisions.

It follows from this that the development of the law relating to charitable status has *de facto* been in the Charity Commissioners' hands for the past forty years. That this task would effectively fall upon them as a consequence of their taking responsibility for the Register was foreseen by the Commissioners themselves in 1966, when they anticipated that there might not be a regular flow of appeals to the courts, and that if they were to try progressively to meet the evolving needs of society, their decisions would inevitably move further away from cases decided by the courts.[57] In practice, they have sought to carry out this task by adopting the courts' own approach to determining charitable status, which is to follow binding judicial precedents when they are in point, and to analogize with previous cases where no direct precedent can be found.[58] In other words, to determine whether a proposed purpose is charitable the Commissioners have

[54] Between 1961 and 1986, only six refusals of charitable status by the Commissioners went to the courts on appeal, discussed in J M Fryer, "Charity Appeals to the High Court: Practice Problems and Reform", (1986) 136 *NLJ (Ann Charities Rev)* 20. Since then there has been *Southwood* v. *A-G* [1998/99] ITELR 119, affirmed *The Times*, 18 July 2000, and the Church of Scientology is currently appealing from the Commissioners' decision at the end of last year to refuse it registered status: *The Times*, 10th Dec 1999, 6. Chesterman, above n 44, 131, states that only three revenue appeals reached the courts between 1961 and 1979: *Incorporated Council of Law Reporting for England and Wales* v. *A-G* [1972] Ch 73; *Construction Industry Training Board* v. *A-G* [1973] Ch 173; *IRC* v. *McMullen* [1981] AC 1; to this list can now be added *IRC* v. *White* (1980) 55 Tax Cas 651 and *McGovern* v. *A-G* [1982] Ch 321.

[55] J Warburton (ed), *Tudor on Charities* 8th edn (London, Sweet & Maxwell Ltd, 1995), 18: "in practice, if the Charity Commissioners are minded to register an institution they refer the case to the Inland Revenue to give them an opportunity to object." See e.g. (1995) Decisions of the Charity Commissioners 11, 17.

[56] "The Inland Revenue does not appeal just because there is some matter of 'principle' to be determined": Drache, above n 4, 4, citing the Chief Charity Commissioner as his source for this information. Drache also states at 5 that the Charity Commissioners are currently considering whether a bank whose shareholders are all charities can itself be registered as a charity, and that "the Commission tends to registration while the Inland Revenue has serious reservations".

[57] Charity Commission, *Annual Report for 1966*, para 33. See too *Annual Report for 1985*, para 25.

[58] Charity Commissioners, *Annual Report for 1985*, para 26. The broad outlines of the current English legal definition of charity are described elsewhere in this book, by Patrick Ford, at 206–9.

taken the strictly formalistic approach of looking to see whether they or the courts have previously held such a purpose to be charitable, and if they have not, of considering whether to "analogize" between the proposed purpose and some other purpose which has previously been held to be charitable. The Commissioners have declared their intention to act "constructively and imaginatively" and to be "robust" in their search for analogies.[59]

Just as the courts are not rigidly bound by precedent, but may reassess the charitability of particular purposes in the light of changing social circumstances,[60] the Commissioners have a similar power to reexamine whether particular purposes are charitable, even though this question has previously been judicially determined. Indeed, the power to remove charities from the Register on the ground that they are no longer charitable is expressly conferred on the Commissioners by statute.[61] On occasion, the Commissioners have therefore departed from judicial decisions on charitable status: for example, in 1983, when they declined to follow *Re Strakosch*[62] in holding that the promotion of racial harmony could be a charitable purpose;[63] and in 1993, when they declined to follow *Re Stephens*[64] in deciding to refuse registration to the Burnley Rifle Club.[65] As a general rule, however, they have tended to be fairly conservative in their approach to previous judicial decisions, and to respond with caution to invitations to depart from long established principles in order to widen the concept of charity at common law. Thus, for example, in 1997 they considered that such a decision "could only be taken by the court"[66] in the course of rejecting an application for registration by the North Tawton Rugby Union Football Club, on the ground that the promotion of mere sport is not a charitable purpose. In reaching this decision, they followed the Court of Appeal's decision in *Re Nottage*,[67] and various House of Lords dicta to the same effect, even though they considered that the decision in *Re Nottage* could:[68]

> usefully be reconsidered by the court in the light of the role of sport in modern conditions [and in particular] the decrease in the emphasis on, and amount of sport in schools . . . and the increased acceptance of the value from a health point of view of people of all ages taking part in healthy exercise.

Controversially, the Commissioners now consider themselves entitled to interpret an organization's declared purposes by reference to the activities which it proposes to undertake, when determining whether these purposes are charitable. In 1966, they stated that they were "bound by the decision of the

59 *Ibid*, para 27, cited in (1993) 2 Decisions of the Commissioners 5, 9.

60 *Re Foveaux* [1895] 2 Ch 501, 505 (Chitty J); *National Anti-Vivisection Soc* v. *IRC* [1948] AC 31, 42 (Lord Wright); *IRC* v. *McMullen* [1981] AC 1, 15 (Lord Hailsham).

61 Charities Act 1993, s 4(5).

62 [1949] 1 Ch 529.

63 Charity Commission, *Annual Report for 1983*, paras 15–20.

64 [1892] 8 TLR 792.

65 (1993) 1 Decisions of the Charity Commissioners 4.

66 (1997) 5 Decisions of the Charity Commissioners 7, 9.

67 [1895] 2 Ch 649.

68 (1997) 5 Decisions of the Charity Commissioners 7, 13.

courts to base [their] decision whether an institution is a charity upon the words used in its constitution or other instrument of government".[69] But they also said that they would not register a proposed new organization as a legal charity where its governing documents were obscurely drafted and so allowed room for doubt whether its future activities would be exclusively charitable.[70] And they have since moved to the position that they will not register an organization as charitable even though its stated purposes are clearly charitable in law, if they believe that its present and/or likely future activities do not fulfil these stated purposes, and are not themselves in the public interest.[71] Accordingly, they require applicants for registration to fill in a form stating not only what purposes their organization is formed to achieve, but also how it intends to achieve these purposes, and they state on this form that "we need [this information] to consider whether your organization is charitable."[72]

There are obvious practical reasons why the Commissioners have sought to develop the law in this way, namely that refusing to register an organization with charitable purposes but non-charitable activities saves them the bother of registering it and then immediately having to intervene in its affairs, to insist that it pursues different activities. Furthermore, as I shall discuss below in part 3, section C(5), a shift away from a solely purpose-orientated approach to determining charitable status might yet turn out to be a desirable move, if it enables the courts and the Commissioners to assess the spirit in which an institution's purposes are pursued when determining whether or not it is a charity. However, the Commissioners' "activities test" does create the problem for organizations which are given funds for charitable purposes that the donors cannot claim any tax or business relief on those funds in the event that the Commissioners refuse to register them because they dislike their proposed activities.[73] And as a matter of law, it is currently unclear that the Commissioners are in fact entitled to apply an "activities test". Judicial dicta touching on this question are not clear-cut,[74]

[69] Charity Commission, *Annual Report for 1966*, para 34.

[70] *Ibid*, paras 37–40.

[71] See e.g. Charity Commission, *Annual Report for 1996*, para 79: when reviewing applications to register "we consider whether the purposes of the organization are charitable in law and this involves us looking at both its objects and activities". See too Charity Commission, *Starting and Registering a Charity*, leaflet CC 21 (1998), para 63. For applications of this rule, see e.g. Charity Commission, *Annual Report for 1982*, paras 45–51; *Annual Report for 1990*, App A; and *Annual Report for 1996*, para 64: "We also had to decide whether JUSTICE's activities actually fulfilled the proposed purpose and whether they were of a standard that could be regarded as being of public utility."

[72] Charity Commission, *Application Form for Registering a Charity*, leaflet App 1 (London, Charity Commission, 2000), part 4. One of the Commission's charitable status team, Alison Pevely, recently confirmed at the SCVO conference, "Modern Charity—Beginning at Home?", in Edinburgh on 7 September 2000, that she and her colleagues look systematically at the proposed day-to-day activities of applicant bodies, to see whether they are well managed and capable of doing what they say they want to do.

[73] A point made by J Claricoat, quoted in H Picarda, "Charities Require Masters of All Trades", *The Lawyer*, 3rd December 1999, 3, where Lord Phillips' opinion is also quoted, that the Commission's pre-policing activities are "a big problem which is going to have to be curtailed."

[74] Compare *McGovern* v. *A-G* [1981] 3 All ER 493, 514 (Slade J), following *Incorporated Council of Law Reporting for England and Wales* v. *A-G* [1972] Ch 73, 99 (Buckley J); *A-G* v. *Ross* [1986] 1

and in 1991 it was apparently thought necessary to give the courts and the Commissioners an express statutory power to look at an organization's likely future activities when determining its entitlement to charitable status, by inserting a clause to this effect in the Charities Bill 1991.[75] When the bill was debated in the House of Lords, Lord Browne-Wilkinson took the view that the clause would "change the substantive law of charity",[76] and objected to its enactment on the ground that it would commit the courts and the Commissioners to an enquiry into the future intentions of an organization's officers which was essentially impossible, and which would increase the administrative and legal costs to be borne by voluntary organizations generally.[77] The further objections were raised to the clause in debate that it gave very wide powers to the courts and the Commissioners, and that it failed to make clear what criteria they were supposed to apply when determining whether an organization's proposed activities were in the public interest.[78] In the face of these criticisms, the clause was dropped in committee.

The task of assessing the Commissioners' performance as quasi-judicial law-makers presents similar difficulties to those which are encountered when assessing their performance as regulators, to the extent that it requires us to take a position on a number of political questions. At a technical level, I think that all would agree—including the Commissioners themselves—that it is desirable for them to be consistent in their handling of applications for registration, and it is not clear that in practice they have always achieved this, although I am unaware of strong evidence that this is an endemic problem.[79] Also on a technical level, I suspect that the Commissioners are wrong to think, as they appear to think, that the courts generally have the power to take larger steps than the Commissioners themselves in developing the law of charitable status.[80] I shall return to this point below, in part 3, section C(1).

WLR 252, 263 (Scott J); *IRC* v. *Oldham Training and Enterprise Council* [1996] STC 1218, 1243–5 (Lightman J), followed in *Larne Enterprise Development Co Ltd* v. *Commissioner of Valuation for Northern Ireland* [1998] RVR 221; *Southwood* v. *A-G* [1998/99] ITELR 119, 133–4 (Carnwath J) affirmed *The Times*, 18 July 2000, where Chadwick LJ held that a declaration of charitable trust, "like any other written instrument, must be construed with a proper regard to the circumstances in which it came to be executed".

75 Charities Bill 1991, clause 2. In Parliament two years previously, the Home Secretary gave the following answer to the question whether he would give the Charity Commission powers to examine and regulate religious charities before they are registered to ensure that they act in the public interest from the moment of registration: "That is the purpose of registration. Due to the shift in its priorities, the Charity Commission will be increasingly able to monitor and investigate at an earlier stage": *Hansard, HC Debs*, 6th series, vol 153, col 176, 16 May 1989. (D Hurd MP).

76 *Hansard, HL Debs*, 5th series, vol 532, col 836, 19 Nov 1991.

77 *Ibid.*

78 *Ibid*, cols 830–831 (Lord Richard).

79 But cf R Meakin, "Improving the Registration Procedure", (2000) *Trusts and Estates LJ* 24, 24: "the wording of objects clauses of charities which are already on the register can be followed exactly and yet registration still be refused." This apparent inconsistency may derive from the fact that the Commissioners now routinely examine an applicant body's activities as well as its objects clause, as discussed at 184–5 above.

80 See text to n 66 ff, above; and cf Charity Commission, *Annual Report for 1971*, para 10: "The Law is . . . what it is and we cannot change it."

Beyond these observations, however, assessing the Commissioners' achievement as lawmakers requires us to take a position on some political questions. These flow from the fact that decisions on charitable status have resource implications, in the sense that charities are entitled to tax exemptions and a decision to recognize an institution as a charity accordingly deprives the Treasury and rating authorities of tax revenue which the institution would otherwise have had to pay. To test the Commissioners' achievement, we must therefore decide whether we think that the money which has been spent on their own purposes by institutions recognized by the Commissioners as charities over the past forty years would have been better spent on purposes selected by the Government; and by the same token, we must decide whether money which has been paid as tax by institutions not recognised as charities by the Commissioners would have been better spent on these institutions' purposes than on the Government's. These are obviously questions on which great divergences of opinion are possible. The view appears to be fairly widespread within the English voluntary sector that the Commissioners are "timid",[81] "wary and conservative"[82] in their approach to proposed new purposes. But activists whose purposes run in new directions are bound to feel that the Commissioners do not move quickly enough to give them the recognition—and the tax breaks—which they deserve, and the Commissioners are not necessarily wrong to think otherwise. Moreover, a list of the main classes of new purpose which they have recognized as charitable over the past forty years scarcely suggests that the Commissioners have done nothing to acknowledge new ways of supplying people's changing needs. This list includes:[83] (i) social welfare, e.g. the care of drug addicts and AIDS sufferers, counselling and support for members of broken families and for young homosexuals, victim support schemes, and the relief of youth unemployment; (ii) cultural purposes; (iii) education, including pre-school playgroups and parent/teacher and home/school associations; (iv) protection and conservation of the environment, including the protection of historic buildings; (v) religious and cultural teachings of immigrant communities, promotion of racial harmony, and the integration of refugees into national life.

A related but deeper question is whether the Commissioners (and the courts, for that matter) are the appropriate people to take decisions on charitable status at all, given that these decisions have implications for state spending, and so should arguably be taken by an elected body. I propose to return to this

[81] Drache, above n 4, 4.

[82] Institute of Chartered Secretaries and Administrators, *Response to NCVO Charity Law Review Project Briefing Paper* (1998) (www.icsa.org.uk/connvco.html), 2, citing as an example the debate in 1996 over the registration of Justice, an organization which campaigns against miscarriages of justice and for reforms of legal administration.

[83] The following examples are drawn from: Charity Commissioners, *Annual Report for 1978*, para 60; *Annual Report for 1982*, para 30; *Annual Report for 1983*, paras 12–20; *Annual Report for 1986*, paras 35–6; *Annual Report for 1987*, para 14; *Annual Report for 1989*, paras 28–32; *Annual Report for 1991*, paras 73 and 78; *Annual Report for 1993*, para 27. See too the registered purposes of the Ethnic Minority Training and Employment Project, registered no.1050917, which was registered on 22nd Nov 1995.

question in part 4, below. It should be noted here, though, that as far as I am aware, the Commissioners have consistently avoided taking overtly resource-orientated considerations into account when determining charitable status, stating, for example, that it will not affect their decision that an applicant body's purposes are duplicated by an existing charity.[84] And it should also be noted that when challenged on the question whether their formalistic approach is an undesirably artificial way to determine charitable status, their response has always amounted to the statement that "if the judges are going to do it that way, then we are too".[85]

3. THE REVIEW OF THE REGISTER

A. Why the Review was Undertaken

In March 1998, the Select Committee on Public Accounts released a strongly worded report in which it criticized the Commissioners for failing to use their powers to enforce the accountability of charities in a more active manner.[86] This was not the first time that this Select Committee had taken the Commissioners to task: in 1987, it had issued a report which was broadly condemnatory of their "passive" and "complacent" attitude, and their failure to monitor the charity sector effectively,[87] and in 1991, it expressed itself to be "concerned" about the degree of progress made by the Commissioners in bringing the Register up to date and in chasing up recalcitrant charities which had failed to comply with their statutory obligation to file accounts.[88] On this occasion, the Select Committee concluded that it was "unacceptable", among other things, that in 1996 around 37,000 (24%) of registered charities had failed to provide annual returns and 36,000 (31%) had failed to provide annual accounts, and that the

[84] For the argument that the Commissioners should take a lead in planning the shape of the charitable sector, see e.g. R Meakin, *Charity in the NHS: Policy and Practice* (Bristol, Jordans, 1998), 16–17. For the Commissioners' refusal to do so, see Fries, above n 17, 6: "there are concerns that absolute freedom to set up a charity means duplication and proliferation. Our view is that raising standards and accountability is the best approach." In *Starting and Registering a Charity*, leaflet CC 21 (1998), para 44, the Commissioners offer the advice to applicants for registration that they should "think about whether it would be better to offer your services to, or combine with, an existing charity"; it is clear, though, that they would not refuse to register a charity simply on the ground that it duplicated the work of another body.

[85] See e.g. Select Committee on Public Accounts, *16th Report for 1997–98 Session, Minutes of Evidence*, 8 (D A Peach): "if one imports into a judgment in law about what is a charity considerations of value for money or usefulness or effectiveness, then one is starting to go towards a political system . . . [but what] we have with charity is a judicial system. We have a body of case law based on the four traditional heads of charity".

[86] Select Committee on Public Accounts, *28th Report for 1997–1998 Session: Charity Commission—Regulation and Support of Charities*.

[87] Select Committee on Public Accounts, *16th Report for 1987–1988 Session: Monitoring and Control of Charities in England and Wales*, para 4 (summary of conclusions and recommendations).

[88] Select Committee on Public Accounts, *7th Report for 1990–1991 Session: Monitoring and Control of Charities in England and Wales*, para 3 (summary of conclusions and recommendations).

Register was itself only 76% accurate.[89] It found it "unsatisfactory" that the Commissioners had no procedures in place to check that the prospective trustees of newly registering charities had not previously been removed from such posts by the Commissioners or the courts,[90] and it took the view that the Commissioners had failed to strike an appropriate balance between their regulatory and advisory functions, by failing to dedicate more than 8% of their staff to investigation work.[91] The Commissioners made the response to these criticisms that abuse and maladministration is a minor problem in the world of charities, but the Select Committee doubted "how much evidence there [was] for this view given the inaccuracy of the Commission's register of charities, its inability to secure proper accounts from many of them, and the relatively low percentage of its resources applied to monitoring and investigating charities."[92] It also regarded as too low the number of cases involving inefficiency or irregularity identified by the National Audit Office in the first three months of 1996 which had since been rectified (39 out of 232, or 17%),[93] although to some extent it seems to have accepted the Commissioners' response that the way in which their work in this area had been classified was misleading,[94] and it also acknowledged the outcome of surveys conducted by the Commissioners which indicated that 85% of charities were satisfied with the service which the Commissioners provided.[95]

In response to these findings, the Charity Commissioners initiated a number of administrative reforms within their department. More significantly for present purposes, they also announced that as part of their ongoing commitment to maintaining an accurate and up-to-date Register of Charities, they proposed to initiate a Review of the Register, to take "a long hard look" at the questions "whether those organizations which currently benefit from charitable status should continue to do so and whether there is scope to develop further the boundaries of charitable status by the flexible use of the Commission's powers."[96] Given that this initiative was taken in response to pressure from the Select Committee, it seems that it is not wholly accurate to say that the Commissioners are "independent of the political process"[97] when exercising their quasi-judicial power to determine charitable status. It is true that the way in which the Commissioners have gone about the Review, and the policy decisions which they have taken in the course of it, have not been influenced by political pressure in the sense that the Government (or any other political body) has lent on them to widen or narrow the scope of what is legally charitable,

89 *28th Report for 1997–1998 Session*, paras 7 (ii), (iii), and (iv), 26, 27, and 28.

90 *Ibid*, paras 7(vi) and 30.

91 *Ibid*, paras 7(xvii) and 61.

92 *Ibid*, para 8.

93 *Ibid*, para 7(xvi).

94 *Ibid*, paras 50 and 60.

95 *Ibid*, paras 49 and 59.

96 Charity Commission, *Consultation Paper: Review of the Register—Framework for the Review of the Register of Charities* (1998).

97 Text to n 17 above.

either in a general or in a particular way. Nevertheless, it may be said that the Review is obliquely the product of political pressure, insofar as the Commissioners felt obliged to justify their Parliamentary grant by undertaking to perform their quasi-judicial function in a new way. The strangeness of this can perhaps be appreciated if one imagines what the response of the judges would be to a message from the Lord Chancellor that he could no longer justify their salaries to the Select Committee for Public Accounts unless they began to develop the common law in a more imaginative and energetic manner.

B. What Has Emerged from the Review Process to Date

The Commissioners began by issuing a consultation document, seeking comments on their proposals for a Framework for the Review, which was intended to encapsulate the public policy criteria by broad reference to which their future decisions on the charitable status of registered charities would be made. This Framework comprised a list of the characteristics which the Commissioners suggested should be possessed by all organizations entitled to such status, and which included the requirement that their purposes have some "social value".[98] It was unclear whether this "social value" requirement amounted to the same thing as the "public benefit" test which already forms part of the English legal definition of charity. The list of characteristics also appeared to set up criteria for charitable status which went beyond purposes and included feasibility and managerial effectiveness—i.e. it appeared to represent a further drift by the Commissioners towards "pre-policing" by means of an activities test for charitable status which blurred the line between registration and regulation. Following criticism of the Framework document to this effect, the Commissioners therefore split it into two, dropped their references to "social value", and, broadly speaking, put their list of essential characteristics of legally charitable purposes into one leaflet, *The Review of the Register of Charities*,[99] and their guidelines on the way in which charities ought to be run into a second leaflet, *The Hallmarks of a Well-Run Charity*.[100] However, several of the essential characteristics listed in the former document still relate to the manner in which a charity's activities are pursued (for example, the requirement that charity trustees are "independent"[101]), and in the latter document, the Commissioners state that they are prepared to "work with any charity, *whatever its current stage of development*, towards achieving" best management practice,[102] suggesting that they continue to envisage themselves discussing the manner in which an organization is run prior to recognizing it as a charity.

[98] Charity Commission, *Consultation Paper: Review of the Register—Framework for the Review of the Register of Charities* (1998).
[99] Leaflet RR 1 (1999), Part 2.
[100] Leaflet CC 60 (1999).
[101] Above n 99, 6–7.
[102] Above n 100, 1 (emphasis added).

At the same time as they issued the Framework document, the Commissioners also announced that they proposed to tackle the Review issue by issue, and to publish consultation documents for each issue in turn.[103] To date, the discussion papers they have issued have all adopted roughly the same format: summaries of the current law and discussion of the ways in which it fails to reflect current social needs, and/or creates practical difficulties for voluntary organizations, are followed by suggestions for change designed either to expand the boundaries of charitable status in some way, or to alter existing practice with regard to the Commissioners' treatment of particular kinds of activity. These proposals for change have generally been presented by the Commissioners as incremental, and have often been supported by reference to the principles set out in their list of "Essential Characteristics of a Charity" in *The Review of the Register of Charities*. The consultation documents have been sent by the Commissioners to bodies and individuals known by them to have a general or specific interest in the subject-matter covered; they have also been available online at the Charity Commission web-site;[104] and soundings have also been taken at the Commission's road shows around the country.[105] After considering the responses they have received, the Commissioners have then issued policy documents in which they set out their conclusions.

The first consultation documents to appear concerned urban regeneration[106] and unemployment,[107] and following a consultation process these were followed by two policy documents, *Promotion of Urban and Rural Regeneration*[108] and *Charities for the Relief of Unemployment*,[109] in which the Commissioners announced their intention to recognize these purposes as charitable, subject to various limitations.[110] They have also issued three further discussion papers looking at specific purposes, namely community development, the provision of recreational facilities under the Recreational Charities Act 1958, and preservation and conservation,[111] a more general discussion paper on the degree to which

[103] Above, n 98, para 23.

[104] Their website address is: www.charity-commission.gov.uk.

[105] Charity Commission, *The Review of the Register of Charities*, leaflet RR 1 (London, Charity Commission, 1999), paras 6 and 7; for a description of the consultation process "from the inside", by a member of the Commission's "unemployment" team, see P Somerfield, "Reviewing the Register: Unemployment", (1999) 6 *Charity Law and Practice Review* 23.

[106] Charity Commission, *Review of the Register—Promotion of Urban and Rural Regeneration Discussion Document* (London, Charity Commission, 1998).

[107] Charity Commission, *Review of the Register—Unemployment Discussion Document* (London, Charity Commission, 1998).

[108] Leaflet RR 2 (London, Charity Commission, 1999).

[109] Leaflet RR 3 (London, Charity Commission, 1999).

[110] The first charity to be registered under both these new purposes was the Coalfields Regeneration Trust registered no. 1074930, registered on 30th March 1999.

[111] Charity Commission, *Consultation Paper—Review of the Register: The Promotion of Community Development* (London, Charity Commission, 1999); *Consultation Paper—Review of the Register: The Recreational Charities Act 1958* (London, Charity Commission, 1999); *Consultation Paper—Review of the Register: Preservation and Conservation* (London, Charity Commission, 1999).

a charity's purposes should enure to the benefit of the public,[112] a discussion paper on the degree to which central and local government involvement in the activities of a charity can prejudice the charitable nature of its activities,[113] and a discussion paper on the circumstances in which a charity can be removed from the register and the consequences of removal from the register for the funds of the charity.[114]

C. Aspects of the Commissioners' Approach to the Review

I do not propose to assess the Commissioners' specific proposals and findings in the discussion papers and policy documents they have issued so far, but I do propose to consider what the review process has to tell us about five general matters: the Commissioners' conception of themselves as lawmakers; the scope of their statutory power to remove charities from the Register; the significance of the Human Rights Act 1998 for their decisions on charitable status; their understanding of the extent to which public opinion should influence these decisions; and the question whether the purposes of a voluntary body are—and should be—the only relevant issue when assessing its entitlement to charitable status.

1. *The Commissioners as Lawmakers*

A feature of many of the Commissioners' discussion documents—particularly the earlier ones—is that they do not systematically make it clear which of their statements they consider to be statements of current law as declared by the courts, which they consider to be statements of current law as declared by themselves, and which they consider to be statements of desirable changes to the law as they currently understand it. Thus, the Framework document in particular suffered from the Commissioners' failure to make it clear which of the "characteristics of a charity" it set out were taken by the Commissioners to be legally required of charities as a matter of current law, and which the Commissioners merely thought it would be desirable for charities to possess. For example, they stated that a registered charity should be "able to indicate how its activities are, or will be, able to support its charitable aims",[115] without indicating that is debatable whether the judges currently agree that organizations should have to do this;[116] they also stated that a registered charity should be "run by a clearly identifiable body of people who have to take responsibility and are accountable

[112] Charity Commission, *Consultation Paper—Review of the Register: The Public Character of Charity* (London, Charity Commission, 1999).

[113] Charity Commission, *Consultation Paper—Review of the Register: The Independence of Charities from the State* (London, Charity Commission, 1999).

[114] Charity Commission, *Consultation Paper—Review of the Register: Maintenance of an Accurate Register of Charities* (London, Charity Commission, 1999).

[115] Above n 98, Annex A, *What are the Basic Characteristics of a Charity?*, para (f).

[116] See the cases cited in n 74 above.

for the proper running of the charity, including its general management and control",[117] without indicating that they do not have the legal power to remove charities from the register as a result of poor practice.[118] In subsequent documents they have taken greater care to indicate which of their statements they take to be statements of current law, but even so, they still do not indicate with sufficient clarity whether the courts or the Commissioners themselves are the authority on which they rely for these statements. Thus, for example, in the discussion document on *The Independence of Charities from the State*,[119] they state under the heading "The Current Legal Position" that "A body is capable of being a charity even though it has been set up by national or local government to take on government functions",[120] and also that "A body which exists to promote the interests of the State cannot be a charity".[121] The first of these statements can be directly supported by a judicial decision, *Construction Industry Training Board* v. *A-G*;[122] but the second appears to be the Commissioners' own formulation of what the law should be in principle.[123]

Perhaps because they are not in the habit of thinking of themselves as judges, the Commissioners do not seem to have attached much importance to these distinctions. As has been discussed above, however, the Commissioners have judge-like powers to change the law when they reach decisions on charitable status,[124] and it would be desirable if they were to display a greater consciousness of this fact when issuing policy discussion documents which purport both to summarize the current law and to propose changes to it. It may also be that to the extent that they do reflect upon their role as lawmakers, the Commissioners conceive themselves to be engaged in a process of "discovering" the law rather than "inventing" it. This at any rate appears to be the thought which underlies the statement by one of the Commissioners' Review team, that:[125]

> We were very surprised to see comment from some quarters which appeared to indicate that the Commissioners were intending to use the review process as an opportunity to reinvent the law.

However, judges—and Charity Commissioners when they act as judges—"reinvent" the law the whole time, and the view to the contrary, that they "discover" it in some Aladdin's cave of previously unarticulated legal principles is a

117 Above n 98, Annex A, *What are the Basic Characteristics of a Charity?*, para (d). See too Annex A, *What are the Additional Characteristics of a Well Run Charity?*

118 See n 130 below.

119 Above n 113.

120 *Ibid*, para 15.

121 *Ibid*, para 17.

122 [1973] 1 Ch 173.

123 For further discussion, see J Garton, "Charities and the State", (2000) 14 TruLI 93, 97–8.

124 Text to nn 45 ff above.

125 Somerfield, above n 105, 24. Cf the sources cited above n 46, affirming that registration does not confer charitable status.

"fairy-tale" in which no-one believes, as the House of Lords itself recently confirmed in *Kleinwort Benson Ltd* v. *Lincoln CC*.[126]

A final point relating to the Commissioners' conception of themselves as law-makers is that they apparently consider themselves to possess less power than "proper judges" to develop the law of charitable status on the ground of changing social circumstances. This emerges from their recent decision not to register the North Tawton Rugby Union Football Club, as I have already discussed,[127] and it is also made plain by the Commissioners in their leaflet on *The Review of the Register of Charities*, where they state that:[128]

> We do not have the power to change the law beyond the flexibility which is implied in the decisions of the courts. Any changes beyond that would need to be made by the higher courts or by Parliament.

An obvious problem with this is that it is quite unpredictable when the Commissioners (and the courts for that matter) will think the point has been reached, where a decision to change the law must be made by the courts rather than the Commissioners. It is notorious that different judges have different conceptions of when changes to the law of charitable status cease to be permissibly incremental and so within the courts' power rather than a matter for the legislature,[129] and by the same token, there seems no reason to suppose that the Commissioners and the courts will agree where the dividing line between the Commissioners' and the courts' respective spheres of authority might lie. But that aside, the more fundamental point must also be made, that if the Commissioners truly possess the power "to change the law [within] the flexibility implied in the decisions of the courts", then this must include the power to invoke changing social circumstances as a ground for changing the law. And this suggests that the true reason why the Commissioners have failed to develop the law in response to applications such as that of the North Tawton RUFC is not that they lack the legal power to do so, but that they lack the political nerve.

2. *Removal from the Register*

It is well established that the Commissioners do not have the legal power to remove charities from the Register as a result of poor practice or the misappli-

[126] [1999] 2 AC 349, 358 (Lord Browne-Wilkinson), and 410 (Lord Hope), both quoting from Lord Reid, "The Judge as Law-Maker" (1972–1973) 12 *JSPTL (NS)* 22.

[127] See text to n 66 above.

[128] Leaflet RR 1 (London, Charity Commission, 1999), para 12.

[129] It is instructive in this connection to compare the majority and minority judgments of the Supreme Court of Canada in *Vancouver Society of Immigrant and Visible Minority Women* v. *Minister of National Revenue* (1999) 169 DLR (4th) 34, both with one another, and with the Canadian Federal Court of Appeal's decision in *Vancouver Regional FreeNet Assoc* v. *Minister of National Revenue* (1996) 137 DLR (4th) 206, esp 213–15, where Hugessen JA held that the provision of free access to the Internet "information superhighway" was a charitable purpose by analogy with the provision of public highways and bridges mentioned in the Preamble to the Statute of Charitable Uses 1601.

cation of charity funds.[130] But it seems that in extreme cases of maladministration they may use their scheme-making powers to "dissolve a charity, transferring its resources to a comparable charity operating effectively",[131] and it is also provided by the Charities Act 1993, s 3(4), that:

> Any institution which no longer appears to the Commissioners to be a charity shall be removed from the register, with effect, where the removal is due to any change in its purposes or trusts, from the date of that change; and there shall also be removed from the register any charity which ceases to exist or does not operate.

The scope of this sub-section is touched upon in the Commission's discussion paper, *Maintenance of an Accurate Register of Charities*,[132] in which the Commissioners seem to contemplate that, aside from the situation where a charity has ceased to exist or operate, there are five grounds on which they can remove a charity from the Register. These are: (i) because they were supplied with false or misleading information with the application for registration, and so mistakenly believed that the institution was formed for purposes other than those for which it was actually formed;[133] (ii) because they overlooked a binding legal authority in existence at the time of the application which should have led them to hold that the institution in question was not a charity;[134] (iii) because they registered the institution as a charity in accordance with "a widely held view of the law" which prevailed at the time, but which the court subsequently declares to have been wrong;[135] (iv) because social circumstances have changed since registration in such a way that purposes which were formerly regarded as charitable have ceased to be charitable;[136] and (v) because there has been a change to the charity's constitution which commits it to the pursuit of some non-charitable purpose.[137]

Of these grounds for removal, ground (v) is uncontroversial, since it is expressly contemplated by the sub-section, and grounds (i) and (ii) are also uncontroversial, since they amount to mistakes made by the Commissioners at the time of registration, and it was accepted by Walton J in *Holmes* v. *A-G*[138]

130 Charity Commission, *Annual Report for 1997*, para 60. See too R Venables and J Morris, "Private Benefit: A Conundrum", (1999) 6 *Charity Law and Practice Review* 31, 33 n 5, glossing (1993) 1 Decisions of the Charity Commissioners 19. But cf the letter sent by the Charity Commission on 18th April 1996 to the Pagan Hospice and Funeral Trust (published by the Trust at www.demon.co.uk/charities/PHFT/letter-from.html), stating that in light of its continuing non-charitable activities "the Commission must consider the continued registration of the Trust as a charity"; the Trust was removed from the Register on 14th October 1998 for the reason that it had by then ceased to exist.

131 Fries, above n 17, 7.

132 Above n 114.

133 *Ibid*, para 13.

134 *Ibid*.

135 *Ibid*.

136 *Ibid*, para 17.

137 *Ibid*, para 18.

138 [1981] *The Times*, 12th Feb. Another case in which the Commissioners removed an institution from the Register on the ground that they had made a mistake at the time of registration is *The Scott Bader Commonwealth Ltd*, discussed in Charity Commission, *Annual Report for 1967*, App D, part III.

that as a matter of principle the Commissioners have the power to remove institutions from the Register on this ground (although he went on to hold that in fact the Commissioners had not made a mistake at the time when they registered the Deed in question). However, grounds (iii) and (iv) are less straightforward. To understand why, it must be appreciated that in principle judicial decisions which change the law can be made to take effect either prospectively, or both prospectively and retrospectively. In other words, a judge (or Charity Commissioner) can hold either that the law shall henceforth be different from what it was before, or alternatively that it shall henceforth be different and that moreover it shall be fictionally deemed always to have been different from what it was before. A decision to remove a charity from the register on the ground that social circumstances have changed—i.e. ground (iv)—would take prospective effect only, since it would amount to a declaration that the institution was a charity in law up until the date of the decision, but is a charity no longer. However, a decision to remove a charity from the register on the ground that it was not a charity at the time of registration, even though its charitable nature might have been supported at the time of registration by the invocation of legal authority—i.e. ground (iii)—would take retrospective effect, since it would amount to a declaration that the institution is not, and never has been, charitable.

Why does this rather abstract and technical distinction matter? The answer is that it can make a difference to what should happen to an institution's funds in the event that it is removed from the Register. For if it were removed on the ground that it was once, but is no longer charitable, then it would appear that its funds would have to be applied cy-près; on the other hand, if it were removed on the ground that it was never charitable, then prima facie the institution would get to keep them. In the latter case, though, the further question might then arise whether donors to the institution should be allowed to recover their money on the ground that they had mistakenly supposed it to be a charity at the time of making their donations. On one view, a restitutionary claim to recover on the ground of "retrospective mistake of law" would lie in these circumstances following the *Kleinwort Benson* case.[139] However, the better view is probably that the donors would be debarred from recovery by the Charities Act 1993, s 4(1), where it is stated that:[140]

> An institution shall for all purposes other than rectification of the register be conclusively presumed to be *or to have been* a charity at any time when it is *or was* on the register of charities.

That this sub-section would debar donors from recovering their money on the ground of mistake is supported by the fact that the Government seems to have contemplated that this should be its effect at the time when its statutory precursor was enacted as part of the Charities Act 1960.[141]

[139] Above n 126.
[140] Emphasis added.
[141] *Hansard, HC Debates,* 5th series, vol 627, cols 862–4, 21 July 1960 (Sir J Simon MP).

Finally, however, it must also be noted that the Commissioners themselves are the only source of authority for the view that s 3(4) empowers them to remove a charity from the Register on the ground that they have adopted a new interpretation of the law according to which its purposes are no longer charitable. And Picarda has argued to the contrary, that the Commissioners' statutory power to deregister an institution which no longer appears to be a charity is "confined, where it is a matter of the Commissioners' own initiative, to cases where an objection is raised about a change in the purposes or trusts of the institution or where there is an objection by a person affected by the registration who applies for it to be removed".[142] The opportunity to test this point arose in the wake of the Commissioners' decision that the purposes of the Burnley Rifle Club were not charitable,[143] since the gun clubs which were registered as charities at the time were then informed that the Commission proposed to remove them from the Register. However, none of the clubs challenged the Commissioners' power to do this, and the matter therefore remains untested in the courts.

3. *The Human Rights Act 1998*

The Commissioners say very little in their discussion documents about the way in which the Human Rights Act 1998 might affect their determination of charitable status, although it seems likely that they are subject to the prohibition in section 6 against public authorities acting contrary to the European Convention on Human Rights. The only reference to the statute I have found comes in the discussion document on *The Public Character of Charity*,[144] where the Commissioners take the point that an institution's human rights might conceivably be infringed if it were deemed non-charitable on the basis that the section of people it served was described in a different way from the section of people served by a registered charity with identical purposes, even though the sections of people served in both cases were essentially the same. Presumably the articles of the European Convention on Human Rights which might be breached in such a case would be Article 9, which provides the right to freedom of thought, conscience and religion, or Article 11, which gives the right to freedom of association and expression, along with Article 14, which provides the right to enjoyment of Convention rights free from discrimination. Whether disappointed applicants can rely on these Articles against the Commissioners should soon become clearer, as it seems likely that they will form part of the appeal by

[142] H Picarda, "Charity Review is a Review Too Far", [1998] *The Lawyer*, 9th June. See too NCVO, *Comments on the Charity Commission Review of the Register Draft Consultation Paper* (NCVO, London, 1997), para 3.

[143] See text to n 65 above. See too J Claricoat and H Phillips, "Removal from the Register", (1997/98) 5 *Charity Law and Practice Review* 13, 13, reporting a recent statement by "a spokesman for the Commissioners", that five registered charities set up to facilitate the payment of school fees "no longer qualify for this status, so we will simply remove them."

[144] Above n 112, Annex B, para B10.

the Church of Scientology against the Commissioners' refusal to register it as a charity last December.[145] In this connection, though, it is worth noting that Strayer JA recently gave short shrift to a similar argument founded upon the right to freedom of expression in the Canadian Charter of Rights and Freedoms,[146] in a case in the Canadian Federal Court of Appeal, *Human Life International of Canada Inc* v. *Minister of National Revenue*:[147]

> With respect to the Charter argument based on alleged infringement of freedom of expression, the basic premise of the appellant is untenable. Essentially its argument is that a denial of tax exemption to those wishing to advocate certain opinions is a denial of freedom of expression on this basis. On this premise it would be equally arguable that anyone who wishes the psychic satisfaction of having his personal views pressed on his fellow citizens is constitutionally entitled to a tax credit for any money he contributes for this purpose. The appellant is in no way restricted by the Income Tax Act from disseminating any views or opinions whatever. The guarantee of freedom of expression in paragraph 2(b) of the Charter is not a guarantee of public funding through tax exemptions for the propagation of opinions no matter how good or sincerely held.

4. *Public Opinion*

At the outset of the Review, the Commissioners indicated that they would take public opinion into account as a relevant consideration when they came to formulate policy principles as part of the review process,[148] and they have since reiterated their view that public opinion constitutes:[149]

> an important factor to be taken into account in the shaping of the legal understanding of charity . . . in so far as it represents . . . a general consensus; or people's views on what should as a matter of ethics be regarded as beneficial; or a common understanding of informed opinion.

It is hard to find fault with these statements to the extent that they represent a declaration of intent by the Commissioners to keep pace with changes in social values, whether or not they might also be interpreted as an indicator of the Commissioners' sensitivity to the accusation that they are an unrepresentative body effectively taking decisions about the allocation of public resources. However, the use of public opinion as a benchmark for charitability—assuming

[145] See n 54 above, and on this aspect of the case, see J Warburton, "Human Rights and Charity Law" (2000) 144 *Sol Jo (Spring Charities and Apps Supp)* 24.

[146] (Canadian) Constitution Act 1982, Part 1, being the (English) Canada Act 1982, Sched B. The equivalent article in the European Convention is article 10, considered in passing by Michael Chesterman in this book at 263

[147] [1998] 3 FC 202, 220–221. Leave to appeal to the Supreme Court of Canada was refused on 21st Jan 1999 (unreported, file number 26661).

[148] Charity Commission, *Consultation Paper: Review of the Register—Framework for the Review of the Register of Charities* (London, Charity Commission, 1998), Annex E.

[149] Charity Commission, *The Review of the Register of Charities*, leaflet RR 1 (London, Charity Commission, 1999), paras 13–14.

that it is possible to determine what it is[150]—creates the obvious danger that the wishes of the majority will come to dominate the determination of charitable status, and that in the process a vital part of charitable action will be suppressed. Thus, for example, NCVO has argued that requiring organizations to show that they have public approval:[151]

> could be extremely damaging for a sector that sees its strength and diversity in large measure in its ability to respond to new needs, and develop innovative ways of meeting that need. . . . Charities have often had their greatest success and made the greatest contribution when they have attempted to change public opinion by education and example.

And the same point has been made by a Canadian judge, Decary J:[152]

> To define charity through public consensus would be a most imprudent thing to do. Charity and public opinion do not always go hand in hand; some forms of charity will always precede public opinion while others will often offend it. Courts are not well equipped to assess public consensus, which is a fragile and volatile concept. The determination of the charitable character of an activity should not become a battle between pollsters. Courts are asked to decide whether there is an advantage for the public, not whether the public agrees that there is such an advantage.

The Charity Commissioners are obviously aware of these dangers, and have stressed in oral presentations on the Review that it is "not a popularity contest".[153] They have also stated in their gloss on the "Essential Characteristic of a Charity" that its aims should be "directed to the provision of something of clear benefit to others in society", that:[154]

> Another element of the benefit that many charities contribute to society is their ability to inspire others to volunteer to work on the charity's behalf, to offer financial support to achieve its aims or just to support, in general terms, the cause. *This is especially so of charities that are innovative, risk taking or fund research which can inspire others by their own example or by a direct appeal for public support.*

The dangers of deference to public opinion are worth emphasising, nonetheless, and those who would doubt this might wish to consider the criticisms which have been made of the grants to a range of organizations including refugee

[150] Cf H Picarda, "Charity Review is a Review Too Far", [1998] *The Lawyer*, 9th June: "Consultation with 'Joe Public', while possibly concordant with a 'touchy-feely' approach to government, is an inappropriate way of deciding what is in the public interest. Judges act on evidence, usually expert evidence, on the educational benefit of an educational object said to be charitable. . . . There should be no room for evidence gained through canvassing for opinions, especially where it is collected by unreliable opinion polls. Decisions on charitable status must be determined on legally relevant evidence and well-established principle and not on unclear criteria or popular soundings."

[151] NCVO, *Comments on the Charity Commission Review of the Register Draft Consultation Paper* (London, NCVO, 1997), para 4.

[152] *Everywoman's Health Centre Society (1988)* v. *Minister of National Revenue* [1992] 2 FC 52, 68–69.

[153] Richard Carter, addressing the Charity Law Association's Fifth Annual Conference, in York on 14th October 1999.

[154] Charity Commission, *The Review of the Register of Charities*, leaflet RR 1 (London, Charity Commission, 1999), part 2, para (a)(i) (emphasis added).

groups, minority ethnic groups, and gay and lesbian groups, by the National Lottery Charities Board, the body charged with distributing National Lottery money to voluntary organizations in the United Kingdom.[155] The most extreme criticisms—described by the Directory of Social Change as "virulent, bigoted and even racist"[156]—appeared in the tabloid press, but broadsheet journalists were equally happy to attack "controversial" grants, as was the former Prime Minister, John Major, who let it be known in 1995—no doubt for political reasons of his own—that some of the awards made by the Board "do not in my judgement reflect the way Parliament and the public expected the lottery money to be spent. From time to time, I think they make awards that are ill-founded and ill-judged."[157] The Board's director of communications has observed of these criticisms that:[158]

> There was an enormous amount of hoo-ha of a very emotive nature, you know, little kiddy-winkies are dying of leukemia and the horrid charities board is funding refugees and gays and it's all wicked. If you're a general purpose grant-maker, if you're making grants reaching out to some of the more challenging and difficult areas of society, not every grant is going to be warm and cuddly. . . . As [the board's chairman] observed in a rather acrid moment when we were having a going-over from the tabloids: "If we'd wanted a quiet life, we would have given the whole bloody lot to Guide Dogs for the Blind." Then everyone would have been happy.

5. *Purposes and Activities*

As I have said already, the Commissioners now routinely look at the means by which an organization proposes to carry out its purposes as well as the purposes themselves, when determining whether it is entitled to charitable status,[159] and they have carried this approach over into the Review.[160] As I have also said, the Commissioners have been criticized for this, on the grounds that their approach improperly blurs the line between registration and regulation, and that a body whose purposes are charitable should always be entitled to charitable status, regardless of the way in which it pursues these purposes.[161] The assumption underlying these criticisms, that a body's purposes and its activities can meaningfully be disentangled, seems questionable to me. But leaving that point for another day, I would like to suggest here that in any case it may be a mistake to suppose that charitable status should be determined by focussing exclusively upon a body's formal stated purposes. This is not to deny that the English courts have generally done it this way in the past, and have held, for example, that the motive of a donor is immaterial to the question whether her gift is a charitable

[155] Discussed in R Snoddy and J Ashworth, *It Could Be You: The Untold Story of the UK National Lottery* (London, Faber & Faber, 2000), 170–174.

[156] Quoted with approval in the Deakin Report, above n 34, para 2.6.7.

[157] Quoted in Snoddy and Ashworth, above n 155, 171.

[158] Quoted in Snoddy and Ashworth, above n 155, 172.

[159] Text to nn 69 ff.

[160] Text to n 99 ff.

[161] Above, n 73.

one.[162] My point is rather that the *spirit* in which voluntary action is undertaken is an important part of what makes this action "charitable" in a moral sense,[163] and that the law's failure to take this into account when defining what is legally "charitable" contributes to the public perception that the law is out of step with what "charity" is all about. Whatever the rights and wrongs of the Charity Commissioners' desire to "pre-police" organizations applying for entry onto the Register, therefore, it seems to me that the real importance of their drift away from an exclusively "purpose-orientated" approach to determining charitable status is that it may enable them in the future to take the motives and the spirit of an institution into account when deciding whether it merits legal charitable status. Indeed, it may be argued that they already do this, to the extent that they will not register bodies whose constitutional documents contain a trustee remuneration clause, unless they can be persuaded that this is necessary for the bodies' proper administration.[164]

4. HOW ENGLISH CHARITY LAW IS MADE

When the Charity Commissioners first announced the Review of the Register, they seem to have been caught between a number of contradictory impulses, which nicely illustrate the quirky nature of their status as civil servants vested with quasi-judicial powers to develop the law. On the one hand, they wished to be seen to be responding in a positive way to the criticisms of the Select Committee on Public Accounts, that they had not done enough to maintain the credibility of the Register,[165] and therefore were not altogether unhappy to concede that the idea of developing the Framework for the Review as a statement of policy principles "backed up . . . by an informed consensus" was "admittedly novel".[166] On the other hand, they also wished to downplay the revolutionary nature of their undertaking so as to head off claims that they were acting without a democratic mandate and/or beyond the scope of their power to make incremental changes in the law. Thus, they stated in their Framework document that "the Review is about the law of charities as it is today and not about any radical changes to that law which are a matter for Ministers and Parliament",[167] they stressed in their accompanying press release that "this is not a revision of the law of charitable status . . . the aim of the Review is to see whether there is

[162] See e.g. *Hoare* v. *Osborne* (1866) LR 1 Eq 585; *Re King* [1923] 1 Ch 243.

[163] This seems to me to emerge most strongly from the chapters in this book written by John Gardner (chap 1), David Stevens (chap 2), and Sue Moody (chap 4).

[164] Pevely, above n 72; Charity Commission, *Trustee remuneration Consultation Document* (London, Charity Commission, 1999), para 25. For further discussion, see Sue Moody's contribution to this book at 89–93.

[165] See text to nn 42–49, supra.

[166] Charity Commission, *Consultation Paper: Review of the Register—Framework for the Review of the Register of Charities* (1998), para 29.

[167] Charity Commission, *Consultation Paper: Review of the Register—Framework for the Review of the Register of Charities* (1998), para 6.

scope to develop further the boundaries of charitable status by the flexible use of the Commission's existing powers",[168] and they stated truthfully but perhaps rather misleadingly (since it cannot honestly be said that the courts have been assiduous in this respect) that "the courts are increasingly setting out the underlying principles when deciding cases on charitable status and providing guidelines for future cases" and that it was therefore appropriate for them to do the same thing.[169] In their current leaflet on *the Review of the Register of Charities*, moreover, they continue to stress that there is "nothing new" about the review process,[170] save perhaps for the fact that issues are looked at in a systematic way on the Commissioners' own initiative, rather than in a piecemeal fashion, in response to individual applications.

The question therefore obviously arises, just how "new" the Review of the Register has turned out to be. My own view is that it marks an important new departure for English charity law, because the policy discussions contained in the Review of the Register discussion documents, and the consultation process in which the Commissioners have engaged, have rendered the development of the English law of charitable status significantly more transparent than was previously the case. The criticism has often been made in the past, that the English law of charitable status is "artificial",[171] because the courts and the Charity Commissioners have generally failed to make explicit the policy calculations which underpin their decisions on charitable status, and have instead played out an elaborate and "intellectually dishonest"[172] "charade",[173] in which the process of analogizing from previous charity cases has been treated as an adequate substitute for a policy-based analysis of proposed purposes, to determine whether they merit the advantages which flow from charitable status.[174] The courts and the Commissioners have always obviously been aware of the practical significance of their decisions to recognize charitable status, and from time to time they have remarked upon it,[175] or commented on the fact that social

[168] Charity Commission, *Press Release: Looking Forward to Charity*, 28th April 1998.

[169] Charity Commission, *Consultation Paper: Review of the Register—Framework for the Review of the Register of Charities* (1998), Annex D, *Charity Commission Powers to Determine Charitable Status*, para 8. The same wording is used in Charity Commission, *The Review of the Register of Charities*, leaflet RR 1 (London, Charity Commission, 1999), para 9.

[170] Leaflet RR 1 (London, Charity Commission, 1999), para 11.

[171] *Re Howley's Estate* [1904] IR 109, 114 (Gavan Duffy J).

[172] N P Gravells, "Public Purpose Trusts", (1977) 40 *MLR* 397, 401.

[173] P C Hemphill, "The Civil-Law Foundation as a Model for the Reform of Charitable Trusts Law", (1990) 64 *ALJ* 404, 409: "The claim that the courts do not decide these cases on the basis of public policy and the charade of pretending to find a body of law in the interpretation by analogy on analogy of a long-since repealed preamble to a statute of 1601 form . . . a blot on our jurisprudence."

[174] J Hackney, "The Politics of the Chancery", [1981] *CLP* 113, 119; S Gardner, *An Introduction to the Law of Trusts* (Oxford, Clarendon Press, 1990), 101–110. See too Quint, above n 38, 212: "a good deal of the law relating to charitable status is primarily instinctive, the rationalization being secondary. It is in the instinctive reaction that this or that purpose should be treated as charitable, and thereby favoured, that the true rationale for charity law is to be discerned."

[175] As in e.g. *Re Hobourn Aero Components Ltd's Air Raid Distress Fund* [1946] 1 Ch 194, 208 (Morton LJ); *Re Compton* [1945] 1 Ch 123, 137 (Lord Greene MR); *McGovern* v. *A-G* [1981] 3 All ER 493, 502 and 519 (Slade J). Cf *NZ Soc of Accountants* v. *CIR* [1986] 1 NZLR 147 (Somers J).

ideas and policy change, with the result that it might now be inappropriate to hold that a purpose is legally charitable which was held to be legally charitable a century ago.[176] In a well-known case, Lord Cross even held that "in answering the question whether any given trust is a charitable trust the courts . . . cannot avoid having regard to the fiscal privileges accorded to charities",[177] although three of the other law lords in the case disassociated themselves from these remarks.[178] However, it has been said that such cases are not the norm, that it remains broadly true that when determining "the vital issue whether or not an object is charitable . . . it is primarily to the Statute of Elizabeth and not behind it that the court [looks] for guidance,"[179] and that the effect of this has been to deny people the opportunity to challenge the unarticulated, underlying policy basis on which the courts and the Commissioners have decided that particular purposes do or do not merit charitable status. In my opinion, the force of these criticisms has been considerably diminished by the Commissioners' initiative in undertaking the Review, and by the opportunity which they have given to interested parties to debate the desirability of recognizing new charitable purposes on policy grounds.

The further criticism has been made of English charity law, that the resource implications of decisions on charitable status render the courts and the Commissioners unsuitable bodies to make these decisions, because they have no mandate from the taxpayers whose money they effectively spend when they declare voluntary organizations to be entitled to the tax rebates associated with charitable status.[180] I do not think that the Commissioners' actions in undertaking the Review have really met the force of this criticism, notwithstanding their statements that they propose to take public opinion into account. However, it should be borne in mind that the possession of a democratic mandate and accountability are not the only criteria by reference to which one might wish to assess the legitimacy of rules issued by a body such as the Charity Commissioners, and they would score much more highly if judged against the

[176] As in e.g. *Re Foveaux* [1895] 2 Ch 501, 505 (Chitty J); *IRC* v. *McMullen* [1981] AC 1, 15 (Lord Hailsham).

[177] *Dingle* v. *Turner* [1972] AC 601, 624.

[178] *Ibid*, 614 (Lord Dilhorne, Lord MacDemott, and Lord Hodson). At 614 Lord Simon briefly concurred with Lord Cross. For other cases in which judges have turned down invitations to enter into policy discussions, see e.g. *IRC* v. *Yorkshire Agricultural Soc* [1928] 1 KB 611, 634–5 (Atkin LJ); *Camille and Henry Dreyfus Foundation Inc* v. *IRC* [1954] 1 Ch 672, 704 (Jenkins LJ); and cf *D V Bryant Trust Board* v. *Hamilton CC* [1997] 3 NZLR 342, 351 (Hammond J).

[179] *Gilmour* v. *Coats* [1949] AC 426, 442 (Lord Simonds).

[180] It is interesting to note in this connection that when the Inland Revenue Commissioners began to reduce the scope of tax exemption afforded to religious and educational trusts in the 1880s, their policy triggered a protest from *The Times*, that they were attempting to fill the gap created by the absence of legal principles governing charitability to develop their own criteria at the cost of usurping a function of Parliament: *The Times*, 4th Sept 1888, quoted in D Owen, *English Philanthropy 1660–1960* (London, 1965), 334. This also struck Lord Macnaghten as offensive, in *Commissioners for Special Purposes of Income Tax* v. *Pemsel* [1891] AC 531, 591: "To my mind it is rather startling to find the established practice of so many years suddenly set aside by an administrative department of their own motion."

different criteria of fairness, expertise, and efficiency, for example.[181] Moreover, the effect of taking the decision out of the Commissioners' hands and placing it in the hands of a democratically elected body would be to prioritize the opinion of the majority,[182] with the real danger that various aspects of charitable action which have been identified by other contributors to this collection as comprising integral functions and virtues of charity might be eliminated or marginalized, as incompatible with the majority view, or indeed with the whole process of treating the question of where charitable funds should go as a matter of public policy: for example, the roles which charitable action plays of empowering disadvantaged and dispossessed minorities, fostering spontaneity of response to the misfortunes of others, and enabling self-giving.[183] This would not happen, if the majority attached such a large value to living in a diverse society of altruistic people who desire to give their time, energy, and money to others, who desire to give their money to the state for the public good, and who are encouraged by generous provision to initiate new and valuable ways of meeting social needs, that they think the maintenance of such a society is worth the cost of supporting particular voluntary activities which they think are valueless in themselves. I doubt whether that is currently a majority view. It is therefore hard to resist the conclusion that any reform of the law whose effect is explicitly to prioritize community values over individual values will leave these integral charitable virtues out of account.

[181] For discussion of these assorted criteria, and for the point that it is unrealistic to expect a rule-making body to fulfil them all, see R Baldwin, *Rules and Government* (Oxford, Clarendon Press, 1995) Chap 3, esp 41–57.

[182] Cf S Gardner, *An Introduction to the Law of Trusts* (Clarendon Press, Oxford, 1990), 112: "At least in societies which employ the democratic system, questions of social priorities are regarded as matters in which there is no objective truth . . . they are ultimately determined by the people, and in practice by the elected legislature, and by the executive under its supervision." For a classically majoritarian viewpoint, see eg G Cross, "Some Recent Developments in the Law of Charity" (1956) 72 *LQR* 187, 204: "There is . . . a compulsory subsidy of nearly £40 million a year paid by the general body of taxpayers to charities. In so far as the expenditure of charities is expenditure which the State would feel it proper to incur itself if it was not defrayed by charity, the exemption from tax is plainly justified. But although most expenditure on the part of charities is no doubt 'money well spent', it is hardly possible—especially in view of the breadth of the meaning of the word—to maintain that all income applied for charitable purposes deserves a subsidy of this sort."

[183] See variously, the contributions of Alison Dunn (chap 3), John Gardner (chap 1) and Sue Moody (chap 4).

8

Public Benefit Versus Charity: A Scottish Perspective

PATRICK J FORD

1. INTRODUCTION

THE ENGLISH LEGAL definition of charity has its admirers and its detractors, but the intention of this chapter is not to take sides. It is simply to present the definition from a Scottish perspective, to describe by way of comparison the equivalent Scots law concept of "public benefit", and to offer in the light of the comparison a tentative redefinition of charity which seeks to give effect to the recommendations of the Deakin and Kemp Reports.[1]

Both reports suggest that reform should be based on the concept of "public benefit".[2] Neither provides a draft redefinition as such, though the Deakin Report sketches out its essentials in some detail, recommending:[3]

> that the existing four "heads" of charity should be abolished and a single overarching charitable category be established, formulated in terms of benefit to the community. This definition would aim to be clear, workable and flexible. It would embody the essential altruism implicit in an organisation being established for the benefit of the community rather than for any private or sectional interest. The "community" in this context would be a sufficiently important section of the public and would include any identifiable Black and minority groups.

The Kemp Commission agrees "that a new UK legal statutory definition of charity is needed",[4] and proposes that a new definition:[5]

> should entrench, on a UK basis, the concept of public interest already central to the approach of both jurisdictions but should not be narrowly codified.

[1] Commission on the Future of the Voluntary Sector ("Deakin Commission"), *Report: Meeting the Challenge of Change—Voluntary Action in the 21st Century* (London, NCVO, 1996) ("Deakin Report"); Commission on the Future of the Voluntary Sector in Scotland ("Kemp Commission"), *Report: Head and Heart* (Edinburgh, SCVO, 1997) ("Kemp Report").

[2] Deakin Report, above n 1, Part Six: Summary of Recommendations, para 10; Kemp Report, above, n 1, para 7.16.3.

[3] Deakin Report, above n 1, para 3.2.6. The report also envisages (*ibid*) "that the fundamental test of charitability would remain an organisation's establishment for charitable purposes" (however defined), and should not include criteria related to achievements or activities.

[4] Kemp Report, above n 1, para 7.14.3.

[5] Kemp Report, above n 1, para 7.16.3.

These recommendations open the discussion rather than close it—or, more accurately, they continue a long-running discussion of which this book is a yet further instalment.[6] It is hoped that this chapter may provide useful new material for participants south of the Border by offering a Scot's-eye view of the existing English definition and showing how the concept of public benefit works in practice in the established Scottish system of public trusts. It points up the main areas of difference and overlap between the English and Scots approaches, and concludes by considering how a statutory redefinition of charity based on the Scottish concept might fare as a substitute, within the English system itself, for the existing English definition enshrined in the case law. Might this be what the Deakin Commission and the Kemp Commission and countless other reformers have been looking for all along?

The chapter begins with a brief account of the English definition and of its functions in both England and Wales and in Scotland; introduces the Scottish concept with a note on background, an outline definition, a summary of functions, and a note on certainty and the meaning of "charitable" in Scots common law; describes the Scottish concept more fully by reference to the decisions of the Court of Session and by comparison with appropriate English case law, concentrating first on the scope of Scottish "public" purposes, then on the Scottish understanding of "a section of the public"; summarises the points of difference and similarity between Scottish "public" and English "charitable" purposes; then proposes a statutory redefinition of charity based on the Scottish concept.

2. THE ENGLISH DEFINITION

It may be helpful for comparative purposes to outline at the outset the main features and functions of the existing English definition. As will be seen shortly, the definition is of great practical significance in Scotland, but it is undoubtedly still generally acknowledged by Scots lawyers as lying within a peculiarly English field of expertise.[7] The account given of it here, therefore, is not intended to say anything new.[8] It adopts an analysis found in one form or another in the major English textbooks,[9] and in consultation and guidance documentation issued by the Charity Commissioners.[10]

[6] For a recent summary of criticisms and proposals for reform see C Mitchell, "Redefining Charity in English Law", (1999) 13 *Tru LI* 21, 36–47.

[7] *IRC* v. *City of Glasgow Police Athletic Association* [1953] AC 380, 392 (Lord Normand); *Guild* v. *IRC* [1992] 2 AC 311, 323 (Lord Keith); Kemp Report, above n 1, para 7.15.3.6.

[8] For a general critique of the English definition, however, see David Stevens' discussion in this book, esp, at 47–9, and also Michael Chesterman's discussion at 253–61.

[9] See in particular J Warburton and D Morris (eds), *Tudor on Charities* 8th edn (London, Sweet and Maxwell, 1995) ("Tudor"); G Moffat, *Trusts Law: Text and Materials* 3rd edn (London, Butterworths, 1999) ("Moffat"); J Martin (ed), *Hanbury and Martin's Modern Equity* 15th edn (London, Sweet and Maxwell, 1997) ("Martin").

[10] For example, Charity Commission, *The Review of the Register of Charities*, leaflet RR 1

A. Definition

A working summary of the English definition can be obtained by putting together two well-known judicial statements, both, as it happens, pronounced in Scottish taxation appeals to the House of Lords. The first stipulates that:[11]

> The purposes in question, to be charitable, must be shown to be for the benefit of the public, or the community, in a sense or manner within the intendment of the preamble to the statute 43 Eliz. 1, c. 4.[12] The latter requirement does not mean quite what it says; for it is now accepted that what must be regarded is not the wording of the preamble itself, but the effect of the decisions given by the courts as to its scope, decisions which have endeavoured to keep the law as to charities moving according as new social needs arise or old ones become obsolete or satisfied.

The second states that:[13]

> it is not enough that one of the purposes of a body of persons is charitable: . . . it must be established for charitable purposes only.

This composite definition can be broken down into the following constituent requirements: the type of benefit involved must fall within the intendment of the preamble to the Charitable Uses Act 1601; the benefit must be public in character, in the double sense that its value to the public at large must be demonstrable,[14] and that those eligible to enjoy the benefit directly must constitute either the public as a whole or a section of the public;[15] and, if a charitable organisation is to have more than one purpose, each of its purposes must be charitable.

1. *Types of Benefit*

The benefit bestowed on the public by a charitable purpose must fall within the intendment of the preamble to the Charitable Uses Act 1601. A convenient starting point for assessing whether or not a given purpose meets this test is to see whether or not it falls within one or more of the four categories of Lord Macnaghten's "classification of convenience"[16] in *Commissioners for Special Purposes of the Income Tax* v. *Pemsel*.[17] The "Macnaghten categories" are the relief of poverty, the advancement of education, the advancement of religion

(London, Charity Commission, 1999); Charity Commission, *Consultation Paper—Review of the Register: The Public Character of Charity* (London, Charity Commission, 1999).

[11] *Scottish Burial Reform and Cremation Society* v. *Glasgow Corporation* [1968] AC 138, 154 (Lord Wilberforce).

[12] i.e. the Charitable Uses Act 1601 (my footnote).

[13] *IRC* v. *City of Glasgow Police Athletic Association* [1953] AC 380, 402 (Lord Reid).

[14] Or "provable": G S Plowright, "Public Benefit in Charitable Trusts", (1975) 39 *Conv (NS)* 183.

[15] Tudor, above n 9, 5.

[16] So described in *Scottish Burial Reform and Cremation Society* v. *Glasgow Corporation* [1968] AC 138, 154 (Lord Wilberforce).

[17] [1891] AC 531.

and other purposes beneficial to the community not falling within the first three heads.[18]

The fourth category is not, as might appear at first sight, a catch-all provision which allows any purpose beneficial to the community to be considered charitable: the type of benefit involved must be one which has previously been held to be charitable, or can be shown to be analogous to a form of benefit previously held to be charitable, or in the last resort can be connected back in some way with the list of charitable uses contained in the preamble to the 1601 Act. This requirement, therefore, acts as a restriction on the types of benefit which can be regarded from time to time as charitable.[19]

2. *Public Benefit: Demonstrable Benefit to the Public*

The requirement that, to be charitable, a purpose must be of demonstrable benefit to the public means normally that the benefit must be tangible and objective, but it may be enough that it is approved by "the common understanding of enlightened opinion for the time being".[20] The requirement may vary according to which of Lord Macnaghten's four categories of benefit is involved: the generally accepted rule is that benefit to the public is presumed under the first three heads—though the presumption may be rebutted—but must be proved under the fourth head.[21]

3. *Public Benefit: Section of the Public*

Those who are eligible to benefit directly from a purpose must be either the public as a whole or, in practice more commonly, an "appreciably important class of the community".[22] The point of this requirement is to prevent the direct advantages of charitable status accruing, not to the public at large or to some identifiable part of it, but to a "fluctuating body of private individuals".[23] It is accepted, however, that the difference between a fluctuating body of private individuals and a section of the public can in any given case be difficult to pin down. In particular, there are doubts about whether a "class within a class", or

[18] [1891] AC 531, 580 (Lord Macnaghten).

[19] It should be added that the scope of what is considered charitable does not rest entirely on the preamble to the 1601 Act and subsequent case law. The Recreational Charities Act 1958 was passed to confirm the "charitable nature of certain trusts and institutions which exist for the purposes of providing recreational or similar facilities, or whose purposes include the provision of such facilities in the interests of social welfare": Tudor, above n 9, 112. The charitable status of such organisations had been put in doubt by the House of Lords in *IRC* v. *City of Glasgow Police Athletic Association* [1953] AC 380 and *IRC* v. *Baddeley* [1955] AC 573.

[20] *National Anti-Vivisection Society* v. *IRC* [1948] AC 31, 49 (Lord Wright).

[21] Tudor, above n 9, 5.

[22] *Verge* v. *Somerville* [1924] AC 496, 499 (Lord Wrenbury).

[23] *Ibid.* See also *Dingle* v. *Turner* [1972] AC 601, 624 (Lord Cross).

a group of persons connected by "personal nexus", may be treated as a section of the public in the required sense.[24]

4. *Exclusively Charitable*

If an organisation has more than one object, then, to be charitable, all of its objects must be charitable. The purpose of the rule is to prevent the privileges of charitable status being allowed by association to activities which, considered on their own, would not be charitable. The rule is not absolute, however. In particular, some non-charitable benefit to the individual members of an organisation may be permissible if it is "of a subsidiary or incidental character."[25]

B. Functions in England and Wales

The definition of charity performs in English law functions which for analytical purposes can be treated as distinct: a trust law function, a supervisory function, and a fiscal function.

1. *Trust Law Function*

The definition marks out trusts with charitable purposes as different both from trusts for persons—trusts constituted for the benefit of ascertainable individuals—and from "private purpose" trusts—that is, trusts for the furtherance of purposes (rather than directly for the benefit of ascertainable individuals) which are not charitable.[26] Charitable trusts enjoy privileges under trust law not accorded to the other two classes of trust, the most significant of which in the context of this chapter is that a charitable trust is the only form of purpose trust which is enforceable by the court. By operation of the "beneficiary principle" of English trust law, a "trust must have a definite object. There must be somebody in whose favour the court can decree performance."[27] Trusts for charitable purposes are enforceable by the Attorney-General acting on behalf of the Crown as *parens patriae*,[28] but private, non-charitable purpose trusts are treated as unenforceable and are therefore, on a strict view of the beneficiary principle, void.[29]

Also of significance for the purposes of this chapter is the privileged treatment of charitable trusts under the English perpetuity rules. What this amounts to in non-technical terms is that a charitable trust, unlike a trust for persons (or a private purpose trust), may last forever. In the nature of things, a charitable trust

[24] See *Oppenheim* v. *Tobacco Securities Trust Co Ltd* [1951] AC 297; *IRC* v. *Baddeley* [1955] AC 573; *Dingle* v. *Turner* [1972] AC 601.

[25] *IRC* v. *City of Glasgow Police Athletic Association* [1953] AC 380, 402 (Lord Reid).

[26] Martin, above n 9, 347–359.

[27] *Morice* v. *Bishop of Durham* (1804) 9 Ves Jun 399, 404 (Sir William Grant MR).

[28] Tudor, above n 9, 324.

[29] Moffat, above n 9, 295–303.

established in perpetuity may require periodic reorganisation as social and financial conditions change, and the Chancery Division of the High Court (and the Charity Commissioners) may make a scheme adjusting either its purposes, or its administrative provisions, or both.

2. *Supervisory Function*

The roles of the Attorney-General and the High Court in the supervision of charitable trusts are ancient in origin but are supported by a statutory system[30] of supervision of "charities"[31] applicable not only to charitable trusts but also to organisations with charitable objects formed otherwise than as trusts. The system is overseen by the Charity Commissioners, who maintain a public register of charities and enjoy extensive advisory, investigatory, protective, remedial and disciplinary powers. The Commissioners' task of registration is a quasi-judicial one which involves applying the English definition of charity as it has been developed by the courts. In effect, however, because few cases on the definition reach the courts, the Commissioners have themselves acquired a key role in keeping "the law as to charities moving according as new social needs arise and old ones become obsolete or satisfied."[32]

3. *Fiscal Function*

The House of Lords established beyond doubt in *Commissioners for Special Purposes of the Income Tax* v. *Pemsel* that:[33]

> the expression "trust for charitable purposes" [in an income tax statute], and the other expressions [in such a statute] in which the word "charitable" occurs, must be construed in their technical meaning in English law.

The rule has been extended to other taxation statutes,[34] and to organisations with charitable objects other than trusts, with the result that the definition is the principal criterion by reference to which eligibility for relief from direct taxes is granted to voluntary organisations. Accordingly, an organisation which can show that it is established for charitable purposes only will be automatically eligible for a wide range of valuable tax reliefs.

[30] Now provided for by the Charities Acts 1992 and 1993.

[31] Defined in the Charities Act 1993, s. 96(1).

[32] *Scottish Burial Reform and Cremation Society* v. *Glasgow Corporation* [1968] AC 138, 154 (Lord Wilberforce). For commentary on the role of the Charity Commissioners in general see Charles Mitchell's chapter in this book (chap 7), esp at 176–88.

[33] [1891] AC 531, 587 (Lord Macnaghten).

[34] VAT is differently treated, however.

C. Functions in Scotland

The functions performed by the English definition in Scotland are at first sight very similar to those it performs in England and Wales. The trust law function has no place in Scots law, but the fiscal function is in principle the same, and there is a parallel supervisory function. The definition has an additional role in Scotland, however, which has, and can have, no counterpart in England—that of delimiting the legislative competence of the Scottish Parliament in the area of voluntary sector law.

1. *Fiscal Function in Scotland*

It may be best to deal with the fiscal function first, as the one which has received the most judicial attention. The effect of *Pemsel* in Scotland is the same as in England and Wales, in the sense that a body of persons established in Scotland for charitable purposes only, in the English meaning of the term, will be entitled to the same range of tax reliefs as its English counterpart. But the decision has some peculiar implications for the Scottish courts.

These were considered in full in *IRC* v. *City of Glasgow Police Athletic Association*,[35] which began as an appeal to the Court of Session from a determination of the Special Commissioners of Income Tax on eligibility for charitable tax relief. The judges of the First Division[36] refused to make any determination of their own, allowing the Special Commissioners' interpretation of English charity law to stand, on the ground that *Pemsel* demanded the application of English law in Scotland, which was foreign law. The Court of Session could treat the doctrines of English charity law only as inferences of fact, and could not, in the words of Lord President Cooper, "invest itself with the unique attributes, traditions and duties of the Chancery Division".[37]

When the Inland Revenue Commissioners took the appeal to the House of Lords, the Scottish judges, Lord Normand and Lord Reid, were sympathetic to their countrymen in the Court of Session, but recalled them to their duty. Lord Reid explained the true effect of *Pemsel*:[38]

> In my judgment holding that ["charity" and "charitable"] must be interpreted according to English law must mean that it is to be held that Parliament enacted that on that

[35] 1952 SC 102.

[36] The Court of Session (which deals with civil cases in Scotland) is divided into an Inner House and an Outer House. Judges in the Outer House sit alone, judges in the Inner House normally in benches of three known as "Divisions". There are two permanent Divisions, but occasionally three judges will sit as an Extra Division. The Inner House normally acts as an appeal court, but may deal with certain types of case at first instance. Judges in the Outer House hear cases at first instance and their decisions are liable to appeal to the Inner House. Decisions of the Inner House are liable to appeal to the House of Lords.

[37] *IRC* v. *City of Glasgow Police Athletic Association* 1952 SC 102, 118.

[38] *IRC* v. *City of Glasgow Police Athletic Association* [1953] AC 380, 403.

> matter the law of England should also become the law of Scotland, and it must follow that Parliament must be held to have placed on the courts of Scotland the duty of administering what was formerly only the law of England but what has been made by Act of Parliament the law of both countries.

Lord Normand dwelt on the role of the Scottish court in greater detail:[39]

> The Court of Session is not reduced to the role of an obsequious follower of decisions either of a judge of first instance or of the Court of Appeal, though it is only good sense to pay special regard and respect to the decisions and opinions pronounced by the English courts on a branch of the law built up by English judges, and familiar to them by long training and experience.

The English definition of charity is, therefore, something of a cuckoo in the Scottish legal nest.[40] The Scottish judges are bound to nurture it as their own, substituting themselves as best they can for its true parent, the English chancery judge.[41] In practice, however, the Scottish courts are subjected to this indignity comparatively rarely. On an everyday basis, eligibility for charitable tax relief is determined by the Financial Intermediaries and Claims Office of the Inland Revenue in Edinburgh, and appeals to the court are unusual.

2. *Supervisory Function in Scotland*

Lord Reid remarked in the *Glasgow Police Athletic Association* case that the duty placed on the Scottish courts by the rule in *Pemsel* could only be removed by legislation.[42] Parliament has compounded the problem, however, if it is one, by taking the rule as the foundation for the new statutory system of supervision for "Scottish charities" introduced under the Law Reform (Miscellaneous Provisions) (Scotland) Act 1990. Here, again, the role of the Inland Revenue is pivotal in practice.

Until Part I of the 1990 Act came into force,[43] Scotland had no system of direct supervision of "charities", in the sense of bodies entitled to tax relief by reference to the English definition of charity. Supervision relied on the general compliance procedures of the tax system, and indirect application of other regimes, such as the regime of the Companies Acts in the case of charitable organisations formed as companies limited by guarantee. This meant that the bodies eligible for charitable tax relief in Scotland were under-supervised by comparison with their equivalents in England and Wales.

[39] *IRC* v. *City of Glasgow Police Athletic Association* [1953] AC 380, 394.

[40] See T B Smith, *Studies Critical and Comparative* (Edinburgh, W Green & Son Ltd, 1962), 213.

[41] In *Guild* v. *IRC* [1992] 2 AC 310, 323, Lord Keith applied the principle to the taxpayer's advantage when he held that a Scottish judge, in considering the effect of an instrument in the context of charitable tax relief, should adopt the same benignant approach to construction as an English judge would in considering the validity of a charitable gift.

[42] Above, n 38, 403.

[43] On 4 July 1992.

Responding to a note of warning sounded in the Woodfield Report,[44] the 1990 Act imposed a new system of accountability on "recognised bodies"—that is, bodies established under the law of Scotland, or wholly or mainly managed or controlled in or from Scotland, and recognised by the Inland Revenue as eligible for income tax relief under section 505 of the Income and Corporation Taxes Act 1988. Recognition under section 505 is accorded by reference to the term "charitable purposes only", which must, of course, according to *Pemsel*, be read in its English meaning.[45]

Only a recognised body may properly call itself a "Scottish charity",[46] so that the effect of the 1990 Act has been to create for supervisory purposes a class of "Scottish charities" defined, via *Pemsel*, by reference to the English definition of charity. The regime of the 1990 Act is altogether less ambitious than the English system overseen by the Charity Commissioners,[47] although it has introduced important new opportunities for public scrutiny of charitable activity in Scotland.[48] What is significant for the purposes of this chapter, however, is that it is the English definition of charity, not the Scottish concept of public benefit, which determines the ambit of the regime.

3. *Constitutional Function in Scotland*

The newest function of the English definition of charity in Scotland is what might be described as its constitutional function. Under the Scotland Act 1998, the definition marks out the boundaries of the legislative competence of the Scottish Parliament in the area of voluntary sector law.

The principle of the Scotland Act is that the Scottish Parliament may legislate in all areas not specifically reserved to the United Kingdom Parliament.[49] One of the areas specifically reserved to Westminster is "the creation, operation, regulation and dissolution of types of business association".[50] "Business association" is defined as including non-profit associations carrying on any kind of business, and "business" is in turn declared to include "the provision of benefits to the members of an association".[51] Nothing is said about the provision of

[44] Sir P Woodfield, *Efficiency Scrutiny of the Supervision of Charities* (London, HMSO, 1987), paras 3 and 144.

[45] The device used in the 1990 Act of reference to the English definition of charity, via the combination of tax legislation and *Pemsel*, was not wholly new: it appears in Part VI of the Education (Scotland) Act 1980 as an element in the definition of an "endowment": see s 122(1).

[46] Law Reform (Miscellaneous Provisions) (Scotland) Act 1990, ss. 1(7) and 2(1).

[47] See C R Barker, "The Regulation of Charities in Scotland", in A Dunn (ed), *The Voluntary Sector, The State and the Law* (Oxford, Hart Publishing, 2000) 87; also P J Ford, "Scottish Charity Law Reform: An Agenda for Coherence", (1999) 5 *Charity Law & Practice Review* 187.

[48] The IRC maintain an index, available to the public, of bodies which have been recognised as eligible for income tax relief, and the Lord Advocate and the Court of Session are given new powers of investigation and of protective, remedial and disciplinary action. There is no body, however, which is truly equivalent to the Charity Commission.

[49] See generally A Page, C Reid and A Ross, *A Guide to the Scotland Act 1998* (Edinburgh, Butterworths, 1999).

[50] Scotland Act 1998, Sched 5, Head C, Section C1.

[51] *Ibid.*

benefits to persons who are not members. "Charities", in any event, are excepted from the reservation. It is submitted that "charities" is to be read here in its technical meaning in English law.[52]

What exactly these provisions are intended to mean in practice cannot be tackled here, and may ultimately have to be resolved by the Judicial Committee of the Privy Council.[53] It seems, however, that the new Parliament has power to legislate comparatively freely for "charities"—in the English sense—but that legislative control of any other type of non-profit organisation describable as carrying on a "business" remains with Westminster. Whatever their exact import, however, the provisions illustrate yet further the way in which the English definition of charity has acquired increasing significance in Scotland at the expense of the Scottish concept of public benefit.

4. *A Scottish Contribution to the Reform Debate*

If there is interest in England and Wales in the reform of the English definition, therefore, there is much reason for it to be shared in Scotland. Perhaps there is an opportunity for Scots lawyers to make a distinctive contribution to the debate, especially if it can be shown—as will be attempted in the rest of this chapter—that the Scottish concept displays many of the characteristics which the Deakin and Kemp Commissions identify as the essentials of a reformed definition.

3. SCOTTISH PUBLIC BENEFIT: INTRODUCTION

So great is the significance of the English definition of charity in Scotland that even Scots lawyers are prone to lose sight of their native law in this area. Periodic admonitions have been issued from the bench,[54] one of the most trenchant of which is Lord President Cooper's in *Wink's Executors* v.*Tallent*:[55]

> In England the whole subject is overshadowed by the statute of Elizabeth and the artificial structure which has been erected upon it; but that statute is unknown to Scots law. The Scottish rules affecting charitable and public trusts are the product of our

[52] *Commissioners for Special Purposes of the Income Tax* v. *Pemsel* [1891] AC 531; *Camille and Henry Dreyfus Foundation* v. *IRC* [1956] AC 39; *Ashfield Municipal Council* v. *Joyce* [1978] AC 122.

[53] The Privy Council is the final court of appeal for "devolution issues" under the Scotland Act 1998.

[54] e.g. *MacKintosh's Judicial Factor* v. *Lord Advocate* 1935 SC 406, 409 (Lord President Clyde); *Russell's Executor* v. *Balden* 1989 SLT 177, 179 (Lord Jauncey).

[55] 1947 SC 470, 476. The "Officials" are the officials or "commissars" of the bishops' courts who had effective jurisdiction over matters of succession until the Scottish Reformation. They were replaced by an Act of the (old) Scottish Parliament of 1563 by secular Commissary Courts exercising a similar jurisdiction, but subject to review by the Court of Session. The court did not acquire a first instance jurisdiction in substantive matters of succession until the nineteenth century, by a series of statutes culminating in the Court of Session Act 1850: J Currie and A E McRae, *Currie on Confirmation* 7th edn (Edinburgh, W Green & Sons, 1973), 1–5.

common law without significant interference by the Legislature; and they are of comparatively recent growth, for the subject was largely the province of the Officials and the Commissary Courts until the 19th century. The English law of mortmain is unknown in Scotland. The English rule against perpetuities is not only unknown to the common law of Scotland but with us the attitude to perpetuities has from the first been one of benevolence and not of distaste. The jurisdiction of the Court of Session over trusts is radically different from that of the Court of Chancery.

The passage serves as a convenient introduction to the law of public trusts in Scotland—charitable trusts in Scots law being simply one class of public trusts among others.[56] The most important point, perhaps, is that the reported cases dealing with Scottish public trusts have been far fewer than the English charity cases, and have been built up over a much shorter time. They have not been complicated by the tension between the 1601 Act and the English Mortmain Acts,[57] or nervousness about a private purpose trust continuing in perpetuity.[58] Nor, though the point is not made expressly by Lord President Cooper, have the Scottish rules as to public trusts been influenced by any fiscal implications, as—at least on one authoritative view[59]—have the English decisions on the definition of charity.

A. Background

More generally, it is helpful to remember that the law of trusts in Scotland, historically and conceptually, is quite different from the law of trusts in England and Wales.[60] Scotland has never known the separation between courts of law and courts of equity on which the English distinction between legal and equitable rights is founded. The right of a beneficiary in a Scottish trust amounts simply to a right to have the trust enforced.[61] There is no question of a beneficiary of a Scottish trust having a right of property in the trust assets, of an equitable or any other kind.

It is true that the Court of Session has a limited "equitable jurisdiction" under the *nobile officium*.[62] That jurisdiction enables the court to provide a remedy

[56] See section D of this part, below.

[57] See Moffat, above n 9, 680–688.

[58] *Ibid*, 242–7.

[59] *Dingle* v. *Turner* [1972] AC 601, 624 (Lord Cross).

[60] *IRC* v. *Clark* 1939 SC 11, 23 (Lord President Normand), and 26 (Lord Moncrieff); Smith, above n 40, 199–228; R Burgess, "Thoughts on the Origins of the Trust in Scots Law", [1974] *JR* 196. For modern accounts of the law of public trusts in particular, see *Stair Memorial Encyclopaedia of the Laws of Scotland*, vol 24 (Edinburgh, Law Society of Scotland/Butterworths, 1994) ("Stair, vol 24"), paras 85–111; W Wilson and A G M Duncan, *Trusts, Trustees and Executors* 2nd edn (Edinburgh, W Green and Son, 1995), chaps 14 and 15.

[61] *IRC* v. *Clark* 1939 SC 11, 22 (Lord President Normand).

[62] A loose translation would be "equitable function". The term refers to "the residual equitable power of the supreme court to order justice to be done in circumstances in which to rely on existing rules would not achieve this": *Stair Memorial Encyclopaedia of the Laws of Scotland*, vol 1 (Edinburgh, Law Society of Scotland/Butterworths, 1987) ("Stair, vol 1"), para 332.

where one would not otherwise exist under the general law, but the court has been unwilling to extend its exercise beyond established situations. One of these, certainly, is the reorganisation of a public trust, and the approval of cy-près (or "approximation"[63]) schemes is one of the best known uses of the *nobile officium*. Lord Cunninghame's description of the Court of Session as "the Supreme Court of Equity in Scotland"[64] is perfectly accurate, therefore, but it would be misleading to push the analogy with the English chancery jurisdiction too far. The law of public trusts does not form a "distinct head of equity", or anything like it, as Lord Macnaghten explained in *Pemsel* is the case with English charitable trusts.[65]

Public trusts, certainly, have by their nature elicited some differences of treatment by the Court of Session from private trusts, but they remain recognisably only a variation of the same trust concept. As Lord Watson, the Scottish judge in *Pemsel*, pointed out:[66]

> Ever since its institution the Court has exercised plenary jurisdiction over the administration of all trusts, whether public or private, irrespective of the particular purposes to which the estate or income of the trust may be appropriated.

To a large extent, in other words, public and private trusts in Scotland are governed by the same rules.[67]

Since Lord President Cooper's time, the law of public trusts in Scotland has fallen more profoundly still under the shadow of the English definition, as donors and advisers have concentrated on the increasing importance of charitable tax relief. As will be seen, a Scottish trust whose purposes are charitable in the English sense will in most cases be a public trust in Scots law, with the result that, at the stage of constitution of a trust, the modern focus is almost entirely on the tax dimension.[68] If the charitable status is got right, the public trust status will follow. There is no requirement in Scotland to register public trusts as such, and correspondingly no body of "Commissioners for Public Trusts" equivalent to the Charity Commissioners in England and Wales.

In consequence, the world of Scottish public trusts remains a comparatively obscure one. Scots lawyers who investigate it, and compare it with the world of English charity law, are forced to the same conclusion as Lord Skerrington:

[63] The term "cy-près", originally adopted into Scots law from English law, is generally used today in preference to the alternative "approximation" favoured by certain Scottish judges: e.g. *Trustees of Carnegie Park Orphanage, Petitioners* (1892) 19 R 605, 608 (Lord McLaren); *Trustees of Glasgow Domestic Training School, Petitioners* 1923 SC 892, 895 (Lord President Clyde).

[64] *Ross* v. *Heriot's Hospital* (1843) 5 D 589, 609.

[65] *Special Commissioners for the Purposes of Income Tax* v. *Pemsel* [1891] AC 531, 580.

[66] *Ibid*, 560.

[67] Stair, vol 1, above n 62, para 85. It is an illustration of the proposition that public and private trusts are simply variations of a single trust concept that in a recent case trustees were able to seek, and obtain, authority to sell heritable property (a country house and estate) without the court's having to express a final view on whether the trust was a public or a private one. The petition was presented under the Trusts (Scotland) Act 1921, which applies equally to public and private trusts: *Tod's Trustees, Petitioners* 1999 SLT 309.

[68] This was certainly the author's own experience as a trust practitioner in Scotland.

"The law of charities in England bristles with technicalities for which no analogies exist in our law."[69] It is possible, therefore, that an English charity lawyer may find the Scottish concept of public benefit disappointingly straightforward, but its very simplicity may have something to contribute to the debate on reform.

The Scottish public benefit concept is to public trusts what the English definition of charity is to charitable trusts. It may be helpful, therefore, to preface substantive treatment of the Scottish concept with an outline definition of a public trust, together with a note of the functions the concept performs in the Scottish system. It may also be helpful to deal briefly with the issue of certainty, and to clarify the significance of the term "charitable" in Scots common law.

B. Outline Definition

In a recent case,[70] Lord Justice-Clerk Ross cited the following statement from the *Stair Memorial Encyclopaedia of the Laws of Scotland* by way of a working definition of a public trust: "In a public trust, the beneficial interest is intended for the benefit of a section of the public."[71] To this should be added the riders that the validity of the trust will depend on whether the intention to benefit a section of the public is specified with sufficient certainty,[72] and that the benefit intended must be lawful and useful.[73] The central concept, therefore, is one of lawful and useful benefit to a section of the public. The beneficial interest—the right to have the benefactor's (or the "truster's"[74]) project enforced—lies with the section of the public the truster intends should benefit from it.

C. Functions

It should be emphasised, first of all, that the Scottish concept has no fiscal function. As we have seen, voluntary sector tax relief in Scotland, as in the rest of the United Kingdom, is applied principally by reference to the English definition of charity.[75] On the other hand, the concept has both trust law and supervisory functions, although it is perhaps artificial to distinguish between them, since the supervisory function applies only to trusts and has no application, unlike the

69 *Anderson's Trustees* v. *Scott* 1914 SC 942, 956.

70 *University of Edinburgh* v. *The Torrie Trustees* 1997 SLT 1009, 1014.

71 Stair, vol 1, above n 62, para 86.

72 Mackenzie Stuart, *The Law of Trusts* (Edinburgh, W Green and Son, 1932), 110.

73 J McLaren, *The Law of Wills and Succession* 3rd edn (Edinburgh, Bell and Bradfute/Sweet and Maxwell, 1894), 917.

74 "Truster" is the Scottish equivalent of the English term "settlor", meaning the person who sets up a trust.

75 The Scottish Parliament does, however, have power to alter the basis of relief from local government taxation: Scotland Act 1998, Sched 5, Head A, Section A1.

supervisory function of English charitable status, to bodies constituted otherwise than as trusts, except in so far as a trust, or a *quasi*-trust, can be implied.[76] For analytical purposes, however, it may be useful to make the distinction.

1. *Trust Law Function*

The principal function of the public benefit concept is to distinguish public trusts from private trusts—to distinguish, as Lord McLaren put it in his *Wills and Succession*:[77]

> between private trusts or bequests, in which only the individuals named or designed can claim an interest, and those which are intended for the benefit of a section of the public, and which may be enforced by *popularis actio*.

Once that distinction has been made, a public trust is treated differently from a private trust in a number of limited but important respects.[78] Most significant for the purposes of this chapter is the availability of the *popularis actio* referred to by Lord McLaren. This is the name sometimes given to the right of individual members of the section of the public intended to benefit from a trust to raise an action for its enforcement. The action is an "action of the people" in the sense described by Lord Watson in *Andrews* v. *Ewart's Trustees*:[79]

> They do not . . . sue in their own private interest, but in the interest of all members of the public who have, or may have, occasion to avail themselves of [the benefit concerned].

The proposition can be stated more widely still, to the effect that "any person interested in the carrying out of the truster's directions, is entitled to enforce fulfilment of the trust".[80] The heirs of the truster may also enforce the trust, although their financial interest is perhaps more likely to lead them to challenge a bequest than to seek to have it upheld.[81] And the Lord Advocate may raise an action to enforce the trust in the public interest.[82]

[76] There is some authority for the view that voluntary associations and corporate bodies whose object is to serve a section of the public may hold their assets in trust or *quasi*-trust for the section of the public concerned: *D & J Nichol* v. *Dundee Harbour Trustees* 1915 SC (HL) 7, 13 (Lord Dunedin).

[77] Above, n 73, 917.

[78] Stair, vol 24, above n 60, para 85; P J Ford, "Charitable Trusts" in C R Barker et al (eds), *Charity Law in Scotland* (Edinburgh, W Green/Sweet and Maxwell, 1996), 54.

[79] 1886 SC 69, 73.

[80] *Aitken's Trustee* v. *Aitken* 1927 SC 374, 387 (Lord Ashmore). See also *Ross* v. *Heriot's Hospital* (1843) 5 D 589. Cf *Mohammed Shariff and Another, Petitioners* (unreported: Lord Nimmo Smith's opinion of 23 June 1999 is available at www.scotcourts.gov.uk.): Lord Nimmo Smith, in the Outer House, suggested that the right to petition for removal of the trustee of a public trust might be restricted to members of the relevant section of the public able to establish "a substantial connection" with the trust.

[81] *Hill* v. *Burns* (1826) 2 W & S 80, 91 (Lord Gifford); *McLeish's Trustees* v. *McLeish* (1841) 3 D 914.

[82] *Mitchell* v. *Burness* (1878) 5 R 954, 959 (Lord Deas); *Aitken's Trustee* v. *Aitken* 1927 SC 374, 387 (Lord Ashmore).

To judge from the reported cases, however, invocation of the *popularis actio* is comparatively rare, and much more commonly used in practice are the special rules for the variation of public trusts. As already mentioned, since public trusts may continue in perpetuity, the Scottish courts have had to develop under the *nobile officium* the same device as applied by the English courts to charitable trusts, that of authorising reorganisation of redundant or ineffective trusts by a scheme "for setting the charity agoing again for its original purposes, or as near thereto as practicable."[83]

2. *Supervisory Jurisdiction*

The role of the Court of Session in the supervision of public trusts is, as Lord Watson said in *Pemsel*,[84] simply one aspect of the court's plenary jurisdiction over all trusts, though the court has adapted its supervisory response to meet their special characteristics. Schemes of reorganisation may adjust administrative provisions as well as purposes, and additionally under the *nobile officium* the court may remove and appoint trustees and give directions to trustees on petition.[85] Generally speaking, however, the court has been reluctant to become involved in the administration of a public trust unless strictly necessary,[86] but has become more flexible in the exercise of the cy-près jurisdiction in recent years.[87] The court's powers under the *nobile officium* have in any case been considerably supplemented by statute,[88] in particular by additional provisions for the reorganisation of public trusts under the Law Reform (Miscellaneous Provisions) (Scotland) Act 1990.[89]

[83] This is the picturesque phrase of Lord Deas in *Mitchell* v. *Burness* (1878) 5 R 954, 959. Lord Deas exhibits the tendency of some nineteenth century (and later) Scottish judges to use the term "charity" as a substitute for "public trust". The applicability of the cy-près jurisdiction to all public trusts, whether or not charitable in the non-technical sense of the term in Scots common law, was established beyond doubt in *Anderson's Trustees* v. *Scott* 1914 SC 942.

[84] *Commissioners for Special Purposes of the Income Tax* v. *Pemsel* [1891] AC 531, 560.

[85] *Ross* v. *Heriot's Hospital* (1843) 5 D 589. For a modern application see *Mohammed Shariff and Another, Petitioners* (unreported: Lord Nimmo-Smith's opinion of 23 June 1999 is available at www.scotcourts.gov.uk).

[86] For instance, in *Edinburgh Young Women's Christian Institute, Petitioners* (1893) 20 R 894 and *Leven Penny Savings Bank, Petitioners* 1948 SC 147, the court refused petitions seeking endorsement of proposed transactions considered to be within the powers of the trustees. See also Wilson and Duncan, above n 60, 251. Traditionally, also, the *nobile officium* could only be exercised by the Inner House of the Court of Session, that is by a bench of at least three judges, but the jurisdiction may now be exercised by a single judge in the Outer House, with power to refer a petition at any stage to the Inner House: RC 14.2, 63.9.

[87] *Mining Institute of Scotland Benevolent Fund Trustees, Petitioners* 1994 SLT 785, 786 (Lord President Hope).

[88] As in the case of private trusts, petitions for directions and for additional powers may be brought under the Trusts (Scotland) Act 1921.

[89] Section 9. These provisions supplement, rather than replace, the traditional cy-près jurisdiction. Section 10 enables the trustees of "small" public trusts to reorganise trust purposes by resolution, subject to the consent of the Lord Advocate.

The Lord Advocate has, at common law,[90] a supervisory role in relation to public trusts which has much in common with that of the Attorney-General in relation to charitable trusts. But the analogy should not be taken too far.[91] The Lord Advocate acts for the Crown in the public interest, but there is no suggestion in the cases that the jurisdiction arises from the Crown's role as *parens patriae*.[92] On the contrary, the Lord Advocate is just as likely to appear for the Crown as *ultimus haeres*,[93] with the object of defeating the trust rather than supporting it.[94] The availability of the *popularis actio*, to say nothing of the heirs' right to implementation, means that enforcement of a public trust does not depend entirely on the Lord Advocate. A picture can legitimately be painted, therefore, of public trusts as a class of trusts which, like private trusts, are enforceable by the courts at the instance of their own beneficiaries: the beneficiaries may on occasion receive the assistance of the Crown, and the Crown may choose to proceed independently of the beneficiaries, but the protection of public trusts in Scotland is very far from being—at least at the level of theory—the exclusive business of the state.

It should be emphasised that the supervisory arrangements for public trusts remain a function of trust law, and have never been adapted by statute to produce a more general regime of compliance for bodies constituted in other legal forms but with "public objects".[95] Whether the Scottish public benefit concept could be successfully used as the basis for a wider statutory regime along the lines of the English charities regime is, accordingly, an open question.

D. Certainty

The object of the certainty requirement is to ensure that the trustees are given adequate directions. That issue is distinct from the question of whether those directions, once established as a clear expression of a truster's intention, are acceptable to the court as "lawful and useful". The parallel distinction in English law tends (at least to a Scottish eye) to be clouded by the dual function of the word "charitable": a trust for "charitable purposes" satisfies the requirement of certainty,[96] and trusts for "charitable purposes" are the only class of purpose trusts accepted as enforceable.

[90] The powers of the Lord Advocate at common law should be distinguished from those under the Law Reform (Miscellaneous Provisions) (Scotland) Act 1990.

[91] *Camille and Henry Dreyfus Foundation* v. *IRC* [1956] AC 39, 47 (Lord Normand).

[92] For a general account of the *parens patriae* jurisdiction see Lord President Hope's opinion in *Law Hospital NHS Trust* v. *Lord Advocate* 1996 SC 301. Proceedings relating to a public trust do not require the consent of the Lord Advocate. Cf Charities Act 1993, s 33.

[93] "The ultimate heir".

[94] e.g. *Smith* v. *Lord Advocate* (1899) 1 F 741; *Anderson's Trustees* v. *Scott* 1914 SC 942; *Mackintosh's Judicial Factor* v. *Lord Advocate* 1935 SC 406.

[95] As distinct from bodies with "charitable objects" in the English sense, which are subject to the regime introduced under the Law Reform (Miscellaneous Provisions) (Scotland) Act 1990.

[96] Martin, above n 9, 379.

1. *Adequate Specification Distinguished from Acceptability*

Mackenzie Stuart's classic statement of the certainty requirement concentrates on definition of the class:[97]

> When a trust is for the benefit of a section of the public, the validity of the trust depends on whether the class is described with sufficient definition; if it is described in general terms the words used must not be so vague as to leave the trustees full power to do with the trust estate as they please.

The description of the class need not be express, but may be implied by specification of the benefit to be enjoyed. Thus, in *Russell's Executor* v. *Balden*,[98] Lord Jauncey identified as "the local sporting community" the section of the public to be benefited by a bequest to "the Town Council of North Berwick for the use in connection with the Sports Centre in North Berwick or some similar purpose in connection with sport". There was sufficient definition of the class to constitute a valid public trust, there being no suggestion in Scots law that the provision of sporting facilities is not a lawful and useful form of benefit to the public.

When general phrases are used, however, there is a danger of invalidity from uncertainty. In Scots law, for instance, the objection to the phrase "social purposes" as an expression of a testator's wishes is simply that it is too vague to be acted on,[99] not, as in English law, that it would allow the trustees to apply funds to non-charitable purposes.[100] There would be no objection in principle in Scots law to including activities which might in general terms be described as "social" as part of a project in favour of an adequately defined section of the public. The provision of social facilities is no more objectionable in itself than the provision of sporting facilities.

Similarly, in Scots law, a direction to apply funds for "public purposes"[101] is insufficiently certain to create a valid trust, but that is not to say that purposes which might be described in general terms as "public" may not, if adequately specified, be regarded by the court as wholly lawful and useful. The object is not to restrict the ways in which a benefactor may benefit the public, but to ensure that the benefactor's project is sufficiently described to be given genuine effect.

2. *"Charitable Purposes" in Scots Law*

The phrase "charitable purposes" is, however, different from other general expressions in that it is treated as in itself a sufficient set of directions to trustees. This is perhaps the clearest instance of "the general benevolence which the law shows towards trusts of a public nature",[102] which has been said to apply

97 Above n 72, 110.
98 1989 SLT 177.
99 Wilson and Duncan, above n 60, 218.
100 Cf *IRC* v. *Baddeley* [1955] AC 572.
101 Wilson and Duncan, above n 60, 217.
102 *Russell's Executor* v. *Balden* 1989 SLT 177, 179 (Lord Jauncey).

particularly, if not exclusively, to charitable trusts.[103] There is something of a paradox here. The Scottish courts have consistently held that trustees directed to apply funds for "charitable purposes" are given sufficiently clear directions, but they have never themselves defined with any real clarity exactly what those directions mean.[104] The most authoritative attempt by a Scottish judge is probably that of Lord Watson in *Pemsel*, in which he concluded a review of the Scottish cases as follows:[105]

> These authorities seem to me to go this length. In the first place, they establish positively that charity is not limited to relief of the physical wants of the poor, but includes their intellectual and moral culture; and, in the second place, they suggest very strongly that purposes which concern others than the poor may nevertheless be charitable purposes in the sense of Scotch law.

Whatever the meaning of charitable in Scots law, however, it is axiomatic that trusts for charitable purposes—in the Scottish sense—are just one species of public trust among others, and governed by the same rules, once established, as the rest. Any special favour the courts may show to them—over and above that shown to trusts of a public nature generally—is confined to questions of construction.[106] Subject to this qualification, the well-known passage from Lord McLaren's *Wills and Succession* remains an accurate statement of the law:[107]

> The term "charitable trust" is a convenient general name, but it must be kept in view that the law of Scotland (as hitherto understood and administered) recognises no distinction either as to construction or principles of administration between gifts to charitable uses properly so called, and gifts to purposes which, though not charitable, are lawful and useful.

4. SCOTTISH PUBLIC BENEFIT: "PUBLIC PURPOSES"

How does the court decide what is lawful and useful? It is clear, first of all, that the truster's own opinion is not the determining factor.[108] The warning should also be issued that the phrase "lawful and useful" is not a Scottish version of the Macnaghten classification. While adopted from time to time in the cases, the expression has not been the subject of exhaustive analysis.[109]

The "lawful" can perhaps be taken as a reference to the general principle that a trust, public or private, may not be illegal, *contra bonos mores*,[110] or other-

[103] *Blair* v. *Duncan* (1901) 4 F HL 1, 6 (Lord Robertson).
[104] *IRC* v. *City of Glasgow Police Athletic Association* [1953] AC 380, 393 (Lord Normand).
[105] *Commissioners for Special Purposes of the Income Tax* v. *Pemsel* [1891] AC 531, 561.
[106] *Blair* v. *Duncan* (1901) 4 F HL 1, 6 (Lord Robertson).
[107] Above, n 73, 917.
[108] *McCaig* v. *University of Glasgow* 1907 SC 231, 240 (Lord Justice-Clerk Macdonald).
[109] e.g. *Ness* v. *Mill's Trustees* 1923 SC 344, 355 (Lord Skerrington); *Clarke* v. *Ross* 1976 SLT (Notes) 62, 63 (Lord Wheatley).
[110] "Against good morals".

wise contrary to public policy.[111] The "useful" perhaps refers to what might be described as the Scottish "beneficiary principle": a trust must benefit somebody, whether an ascertainable private individual or individuals, or a section of the public. In practice, however, it is probably best to look at the two elements of the phrase together: "lawful and useful" is a convenient description of the range of activities which a benefactor is free to promote by means of a public trust—that is, of "public purposes".[112] The range of possible purposes certainly includes purposes which are charitable in the non-technical Scottish sense, but otherwise is restricted only by the court's public policy veto,[113] which in turn incorporates the Scottish version of the beneficiary principle.

A. Public Policy Veto

The best place to begin an explanation of the public policy veto is in Oban, with the notorious *McCaig* cases.[114] In the first of these, *McCaig* v. *University of Glasgow*,[115] the Court of Session set aside as invalid a testator's directions that his substantial highland properties were to be held by trustees in perpetuity: the rental income was to be devoted to the erection of costly statues of the testator and members of his family on top of an existing tower on a hill above Oban, and to the building of further artistic towers (apparently without limit of number) on prominent points on the different estates. In the second case, *McCaig's Trustees* v. *Kirk Session of the United Free Church of Lismore*,[116] the court set aside testamentary directions of the first testator's sister, who had successfully challenged her brother's settlement, to convert the existing tower above Oban into a private enclosure, to erect in it, in accordance with an elaborately conceived design, costly bronze statues of herself, parents and collaterals, and to maintain the tower and the statues in all time coming.

1. *Scottish Beneficiary Principle*

In the first *McCaig* case, the court founded its decision on:[117]

> the cardinal principle that by the law of Scotland there can be no divestiture of a man's heirs or next of kin, except by means of beneficial rights, validly constituted in favour of third parties.

111 Mackenzie Stuart, above n 72, 76 ff.

112 See *Davidson's Trustees* v. *Arnott* 1951 SC 42, 60 (Lord Patrick).

113 Stair, vol 1, above n 62, para 87.

114 The issue of whether "ludicrous purposes" could be given effect as "useful and proper" trust objects was already familiar to the court: see Lord President Inglis' derisive reference to a trust for "the maintenance of an army of cats" in *Dundas and Others, Petitioners* (1869) 7 M 670, 675. See generally Wilson and Duncan, above n 60, 199–201.

115 1907 SC 231.

116 1915 SC 426.

117 Above, n 115, 242 (Lord Kyllachy).

It was held that the testator's directions created "no beneficial interest in any third person, or body of persons—even including in the latter category the general public."[118] The later case of *Ness* v. *Mill's Trustees*[119] provides an illustration of the positive, rather than the negative, application of the principle, the court treating as valid directions to build and maintain a community observatory in Dundee. The testator's object was to enable contemplation of "the wonders and beauty of the works of God in creation" such as to yield "rational and innocent entertainment of the highest kind." Lord President Clyde explained and applied the first *McCaig* case as follows:[120]

> [I]f a residuary bequest is to have the effect of disinheriting the heir, it must be such as to create some beneficial interest of an intelligible and tangible character in favour of some definite third party. There must in short be a valid gift and an effectual nomination of a donee who is to take preferably to the heir. Here there is a perfectly valid gift. The provision of the means for rational and innocent public entertainment is an intelligible and tangible object of public utility. And there is no doubt about the donee, namely the community of the testator's native city.

2. *"Grotesque, Extravagant, Wasteful or Futile"*

The main ground of judgment in the first *McCaig* case, therefore, was that the bequest created no beneficial interest in anyone, but the wider ground of public policy was also discussed. Lord Kyllachy suggested that the beneficiary principle might ultimately be founded on public policy,[121] and in the second *McCaig* case public policy became the main ground of decision. The court conceded that there was an established exception to the beneficiary principle in favour of memorials to the dead, "but so far only as these are customary or rational".[122] Miss McCaig's directions were not, therefore, invalid because they benefited no one—though there were in fact no family members surviving who might wish to admire the statues in private, and the public were to be shut out from the tower altogether—but because they were "a sheer waste of money",[123] "an absurd whim which has neither reason nor public sentiment in its favour",[124] and

[118] *Ibid,* (Lord Kyllachy).

[119] 1923 SC 344.

[120] *Ibid*, 353.

[121] Above, n 115, 242, where Lord Kyllachy was sympathetic to the view that "if it is not unlawful, it ought to be unlawful, to dedicate by testamentary disposition, for all time, or for a length of time, the whole income of a large estate . . . to objects of no utility, private or public, objects which benefit nobody, and which have no other purpose or use than that of perpetuating at great cost, and in an absurd manner, the idiosyncracies of an eccentric testator." Lord Low *(ibid*, 247), on the other hand, considered the directions to be "whimsical and of no utility", but "perfectly lawful" and impossible to regard as contrary to public policy.

[122] Above, n 116, 438 (Lord Guthrie); see also 433 (Lord Salvesen).

[123] *Ibid*, 434 (Lord Salvesen).

[124] *Ibid* (Lord Salvesen).

"unnatural, contrary to custom, and unreasonable".[125] Lord Guthrie stated the general principle as follows:[126]

> If the law of mortmain is to be allowed at all, it is not unreasonable to say that it must not result in a large measure of useless waste. Therefore, without being illegal in the sense of being contrary to any express rule of the common law or contrary to any statute, the principle of public policy will prevent such post-mortem expenditure. Whether the act is sufficiently contrary to public policy to warrant the Court's interference must depend on the degree to which it is against public policy.

In the later case of *Mackintosh's Judicial Factor* v. *Lord Advocate*,[127] Lord President Clyde produced a rather more striking formulation of the same principle. A testator had directed that the remains of two persons, described by her as her "aunt" and "uncle" but not legally related to her, were to be exhumed and reburied with her in a granite vault on whose construction and maintenance the whole of her (substantial) personal estate was to be expended. His Lordship acknowledged the long-established principle of Scots law permitting a bequest for construction of a memorial to a deceased testator—though there might be no direct benefit to anyone living—and conceded that even a substantial sum might properly be devoted to such a purpose. He held, however, that the direction for exhumation, which was inseparable from the rest of the project, rendered it invalid as a whole. Drawing on the *McCaig* cases, he formulated the following question for the court—which he answered in the affirmative:[128]

> Is the [testator's project] so grotesque, so extravagant, so wasteful, or so futile—in a word, so mad—that her direction must be declared a nullity?

3. *Beneficiary Principle and Public Policy Veto Combined*

While it is possible, therefore, to make a distinction between the beneficiary principle as such and wider considerations of public policy, in practice the courts have come to adopt a "belt and braces" approach and to justify their decisions on both grounds. In *Aitken's Trustees* v. *Aitken*, Lord Sands had already attempted a reconciliation of the *McCaig* cases:[129]

> The difference between the rules applied in the two *McCaig* cases is dialectical, and, in my view, devoid of substance. In the first case the Court affirmed: "This bequest confers no benefit on anybody, therefore it is ineffectual to oust the heir." In the second case they affirmed: "This bequest confers no benefit on anybody, accordingly it is unreasonable and wasteful, and therefore it fails as being contrary to public policy." . . . Accordingly, I take the law applicable to the present case as based upon the *McCaig* cases to be that, if testamentary directions are unreasonable as conferring

[125] *Ibid*, 436 (Lord Guthrie).

[126] *Ibid*, 438. There is no statutory law of mortmain in Scotland, but the court has a common law power to control post-mortem expenditure.

[127] 1935 SC 406: the Lord Advocate appeared for the Crown as *ultimus haeres*.

[128] *Ibid*, 411.

[129] 1927 SC 374, 380.

> neither a patrimonial benefit on anybody nor a benefit upon the public or any section thereof, the directions are invalid.

Lord Sands went on to explain the apparent exception to the beneficiary principle in favour of memorials to the dead in terms of the moral benefit to the living arising from pious feelings.[130] Similarly, monuments to public figures, national or local, could be regarded as beneficial in terms of the civic feeling generated in the public.[131]

The directions in *Aitken's Trustees* were for the erection and maintenance in all time coming of a massive bronze equestrian statue of the testator, a farmer and butcher by trade. His family had long been connected with the small town of Musselburgh, and the statue was to depict him in the traditional guise of "Champion of the Riding of the Town Marches". It was to be of "artistic merit"—although a photograph of the testator produced to the court suggested that it might excite ridicule rather than admiration. A prominent site for the statue was to be cleared by demolition of valuable commercial and domestic property in the town which formed part of the testator's estate. Lord Sands held that the purposes—commemorating local civic customs and honouring the testator's and his family's long association with the town—were not unreasonable in themselves. They were not incapable in principle of benefiting a section of the public, but, taken as a whole, the project was "irrational, futile and self destructive",[132] and the bequest was invalid.

Lord Sands acknowledged that such a judgment involved "a somewhat delicate exercise of judicial discretion".[133] He was fortified in his conclusion, however, by evidence—in the form of a resolution of the Town Council—that the local community was strongly opposed to the scheme. Such indications did not bind the court, but at the same time:[134]

> the Court is not to make itself judge of what is for the public benefit. It is enough that the object is one, not immoral or contrary to public order, which a certain section of opinion may regard as of public benefit.

It was clear in this case, however, that no section of opinion could be found which supported the testator's project. The other judges arrived at the same result, Lord Blackburn holding expressly that the directions were contrary to public policy,[135] and Lord Ashmore that they were invalid as conferring no benefit on anyone.[136] Both, however, took into account the views of the Town Council.

A similar double-barrelled approach is found in the First Division's decision in *Lindsay's Executor* v. *Forsyth*.[137] There it was held that a bequest to a par-

[130] 1927 SC 374, 381.
[131] *Ibid*, 382.
[132] *Ibid*, 383.
[133] *Ibid*, 382. See also Lord Ashmore at 387.
[134] *Ibid*, 381.
[135] *Ibid*, 386.
[136] *Ibid*, 388.
[137] 1940 SC 568.

ticular church to provide a bi-weekly mass for the testator's mother and herself was valid, but that a (separable) bequest for providing a weekly supply of fresh flowers to be placed on their graves in perpetuity was invalid. The first bequest was in effect a gift in perpetuity for religious purposes, which conferred a benefit on a section of the public by enabling a ritual act of public worship to be performed. The second, however, was both "extravagant to the point of caprice" and conferred no benefit on anyone.[138]

Again, in *Campbell Smith's Trustees* v. *Scott*[139] Lord Russell, in the Outer House, after a full review of the cases, relied on both principles in treating as valid a bequest of residue, worth thirty thousand pounds in 1943, to be paid to the trustees of the Royal Scots Club as the basis of a fund for creating "a worthy public monument in a suitable conspicuous locality in Edinburgh in commemoration of the past services of the regiment". Lord Russell found both that the bequest conferred "what may well be regarded as a useful public benefit in the opinion of large sections of the public",[140] and that it was not "extravagant, wasteful, or irrational, or contrary to public policy."[141]

4. *Assessment of Benefactor's Project as a Whole*

The case of *Sutherland's Trustee* v. *Verschoyle*[142] shows that this double test, developed largely in the memorial cases, can be applied more generally, and to projects of a more complex kind. The testator had directed that her "valuable art collection" should be transferred from Edinburgh to Saint Andrews to be exhibited in perpetuity there, in a house "of a certain size and dignity" and under the charge of a resident caretaker. There was expert opinion to the effect that even the best items did not form a collection suitable for public exhibition and that of themselves they would not justify the establishment of a house for their display. Such a project would have tied up the whole of the deceased's estate—of which the value of the collection represented only a fraction. The testator gave the trustees no power to split the collection, but obliged them to house the collection as a whole. Lord Justice-Clerk Grant, with whom the other judges of the Second Division agreed, conceded—in a reference to *Re Pinion*[143]—that the collection was not just a "mass of junk". In holding the bequest invalid, however, he adopted the following approach:[144]

> One must accordingly look, in my opinion, at the merits of the collection as a whole and its viability as a collection to be publicly exhibited as a unit in St Andrews in perpetuity. The collection, it seems, is a heterogeneous conglomeration with no group of material sufficient to provide or illustrate any historical or educational theme such as

[138] *Ibid*, 572.
[139] 1944 SLT 198.
[140] *Ibid*, 200.
[141] *Ibid*, 202. Lord Russell also rejected a claim that the directions were uncertain.
[142] 1968 SLT 43.
[143] [1965] Ch 85.
[144] Above n 142, 46.

> might attract scholar, student or even the general public. . . . As a whole it is "not such as to sustain [the] interest of any section of the public over a period of time". While it is only in the most exceptional circumstances that the courts will interfere with the expressed wishes of a testator, I have come to the conclusion that in the present case we ought to do so. Even if any public benefit would arise from implementing the purported bequest, it would be so minimal that to apply the deceased's estate to such implementation would, in my opinion, be so grossly extravagant and so completely wasteful as to be contrary to public policy.

5. *Summary*

Taken overall, the cases tend to confirm Lord Sands' analysis that the court's public policy veto and the beneficiary principle—the "lawful" and "useful" elements of the Scottish public benefit concept respectively—are, if not indistinguishable, then all but inseparable in practice. The beneficiary principle can itself be explained as arising from public policy, but the public policy considerations are wider. A project might be found to confer some benefit on a section of the public, yet still be sufficiently "grotesque, extravagant, wasteful or futile" to be declared a nullity. The court's object, in any event, is to exclude from the category of "lawful and useful" purposes any purposes which are manifestly harmful or useless.

Usefulness is conceived primarily in terms of benefit to living human beings—trusts for tombs, monuments and animals being explicable in terms of the moral benefit to the living arising from pious, civic and humane feelings.[145] The court, in assessing whether to use its veto, looks at the testator's project as a whole, and is guided, not by the personal views of the judges, but by what a "certain section of opinion" may consider to be publicly beneficial. The veto is invoked only with reluctance and in circumstances which cry out for it. The range of permissible benefit to the public is otherwise unrestricted.

The public policy veto has been developed in the context of testamentary directions: the question has been whether a testator should be permitted to devote assets to a project which will be given effect only after his or her death and may continue in perpetuity. As Lord Salvesen pointed out in the second *McCaig* case, human nature can usually be relied on (in Scotland, at least) to prevent people from throwing their money away on useless projects during their lifetimes—though they are perfectly free to do so.[146] Even if they do, their profligacy normally dies with them, and the control of the court is needed only in the case of wasteful expenditure programmed for after death. It is submitted, how-

[145] *Aitken's Trustees* v. *Aitken* 1927 SC 374, 381 (Lord Sands). The benefit to a section of the public must, however, normally be more than indirect: it is not enough that workmen and others may benefit from the construction of otherwise useless and unwanted follies: *McCaig* v. *University of Glasgow* 1907 SC 231, 245 (Lord Stormonth-Darling).

[146] In *McCaig's Trustees* v. *Kirk of Session of the United Free Church of Lismore* 1915 SC 426, the court was told that both McCaigs had considered elaborate plans for converting the tower during their lifetimes, but "could not bring themselves to part with the money" (434, Lord Salvesen).

ever, that there is no technical reason[147] why the approach of the Scottish courts should not be applied more widely: as is suggested later in the chapter, it might be adopted, for instance, by the Charity Commissioners, as the basis of a new test of "charitability" for the purposes of registering an organisation in the English register of charities.

6. *Examples*

Scottish "public" purposes can be said, therefore, to embrace all objects intended to benefit a section of the public which are not excluded by the public policy veto. As we have seen, such purposes range from the building of a community observatory to the provision of sporting facilities. As we will see later in the chapter, an organisation providing savings account facilities in an area not serviced by conventional banks has been described, tentatively at least, as a public trust,[148] while a bequest for promoting the total abolition of vivisection has been treated, without hesitation, as a public trust,[149] as also has a miners' strike fund.[150]

Further examples can be taken from reported cases of the past decade or so: a group of educational trusts administered by the University Court of the University of Glasgow for the benefit of the university;[151] a trust for the relief of poverty "through or for behoof of" former members of the Mining Institute of Scotland, or members or former members of the Institute of Mining Engineers with a qualifying Scottish connection, and their spouses, parents or children;[152] a trust to provide "a school for boys and girls in or near the parish of Dollar";[153] a bequest to trustees of a collection of works of art "for the purposes of laying a foundation for a Gallery for the encouragement of the Arts";[154] a trust for providing "rest and change of air" for professional persons;[155] a trust for "building and erecting a school for the education of children of Roman Catholic parents principally in or near Aberdeen";[156] and a trust "to provide for the advancement of the teaching and study of Islam".[157] From these examples it will be obvious

147 Reasons of policy, of course, are another matter, because the Scottish approach would considerably widen the existing scope of charity: see part 7 below.

148 *Leven Penny Savings Bank, Petitioners* 1948 SC 147.

149 *Glasgow Society for Prevention of Cruelty to Animals* v. *National Anti-Vivisection Society* 1915 SC 757.

150 *Clarke* v. *Ross* 1976 SLT (Notes) 62.

151 *University of Glasgow, Petitioners* 1991 SLT 604.

152 *Mining Institute of Scotland Benevolent Fund Trustees, Petitioners* 1994 SLT 785.

153 *Governors of Dollar Academy Trust* v. *Lord Advocate* 1995 SLT 596.

154 *University of Edinburgh* v. *The Torrie Trustees* 1997 SLT 1009. The trust was created by a will of 1824.

155 *Tod's Trustees, Petitioners* 1999 SLT 308. The court was not called upon to decide finally whether the trust was public or private, but clearly considered that a trust for these purposes was capable of being a public trust.

156 *Winning and Another, Petitioners* 1999 SC 51. The trust was established in 1823.

157 *Mohammed Shariff and Another, Petitioners* (Unreported: Lord Nimmo-Smith's opinion of 23 June 1999 is available at www.scotcourts.gov.uk.).

that Lord President Clyde's phrase in *Ness* v. *Mill's Trustees*[158] should not be understood in any restrictive sense: "an intelligible and tangible object of public utility" may clearly take the form of a moral or spiritual benefit as well as a purely material one.

B. Types of Benefit

From what has been said so far in this part it will be clear that, although many of the purposes falling within the scope of the Scottish public benefit concept may happen also to be charitable in the English sense, the preamble to the 1601 Act, the Macnaghten categories, and landmark English decisions such as *Re Nottage*[159] are wholly irrelevant to the question of what is "lawful and useful". It is true that trusts for the relief of poverty, for the advancement of education, for the advancement of religion, and otherwise for the benefit of the community may all be public trusts in Scotland, but nothing hangs on their falling into any one or more of those categories. It is almost as if the liberal approach to the spirit and intendment of the preamble proposed by Russell LJ in *Incorporated Council of Law Reporting for England and Wales* v. *Attorney-General*[160]—that "the proper question to ask is whether there are any grounds for holding [a purpose] to be outside the equity of the Statute"—had been taken to its logical conclusion, to create the "single overarching charitable category" recommended by the Deakin Commission.[161]

The question for Scots law is not whether the benefit under discussion can be fitted within certain pre-set categories of permissible benefit, but whether there is any pressing public policy reason for rejecting an ostensibly beneficial project, whatever form it may take: hence the absence of prejudice against sport[162] and recreation[163] as possible forms of benefit. There would be no need to disqualify a project simply because it included "social" purposes,[164] provided the directions of the truster were clear and the project as a whole was not wasteful or extravagant. Likewise, there is no obligation to bring trust purposes within the ambit of specific wordings in the preamble, such as the "relief" of the aged,[165] or of Lord Macnaghten's classification in *Pemsel*, such as the "advancement" of religion.[166] Nor are Scottish judges bound to articulate their rejection of a manifestly useless

[158] 1923 SC 344: see passage quoted in the text to n 120 above.

[159] [1895] 2 Ch 657: authority for the proposition that "mere sport" is not charitable in English law.

[160] [1972] Ch 73, 88.

[161] Deakin Report, above n 1, para 3.2.6.

[162] Cf *Re Nottage* [1895] 2 Ch 657.

[163] Cf *IRC* v. *City of Glasgow Police Athletic Association* [1953] AC 380.

[164] Cf *Williams' Trustees* v. *IRC* [1947] AC 447; *IRC* v. *Baddeley* [1955] AC 572.

[165] Cf *Joseph Rowntree Memorial Trust Housing Association Ltd* v. *Attorney-General* [1983] Ch 159. A trust for "the aged millionaires of Morningside" might well be held invalid by a Scottish court under the public policy veto.

[166] Cf *Keren Kayemeth Le Jisroel* v. *IRC* [1931] 2 KB 465; [1932] AC 650.

project in terms of the Macnaghten categories,[167] nor do those categories pre-condition their assessment of whether a particular project offers sufficient benefit to the public: for instance, by virtue of a rule that the "benefit" element in a trust for the advancement of religion need only be minimal, and certainly less than for one falling under the fourth head.[168] It is no objection to a public trust in Scotland that, although it can be seen to benefit a sufficiently designated section of the public in a lawful and useful way, room still cannot be found for it under any of the four heads of charity.[169] There is no need for a Scottish court to proceed painstakingly from one analogy to another in order to treat a new type of beneficial activity as within the scope of "public": if the activity is not deliberately excluded by the public policy veto, it is automatically included.

C. Demonstrable Benefit to the Public

Scottish public purposes are less restrictive than English "charitable" purposes in another sense. The Court of Session's public policy veto performs, on the face of it, a similar function within the Scottish concept as the English rule that a charitable purpose must benefit the public at large. That rule has both a negative and a positive aspect: it both excludes the harmful and requires that some positive benefit should accrue, directly or indirectly, and in a form perceptible to the court, to the public at large.[170] The Scottish approach, however, is concerned principally with excluding the harmful and the useless: utility is presumed unless the court has no choice but to declare its absence. In a sense, therefore, there is a presumption of benefit in every case which is similar to the presumption of benefit in English law under the first three heads of charity. But if the presumption of benefit is challenged, the test proposed by Lord Sands in *Aitken's Trustees*,[171] and applied by Lord Russell in *Campbell Smith's Trustees*,[172] is not that of demonstrable benefit to the public at large, but that of what "a certain section of opinion may regard as of public benefit."[173]

1. *"Section of Opinion"*

The formula is crucially different from Lord Wright's in *National Anti-Vivisection Society* v. *Inland Revenue*,[174] by which purposes falling under the

[167] Cf *Re Shaw* [1957] 1 WLR 729; *Re Pinion* [1965] Ch 85.

[168] Cf *Re Watson* [1973] 1 WLR 1472.

[169] As was formerly the case, for instance, with charities for the promotion of urban and rural regeneration (see Charity Commission, *Promotion of Urban and Rural Regeneration*, leaflet RR 2 (London, Charity Commission, 1999)) and the relief of unemployment (see Charity Commission, *Charities for the Relief of Unemployment*, leaflet RR 3 (London, Charity Commission, 1999)).

[170] Tudor, above n 9, 5.

[171] 1927 SC 374.

[172] 1944 SLT 198.

[173] *Aitken's Trustees* v. *Aitken* 1927 SC 374, 381 (Lord Sands).

[174] [1948] AC 31.

fourth head of charity, if not tangibly and objectively beneficial, must be approved by "the common understanding of enlightened opinion for the time being"[175] or "the general consensus of opinion or understanding".[176] In Scots law—though it should be said that the point has not been exhaustively discussed—it seems clear that a sectional opinion will do.

Thus, in an earlier Scottish anti-vivisection case, *Glasgow Society for Prevention of Cruelty to Animals* v. *National Anti-Vivisection Society*,[177] the issue before the court was which of a number of societies for the prevention of cruelty to animals, each with a different policy on anti-vivisection, should administer a fund left in trust for the total abolition of vivisection. No question arose as to the validity of the trust: the testator's directions were clear, and were presumed, without argument, to be lawful and useful. The competing societies were treated, again without argument, as societies constituted with public objects. The court's sole concern was to ensure that the testator's wishes were given effect in the way most closely matching her directions, and a scheme was settled accordingly.

Not too much should be read into the decision, perhaps, and it may be that the court's acceptance of the public character of the societies was influenced by previous English decisions such as *Re Foveaux*,[178] though none of these was cited. Describing the case in Lord Sands' terms, however, one might say that it was enough for the court that each society represented a different section of opinion on the controversial question of vivisection. The court was not concerned with the merits of the competing views, and was not bound to take any position of its own on the issue.[179]

The Scottish approach is much closer, therefore, to that of Chitty J in *Re Foveaux*[180] than to Lord Wright's. Chitty J held that an anti-vivisection society was charitable, on the basis that it was not for the court to take sides between the supporters and the opponents of vivisection, since the views on both sides were rationally held, and it was the intention of an anti-vivisection society to

175 [1948] AC 31, 49.

176 *Ibid*, 47. See also Charity Commission, *Consultation Paper—Review of the Register: The Public Character of Charity* (London, Charity Commission, 1999), Annex A, para A4.

177 1915 SC 757.

178 [1895] 2 Ch 501.

179 Cf the neutral position described in the American Law Institute, *Restatement of the Law of Trusts*, § 374, comment 1, quoted in Martin, above n 9, 400:

> The courts do not take sides or attempt to decide which of two conflicting views of promoting the social interest of the community is better adapted for the purpose, even though the views are opposed to each other.

Cf also Moffat, above n 9, 757, quoting *Gilmour* v. *Coats* [1949] AC 426, 459 (Lord Reid):

> where a particular belief is accepted by one religion and rejected by another, the law can neither accept nor reject it. The law must accept the position that it is right that different religions should each be supported, irrespective of whether or not all its beliefs are true.

Moffat suggests that by parity of reasoning other, non-religious campaigning organisations might be held charitable.

180 [1895] 2 Ch 501.

benefit the community. That approach was disapproved by Lord Wright in the *National Anti-Vivisection Society* case on the grounds that it was subjective, in the sense that it allowed the benefactors—the contributors to such a society—to determine what was or was not charitable.[181] But on Lord Sands' test it is not the benefactors' view that determines what is or is not beneficial, but the view of a "certain section of opinion", established by the court if necessary with the aid of objective evidence.

Lord Wright's test was, of course, formulated only with the fourth head of charity in mind, and it has been frequently emphasised that the requirement for benefit to the public at large differs under each of the four heads. But in Scots common law the Macnaghten categories are irrelevant, and Lord Sands' test of the approval of a section of opinion, subject always to the public policy veto of the court, can be said to apply to all types of benefit which might come into consideration. How might it be applied to a gift to Carmelite sisters such as the one discussed by the House of Lords in *Gilmour* v. *Coats*?[182] There Lord Simonds described the benefit to the wider public of intercessory prayer as "manifestly not susceptible of proof".[183] Leaving aside for the moment the separate question of whether the sisters themselves could be described as a "section of the public", one might suggest that the "certain section of opinion" represented by the Roman Catholic Church would be sufficient to establish the publicly beneficial character of the Carmelite way of life. It would be a bold court, surely, that would characterise such a life as "grotesque, extravagant, wasteful or futile".

2. *Campaigning Organisations*

Lord Sands' approach has obvious implications for the treatment of campaigning organisations. A trust for the promotion of law reform, such as the total abolition of vivisection, may be a public trust. Such an object is lawful, and in a democratic society must surely also be considered useful, provided—according to Lord Sands' test—a section of opinion can be found which regards the reform proposal as beneficial. One might argue that the section of the public intended to benefit from the activities of an anti-vivisection society consists of those who hold the specific beliefs espoused by the society, rather than those who may be morally improved by the humane feelings the society may generate. Such "believers" may join the society and participate actively in the promotion of those beliefs, or they may remain passive beneficiaries of the society's efforts. In any event, there is no need for the court to make a judgment on the beliefs on behalf of the public as a whole, and the court need reject them only if they justify application of the public policy veto as "grotesque, extravagant, wasteful or futile". It is significant that in *Glasgow Society for Prevention of Cruelty to*

[181] *National Anti-Vivisection Society* v. *IRC* [1948] AC 31, 46. See also Lord Simonds, 67.
[182] [1949] AC 426.
[183] *Ibid*, 446.

Animals v. *National Anti-Vivisection Society*[184] the court expressed no doubts as to the validity of the bequest, although a recent Royal Commission on Vivisection had held out minimal prospects of a change in the law.

More recently, the court has taken a similarly relaxed attitude to a trust with a campaigning dimension of a different kind. In *Clarke* v. *Ross*,[185] the purposes of a miners' strike fund were described as "lawful and useful" and a scheme was approved by the Second Division under which the unexpended balance of the fund would be applied, among other objects:

> To promote the interests of the members of the National Union of Mineworkers resident in Fife during and consequent upon official strikes called by said union.

It seems, therefore, that purposes which would, it is submitted, be too "political" to be "charitable" in England and Wales may quite properly be "public" in Scotland.[186] Tentatively, therefore, one might put forward the view that a campaigning organisation having as its principal object the promotion of law reform, or the support of political activity in the general sense of the pursuit of citizens' rights, is an organisation with a lawful and useful public object in the sense of Scots law. It is submitted that the line of authorities which prevents such organisations from being classified as charities in English law forms no part of, and has no parallel, in Scottish public trust law.[187]

3. *Relevance of Fiscal Dimension*

The difference between the English and Scottish approaches is perhaps attributable, at least in part, to the fact that no fiscal consequences attach to Scottish public trust status.[188] Where taxpayers' money is at stake, there is obvious pressure for reliefs to be applied towards objects approved by reference to some form of "common understanding", or at least majority view, across the nation at large. Where no public funding is involved, on the other hand, there is no need for the court, or any other central authority, to "make itself judge of what is for the public benefit."

5. SCOTTISH PUBLIC BENEFIT: SECTION OF THE PUBLIC

"In a public trust, the beneficial interest is intended for the benefit of a section of the public."[189] The fact that the Scottish public benefit concept performs no

[184] 1915 SC 757.

[185] 1976 SLT (Notes) 62.

[186] Cf *Attorney-General* v. *Ross* [1986] 1 WLR 252.

[187] Cf *Bowman* v. *Secular Society* [1917] AC 406; *National Anti-Vivisection Society* v. *IRC* [1948] AC 31; *McGovern* v. *Attorney-General* [1982] Ch 321; see also *Baldry* v. *Feintuck* [1972] 1 WLR 552. For discussion of the current English law, see Alison Dunn's chapter in this book (chap 3), and also Michael Chesterman's chapter (chap 9), at 261–9.

[188] See Moffat, above n 9, 757 for comment on the influence of fiscal privileges on the development of the English definition.

[189] Stair, vol 1, above n 60, para 86.

fiscal function partly also explains, perhaps, why the Scottish courts have been able to take a comparatively uncomplicated approach to the question of what is and what is not a "section of the public".

There is no particular advantage to be gained under Scots common law from presenting a "fluctuating body of individuals" as a section of the public. If anything, there is a disadvantage, in that, in the event of failure of the trust, it will fall to be reorganised under the *nobile officium* or under the supplementary statutory provisions, and the assets will not revert to the truster's estate or, in the case of an association's assets, be distributable among the members for the time being.[190] The distinction between a public and a private class has not, therefore, received the same close attention in Scots law as in the well-known English charity taxation cases.[191] Nor in Scots law does the validity of trusts for poor employees and for the education of employees' children hang on their being classed as public rather than private.[192] And the conceptual half-way house of an invalid "private" purpose trust, which may purport to confer benefit on a section of the public, but not in a way which is charitable, has no equivalent in Scots law.[193] In Scots law, the crucial point is that a trust must benefit somebody. If it does not benefit individuals named or designed, the presumption must be that it benefits a section of the public.

The main concern of the Scottish court is not, therefore, to prevent a benefactor from passing off a private gift as a public one in order to gain unmerited advantages for family or employees, so much as to discern what the true intention of the benefactor really is. Is the trust "intended to create [a] beneficial right of a private kind in the persons of [the beneficiaries]" or is it "intended to benefit a section of the public in all time coming, in which the public possesses an interest . . ."?[194] Thus, while the opinion of the benefactor will not, as we have seen, determine whether a particular project will be regarded by the court as beneficial—the benefactor's own view is always subject to the "section of opinion" test and to the court's overriding public policy veto—none the less the intention of the benefactor, so far as it can be discerned, will be the court's main guide as to whether the supposed benefit—if it is one—is conferred on a private class or on a section of the public.

[190] *Stair Memorial Encyclopaedia of the Laws of Scotland*, vol 2 (Edinburgh, Law Society of Scotland/Butterworths, 1988) ("Stair, vol 2"), para 811.

[191] e.g. *Williams Trustees* v. *IRC* [1947] AC 447; *IRC* v. *Baddeley* [1955] AC 572; *IRC* v. *Educational Grants Association Ltd* [1967] Ch 993.

[192] Cf *Oppenheim* v. *Tobacco Securities Trust Co* [1951] AC 297; *Dingle* v. *Turner* [1972] AC 601.

[193] Cf *Re Astor's Settlement Trusts* [1952] Ch 534; *R.* v. *District Auditor, ex p. West Yorkshire Metropolitan County Council* [1986] RVR 24.

[194] These questions are drawn from the language of Lord Skerrington in *Anderson's Trustees* v. *Scott* 1914 SC 942, 950, 955.

A. Examples

In practice, in any event, the difference between a public and a private trust seems usually to be reasonably clear to the Scottish courts.[195] A sample of "sections of the public" from the cases may give a flavour of their approach.

First of all, while the usual formulation of the Scottish public benefit concept refers to a "section of the public", the benefit in a public trust may none the less be conferred on the Scottish public as a whole.[196] The section of the public may be part of a "public" outside Scotland,[197] even in England.[198] Very commonly, the section of the public is defined by locality, the definition being implied in some cases by a gift to a particular institution which by its nature serves only a local catchment area.[199]

Also capable of being treated as public are trusts for the benefit of persons of a particular profession,[200] or of professional persons generally;[201] or of a class of disadvantaged persons,[202] or of disadvantaged persons selected by reference to a particular profession;[203] or of "young gentlemen who are not objects of charity in the narrow sense of the word, but who could not obtain the advantages of a public school or university education" without the assistance of a bursary,[204] or of students studying particular subjects at a particular university;[205] or of the families and dependants of those lost in a particular natural disaster.[206]

[195] In *Mohammed Shariff and Another, Petitioners* (unreported: Lord Nimmo Smith's opinion of 23 June 1999 is available at www.scotcourts.gov.uk.), Lord Nimmo Smith was able to say, in the second paragraph of his opinion, of a trust for the advancement of the teaching and study of Islam whose benefits were mediated through an informally constituted association: "Scots law distinguishes between public and private trusts and this trust is clearly a public one." Cf *Glentanar* v. *Scottish Industrial Musical Association* 1925 SC 892; *Tod's Trustees, Petitioners* 1999 SLT 308.

[196] In *Aitken's Trustees* v. *Aitken* 1927 SC 374, 382, Lord Sands gives the example of the Scott Monument in Edinburgh. See also *Campbell Smith's Trustees* v. *Scott* 1944 SLT 198.

[197] *Ewing* v. *McGavin* (1831) 9 S 622 (New Brunswick); *National Bible Society of Scotland* v. *Church of Scotland* 1946 SLT (Notes) 26 (British South Africa Rhodesia).

[198] *Neech's Executors, Petitioners* 1947 SC 119.

[199] *Ness* v. *Mills Trustees* 1923 SC 344 (Dundee); *Lindsays Executors* v. *Forsyth* 1940 SC 568 (RC Parish of St Cuthbert's, Edinburgh); *Leven Penny Savings Bank, Petitioners* 1948 SC 147 (Leven, Fife); *Davidsons Trustees* v. *Arnott* 1951 SC 42 (Girvan); *Sutherland's Trustees* v. *Verschoyle* 1968 SLT 43 (Saint Andrews).

[200] *Cuthbert's Trustees* v. *Cuthbert* 1958 SC 629 (a bequest of a country house as a holiday home for nurses).

[201] *Tod's Trustees, Petitioners* 1999 SLT 308.

[202] *Clyde Industrial Training Ship Association, Petitioners* 1925 SC 676 ("orphans or fatherless boys who are left destitute"); *Trustees of Scotstown Moor Children's Camp, Petitioners* 1948 SC 630 (holidays for "needy and ailing children"); *Craig's Trustees* v. *Hunter* 1956 SLT (Notes) 15 ("orphans of Scottish parentage exclusively").

[203] *Tod's Trustees* v. *The Sailors' And Firemen's Orphans And Widows' Society* 1953 SLT 72 ("old and infirm officers of the mercantile marine").

[204] *Anderson's Trustees* v. *Scott* 1914 SC 942, 954 (example given by Lord Skerrington).

[205] *Grigor Medical Bursary Fund Trustees, Petitioners* (1903) 5 F 1143; *McCrie's Trustees, Petitioners* 1927 SC 556.

[206] *Gibson and Others, Petitioners* (1900) 2 F 1195 (a shipwreck).

Narrower, even eccentric (but not "grotesque or extravagant"), criteria of selection are acceptable, for instance, that section of the public "who have lived worthy lives and have had to struggle against adverse circumstances—pious persons who are not and have not been spendthrifts".[207]

B. Class Within a Class

There is no objection in principle to a class within a class,[208] and there is little doubt that a trust for "old Presbyterian persons"[209] (a class not unfamiliar in Scotland) would be a valid public trust.[210] A trust for "rebuilding a bridge in Ayr"[211] "to be crossed only by impecunious Methodists"[212] might well be invalid, not so much because of the selectivity of the class as such, but because, taken as a whole, the project might be regarded as extravagant and wasteful, even capricious. It is submitted, however, that a trust for a community centre for Methodists and potential Methodists resident in Edinburgh[213] would be both valid and public: if the centre were to fail for any reason, the disposal of the trust assets would be settled by a scheme approved by the court, not by distribution among the members as individuals. The same would be true, it is also submitted, of an institute promoting "the moral, social, spiritual and educational welfare of Welsh people" in Glasgow, on the assumption that the nature of the project was sufficiently defined.[214]

C. Personal Nexus

The distinction between a private and a public trust in Scots law is not clouded by special treatment of trusts for poor relations or poor employees. Lord President Cooper, once again emphasising the differences between Scots and English law, made the position clear when the First Division considered the validity of a bequest to "poor relations" and others in *Salvesen's Trustees* v. *Wye*:[215]

[207] *Donaldson's Trustees* v. *Lord Advocate* 1938 SLT 106.

[208] *Trustees of Prime Gilt Box Society, Petitioners* 1920 SC 534 ("old and disabled mariners belonging to the port of Kirkcaldy and their widows and children"); *Grigor Medical Bursary Fund Trustees, Petitioners* (1903) 5 F 1143 (young men native of the county of Nairn, for the study of medicine at Edinburgh).

[209] See N Dawson, " 'Old Presbyterian Persons'—A Sufficient Section of the Public?" [1987] *Conv* 114.

[210] *Robertson's Trustees, Petitioners* 1948 SC 1 ("convalescent rest home for the benefit of members of churches associated in the Baptist Union of Scotland").

[211] *Burgh of Ayr* v. *Shaw* (1904) 12 SLT 126.

[212] *IRC* v. *Baddeley* [1955] AC 572, 592 (Lord Simonds).

[213] i.e. "a community centre in which social intercourse and discreet festivity may go hand in hand with religious observance and instruction": *IRC* v. *Baddeley* [1955] AC 572, 586 (Lord Simonds).

[214] Cf *Williams' Trustees* v. *IRC* [1947] AC 477.

[215] 1954 SC 440, 447: see also *Caledonian Employees Benevolent Society, Petitioners* 1928 SC 633.

> According to Scots law the mere introduction of the adjective "poor" as a qualification of "relations, friends or acquaintances of mine" will not suffice to impart to this bequest the special qualities and privileges of a trust for charitable uses. It remains a private trust; and I can give no further or other effect to the word "poor" than a narrowing of the class by a requirement that its members should be in need of financial assistance. The dominant determining factor is not that the beneficiaries should be a section of "the poor" in the common and now obsolescent sense of that expression, but that they should answer the description of being connected with the testator as relations, friends, acquaintances or former employees or the wives of such employees.

His Lordship went on to hold, with the other judges, that the vagueness of the word "acquaintances" rendered the bequest void from uncertainty.

1. *Nexus by Family Relationship or Employment*

There is an obvious similarity between Lord President Cooper's criterion of "personal connection" with the testator and Lord Simonds' "personal nexus" test in *Oppenheim* v. *Tobacco Securities Trust Co.*[216] Lord Simonds held that, though a designated group of persons might be numerous, "if the nexus between them is their personal relationship to a single *propositus* or to several *propositi*, they are neither the community nor a section of the community".[217] One might suggest, however, that Lord President Cooper's term "dominant determining factor" is in itself an acceptance that the distinction between "public" and "private" is one of balance and interpretation in each case. The task of the court is to interpret the language of the testator, and Lord President Cooper's main concern is that the anomalous English rules as to poor relations and poor employee trusts should not be allowed to confuse the issue.

2. *Nexus by Contract*

Similarly, it will be a question of balance and interpretation in each case whether the existence of a contract between the beneficiaries of a trust will make the trust private rather than public. Many of the Scottish public trust cases involve the property of what Lord McLaren calls "voluntary societies constituted for public objects":[218] these are associations established with the intention of benefiting a section of the public, and in so far as funds may be contributed by the members and others to furthering their objects they amount to "trusts for public uses".[219] These are organisations founded to confer a benefit on a section of the public other than the members themselves: the members will be bound

[216] [1951] AC 297.
[217] *Ibid*, 306.
[218] Above, n 73, 917.
[219] *Ibid*.

together by a contract of association, but will derive no personal benefit from the association.[220] They are associations of benefactors, not beneficiaries.

Such organisations are to be distinguished from self-help organisations, which not only confine their benefits to their own members but also restrict access to membership by demanding a set contribution which amounts to payment for future benefit.[221] The benefactors and beneficiaries of such organisations, in other words, are to all intents and purposes identical. The organisation's assets are held solely for the benefit of the members for the time being, and subject to the contractual rights of members.[222] Consistently with the approach of Lord President Cooper in *Salvesen's Trustees*, there is no anomalous exception in Scots law in favour of a "closed" self-help organisation of this kind whose object is the relief of the poverty of its members.[223] In such cases, there is no intention to benefit a wider public beyond the membership, and there is no public trust.

In the middle of the spectrum, however, lie organisations which might be described as "mixed": they offer benefits to a section of the public, but their members may themselves enjoy those benefits. There is authority in a dictum of Lord Dunedin, in *D & J Nichol* v. *Dundee Harbour Trustees*,[224] for the view that such an organisation is itself a trustee, or *quasi*-trustee, for the wider public the organisation is intended to serve. The members, in so far as they may influence the disposal of the organisation's assets through its internal decision-making procedures, must do so strictly in accordance with the fiduciary duty they owe to the wider section of the public of which they are themselves representatives. The same idea was put in another way by Lord Skerrington in *Anderson's Trustees* v. *Scott*,[225] when he described a small congregation of dissenting Presbyterians as the "primary beneficiary" of the public trust in which its church and manse were held, the "secondary beneficiaries" being the wider section of the public who might at any time choose to join the congregation in its particular form of worship.[226] As a voluntary association in Scots law, the congregation would have been regulated by a contract among its members, yet the day-to-day enjoyment and control of the trust's assets by the congregation did not deprive the trust of its public character.

[220] Examples are an association to relieve the victims of a natural disaster (*Ewing* v. *McGavin* (1831) 9 S 622), or the financial needs associated with old age or disablement (*Trustees of Prime Gilt Box Society, Petitioners* 1920 SC 534), or to provide a school for destitute children (*Trustees of Falkirk Certified Industrial School* v. *Ferguson Bequest Fund* (1899) 1 F 1175), or promote the spiritual and temporal welfare of young women (*Edinburgh Young Women's Christian Institute, Petitioners* (1893) 20 R 894).

[221] *Mitchell* v. *Burness* (1878) 5 R 954; *Smith* v. *Lord Advocate* (1899) 1 F 741. Cf *Hobourn Aero Components Air Raid Distress Fund* [1946] Ch 169.

[222] Stair, vol 2, above n 190, para 810.

[223] *Smith* v. *Lord Advocate* (1899) 1 F 741.

[224] 1915 SC (HL) 7, 13.

[225] 1914 SC 942.

[226] *Ibid*, 950, 955.

Arguably, adoption of a similar approach might have contributed to a different result in *Gilmour* v. *Coats*,[227] the case in which the House of Lords held that a gift to a closed Carmelite community was not charitable. Might it not have been possible to say that the community of sisters was, like the congregation in *Anderson's Trustees*, simply the primary beneficiary of the intended bequest, of which those who might choose to join the community in the future were the secondary beneficiaries? The community was closed, in the sense that the nuns had no day-to-day contact with the outside world, but open in the sense that postulants would always have been warmly welcomed. In Lord Dunedin's terms, the community for the time being would have owed a fiduciary duty as *quasi*-trustee to its own future members. The section of the public benefited in such a case would be, it is suggested, not so much those who might (or might not) be assisted by the nuns' intercessory prayer, but those members of the public who might from time to time be attracted to their way of life.

That a similar analysis can be applied in a secular context seems clear from *Leven Penny Savings Bank, Petitioners*,[228] in which the trustees of an organisation of indeterminate legal form petitioned the Court of Session for approval of a scheme for disposal of its assets on dissolution. The object of the organisation had been to provide savings account facilities to the people of Leven, but the enterprise had become gradually redundant as a result of the arrival of conventional banking facilities in the town. Lord Keith, while agreeing with the other judges that the petition should be dismissed as unnecessary, warned that the entity was, in his view, a "trust of a public character" and that any scheme of dissolution approved by the members (i.e. depositors) under its existing rules should dispose of any surplus not simply among the members themselves, but "by a scheme of a more public or charitable character".[229]

There is a fine line, no doubt, between an organisation of this mixed type and a self-help organisation proper, but what seems to distinguish them is that—though both types are non-profit organisations—membership of the mixed organisation is open without restriction to an identifiable section of the public. Membership of the organisation is simply the mechanism by which the intended benefit is mediated to the section of the public in question.[230] The *Leven Penny Savings Bank* case, therefore, seems capable of bringing organisations such as a credit union within the scope of the Scottish public benefit concept.[231]

[227] [1949] AC 426.

[228] 1948 SC 147.

[229] *Ibid*, 153.

[230] Cf Charity Commission, *Consultation Paper—Review of the Register: The Recreational Charities Act 1958* (London, Charity Commission, 1999), para 29.

[231] Cf Charity Commission, *Consultation Paper—Review of the Register: The Promotion of Community Development* (London, Charity Commission, 1999), para A 21, n 31.

D. Summary

The *Leven Penny Savings Bank* case is, however, something of a curiosity, and the truth is that generally the Scottish courts have had little difficulty in practice in distinguishing public from private trusts.[232] Their object is to establish the intention of the benefactors in each case, and they have neither devised nor felt the need to devise any foolproof test of what makes a class of beneficiaries a "section of the public", not a private class. The absence of a family or employment nexus to a "single *propositus*" is undoubtedly a guide, but the existence of a contract of association among the beneficiaries does not in itself settle the question either way. There may well be cases in which—to paraphrase Lord Cross in *Dingle* v. *Turner*[233]—the Scottish judges are left, like their English counterparts, "with the bare contrast between 'public' and 'private'" and the sense that the distinction may in practice be nothing more than "a question of degree".[234] The difference between the two systems, however, is that very much more hangs on the distinction in England and Wales than in Scotland, and that the Scottish judges have had to labour over it correspondingly less. They have been free, in short, to adopt the working assumption that if a trust is not obviously a private trust it is a public trust.

6. SCOTTISH PUBLIC BENEFIT: "EXCLUSIVELY PUBLIC"

For similar reasons, the Scottish courts have not had to labour, either, over the question of whether the purposes of a public trust must be exclusively public. There is no true equivalent in Scots law of the rule that, to be classed as a charitable trust, all the purposes of a trust must be charitable. Where trustees are given a discretion to apply funds among a number of objects, some of which are specified with certainty and others not, the whole gift will fall from uncertainty.[235] But where trustees are given a discretion to apply funds among a number of objects, all specified with certainty, but some private and some public, the trust as a whole is valid.[236] Such an approach is possible in Scots law, as it is not in the English law of charities, largely because—as already pointed out—the distinction between public and private trusts in Scots law does not impact on questions of validity and fiscal treatment in the same way. It should be emphasised, however, that a "hybrid" public and private trust is rare, and that the norm in Scotland is to find trusts which are clearly either public or private.

It must be conceded, however, that if fiscal privileges were to be attached to public trust status in the future—or if English charitable status were to be

[232] See n 195 above.
[233] [1972] AC 601.
[234] *Ibid*, 624, 625.
[235] *Salvesen's Trustees* v. *Wye* 1954 SC 440.
[236] *Ibid*. See also *Glentanar* v. *Scottish Industrial Musical Association* 1925 SC 892; *Ossington's Trustees, Petitioners* 1965 SC 410.

redefined in terms of Scottish public benefit but were to retain its existing fiscal function—an exclusivity rule on the model of the current English rule would have to be introduced. That would be the only way of ensuring that tax incentives intended to encourage publicly beneficial activity were not exploited for private benefit. For membership organisations "constituted for public objects" the effect of the rule would no doubt be that any private benefit to members would be limited to benefit "of a subsidiary or incidental character".[237]

7. OVERLAP AND DIFFERENCES BETWEEN SCOTS "PUBLIC" AND ENGLISH "CHARITABLE"

From what has gone before it will be obvious that there are considerable areas of overlap between the Scottish concept of public benefit and the English definition of charity, but also that there are considerable differences. It may be helpful to restate the position briefly.

The Scottish concept is inclusive rather than exclusive. A purpose is public if it benefits a section of the public in a lawful and useful way. The purpose must not be illegal or immoral, but the threshold of what is "useful"—the point at which the court will intervene to exclude what is "grotesque, extravagant, wasteful or futile"—is generally set low. Beyond applying its public policy veto, the court is under no obligation to judge whether or not a purpose will benefit the public at large, so long as a "certain section of opinion" can be seen to support it. Trusts promoting law reform, or campaigning organisations pursuing the interests of an identifiable section of the public, can therefore be said to be included in the concept rather than excluded. The benefactor's own opinion as to what is beneficial, on the other hand, is not a determining factor.

No very sophisticated test has been devised of what is or is not a "section of the public", nor has one been required. It can be said, however, that a link between beneficiaries by personal nexus with the truster is characteristic of a private rather than a public trust, and that the anomalous exception in favour of trusts for the relief of poverty in English charity law has no counterpart in Scottish public trust law. In this context, however, it is the intention of the benefactor which determines the nature of the trust: if the intention is to set up a permanent trust which will benefit persons unconnected with and unknown to the benefactor, the trust will almost certainly be a public trust. Self-help organisations, on the other hand, are not public trusts, even where their object is the relief of poverty, but funds held ostensibly for the members of an association as "primary beneficiaries" may truly be held in public trust for a wider section of the public as "secondary beneficiaries". A hybrid trust with both public and private purposes is not unthinkable in Scots law, though in practice rare.

[237] *IRC* v. *City of Glasgow Police Athletic Association* [1953] AC 380, 402 (Lord Reid). Benefit to members of a "mixed" organisation would not, of course, be regarded as private if the benefit were open equally to a wider section of the public through the machinery of membership.

In practice, almost all trusts which are charitable in the English sense are likely to be public in the Scottish sense. The scope of "public" is not conditioned by the preamble to the Charitable Uses Act 1601 or the Macnaghten categories, but is certainly wide enough to include all types of activity covered by the preamble and by the four heads of charity. The English requirement for demonstrable benefit is stricter than the equivalent Scottish test, and, except in the case of trusts for the relief of poverty, the English test of what amounts to a "section of the public", even in its most flexible form, is almost certainly also stricter.

A Scottish public trust, on the other hand, will not necessarily be charitable in the English sense.[238] Some public purposes will be excluded because they do not fall within the spirit and intendment of the preamble; others because they lack the required element of benefit to the public at large, or at least because the court cannot judge whether they are beneficial to the public at large or not; others because they benefit a body of persons which fails to meet the stricter English test of what is a "section of the public"; and still others because they are not constituted exclusively for charitable purposes, or because they undertake law reform or other "political" activities of a kind stigmatised as non-charitable.

At least some of the differences can be explained by the fact that the Scottish public benefit concept carries no fiscal implications. Those are carried in Scotland by the English definition of charity. The Scottish courts are therefore able to distinguish all the more clearly between what Lord Cross described in *Dingle* v. *Turner* as "really two quite different questions": namely, "the question whether a trust to further some purpose is so little likely to benefit the public that it ought to be declared invalid and the question whether it is likely to confer such great benefits on the public that it should enjoy fiscal immunity".[239]

8. PROPOSAL FOR A REDEFINITION OF CHARITY

Is it possible, then, that the Scottish concept of public benefit might be adapted to produce a statutory redefinition of charity fitting the Deakin and Kemp specifications quoted at the beginning of this chapter? A "charity" is defined in English law by reference to its purposes,[240] and so the real requirement is for a redefinition of "charitable purposes".

[238] *Trustees for the Roll of Voluntary Workers* v. *IRC* 1942 SC 47, 53 (Lord President Normand).

[239] *Dingle* v. *Turner* [1972] AC 601, 624.

[240] However, note Charles Mitchell's argument in this book at 200–1, that the Charity Commissioners have now effectively moved beyond an exclusively purpose-orientated approach, to make legal charitable status contingent on proof that a body seeking registration as a charity will pursue its purposes in particular ways.

A. A Redefinition

Perhaps it might go something like this:

> In the law of England and Wales "charitable purposes" shall mean purposes which are exclusively public, being purposes which are intended to benefit a section of the public and which are lawful and useful.

A proviso might be added to the effect that the constituent terms of the definition should be interpreted according to the law of Scotland, but subject to the further qualification that—in the language of Lord Normand—the English courts need not be "obsequious followers" of the decisions of the Court of Session.[241]

Such a definition would, it is submitted, establish the "single overarching charitable category" envisaged by the Deakin Commission, "formulated in terms of benefit to the community"—"community" being understood, as also envisaged by the Deakin Commission, in the sense of "a sufficiently important section of the public".[242] If applied as the Scottish courts have applied the existing Scottish concept, there is no reason, it is submitted, why the new definition should not be prove to be "clear, workable and flexible". It would embody, it is also submitted, the "essential altruism" implicit in an organisation being established for the benefit of a section of the public rather than for the private benefit of a closed membership.

The new definition would meet the requirement suggested by the Kemp Commission[243] that it "should not be narrowly codified"—though the "concept of public interest" which the Kemp Commission identifies as "central to the approach of both jurisdictions" would be the inclusive Scottish version formulated by Lord Sands in preference to the more demanding tests of Lord Simonds and Lord Wright.

Lest, however, the same criticism were to be directed at the new definition as can be—and has been[244]—directed at the English definition, namely that it is meaningless to a person who has no knowledge of the case law, the following practical guidance as to its application might be issued. A person wishing to establish whether a particular organisation was charitable would ask the following questions:

- Is the benefactor's project defined with certainty?
- Does it evidence an intention to benefit (to the exclusion of private interests) a section of the public?
- Is the benefit such as a certain section of opinion may regard as of public benefit?

241 *IRC* v. *City of Glasgow Police Athletic Association* [1953] AC 380, 394.
242 Deakin Report, above n 1, para 3.2.6(a).
243 Kemp Report, above n 1, para 7.16.3
244 C Mitchell, "Redefining Charity in English Law", (1999) 13 *Tru LI* 21, 36.

- Can application of the public policy veto be excluded: because there is nothing illegal or immoral about the project, nothing contrary to public order, nothing grotesque, extravagant, wasteful or futile?
- Does the class of persons intended to benefit from the project amount to a section of the public?
- Is the dominant determining factor in the definition of the class something other than a personal connection with the benefactor?
- Where *beneficiaries* belong to a membership organisation, is the membership open, and is membership simply a mechanism for mediating benefit to a wider section of the public?
- Where *benefactors* belong to a membership organisation constituted primarily to serve a section of the public (not the members), is any private benefit to members purely subsidiary or incidental?

If the answer to all of these questions was "yes", the organisation would be regarded as "charitable" within the new definition.

B. Deakin and Kemp Criticisms

The new definition would, it is submitted, meet at least some of the criticisms directed at the present definition by the Deakin Commission: its inclusiveness would automatically keep it abreast of changing social conditions,[245] and few organisations popularly regarded as contributing to the public good would be excluded.[246] There is no reason in principle why the definition should not cover, in particular, community development organisations, enterprise schemes, programmes to help the unemployed, credit unions and sporting organisations,[247] provided that the benefits offered were freely available to all comers, and that the membership and management of any organisation mediating the benefit to a wider public conducted themselves as *quasi*-trustees as well as "primary beneficiaries". As the Deakin Commission recommends specifically, identifiable black and minority groups would be included,[248] as would human rights and environmental groups[249]—even those campaigning for changes in government policy and the law.

On the other hand, certain organisations "which some might think are not truly deserving of charitable status"[250] would inevitably retain it—such, perhaps, as schools for the children of the well-off. The definition would not resolve at a stroke the problems associated with the term "section of the

[245] Deakin Report, above n 1, para 3.2.2.

[246] *Ibid*, para 3.2.1.

[247] *Ibid*.

[248] *Ibid*, para 3.2.6(a). See *Mohammed Shariff and Another, Petitioners* (unreported: Lord Nimmo Smith's opinion of 23 June 1999 is available at www.scotcourts.gov.uk.).

[249] *Ibid*, para 3.2.1.

[250] *Ibid*.

public",[251] nor the question of reconciling "public" with any possible "private" benefit.[252] The fine line between, on the one hand, an avowedly mutual or self-help organisation, restricting its benefits to those who have purchased a right to them—excluded from the definition—and, on the other, an organisation mediating a service open to all but enjoyed primarily by its own membership—included in the definition—would become no less fine, although Lord Dunedin's concept of *quasi*-trustees, and Lord Skerrington's of primary and secondary beneficiaries, might provide additional aids to analysis in particular situations. The loss from the charitable fold of poor relations and employee trusts, and of self-help organisations for the relief of poverty, might well be widely regretted.[253]

The additional criticism made by the Kemp Commission that "charity" is nowadays a "slightly patronising" word, and inadequate to describe "the nature of many bodies given charitable status",[254] could be met by adopting (or adapting) the suggestion of the Scottish Council for Voluntary Organisations that charities should be renamed "Public Benefit Associations".[255] The Kemp Commission's further point that it is unsatisfactory that a definition of such significance for Scotland should be determined by the rules of another system would, of course, be met in full.[256] Perhaps, though, an equivalent criticism might be voiced on the other side of the Border.

C. Impact on Functions

What impact would the proposed alteration to the definition have on the functions it currently performs in the English system?[257]

1. *Trust Law Function*

At the level of trust law, the new definition would go some way, perhaps, to reducing the judicial effort required to decide what is and what is not a valid charitable trust. Public policy decisions would no longer have to be couched in the specialist language of English charity law, but could be acknowledged for what they are—"a somewhat delicate exercise of judicial discretion".[258] The

[251] *Ibid.*

[252] *Ibid.*

[253] But see Report of the Goodman Committee: *Charity Law and Voluntary Organisations* (London, NCVO, 1976), para 28.

[254] Kemp Report, above n 1, para 7.14.1.

[255] *Ibid*, para 7.14.3.

[256] *Ibid*, para 7.15.3.6.

[257] For similar conclusions arrived at by a different route, see S Bright "Charity and Trusts for the Public Benefit—Time for a Rethink?" [1989] *Conv* 28.

[258] *Aitken's Trustees* v. *Aitken* 1927 SC 374, 382 (Lord Sands). Cf *R* v. *Registrar General, ex parte Segerdal* [1972] 2 QB 697, and also the Charity Commissioners' recent refusal of an application for registration as a charity by the Church of Scientology (available on the Charity Commission website: www.charity-commission.gov.uk).

new definition would do away with private, non-charitable purpose trusts, but, more importantly, it would remove restrictions—largely historical in justification—on the freedom of individuals to confer benefit on a section of the public through the medium of a trust.

2. *Supervisory Function*

At the level of supervision, the inclusiveness of the new definition would widen the jurisdiction of the Charity Commissioners, and presumably increase their workload. Adjustments might have to be made to the compliance regime to accommodate additional numbers, but the supervisory role of the public itself might be enhanced by the introduction of a general right to enforce along the lines of the *popularis actio*. On the other hand, the task of assessing applications for registration would, it is submitted, become simpler. The presumption would be in favour of registration, and consultations associated with future reviews of the register would concentrate on what not to include rather than on how the existing definition could be "extended and developed" to reflect "changes in social conditions and attitudes".[259] Those changes would be taken account of automatically.

3. *Fiscal Function*

At the level of fiscal privileges, however, the inclusiveness of the new definition might well cause embarrassment. The Deakin Commission considered the "basic link between charitable status and tax benefits . . . a proper one in principle".[260] But the pressure to separate questions of validity and fiscal immunity would surely increase if the definition were widened. The notion of a split-level system of charity might well be revived,[261] with tax privileges accorded only to a favoured layer of organisations identified as specially beneficial to the community as a whole. Such a system already exists, of course, in simple form, in Scotland. The favoured layer consists of bodies which meet the current English definition of charity: the less favoured layer consists of public trusts which have fallen short of charitability in the English sense. Yet, if the fiscal function were the only function of the existing definition of charity throughout the United Kingdom, how long would it resist reform? In other words, if one were designing a system of tax incentives for the voluntary sector from scratch, is the existing definition of charity the place one would start?

[259] Charity Commission, *Review of the Register of Charities*, leaflet RR 1 (London, Charity Commission, 1999), Annex A, para A5.

[260] Deakin Report, above n 1, para 3.2.4.

[261] See The Radcliffe Report: *Final Report of the Royal Commission on the Taxation of Profits and Income*, Cmnd 9474 (London, HMSO, 1955), para 170.

9. CONCLUSION

At the end of the day—to paraphrase Lord Cross again—perhaps one is left with the bare contrast between "public" and "charitable", between the inclusive and the less inclusive. The Scottish public benefit concept has long ago been proved workable and effective by the Scottish courts as a criterion of validity in trust law; it is submitted that it could be made to be workable and effective as the criterion for the supervisory jurisdiction of the Charity Commissioners, especially if the state were willing to accept assistance from the general public in the form of the *popularis actio*; but it is perhaps too blunt an instrument to be used as the criterion for detecting an organisation which is "likely to confer such great benefits on the public that it should enjoy fiscal immunity".[262]

And what of the constitutional function the current English definition performs under the Scotland Act 1998? Its effect is to mark out the limits of the legislative competence of the Scottish Parliament in the area of voluntary sector law: so any increase in the scope of the definition would extend the powers of the Parliament correspondingly. In Scotland, in other words, the wider the definition, the better.

It seems reasonably safe to say, therefore, that a statutory redefinition of charity based on the alternative Scottish concept of public benefit—such as the one proposed in this chapter—would receive a certain amount of support from North of the Border, if, perhaps, from nowhere else.

[262] *Dingle* v. *Turner* [1972] AC 601, 624 (Lord Cross).

9

Foundations of Charity Law in the New Welfare State

MICHAEL CHESTERMAN[1]

1. A MISSION STATEMENT FOR CHARITY LAW

THIS IS SOMETHING of a "back to basics" essay about the peculiar blend of trusts law, tax law and administrative law which we call the law of charities. In general terms, my case is that even though the "new welfare state" may have provided a very different operating environment for charities, one in which both their significance and their resources have seemingly increased, some basic problems remain in charity law. In fact, the importance of solving these problems satisfactorily is another thing that has increased on account of the arrival of new approaches to welfare provision.

About twenty years ago, in the concluding section of my book, *Charities, Trusts and Social Welfare*, I compiled what I fondly hoped was a cogent left-wing critique of the general structure of English charity law.[2] This critique probably now looks distinctly dated. Lodged within it, but not directly expressed, was a set of loosely-formed ideas about what a satisfactory legal regime for charities should seek to achieve. In outline, the set of ambitions, or "mission statement", for charity law[3] which I implicitly had in mind was as follows:

- To provide one or more legal structures (trust, company, etc) whereby the purposes envisaged by the altruistic originators of publicly beneficial, non-profit-distributing enterprises can be formally laid down.

[1] Professor of Law, University of New South Wales, Sydney, Australia. A version of this chapter previously appeared in (1999) 62 *MLR* 333, and it is reproduced here, with minor revisions, with the kind permission of the editor of that journal. Expert research assistance provided by Ms Angela Seow Wee Tan is gratefully acknowledged. I also owe thanks to the Law Foundation of New South Wales for funding this research and to my colleague Associate Professor Philip Burgess for providing critical commentary on a draft.

[2] M Chesterman, *Charities, Trusts and Social Welfare* (London, Weidenfeld & Nicolson, 1979), chaps 14–17.

[3] The "essential characteristics" suggested for charities (not charity law) by the Charity Commission in *The Review of the Register of Charities*, leaflet RR 1 (London, Charity Commission, 1999), part 2, and also the "hallmarks of a well-run charity" set out in *The Hallmarks of a Well-Run Charity*, leaflet CC 60 (London, Charity Commission, 1999), have some similarities to this "mission statement" of mine. See too the Report of the Commission on the Future of the Voluntary Sector, *Meeting the Challenge of Change: Voluntary Action into the 21st Century* (London, HMSO, 1996), part 3.

- To ensure that any processes in which these enterprises, or persons or bodies on their behalf, engage with a view to obtaining funds from government bodies and/or the private sector are carried out in accordance with appropriate standards of honesty and efficiency.
- To ensure that the persons in charge of enterprises of this nature apply their funds and other assets towards fulfilment of their stated purposes, meeting appropriate standards of honesty and efficiency and with some awareness of the desirability of co-operating with other agencies in the same field of welfare provision.
- To provide state support for such enterprises through fiscal privileges, so long as they pursue purposes which can legitimately be expected to benefit a significant group of people who are in need of welfare assistance, and thereby bring about some distribution of society's resources from the rich to the poor.
- To assure to such enterprises a significant measure of independence from state welfare policy, in order that (a) public-spirited individuals will continue to be motivated to establish and maintain them, and (b) any potential which they may have for creative and innovative contributions to welfare provision may be beneficially exploited.

A commentary on my final chapter, published in Australia in 1991,[4] contained the suggestion (with which I agree) that the broad "conundrum" underlying my critique was that of reconciling the "private ordering" which takes place through the creation and perpetuation of charitable enterprises with a number of significant "public interest" considerations. These considerations include efficiency in expenditure of welfare funds, recognition of a hierarchy of needs and co-ordination of welfare activity. The commentary suggested (and again I agree) that total, harmonious reconciliation between these private and public imperatives is impossible, and so some degree of compromise is unavoidable.

In this essay, written two decades later on the topic of "charity law in the new welfare state", what I would like to do is to discuss the extent (if any) to which changes in English charity law and administration over the last twenty years have pursued the fourth and fifth of these broad aims. These aims can be summarised as "promoting wealth redistribution through tax reliefs" and "ensuring relative autonomy" respectively.

I recognise that to specify these two aims—particularly the first of them—as appropriate for charity law may be a touch controversial. But it is my belief that in view of the changes in government welfare policy that are summed up in the phrase "new welfare state", it is even more important now than twenty years ago that charity law should try to achieve them. Virtually every review of wealth distribution in this age of economic rationalism identifies a widening gap

[4] T Carney and P Hanks, "Taxation Treatment for Charities: Distributional Consequences for the Welfare State" in R Krever and G Kewley (eds), *Charities and Philanthropic Organisations: Reforming the Tax Subsidy and Regulatory Regimes* (Melbourne, Comparative Public Policy Research Unit, Monash University and Australian Tax Research Foundation, 1991) 49, 69–71.

between rich and poor. If the institutions that we call charities are not consistently engaged in seeking to narrow this gap, it is difficult to think of a reason why they should deserve to be called "charities".

As my contact with charity law and administration during the last twenty years has almost entirely been in an Australian context, I will unashamedly draw on Australian material when it seems useful.

I will start with a few brief comments on what the arrival of the "new welfare state" seems to have meant for charities.

2. DEVELOPMENTS IN WELFARE PROVISION DURING THE LAST TWO DECADES

There is no point in my trying to describe in detail what is "new" about the "new welfare state". I am not qualified to do so, and quite a few others who are supremely qualified to do so have in fact done so. It is enough for me just to repeat a few familiar generalisations which are relevant to the particular points that I want to make about English charity law.

Twenty years ago the voluntary welfare sector, when matched against the welfare state, was consistently viewed as the "junior partner in the welfare firm"[5] in terms of both overall size and scale of service delivery. It was seen as fulfilling a few distinctive roles appropriate to a "junior partner". In outline, these were the roles of advocate of change, pioneer of new services, provider of complementary, additional or alternative services, and in some instances sole provider of services.[6]

Since then, as is well known, both the balance between state and voluntary provision of welfare and the nature of the voluntary sector's contribution have changed dramatically. In consequence of the "storm tides of the Thatcher years",[7] the proportion of the voluntary sector's provision of welfare services has risen markedly. The most noticeable feature of this shift, according to all the commentators, has been the arrival of contracts to deliver welfare services. To a much greater extent than before, the state has engaged voluntary agencies under contract to provide services in circumstances where central or local government agencies or other governmental or quasi-governmental bodies would previously have provided them. It has also outsourced service provision to private commercial enterprises, with which voluntary agencies have had to

[5] This is the title of D Owen, *English Philanthropy 1660–1960* (Cambridge, Mass, Belknap, 1965), chap 19, in which the relationship of state welfare and private charity following World War I is described.

[6] See e.g. Report of the Wolfenden Committee, *The Future of Voluntary Organisations* (London, Croom Helm, 1978) 43.

[7] R Jones, "Swimming Together: The Tidal Change for Statutory Agencies and the Voluntary Sector", in C Hanvey and T Philpot (eds), *Sweet Charity: The Role and Workings of Voluntary Organisations* (London, Routledge, 1996) 39, 39. See also J Lewis, "Reviewing the Relationship between the Voluntary Sector and the State in Britain in the 1990s", (1999) 10(3) *Voluntas* 255.

compete to secure contracts. The voluntary sector has thus had to come to terms with a new "contract culture".[8]

This has meant, among other things, that the aggregate of direct cash payments from government to charities and the proportion of such payments to total charity income have increased.[9] So too has the proportion of income which charities receive as fees and charges, whether paid by beneficiaries or by government agencies on their behalf. These developments are of course not uniform within the voluntary welfare sector. The proportion of fees and charges within the income of housing associations is much higher, for instance, than in that of most other species of voluntary organisation.

In addition, the range of fiscal privileges associated with charitable enterprises has increased during the last twenty years, notably for the benefit of donors to charity. There is however reason to believe that *inter vivos* donations by individuals to charity are on the decline, with the National Lottery sometimes cited as a contributory factor. The amounts derived from corporate giving and from legacies have increased or more or less stayed the same.[10]

3. BROAD IMPLICATIONS FOR CHARITY LAW

In the result, the "junior partner" metaphor for voluntary welfare is still appropriate in the "new welfare state", though the disproportion between the two "partners" is a good deal smaller. But for my purposes, the significant developments are (a) the increase in state funding for charities through the mechanism of service delivery contracts, and (b) the moves to more favourable fiscal treatment of charities, particularly in relation to donors.

To my mind, the actual impact of these developments has been in many respects detrimental. I realise that it may seem eccentric, if not lunatic, to argue that measures which make charities richer are detrimental. But I have reasons. They stem from the interaction of these measures with two familiar "chestnuts" of English charity law, which (like the poor) seem destined to remain with us.

The first of these "chestnuts" is the principle that, to quote a familiar phrase of Lord Cross in *Dingle* v. *Turner*,[11] validity as a charitable trust and significant "fiscal immunity" continue to "march hand in hand" (the "*Pemsel* principle"[12]). The second is the principle that an enterprise whose purposes include seeking to

[8] For discussion of some of the legal implications, see J Warburton and D Morris, "Charities and the Contract Culture" [1991] *Conv* 419; and for discussion elsewhere in the present collection, see Sue Moody's chapter at 99–101, and Mark Freedland's chapter at 118–21.

[9] See e.g. M Knapp, E Robertson and C Thomason, "Public Money, Voluntary Action: Whose Welfare?", in H K Anheier and W Seibel (eds), *The Third Sector: Comparative Studies of Nonprofit Organizations* (Berlin, Walter de Gruyter, 1990) 183, 186–99.

[10] See e.g. G Moffat, *Trusts Law: Text and Materials* 2nd edn (London, Butterworths, 1994), 627; S Etherington, "To the Millennium: The Changing Pattern of Voluntary Organisations", in Hanvey and Philpot, above n 7, 12–15.

[11] [1972] AC 601, 625.

[12] Laid down in *Commissioners for Special Purposes of the Income Tax* v. *Pemsel* [1891] AC 531.

change some aspect of the law or government policy must be deemed "political" and therefore non-charitable (the "*Anti-Vivisection* principle"[13]).

My argument, in essence, is as follows: so long as these entrenched principles of charity law remain more or less unaltered, their interaction with the phenomena of increased state funding of charities through service contracts and more favourable tax treatment, particularly for donors, impedes, not assists, fulfilment of the two aims for charity law on which I am focusing. This interaction does not promote wealth redistribution through charitable activity and it seriously impairs charity autonomy. It follows, in my view, that reform of these principles—which many people, including myself, have advocated over a long period—is particularly desirable at the present day.

In relation to each of these two principles of charity law—the "*Pemsel* principle" and the "*Anti-Vivisection* principle"—I will now try to explain the steps in my line of argument and to indicate what sort of eminently justifiable changes should be given serious consideration.

4. UNIFORM TAX BENEFITS FOR CHARITIES AND CHARITABLE DONORS (EVEN WHEN THEY BENEFIT THE RICH): "THE *PEMSEL* PRINCIPLE"

A. The Regressive Effects of the Uniform Tax Benefits Currently Available

The charity and the voluntary welfare sectors are not the same. One of the major arguments in my 1979 critique of charity law[14]—and I was not alone in making it at that time[15]—was that they should be brought closer together, at least in the fiscal domain. I argued that the tax reliefs and other "privileges" associated with charitable status should not be enjoyed, in the name of charity, by organisations, such as "public" schools and private hospitals, which on any popular understanding of the relevant terms were neither charitable in orientation nor engaged in welfare provision for persons of lesser or middle-range means. They should instead be reserved for organisations whose welfare programs achieved some measure of wealth redistribution by benefiting the poor and could therefore be genuinely deemed altruistic.[16] Put in these terms, this argument directly attacked the tax law dimension of the House of Lords' decision in *Pemsel's case*.[17]

[13] Laid down in *National Anti-Vivisection Society* v. *IRC* [1948] AC 31.

[14] Above n 2, 349–50, 403–4.

[15] See e.g. B Whitaker, "Minority Report", in National Council of Voluntary Organisations, *Charity Law and Voluntary Organisations* (the "Goodman Report") (London, NCVO, 1976) paras 6–10.

[16] For an argument in similar terms (though lacking the specific concern with tax policy), see A Ware, "Meeting Needs through Voluntary Action: Does Market Society Corrode Altruism?", in A Ware and R E Goodin (ed), *Needs and Welfare* (London, Sage, 1990) 185, 197–202. See too sources cited in C Mitchell, "Redefining Charity in English Law", (1999) 13 *Tru LI* 21, 46.

[17] Above, n 12.

As I have indicated, the extensions of tax relief that now particularly concern me affect *inter vivos* donations to charities. Since 1990, one-off gifts of money to a charity have attracted relief for income tax on the part of the donor, whether individual or corporate.[18] Since 1991, no upper limit has applied to the amount donated.[19] This form of relief, whether earned through making such a gift or under a voluntary covenant extending over four or more years, exempts the taxpayer from both basic and higher rates of tax.[20] In addition, statutory payroll deduction schemes facilitate the claiming of tax relief by employees[21] and provisions recently enacted introduce income tax relief for the donors of shares.[22]

The overall value of tax reliefs to charities is considerable. A Treasury estimate in 1997 quoted a figure of £1.75 billion.[23]

One clear effect of these extensions of tax benefits for donors to charities is to encourage gifts of significant amounts—i.e. of £250 or more, if made on a one-off basis—and gifts, whether or not of significant amounts, made by people in the higher tax brackets, who now obtain relief at both basic and higher rates. To the extent that these changes have in fact enhanced the scale of donations, they have allowed to be diverted to charities yet more private money that might otherwise have been brought into public revenue as income tax. And the important underlying point, even more important in the light of these changes, is that the state has no means of controlling the amount of tax revenue forgone on gifts or covenants to a charity or indeed income or capital profits realised by a charity. If the prescribed conditions are satisfied, the relevant tax relief can be claimed as of right. What the charity receives is "blanket, automatic, no-strings attached, open-ended aid".[24] It follows also, of course, that there can be no control over the total amount of tax foregone in favour of the charity sector as a whole, though this is not the issue of specific interest here.

In addition, these extensions of donors' tax relief favour richer donors, and the charities which they choose to support, in two distinct ways. First, the new relief in respect of one-off gifts only operates if the amount given is at least £250. Only relatively wealthy people make one-off gifts of this magnitude. Secondly, the relief granted now extends to the income tax that would otherwise be paid by the donor at higher rates. While in many cases the charities which rich donors

18 Income and Corporation Taxes Act 1988, ss 338 and 339; Finance Act 1990, ss 25 and 26, as amended by Finance (No 2) Act 1992, s 26; Finance Act 1993, s 67; Finance Act 2000, s 39(3).

19 Finance Act 1991, s 71. Between 1990 and 2000, the gift had to be of not less than £250, but this requirement has been abolished: Finance Act 2000, s 39(3).

20 Income and Corporation Taxes Act 1988, ss 347A–350, 660, 683; Finance Act 1989, s 59.

21 Income and Corporation Taxes Act 1988 s 202, and Finance Act 1993, s 68. An upper limit of £1200 on payroll giving was recently removed: Finance Act 2000, s 38(5).

22 Finance Act 2000, inserting a new section 83B into the Income and Corporation Taxes Act 1988.

23 HM Treasury, News Release, "Charity Taxation Reviewed", 2 July 1997.

24 S S Surrey, "Federal Income Tax Reform: The Varied Approaches Necessary to Replace Tax Expenditures with Direct Governmental Assistance", (1970) 84 *Harvard LR* 352, 385; and see discussion in R Krever, "Tax Deductions for Charitable Donations: A Tax Expenditure Analysis", in Krever and Kewley, above n 4, 1, 18–19; J G Simon, "The Tax Treatment of Nonprofit Organizations", in W W Powell (ed), *The Nonprofit Sector: A Research Handbook* (New Haven, Yale UP, 1987) 67, 73–81.

favour may genuinely assist the poor, the potential of this "upside-down" factor to direct further state financial support towards fee-charging elitist institutions which by virtue of charging high fees operate almost entirely for the benefit of rich people—for example, elite independent schools[25] or expensive private hospitals—is quite obvious.[26] By contrast, limits can be and of necessity are placed on the amounts paid to individual social welfare charities by or on behalf of the state under granting programs or as fees for providing welfare services.

In this instance, the balance between private "ordering" and "public interest" that I spoke of earlier is clearly tipped towards private "ordering". The decision of a wealthy private donor to make a substantial gift to a charity which benefits only people in the middle and higher income ranges automatically drags with it a significant sum of public money, irrespective of the public interest considerations in issue.

These arguments highlight the weakness of one of the significant propositions appearing in the case-law to justify charitable status for enterprises such as independent schools or private hospitals. I am referring to Lord Wilberforce's statement in *Re Resch's Will Trusts*[27] that in establishing the requisite public benefit (which may be "indirect" as well as direct) to qualify for charitable status, a private fee-charging facility in a field such as health care or education may argue that it relieves pressure on equivalent state facilities.

This principle was invoked in 1982 in *Joseph Rowntree Memorial Trust Housing Association* v. *Attorney-General*.[28] It was held by Peter Gibson J that the provision by a housing association of residential long leases for elderly people, irrespective of their means, was within the fourth class of charitable purposes because the accommodation was specifically designed to meet the particular needs of "the aged". He confirmed prior authority, including the decision in *Resch*, to the effect that the phrase "aged, impotent and poor people" in the Elizabethan preamble should be read disjunctively. His judgment includes a statement, similar to that of Lord Wilberforce, that the provision of such leases conferred "a clear public benefit" on the community in so far as the tenants could "defer the time when they may fall on to state services".[29]

In conformity with this approach, the Charity Commission has on occasions approved objects clauses which envisage lessening of the burden on the National Health Service through the provision of "mainstream" private health facilities.[30]

[25] In a study published in 1989, it was estimated that the value of tax concessions to independent schools was probably between five and ten per cent of their fee income: G Moffat, "Independent Schools, Charity and Government", in A Ware (ed), *Charities and Government* (Manchester, Manchester UP, 1989) 190, 200–2. This study, of course, predated the tax changes of the early 1990s.

[26] Krever, above n 24, at 19–21; see too P R McDaniel, "Federal Matching Grants for Charitable Contributions: A Substitute for the Income Tax Deduction", (1972) 27 *Tax LR* 377, 390–2.

[27] [1969] 1 AC 514, 544 (PC). See critical discussion in Moffatt, above n 25, 199; J Hackney, "The Politics of the Chancery", [1981] CLP 113, 121–2.

[28] [1983] Ch 159. See critical discussion in R Nobles, "Selling Charity", (1983) 46 *MLR* 782.

[29] *Ibid*, 167. The second phrase in quotation marks had appeared in a letter from the Charity Commissioners to the housing association's solicitors, and was cited with approval by Peter Gibson J.

[30] Moffat, above n 10, 664–5.

Yet this principle is contradicted by the Commissioners in their published statements relating to poverty relief charities. They have said in several of their Annual Reports that the funds of these charities should not be used simply to relieve the statutory responsibilities of state welfare authorities.[31]

One cannot always assume, however, that private provision in an area such as health will in fact relieve state expenditure. In some instances, private providers make significant use of state facilities, without paying full value for them.[32] Also, any "public benefit" arising because the relevant charitable organisation reduces pressure on equivalent state services may be substantially offset by the financial support accruing to it through tax concessions. As I have just emphasised, the scale of this support cannot be controlled to any degree by the Treasury. Furthermore, the organisation in question may in addition be receiving cash grants.[33] Accordingly, in the absence of empirical justification, the use of this argument, based on "relief of the burden on state welfare", in order to support charitable status for private facilities in realms such as health, housing and education is highly questionable. As I have just indicated, it is considered dubious by the Charity Commission in the context of relief of poverty.

In any event, even if the private facility does in fact confer a net benefit on the state, the overall level of "handout" to each of the beneficiaries coming from the state (through fiscal exemptions and cash grants) and from the funds raised otherwise by the charity may often be distinctly greater than occurs under any equivalent state scheme, even after the value of the fees and charges paid by the beneficiaries is taken into account. A further ruling in the *Rowntree* case shows how charity law's interpretation of "public benefit" leaves scope for this. Peter Gibson J held that various schemes for providing long leases which the association had proposed for approval by the association were charitable in law and valid. This was the case even though the tenants, on exercising a right to surrender their leases, might derive a profit because the lease had increased in value during their tenancy. Because any such profit was "at most incidental to the charitable purpose",[34] it did not matter that the schemes provided, in essence, an opportunity for investment by the beneficiaries as well as accommodation specially designed to meet their specific needs.

There is in fact no clear limit to the level of generosity, indeed luxury, to which the benefits dispensed by a fee-charging charitable organisation may aspire. In discussing charity law, one should never forget the swimming-pool that Marlborough College did not need. (My reference here is to *Re Geere (No 2)*,[35] in which a bequest of £10,000, a substantial sum in 1954, to furnish the

[31] Charity Commission, *Annual Report for 1967*, paras 17–20; *Annual Report for 1975*, para 29; *Annual Report for 1991*, Appendix A(b).

[32] Moffat, above n 10, 676.

[33] For discussion in relation to independent schools, see e.g. above n 25, 202.

[34] Above n 28, 176.

[35] [1954] CLY 388; [1954] *The Times*, 19 May; for brief commentary, see above n 2, 335; H Picarda, *The Law and Practice Relating to Charitable Trusts* 2nd edn (London, Butterworths, 1995), 43.

College with "a proper swimming bath and hot water baths" was held charitable and valid, but had to be applied cy-près because the College already possessed these facilities.)

By contrast, less prosperous charitable organisations which provide welfare services, without charge, to less well-off people will inevitably be confined to dispersing meagre benefits. A striking illustration appears in the Charity Commissioners' guidelines indicating how charities for the relief of poverty may engage in "topping up" state social security benefits. The measures listed include "the provision of items [either outright *or, if expensive and appropriate, on loan,* [such as] (a) furniture, bedding, clothing, food fuel, heating appliances; (b) washing machines *for widows with large families* or radio or television sets *for the lonely, bedridden or housebound*".[36] There are shades here of the notoriously moralistic comment of Romer LJ in *Re Cole*, that:[37]

> I cannot regard the provision of television sets, etc, for the benefit of such persons as juvenile delinquents and refractory children in [a local authority home for such people] as coming within any conception of charity which is to be found in the preamble.

In addition, such charities are increasingly operating under relatively strictly-drawn contracts to deliver services on behalf of the state, where again the scale of individual benefits will be distinctly meagre. This is, as I have already said, the "new role" for voluntary welfare.

The problem remains, therefore, that the automatic harnessing, ever since *Pemsel's case*, of tax privileges to the preamble-based trusts law definition of "charitable" continues to contradict my charity law aim of "fiscally promoting wealth redistribution". I hope that I have managed to demonstrate that this contradiction has been accentuated by the tax changes of the last two decades.

One familiar solution, frequently mentioned,[38] for this problem is to exclude from the legal definition of charitable those bodies whose activities cannot in practice confer any significant benefit on people of limited means. Another, which I wish to explore now, is to apply differential tax treatment to different classes of charities. Predictably, my contention is that those charities which genuinely benefit poor people should receive the most favourable tax treatment. This should, I think, extend particularly to the donors to such charities. The enlarged reliefs for donors which England has introduced since the early 1990s should clearly not, in my view, operate indiscriminately amongst all charities.

[36] Charity Commission, *Annual Report for 1991*, Appendix A(b) (emphasis added).

[37] [1958] Ch 877, 888. For criticism, see above n 2, 335–7, and 355; Picarda, above n 35, 44.

[38] See e.g. Whitaker, above n 12, paras 6–10; Moffat, above n 22, 217.

B. A Model for Tax Reform

In Australia, a number of tax laws, including particularly the provisions governing income tax relief for donors, have in fact broken away from the principle that the pursuit of "charitable" purposes, as defined by the majority judges in *Pemsel*, should be the sole password to fiscal privileges so far as philanthropic or welfare-oriented bodies are concerned. There is instead a two-tier set of exemptions, in which "eleemosynary" charities, and the donors to such charities, receive the most favourable treatment.

This process of breakaway began as a consequence of a case in 1926 called *Chesterman* v. *Federal Commissioner of Taxation*.[39] Here the Privy Council reversed a decision of the High Court of Australia[40] to the effect that "charitable", in the context of an exemption from estate duty, should be construed rather along the lines of the minority judgments in *Pemsel*—that is, according to the word's popular meaning, covering only purposes involving relief of poverty. The Privy Council insisted that the definition prescribed by the majority in *Pemsel*, embracing the traditional four categories derived from the Elizabethan preamble, should apply instead.

The response of the Australian Parliament in 1928 was to amend the estate duty legislation so as to grant exemptions to bequests to a different category of recipients, that of "public benevolent institution". This concept is now employed in lieu of "charitable" as a criterion for relief from a number of Commonwealth and State taxes in Australia, including payroll tax, fringe benefits tax, sales tax and income tax payable by donors.[41] The term "charitable" continues to play a fiscal role also: for example, the investment and trading income of charitable institutions and of funds established by will or instrument of trust for "public charitable purposes" are exempt from income tax.[42] Under some provisions,[43] exemptions may be claimed on either ground. In the preparation of a governing instrument of any trust, association or other body operating in a philanthropic or welfare field in Australia, it is now commonplace to try to frame objects which will establish it both as a charitable body and as a "public benevolent institution".

To qualify as a "public benevolent institution", an organisation must be engaged in relief of "poverty, suffering, distress or misfortune"[44] or of "destitu-

[39] [1926] AC 128. The case arose out of a claim for exemption from estate duty for the assets in a testamentary trust (the Peter Mitchell Trust), under which prizes for physical, moral and literary excellence were to be awarded to young men irrespective of their means. The first-named trustee was my grandfather.

[40] (1923) 32 CLR 362.

[41] This last and most significant exemption is conferred by the Income Tax Assessment Act 1997 (Cth), s 30–45.

[42] Income Tax Assessment Act 1997 (Cth), s 50–5.

[43] For example, Local Government Act 1919 (NSW), s 132(1)(d), dealing with liability for rates.

[44] This phrase comes from the judgment of Dixon J in the first High Court case to consider the question of interpretation, *Perpetual Trustee Co Ltd* v. *Commissioner of Taxation (Cth)* (1931) 45 CLR 224, 233–4.

tion or helplessness",[45] or of those "who are in need of [relief] and are unable to care for themselves", namely "the poor, the sick, the aged and the young".[46] In early cases, it was suggested that if fees were to be charged, they would have to be purely nominal or be levied on a sliding scale according to the means of the beneficiary.[47] Later authorities have however held that an institution for the relief of sickness or some other distress or misfortune may be "benevolent" even if it charges fees at a level approaching the value of services rendered.[48] A body which is established, funded and controlled by government and which therefore operates in essence as an arm of the state cannot qualify,[49] but a body which is funded but not controlled by government agencies may do.[50]

In recent years, the phrase has been held to cover an institute established to assist the mentally ill[51] and a co-operative society providing housing, education and employment opportunities for needy Aboriginal people within a defined area and also promoting the development of their culture and identity.[52] On the other hand, the Royal Society for the Prevention of Cruelty to Animals has been held outside the category,[53] even though the court recognised that its activities were beneficial to mankind more or less for the same reasons as appear in the cases holding animal welfare bodies to be charitable.[54]

A significant problem for my overall argument is the fact that income tax relief for donors in Australia, while not available, as I have said, for donors to all charitable bodies, is not restricted to gifts to public benevolent institutions. The relevant statutory provision, section 30–45 of the Income Tax Assessment Act 1997 (Cth), also makes it available for gifts to several other limited categories of institution which have charitable purposes—for example, public educational institutions—or to any one of a large number of individual listed charities (which include, for instance, marriage guidance councils and the RSPCA).

Yet the important concept that charitable status should not be the sole password to tax privileges for bodies of a philanthropic nature and their supporters remains within Australian tax law. The equally significant category of "public benevolent institution" more clearly reflects the popular meaning of "charitable" (and the minority views in *Pemsel*[55]) in its focus on relief of the needs of

[45] *Ibid*, 232 (Starke J).

[46] *Ibid*, 235–236 (McTiernan J).

[47] *Ibid*, 235 (Evatt J); *Lemm* v. *Federal Commissioner of Taxation* (1942) 66 CLR 399.

[48] *Commissioner of Pay-roll Tax (Vic)* v. *Cairnmillar Institute* (1992) 92 ATC 4307.

[49] *Metropolitan Fire Brigades Board* v. *Commissioner of Taxation* (1990) 27 FCR 279.

[50] *Tangentyere Council Inc* v. *Commissioner of Taxes (NT)* (1990) 90 ATC 4352 (revd on other grounds (1992) 107 FLR 470).

[51] *Cairnmillar Institute*, above, n 48.

[52] *Maclean Shire Council* v. *Nungera Co-operative Society Ltd* (1995) 86 LGERA 430 (Court of Appeal, NSW).

[53] *Re Royal Society for the Prevention of Cruelty to Animals, Queensland Inc* [1993] 1 Qd R 571.

[54] *Ibid*, 583 (Thomas J).

[55] i.e. those of Lord Halsbury LC and Lord Bramwell, above n 12, 542, and 564–6. On the similarity between the concept of "public benevolent institution" and the popular notion of charity, see e.g. *Ashfield Municipal Council* v. *Joyce* [1978] AC 122, 137 (PC); *Metropolitan Fire Brigades Board*, above n 49, 283.

poor or disadvantaged people. It provides a model for any common law jurisdiction which wishes, wholly or partly, to confine tax reliefs to bodies within this narrower category and/or to individuals or corporations making gifts or bequests to such bodies.

I must also concede, however, that it is not a perfect model in terms of my "mission statement" for charity law. It is open to criticism[56] on the ground that it implements a distinctly conservative view of charitable activity, according to which only traditional "relief" organisations can qualify as "public benevolent institutions". This means that organisations whose activities are directed at "changing the circumstances which either create or aggravate poverty or distress"[57] are excluded. So too, it would seem, are organisations which engage in research, publication and advocacy with a view to assisting and representing other bodies which dispense relief. Pursuant to the first of these principles, the status of "public benevolent institution" was denied in 1985 to the Australian Council of Social Service, Australia's peak welfare council (the equivalent, more or less, of the National Council for Voluntary Organisations).[58] In the view of one judge, the latter principle also provided a ground for this ruling.[59]

A further ground of criticism is that the court's initial instinct to deny the status of "public benevolent institution" to bodies which charge more than nominal fees has given way to a recognition that fee-charging is not incompatible with "benevolence". For reasons that will have become apparent, I believe this to have been an unfortunate development in the case-law.

If Australia were to set about redefining "public benevolent institution" within in its current tax laws, or if England were to adopt the same general approach to framing tax reliefs, some changes to the definition should therefore, I believe, be made. I have no quarrel with the use of phrases such as "poverty, suffering, distress or misfortune" and "destitution or helplessness" to define the circumstances in which potential beneficiaries must find themselves. But nineteenth century concepts of "relief" should be jettisoned in favour of a more liberal requirement that the purposes of a public benevolent institution must simply entail some form of benefit to a section of the public[60] which qualifies as beneficiaries. The current requirement, for instance, that a body cannot be a "public benevolent institution" unless it directly provides "relief" to the relevant class of beneficiaries is unnecessarily restrictive. In addition, the earlier rulings

[56] See e.g. Carney and Hanks, above n 4, 68–9, and 75–6. For criticism from a rather different perspective, see EB Bromley, "Problems in Defining Charity", in Australian Association of Philanthropy Inc, *Australian Charity at the Crossroads* (Melbourne, Australian Association of Philanthropy, 1994) 38.

[57] *Australian Council of Social Service Inc* v. *Commissioner of Pay-roll Tax* (1985) 1 NSWLR 567, 571, (Priestley JA); and see *Marriage Guidance Council of Victoria* v. *Commissioner of Pay-roll Tax* (1990) 90 ATC 4770.

[58] *Australian Council of Social Service*, above n 57.

[59] *Ibid*, 568–9 (Street CJ).

[60] This means, it will be noted, that benefit solely to "poor relations" or "poor employees" would not suffice, irrespective of decisions such as *Dingle* v. *Turner* (above n 11) to the effect that trusts for these classes of beneficiaries may fall within the legal definition of "charitable purpose".

which apparently insisted that no significant fees could be charged should be reinstated.

The question whether a body might legitimately receive especially favourable tax treatment as a public benevolent institution if its activities are directed to "changing the circumstances which either create or aggravate poverty or distress" brings me directly to the second issue that I have singled out for discussion. This is the status of "political" purposes within the law of charity.

5. "POLITICAL" IS NOT CHARITABLE (EVEN IN A DEMOCRACY): THE "*ANTI-VIVISECTION* PRINCIPLE"

The background to my discussion of this well-known principle of charity law is the emergence of the "contract culture" associated with the "new welfare state". Essentially my argument is that the autonomy and the innovative potential of charities are now threatened from two sides.[61]

On one side, their engagement in contracts with state authorities to deliver welfare services robs them of their freedom to decide for themselves how they might most effectively apply their resources for the benefit of their chosen constituency. They are effectively, or at least potentially, bound to acquiesce in and implement the welfare policies of the governmental or quasi-governmental body with which they are in contract. It has been suggested that the general tendency of the service contract model is indeed to favour larger, longer-established, more specialised and generally more cautious charities.[62]

On the other side, the limits which charity law imposes on "political activities", particularly since the 1982 case of *McGovern* v. *A-G*,[63] significantly inhibit those charities which are not too tightly bound by service contracts from publicly challenging those policies. The legal divide between political and charitable purposes has indeed become deeper as a result of Slade J's ruling in the *McGovern* case that Amnesty International was not a charity.

So far as charities operating in the United Kingdom are concerned, the important aspects of Slade J's judgment are twofold. First, it reinforced the rule that advocating any change in the law was a political and therefore non-charitable purpose. Secondly, and most significantly for my purposes, it confirmed the extension of this rule to pressing for changes in government policies or administrative decisions.[64] The legal justifications provided were familiar: that courts

[61] For a forceful argument along these lines relating specifically to unemployment relief charities, see M Brenton, *The Voluntary Sector in British Social Services* (London, Longman, 1985), 93–100.

[62] See e.g. N Deakin, "Government and the Voluntary Sector in the 1990s", (1991) 12 (3) *Policy Studies* 11; M Taylor, "The Changing Role of the Nonprofit Sector in Britain: Moving Towards the Market", in B Gidron, R M. Kramer and L M. Salamon (eds), *Government and the Third Sector* (San Francisco, Jossey- Bass, 1992) 147; M Taylor, "The Canary in the Coalmine: Issues Facing the Voluntary Sector", (1996) 8 *Social Policy Review* 40.

[63] [1982] Ch 321.

[64] It is generally assumed that opposing changes in the law is also "political" and therefore non-charitable: see *Re Hopkinson* [1949] 1 All ER 346, 350; Picarda, above n 35, 161–2.

have no means of judging whether changes in laws, government policies or administrative decisions would be for the public benefit, and that to decide that the law is not right as it stands would usurp the functions of the legislature.[65] The judgment has been frequently criticised.[66]

The Charity Commissioners' Guidelines on the matter[67] somewhat alleviate the situation for campaigning charities by indicating how they may make the most of the principle that political activity which is merely ancillary to one or more charitable purposes does not endanger charitable status. But many charities dealing with poverty and disadvantage remain convinced that they cannot operate effectively without a significant degree of campaigning. They are inhibited in doing this because it is very difficult to tell in advance whether a campaign will be deemed by the Commission to have gone beyond merely ancillary or subordinate conduct.[68]

A valuable review of the attitudes of twenty-four legal systems to this issue, conducted by Anita Randon and Perri 6,[69] shows clearly that the English rules, along with those of most other "charity law countries", are firmly situated at the restrictive end of the spectrum. Those countries which do not adhere to a common law concept of "charity" appear remarkably relaxed about voluntary welfare organisations engaging in campaigns about welfare issues.

The authors of this article also set out an argument which has been noticeable in critical commentary on the subject during the last couple of decades[70] and which I would now like to develop further. Its starting-point is the proposition that the participation of individual citizens and non-governmental groups in public agitation to change laws and government policies is an integral and beneficial element of democracy. This notion underpins legal guarantees of freedom

[65] Above n 63, 333–7, and 339–40, citing *Bowman* v. *Secular Society* [1917] AC 406, 442 (Lord Parker) and *National Anti-Vivisection Society Ltd* v. *Inland Revenue Commissioners* [1948] AC 31, 62–3 (Lord Simonds) The extension to advocacy of changes in government policy was applied in *Webb* v. *O'Doherty* [1991] *The Times*, 1 February (injunction to restrain students' union, a charity, from spending funds to support a campaign to stop the Gulf War); and in *Southwood* v. *A-G* [2000] *The Times*, 18 July (educational trust held to be propagandist on the issue of disarmament).

[66] See e.g. R Nobles, "Politics, Public Benefit and Charity", (1982) 45 *MLR* 704; F Weiss, "Quot Homines Tot Sententiae or Universal Human Rights: A Propos McGovern v. The Attorney-General", (1983) 46 *MLR* 385, 385–92; D Lee, "Charities and Politics—The Perennial Problem", (1984) 6 *Liverpool LR* 49; C J Forder, "Too Political to be Charitable?", [1984] *Conv* 263; A Dunn, "Charity Law—a Political Scandal?", (1996) 2 *WJCLI*; also sources cited below in nn 70 and 75, and Alison Dunn's discussion in her chapter in the present collection (chap 3).

[67] Charity Commission, *Political Activities and Campaigning by Charities,* leaflet CC 9 (London, Charity Commission, 1997).

[68] For a recent affirmation of this point, see F Bates and J Pitkeathley, "Standing Up to be Counted: Campaigning and Voluntary Agencies", in Hanvey and Philpot, above n 7, 82.

[69] "Constraining Campaigning: The Legal Treatment of Non-Profit Policy Advocacy Across 24 Countries", (1994) 5(1) *Voluntas* 27.

[70] See *ibid*, 38; D Morris, "Charities, Politics and Freedom of Speech", (1999) 5(3) *Charity Law and Practice Review* 219; G F K Santow, "Charity in its Political Voice—a Tinkling Symbol or a Sounding Brass?", (1999) 18 *Australian Bar Rev* 225 (these last two sources discuss the impact of the Human Rights Act 1998). See also eloquent passages in C E F Rickett, "Charity and Politics", (1982) 10 *NZULR* 169, 170–3; C Rickett, "Politics and Cy-Pres", [1998] *NZLJ* 55, 62.

of speech, whether they take the form of express statements in a country's constitution (as in the USA), or arise as constitutional implications (as in Australia) or are mandated by instruments of international law (such as Article 10 of the European Convention on Human Rights, recently implemented, up to a point, in the United Kingdom under the Human Rights Act 1998). During the last decade, a number of cases in England, notably the decision of the House of Lords in *Derbyshire County Council* v. *Times Newspapers Ltd*,[71] have acknowledged the importance in freedom of public discussion of political matters within a democratic society.

When, however, in a recent English case an opportunity arose to take account of these considerations in a context analogous to charity law, it was not taken up. In the 1996 case of *R* v. *Radio Authority, ex p Bull*,[72] the British Section of Amnesty International (AIBS) challenged a decision of the Radio Authority banning licensed radio stations from broadcasting its advertisements. The ban was imposed on the ground that the advertisements fell within a prohibition in section 92(2)(a)(i) of the Broadcasting Act 1990 covering advertisements "inserted by or on behalf of any body whose objects are wholly or mainly of a political nature". The objects of AIBS were clearly political in the broader sense of seeking to change laws and/or government policies, but were not party-political. The same could be said of the content of a proposed advertisement, relating to human rights abuse in Rwanda and Burundi, which was before the court. In upholding the ban, both the Divisional Court and the Court of Appeal relied on the broad definition of "political" which Slade J had applied in *McGovern* v. *A-G*[73] in ruling that the Amnesty International Trust was not a charity.

The specific circumstances of this case provided a good opportunity for injecting into a judicial definition of "political" some acknowledgment of the importance of freedom of public discussion of political matters within a democratic society. AIBS argued that a legislative policy against party-political advertising was understandable at least, if not positively beneficial (though interestingly in *Australian Capital Television Pty Ltd* v. *Commonwealth*,[74] the Australian High Court had held in 1992 that a legislative ban on all forms of broadcast political advertising generally, including party-political advertisements, was contrary to an implicit principle of freedom of political discussion within the Australian Constitution). But it maintained that the broader definition of "political", embracing advocacy of any changes in law or policy, even when these would promote respect for human rights, should not have been transplanted unquestioningly from charity law into the law regulating media communications. This contention was, however, rejected.

[71] [1993] AC 534, where it was held that a local council, being a governmental body, could not sue for defamation at all.

[72] [1996] QB 169 (DC); [1998] QB 294 (CA).

[73] Above, n 63.

[74] (1992) 177 CLR 106. In the Divisional Court in *Bull*, above n 72, at 181, Kennedy LJ cited a passage from the judgment of Mason CJ (at 145) in this case.

As a valuable commentary on the case in the journal *Public Law* points out,[75] the decision in *R* v. *Bull, ex p Radio Authority* was unfortunate from the point of view of both of these branches of law. In relation to charity law, the authors state:[76]

> Those cases which established that charitable status should not extend to purposes which are political belong to an earlier social era. The fundamental objection to according such status, namely that the law is incapable of judging whether a change in the law or government policy is good or bad, is clearly spurious. In a relativistic age and a mature democracy the law should be able to uphold as charitable objects which are diametrically opposed to each other, provided that they are for the "public benefit" in the view of a sizeable body of adherents. . . . [T]he law of charities . . . should be allowed to evolve so as to encompass the observance of human rights, whether in this country or overseas, and the honouring of international obligations which have been entered. The very fact that the UK has acceded to such obligations should be conclusive evidence of benefit to the community.

A comparable approach to softening the rigour of the *McGovern* decision was in fact adopted in a judgment in 1997 in the Supreme Court of New South Wales. The case, *Public Trustee* v. *A-G for NSW*,[77] concerned the objects of a non-governmental organisation (now defunct) called the Federal Council for the Advancement of Aborigines and Torres Strait Islanders. Citing earlier High Court authority,[78] Santow J drew a distinction[79] between trusts for purposes which are "contrary to the established policy of the law", which are political and automatically fail, and trusts whose object is to "introduce new law consistent with the way the law is tending", which "may survive in Australia as charitable". He suggested, though he did not have to decide, that a trust with "a modest agenda for legislative change" might fall into the latter category where "the change is to promote anti-discrimination legislation conforming to the trend in legislative policy and reinforced by norms of international law . . .".[80]

The important question in charity law is of course not whether advocacy of change in laws or policies should merely be permissible but whether it is of benefit to the public, indeed sufficiently beneficial to attract fiscal privileges. In terms of their strict legal effect, guarantees of freedom of speech—which, it should be said, is also one of the "norms of international law",[81] as indeed of European law[82]—generally address only the former issue.[83] Their chief effect is to proclaim, subject to numerous exceptions and qualifications, that speech should not attract legal sanctions. But in at least one legal context in which the

[75] J Stevens and D J Feldman, "Broadcasting Advertisements by Bodies with Political Objects, Judicial Review, and the Influence of Charities Law", [1997] *PL* 615.

[76] *Ibid*, 622.

[77] (1997) 42 NSWLR 600.

[78] *Royal North Shore Hospital of Sydney* v. *A-G for NSW* (1938) 60 CLR 396, 426 (Dixon J).

[79] Above n 77, 607–608.

[80] *Ibid*, 617; see also 619.

[81] For example, under Article 19 of the International Covenant on Civil and Political Rights.

[82] Under Article 10 of the European Convention on Human Rights.

[83] Cf *Human Life International of Canada Inc* v. *Minister of National Revenue* [1998] 3 FC 203, 220–1 (Strayer JA), quoted by Charles Mitchell in this book at 198.

impact of notions of free speech has been much discussed in recent years, it has in fact been held that public discussion of matters of government or politics or other matters relating to the "public life" of the community is positively beneficial to the community. The relevant area of law is civil defamation.

In England, the significant case is very recent. In *Reynolds* v. *Times Newspapers Ltd*, a defamation case instituted by a former Prime Minister of a neighbouring country (Ireland), the Court of Appeal[84] and the House of Lords[85] held that the defence of common law qualified privilege could protect the makers of defamatory communications to the public at large in a much wider range of situations than had previously been recognised. The long-established justification for this defence is that it serves "the common convenience and welfare of society".[86] It operates to protect defamatory communications, even when they are untrue, if they are made without malice by a person having a legal, moral or social duty or interest to publish the material and the recipients have a reciprocal duty or interest to receive the material.

For present purposes, the important passage in the Court of Appeal's judgment in *Reynolds* is as follows:[87]

> We do not for an instant doubt that the common convenience and welfare of a modern plural democracy such as ours are best served by an ample flow of information to the public concerning, and by vigorous public discussion of, matters of public interest to the community. By that we mean matters relating to the public life of the community and those who take part in it, including within the expression "public life" activities such as the conduct of government and political life, elections . . . and public administration, but we use the expression more widely than that, to embrace matters such as (for instance) the governance of public bodies and companies which give rise to a public interest in disclosure, but excluding matters which are personal and private, such that there is no public interest in their disclosure.

In the leading judgment in the House of Lords, Lord Nicholls of Birkenhead spoke in similar terms.[88]

> My starting point is freedom of expression. The high importance of freedom to impart and receive information and ideas has been stated so often and so eloquently that this point calls for no elaboration in this case. At a pragmatic level, freedom to disseminate and receive information on political matters is essential to the proper functioning of the system of parliamentary democracy cherished in this country. This freedom enables those who elect representatives to Parliament to make an informed choice, regarding individuals as well as policies, and those elected to make informed decisions.

These words appear at the commencement of Lord Nicholls' discussion of a submission by the defendant newspaper that the courts should create a new "generic" category of privileged occasion, covering the communication of

[84] [1998] 3 WLR 862.

[85] [1999] 3 WLR 1010.

[86] *Stuart* v. *Bell* [1891] 2 QB 341, 346 (Lindley LJ), drawing upon *Toogood* v. *Spyring* (1834) 1 CM & R 181, 193 (Parke B).

[87] Above n 84, 909.

[88] Above n 85, 1022–3

political information. The House of Lords rejected this submission, partly because in their view it was anomalous to segregate political information from information on other topics of public importance. But all of their Lordships agreed that on account of the importance of freedom of expression on matters of public concern, the defence of qualified privelege should extend to publications on such matters even when made to the community as a whole. Its availability should depend, said Lord Nicholls, on the circumstances of the individual case. Matters such as the status and course of the information conveyed, the extent to which it related to a matter of public concern, the steps taken by the defendant to verify it and the "tone" of the publication should be taken into account by the court.[89]

An alternative formulation had been developed shortly beforehand by the High Court of Australia. This was in the case of *Lange* v. *Australian Broadcasting Corporation*,[90] another defamation case brought by the former Prime Minister of a neighbouring country (New Zealand). The High Court held that the criterion for determining whether public statements relating to "government and political matters" should be protected by qualified privilege was whether there had been "reasonableness of conduct" in making the publication. In *Reynolds*, Lord Cooke of Thornton suggested that while this approach adopted by the Australian High Court differed significantly from that of the House of Lords, they shared the same "pervading ideals".[91]

The judgments in these cases clearly imply that courts are capable of distinguishing between two categories of statement which contribute to the "flow of information to the public concerning, and [to] vigorous public discussion of, matters of public interest to the community" (to quote the Court of Appeal in *Reynolds*).[92] These are respectively statements that satisfy the flexible criteria laid down by the House of Lords (or, in Australia, are published "reasonably")—which means that publication of them to the world at large sufficiently serves "the common convenience and welfare of society" to attract the defence of qualified privilege—and statements that fail to satisfy these criteria (or, in Australia, are not published "reasonably").

Returning, after this brief excursus, to the topic of charities, it could not be doubted that the subject-matter of public statements urging changes in law or government policy, which the *McGovern* decision[93] treats as "political", is within the broad concept of matters of public concern, as conceived by the House of Lords in *Reynolds*. With this in mind, consider now the legal implications of a hypothetical report, accompanied by a press release, issued by a well-established and well-respected unemployment relief charity.

[89] *Ibid*, 1027.

[90] (1997) 189 CLR 520. In New Zealand, see *Lange* v. *Atkinson* [1998] 3 NZLR 424 (Court of Appeal). Here qualified privilege was held by the New Zealand Court of Appeal to protect any defamatory publication relating to the official conduct of a politician, if honestly made, without any additional criterion of reasonableness.

[91] Above n 85, 1042.

[92] Above n 84.

[93] Above, n 63.

The report and press release vigorously attack the responsible Minister for promulgating regulations lowering the level of youth unemployment benefits, allege that she has systematically misinterpreted data provided to her about the cost of maintaining benefits at pre-existing levels and urge the Government to adopt a much more sympathetic welfare policy towards unemployed young people. The report is based on reasonably careful investigation of the background to the new regulations, and both the charity employees who prepared it and the journalists who disseminate its arguments honestly believe its contents to be true.

Suppose that the Minister takes defamation proceedings against the charity and against the media organisations which published these allegations. In this situation, the defendants might well be able to show that the flexible criteria set out in *Reynolds* were satisfied and that the defence of qualified privilege was therefore available to them. If the court agreed, publication of the report and press release would be implicitly held to serve "the common convenience and welfare of society".

On the other hand, opponents of the stance on unemployment adopted by the charity could use these documents in support of an argument to the Charity Commission that the charity trustees were pursuing political, not charitable, aims. In terms of the Guidelines issued by the Commissioners, they would appear in particular to breach prohibitions against expressing opposition to particular political parties.[94] The Commission could be invited to take steps against the trustees to recover any expenses associated with the report and press release, or indeed to consider deregistration of the charity.[95] As already indicated, the legal principles underpinning this argument include the proposition that advocacy of a change in the law or in government policy cannot constitute a charitable purpose because a court has no means of judging whether the change would be for the public benefit, or because the court cannot usurp the functions of the legislature (the law cannot "stultify itself"[96]) by holding that any change would be beneficial.

In strict terms, this evident contradiction can be reconciled, though only just. The principle of defamation law states that society derives benefit from a "flow of information to the public concerning, and . . . vigorous public discussion of, matters of public interest" such as a past or proposed change in law or government policy. On the other hand, the principle of charity law is not, in its terms, concerned with information flow or public discussion, but with whether the change is or is not beneficial.

Yet in practical terms this distinction is illusory. In the charity cases, the courts regularly and misleadingly describe the impugned trusts as trusts "to

[94] See above n 67, paras 19, 46, 47, 50.

[95] *Ibid*, paras 71–75. As is well known, Oxfam has on occasions considered it necessary to tone down its political activities in response to warnings by the Commission: see e.g. Charity Commission, *Annual Report for 1991*, 19–20; also, the complaints in Parliament by Sir George Gardiner MP relating to the Commissioners' treatment of Oxfam in this connection, which are cited by Charles Mitchell in this book at 180, n 35.

[96] *National Anti-Vivisection Society*, above n 13, 50, (Lord Wright).

change the law", as if nothing more than a decision by the trustees would immediately enact the relevant legislation. At most, however, they are no more than trusts to communicate to relevant government authorities, and to the electorate, arguments in favour of changing the law—i.e. to convey information to government and to the public concerning, and engage in public discussion of, this issue of public interest.

It is wholly contradictory for the courts to say that in certain circumstances this activity serves "the common convenience and welfare of society", in the context of defamation law, but that it cannot in any circumstances be adjudged to be for the public benefit, in the context of charity law. In the former situation, courts must now be prepared to discriminate between those communications to the public which promote "the common convenience and welfare of society" and those which do not. Yet in the latter, they are constrained by authority to declare themselves incapable of drawing any such distinction. The justifications offered are distinctly archaic. They include, for instance, the notion that it is for the legislature alone to say whether a change in the law would be beneficial. This looks very like Lord Reid's "fairy tale"[97] that judges never make the law, but only declare it. They also betray scant regard for the role of popular opinion in a democracy.

A further anomaly is that, within the limits of their powers, the Commissioners do make such a distinction in their Guidelines. In fact, some of the criteria applied by them in determining whether a charity's advocacy of changes in law or government policy crosses the line from legitimate to illegitimate political activity resemble those outlined in the *Reynolds* case. The Guidelines state, for instance, that a charity may carry out such advocacy within the range of its charitable purposes by presenting a "reasoned" written memorandum to the Government, or by seeking to influence public opinion "by well-founded reasoned argument".[98]

The overriding legal principle which the Guidelines seek to elaborate is however that political activity by a charity can only ever be ancillary to its charitable, non-political purposes. Adhering to this principle is, as I have said, difficult for charities because, as the Commission concedes, "the dividing line between proper debate in the public arena and improper political activity is a difficult one to judge".[99] The argument which I am putting here would go a long way towards reducing those difficulties. It is that participation in public debate about changes in law or policy relating to an area of charitable activity should be recognised as beneficial within a democratic society and, within limits, charitable in its own right. Judicial acceptance of this argument would significantly loosen the constraints on campaigning charities.

[97] See "The Judge as Lawmaker", (1972) 12 *JSPTL* 22, 22.
[98] Above n 67, para 36.
[99] *Ibid*, para 10.
[100] Inheritance Tax Act 1984, s 24; Taxation of Chargeable Gains Act 1992, s 260.

This means, of course, that organisations with significantly political orientations could claim tax privileges. This notion is not total heresy: under present law,[100] gifts to political parties attract exemption from inheritance tax and consequential relief under the capital gains tax regime, to the same extent as gifts to charities. But the arguments which I have put forward in the preceding section for differentiating between charities in framing tax reliefs for the charity sector would of course apply to political charities. If, under a differential tax regime, charities which engaged genuinely in activities assisting the poor and disadvantaged obtained more favourable treatment than other charities, they should not lose this fiscal advantage merely because one of their purposes was to campaign for changes in law or government policy within their field of operation.

This last sentence brings together the two general propositions which I am advocating in order to strengthen the foundations of English charity law in the era of the "new welfare state". Whatever novelties may now be on the welfare scene, neither of these propositions is a new one. But if charity law is ever to achieve what in my view are its most valuable aims, each of them has become a good deal more important during the last two decades.

Index